Peterson's

MASTER THE REAL ESTATE LICENSE EXAMS

7th Edition

PETERSON'S

A **nelnet** COMPANY

About Peterson's, a Nelnet company

To succeed on your lifelong educational journey, you will need accurate, dependable, and practical tools and resources. That is why Peterson's is everywhere education happens. Because whenever and however you need education content delivered, you can rely on Peterson's to provide the information, know-how, and guidance to help you reach your goals. Tools to match the right students with the right school. It's here. Personalized resources and expert guidance. It's here. Comprehensive and dependable education content— delivered whenever and however you need it. It's all here.

For more information, contact Peterson's, 2000 Lenox Drive, Lawrenceville, NJ 08648; 800-338-3282 Ext. 54229.

Stephen Clemente, Managing Director, Publishing and Institutional Research; Bernadette Webster, Director of Publishing; Mark D. Snider, Editor; Ray Golaszewski, Publishing Operations Manager; Linda M. Williams, Composition Manager

ISBN-13: 978-0-7689-2820-4
ISBN-10: 0-7689-2820-6

Printed in the United States of America

10 9 8 7 6 5 4 3 2 1   12 11 10

Seventh Edition

By printing this book on recycled paper (40% post-consumer waste) 80 trees were saved.

Petersons.com/publishing

Check out our Web site at www.petersons.com/publishing to see if there is any new information regarding the test and any revisions or corrections to the content of this book. We've made sure the information in this book is accurate and up-to-date; however, the test format or content may have changed since the time of publication.

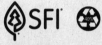

Contents

PART IV: FIVE PRACTICE TESTS

APPENDIXES

Before You Begin

HOW THIS BOOK IS ORGANIZED

You may have bought *Peterson's Master the Real Estate License Exams* because you are thinking about becoming a real estate salesperson and want to see what you will need to learn. Or, you may have bought this book because you have finished your coursework and want to review before taking your salesperson or broker licensing exam. In either case, *Peterson's Master the Real Estate License Exams* will provide you with a thorough review of the exam with chapters on law of agency, types of ownership, contracts and deeds, and much more. In addition, *Peterson's Master the Real Estate License Exams* reviews those aspects of real estate laws, rules, and regulations that may vary by state, the District of Columbia, and the U.S. Virgin Islands.

Peterson's Master the Real Estate License Exams is divided into five parts to facilitate your study.

- **Part I** explains basic information about the real estate licensing exam and offers strategies to help you score high on it.

- **Part II** provides a Diagnostic Test to help you identify your areas of strength and those topics where you need to place more emphasis in your review.

- **Part III,** which is divided into twelve chapters, offers a review of the major content that will appear on the exam. These chapters were developed by reviewing content outlines available from states. Reminders to research state-specific laws, rules, and regulations related to these topics appear from Chapters 3 to 13. Chapter 14 reviews in easy-to-follow, step-by-step explanations the types of math problems that appear on the exam. The chapter also provides sample problems for practice.

- **Part IV** contains five more Practice Tests. Like the Diagnostic Test, the answer section for each Practice Test provides detailed explanations for why the incorrect answers are wrong, so you can quickly identify information you need to review. The major concepts and federal laws related to real estate are assessed in these tests. However, because of the variety of state laws governing real estate, it is impossible to test every aspect of a state's real estate laws, rules, and regulations. At times, a concept may be referred to in a test by a term different from the one used in your state. Be sure that you know what the concept is called in your state. In addition, some states may allow something that your state does not or vice versa. For that reason, the final test in this section is a Do-It-Yourself Test. The topics are provided and you fill in the correct information.

- The **Appendixes** provides a glossary of important real estate terms that will both help you as you study for the exam and provide a quick review of concepts right before the exam. Appendixes B and C also list contact information for the real estate commissions and appraisal boards for the fifty states, the District of Columbia, and the U.S. Virgin Islands.

SPECIAL STUDY FEATURES

Peterson's Master the Real Estate License Exams has several features that will help you get the most out of your study time.

Overview

Each chapter begins with a listing of the major topics in that chapter followed by an introduction that explains what you will be reviewing in the chapter.

Summing It Up

Each chapter ends with a point-by-point summary of the main points of the chapter. It can be a handy last-minute study guide before the exam. The exception is Chapter 14, which ends with some important math test-taking tips as well as review points.

Bonus Information

You will find three types of notes in the margins of *Peterson's Master the Real Estate License Exams* that alert you to important information or remind you to check your own state requirements.

Note

Notes in the margins highlight important information about the real estate profession and remind you to check your state for specific laws, rules, and regulations.

Tip

Tips point out valuable concepts and advice for taking the real estate exam.

Alert!

Alerts caution you about common problems in marketing real estate.

YOU'RE WELL ON YOUR WAY TO SUCCESS

You've made a decision to pursue a career in real estate and have taken a very important step in that process. *Peterson's Master the Real Estate License Exams* will help you increase your score and prepare you for the day of your state's real estate license exam.

FIND US ON FACEBOOK® & FOLLOW US ON TWITTER™

Join the Real Estate License conversation on Facebook® and Twitter™ at www.facebook.com/relexam and www.twitter.com/relexam and receive additional test-prep tips and advice. Peterson's resources are available to help you do your best on this important exam—and others in your future.

Peterson's publishes a full line of books—test prep, education exploration, financial aid, and career preparation. Peterson's publications can be found at high school guidance offices, college libraries and career centers, and your local bookstore and library. Peterson's books are now also available as eBooks.

We welcome any comments or suggestions you may have about this publication. Your feedback will help us make educational dreams possible for you—and others like you.

TOP 10 WAYS TO RAISE YOUR SCORE

1. **Find out about the real estate exam that is given in your state.** If you haven't already, go online to your state's real estate commission (see Appendix B) and find out which test is given in your state, where it's given, how often it's given, how much it costs, how to register for it, and what kind of identification you need to get into the testing site. If you have a choice, decide if you want to take the computer-based test or the paper-and-pencil version. Find out also if you can use a calculator. Download any handbook or content outline that is posted for the exam.

2. **Use the Diagnostic Test as a tool.** Taking the test and studying the answers will help you identify the content that you need to spend the most time reviewing.

3. **Schedule your study time.** Between now and the time you will take the exam, set aside time six days a week to study. Try to give the same amount of time each day. Find a place that is conducive to studying.

4. **Budget your time on the topics.** Don't move too quickly through the material, but don't get bogged down and spend too much time on one or two topics. Be sure that you are comfortable with each topic before you move on to the next one, but be aware that you can spend too much time early in your schedule on just a couple of topics and then have to rush through the end of your review.

5. **PRACTICE, PRACTICE, PRACTICE.** Practice may not get you a perfect score on your test, but it will help you score better. Take the Diagnostic Test, complete each set of exercises in each chapter, and take all five Practice Tests, including the Do-It-Yourself Test on the real estate laws, rules, and regulations specific to your state. Don't assume you know all the information and brush this test aside because it will take time to do.

6. **Get rid of any negative attitude you may have toward tests in general.** A test is not a device designed to trip you up. Rather, it is an evaluation tool.

7. **Find the location of the test center.** If you aren't familiar with the location of the test site, take a trial run to find it and find out how long it takes to get there. If you're driving, locate a parking lot or garage. This may seem like overkill, but who wants to arrive at the testing site out of breath with 5 minutes to spare because you got lost on the way or spent 20 minutes trying to find a parking lot that turned out to be eight blocks away?

8. **Organize what you need for the test.** The night before the test, lay out on your bureau, the table by the door, or wherever you will see the things and won't forget them, the admissions slip/ticket for the testing center, the identification you need, your calculator and extra battery, and whatever else you NEED for the exam. Each testing company has a list of the things you can't bring, such as study materials and calculators that print. Again, organizing ahead of time may seem like a waste of time, but it's better than wasting time the day of the test by rooting around for the admissions slip or having your calculator die because you didn't have time to buy an extra battery.

9. **Carefully read the directions for each section of the exam.**

10. **Be confident.** If you have studied the material and prepared properly, you will do very well on the exam.

PART I

ALL ABOUT THE EXAM

What You Need to Know About the Exam

chapter 1

OVERVIEW

- **What's tested on a typical exam?**
- **How to find out about your state's test**
- **Types of multiple-choice questions**
- **Practice, practice, practice**
- **Summing it up**

Each state requires that real estate brokers and salespeople are licensed. The requirements for eligibility for licensing vary from state to state, the District of Columbia, and the U.S. Virgin Islands. The licensing exams and their test developers also vary. There is no single national test. Most states require some number of hours of coursework to become either a salesperson or a broker. The best way to find out what is required in your state is to consult the Web site for your state's or territory's real estate commission or board.

WHAT'S TESTED ON A TYPICAL EXAM?

Just as there is no single national real estate licensing exam for either a real estate salesperson or a broker, there is no single test developer. Each state chooses its own test developer and mandates its own state-specific content that is tested along with the national content. Among the questions that you will find on the national section are ones that relate to

- the code of ethics that realtors should follow.
- general common law such as contracts.
- federal laws such as hazardous materials, interstate land sales, and banking and consumer credit legislation.
- federal programs such as the Federal Housing Administration and the Veterans Affairs mortgage guarantees.

The state-specific section of an exam will ask questions about the state's real estate licensing laws and its laws, rules, and regulations related to real estate within its borders. Among the topics you will probably find on the exam are

- the powers, purpose, and composition of your state's real estate commission/board.
- your state's licensing requirements for realtors.
- statutory requirements governing the activities of real estate licensees.
- specific state laws relating to the environment, zoning, deeds, and title conveyance.

Throughout *Peterson's Master the Real Estate License Exams,* you will find reminders in the margin to make sure you know how your state deals with certain topics, for example, what kind of foreclosure is used or how a title is warranted.

HOW TO FIND OUT ABOUT YOUR STATE'S TEST

The format of the exam varies by state and the way the exam is administered varies by test developer. The national portion of the exam tends to be 80 questions for both salesperson and broker, and the state section may range from 40 to 60 questions. The allotted time for a test varies from two to four hours.

Some of the test developers offer their exam in both a paper-and-pencil version and a computer-based version. Others offer only a computer-based exam. Some tests are given on computers that use a standard keyboard to input answers, others use a keypad, and still others use computers with touch screens to input answer choices. Test-takers go to special testing centers to take the exam.

Once you know which test developer provides the real estate licensing exam that you need to take, go online to its Web site to find out all you can about the exam. The site will have a handbook or similar documents you can download that describe the exam. They will also provide a content outline specific to your state's testing requirements—both for the national portion of the exam and the state-specific portion. The outline may even have the percentage of questions for each major topic.

Some questions to bear in mind as you search for information are where the test is given, how often it's given, how much it costs, how to register for it, and what kind of identification you need to get into the testing site. If you have a choice, decide if you want to take the computer-based test or the paper-and-pencil version. Find out also if you can use a calculator. Use the checklist below to be sure that you have identified all the relevant information that you need.

WHAT YOU NEED TO FIND OUT ABOUT THE EXAM

Complete the following checklist to help you identify answers to important questions about the exam you will be taking. Check off each item as you write the information on the blank lines.

❑ Number of questions on the exam:

national part of the exam _____

state-specific part of the exam _____

❑ Time allocation:

national part of the exam _____

state-specific part of the exam _____

❑ Exam form:

computer-based _____

paper-and-pencil _____

❑ Question format(s) _____

❑ Passing score _____

❑ How the exam is scored _____

❑ How many times an exam can be taken _____

❑ Fee _____

❑ Nearest testing site _____

❑ Possible dates I could take the exam _____

❑ Registration confirmation received (date) _____

TYPES OF MULTIPLE-CHOICE QUESTIONS

Chances are all the questions on the exam will be multiple choice. They may have four or five answer choices, but the following strategies will work for either format. Questions typically are general knowledge, or they present a scenario or situation. They may be straightforward in how they ask a question or may be a reverse question.

General Knowledge Questions

General knowledge can also be thought of as definition questions and are straightforward. The question stem presents a term followed by four possible meanings. Or, the question stem presents a definition, or explanation, followed by four terms, one of which is correct.

1. In a net lease, the tenant pays
   - **(A)** the base rent only.
   - **(B)** the base rent and some of the expenses of the property.
   - **(C)** a percentage of gross sales.
   - **(D)** rent that escalates over time.

The correct answer is (B). In a net lease, the tenant pays the base rent and some of the expenses of the property.

2. A lease in which the tenant pays the base rent and some or all of the expenses of the property is a
   - **(A)** gross lease.
   - **(B)** percentage lease.
   - **(C)** net lease.
   - **(D)** graduated lease.

The correct answer is (C). When the tenant pays the base rent and some of the expenses of the property, the tenant has a net lease.

Scenario Questions

In this type of question, the stem presents a scenario that the test-taker must interpret in order to find the correct answer. Math questions often set up scenarios.

1. The Yees bought a beachfront property that is 40' × 60'. What is the square footage of the property?
   - **(A)** 2,000 square feet
   - **(B)** 2,200 square feet
   - **(C)** 2,400 square feet
   - **(D)** 2,600 square feet

The correct answer is (C). The fact that this is a beachfront property is not relevant for arriving at an answer. The length and width of the property are all you need to know to arrive at the square footage: $40' \times 60' = 2,400$ square feet.

2. Sally Harper made a formal complaint to the board of health because her apartment had a leak from the upstairs bathroom that was still not repaired after six months. Her landlord tried to evict her. Sally claimed that this was a/an

(A) actual eviction.

(B) retaliatory eviction.

(C) adverse possession.

(D) constructive eviction.

The correct answer is (B). There is a great deal of information in the question, but if you isolate the important information, you will find that the question is asking what kind of eviction does this appear to be from Sally's point of view—the only point of view that we have in the question. Once you strip away the details of the story, the basic information that you need in order to answer the question is very clear.

Signal Word Questions

You may find a few questions that use signal words such as "typically," "generally," "required," "best," and similar qualifying words. Be sure to pay attention to how these words impact the answer.

- Who *typically* pays the transfer tax?
- When asked if there are many children in the complex, which of the following is the agent's *best* response to the client?
- Which of the following actions is *required* of a broker?

Reverse Questions

You may or may not find reverse questions on the test that you take. These use the words NOT and EXCEPT in the question stem so you are looking for what does not fit in a series or situation.

1. Which of the following is NOT one of the four unities required for joint tenancy?

(A) Time

(B) Survivorship

(C) Interest

(D) Possession

OR

A reverse question could also use the word EXCEPT.

2. Each of the following is a component of the four unities of joint tenancy EXCEPT

(A) time.

(B) survivorship.

(C) interest.

(D) possession.

The correct answer for both questions is (B). For both questions, the answer that is not one of the four unities, choice (B), is the correct answer. The other three answers, choices (A), (C), and

(D), are correct in that they are components of the four unities, but that's not what the question is asking for, so they are all wrong answers to the question. This can be confusing if you are trying to answer questions quickly. That's why it's important to really concentrate on what a question is asking as you read it.

Distracters

We are using the term "distracter" in the answer explanations for the Diagnostic Test and Practice Tests to refer to answer choices that seem as though they might be correct because they seem familiar—especially if you are working quickly.

1. When a state takes property for public use, it is called
   (A) escheat.
   (B) eviction.
   (C) eminent domain.
   (D) public domain.

The correct answer is (C). If you read quickly and just focused on "a state takes property," you might have picked choice (A) because that occurs when a person dies without a will and without heirs, so the state takes the property. Choice (B) might snag a few test-takers if they only have a hazy notion of both eminent domain and eviction—after all, eviction has something to do with forcing people off property. Choice (D) may also confuse some test-takers who remember the word "domain," but second guess themselves into thinking that "public" sounds like government, so it must be the right question. As the Test-Taking Tips that follow say, "don't second guess yourself."

PRACTICE, PRACTICE, PRACTICE

Use all the tools that *Peterson's Master the Real Estate License Exams* provides you with to prepare for your exam. Read all the chapters, complete all the questions at the end of the chapters, and take each practice test in the allotted time. Read all the answer explanations—even for the questions that you answered correctly. You will find additional information in many answer explanations.

Good luck with your study and review! And good luck on your exam!

TEN TEST-TAKING TIPS

1. **Take the computer tutorial if you are taking a computer-based exam.** Every program is slightly different and every computer keyboard or keypad can be different, so take the untimed tutorial before beginning the test or pay careful attention to any directions that are given. Instead of a keyboard or keypad, a computer-based exam may use a touch screen similar to your smartphone screen.

2. **Read the test directions and each question carefully to determine exactly what is being said.**

3. **Budget your time.** Figure out how many minutes per question you can spend, for example, 80 questions in 120 minutes equals 1.5 minutes per question. For the computer-based test, if the screen has a clock, you may want to turn it off if you can because you find it distracting, or you may find it helpful to have it clicking down your time. If you're taking the paper-and-pencil version, take your watch off and lay it next to the test. Check it periodically to see how you're doing with time.

4. **Read all the answer choices before you choose one.** You want to move quickly through the test, but not so quickly that you read only to the first answer that seems right, and then move on to the next question. Read all answer choices because an answer may seem right because it seems familiar when the right answer is really the last choice.

5. **Use the process of elimination if you aren't sure about an answer.** Eliminate answers that are obviously wrong until you are left with one or two possible answers. Choose the one that seems the most likely answer.

6. **With a computer-based test, once you click "next" (or whichever button closes the screen), you can't change your answer, so be sure it's the one you want.** However, don't obsess. You need to keep moving.

7. **You can change your answer with a paper-and-pencil test, but don't second guess yourself.** Your first idea is most likely the correct one—with pencil in hand or finger on the mouse.

8. **You can't take scratch paper into the exam, but you may be given some to work out math problems.** Take and use it. You can jot down the information that you know from the question, what you need to find out, the formula you want to use, and then substitute numbers into the formula. You can use your calculator to do the operations.

9. **If you are taking a paper-and-pencil exam, be sure that you mark your answer on the correct line.** You have to stay particularly alert if you skip answering some questions.

10. **Check the exam requirements beforehand to see if wrong answers count against your score.** If not and you are running out of time, choose one answer choice other than choice (A) and mark all the remaining questions with that answer.

SUMMING IT UP

- Each state has its own real estate exam for different real estate licenses, and each exam has both a national section and a state-specific section.

- States hire outside test development companies to write tests to each state's specifications, including content specific to that state's real estate licensing laws and its laws, rules, and regulations related to real estate.

- The exams may be given as paper-and-pencil tests or as computer-based tests. A test-taker may be able to choose which format to take or may not, depending on the test developer.

- Some pieces of information that test-takers needs to find out are the
  - ☐ location of convenient testing sites.
  - ☐ frequency of exam administration.
  - ☐ fee for taking the exam.
  - ☐ procedure for registration.
  - ☐ format of the exam.

PART II
DIAGNOSING STRENGTHS AND WEAKNESSES

CHAPTER 2   Practice Test 1: Diagnostic

Practice Test 1: Diagnostic

Before you begin your review for the real estate exam, it would be helpful to determine what you know well, what you may be a little uncertain about, and what you need to study more thoroughly. Taking the following Diagnostic Test will help you identify your strengths and weaknesses.

Like actual real estate exams, the Diagnostic Test contains multiple-choice questions. Allot three hours for the test and, if possible, complete it in one sitting. When you have finished, check your answers against the answer key. For any incorrect answers, see if you can figure out why you got the answer wrong and why the correct answer is correct. After you have done that, go on and read all the answer explanations.

ANSWER SHEET PRACTICE TEST 1: DIAGNOSTIC

1. Ⓐ Ⓑ Ⓒ Ⓓ	21. Ⓐ Ⓑ Ⓒ Ⓓ	41. Ⓐ Ⓑ Ⓒ Ⓓ	61. Ⓐ Ⓑ Ⓒ Ⓓ	81. Ⓐ Ⓑ Ⓒ Ⓓ
2. Ⓐ Ⓑ Ⓒ Ⓓ	22. Ⓐ Ⓑ Ⓒ Ⓓ	42. Ⓐ Ⓑ Ⓒ Ⓓ	62. Ⓐ Ⓑ Ⓒ Ⓓ	82. Ⓐ Ⓑ Ⓒ Ⓓ
3. Ⓐ Ⓑ Ⓒ Ⓓ	23. Ⓐ Ⓑ Ⓒ Ⓓ	43. Ⓐ Ⓑ Ⓒ Ⓓ	63. Ⓐ Ⓑ Ⓒ Ⓓ	83. Ⓐ Ⓑ Ⓒ Ⓓ
4. Ⓐ Ⓑ Ⓒ Ⓓ	24. Ⓐ Ⓑ Ⓒ Ⓓ	44. Ⓐ Ⓑ Ⓒ Ⓓ	64. Ⓐ Ⓑ Ⓒ Ⓓ	84. Ⓐ Ⓑ Ⓒ Ⓓ
5. Ⓐ Ⓑ Ⓒ Ⓓ	25. Ⓐ Ⓑ Ⓒ Ⓓ	45. Ⓐ Ⓑ Ⓒ Ⓓ	65. Ⓐ Ⓑ Ⓒ Ⓓ	85. Ⓐ Ⓑ Ⓒ Ⓓ
6. Ⓐ Ⓑ Ⓒ Ⓓ	26. Ⓐ Ⓑ Ⓒ Ⓓ	46. Ⓐ Ⓑ Ⓒ Ⓓ	66. Ⓐ Ⓑ Ⓒ Ⓓ	86. Ⓐ Ⓑ Ⓒ Ⓓ
7. Ⓐ Ⓑ Ⓒ Ⓓ	27. Ⓐ Ⓑ Ⓒ Ⓓ	47. Ⓐ Ⓑ Ⓒ Ⓓ	67. Ⓐ Ⓑ Ⓒ Ⓓ	87. Ⓐ Ⓑ Ⓒ Ⓓ
8. Ⓐ Ⓑ Ⓒ Ⓓ	28. Ⓐ Ⓑ Ⓒ Ⓓ	48. Ⓐ Ⓑ Ⓒ Ⓓ	68. Ⓐ Ⓑ Ⓒ Ⓓ	88. Ⓐ Ⓑ Ⓒ Ⓓ
9. Ⓐ Ⓑ Ⓒ Ⓓ	29. Ⓐ Ⓑ Ⓒ Ⓓ	49. Ⓐ Ⓑ Ⓒ Ⓓ	69. Ⓐ Ⓑ Ⓒ Ⓓ	89. Ⓐ Ⓑ Ⓒ Ⓓ
10. Ⓐ Ⓑ Ⓒ Ⓓ	30. Ⓐ Ⓑ Ⓒ Ⓓ	50. Ⓐ Ⓑ Ⓒ Ⓓ	70. Ⓐ Ⓑ Ⓒ Ⓓ	90. Ⓐ Ⓑ Ⓒ Ⓓ
11. Ⓐ Ⓑ Ⓒ Ⓓ	31. Ⓐ Ⓑ Ⓒ Ⓓ	51. Ⓐ Ⓑ Ⓒ Ⓓ	71. Ⓐ Ⓑ Ⓒ Ⓓ	91. Ⓐ Ⓑ Ⓒ Ⓓ
12. Ⓐ Ⓑ Ⓒ Ⓓ	32. Ⓐ Ⓑ Ⓒ Ⓓ	52. Ⓐ Ⓑ Ⓒ Ⓓ	72. Ⓐ Ⓑ Ⓒ Ⓓ	92. Ⓐ Ⓑ Ⓒ Ⓓ
13. Ⓐ Ⓑ Ⓒ Ⓓ	33. Ⓐ Ⓑ Ⓒ Ⓓ	53. Ⓐ Ⓑ Ⓒ Ⓓ	73. Ⓐ Ⓑ Ⓒ Ⓓ	93. Ⓐ Ⓑ Ⓒ Ⓓ
14. Ⓐ Ⓑ Ⓒ Ⓓ	34. Ⓐ Ⓑ Ⓒ Ⓓ	54. Ⓐ Ⓑ Ⓒ Ⓓ	74. Ⓐ Ⓑ Ⓒ Ⓓ	94. Ⓐ Ⓑ Ⓒ Ⓓ
15. Ⓐ Ⓑ Ⓒ Ⓓ	35. Ⓐ Ⓑ Ⓒ Ⓓ	55. Ⓐ Ⓑ Ⓒ Ⓓ	75. Ⓐ Ⓑ Ⓒ Ⓓ	95. Ⓐ Ⓑ Ⓒ Ⓓ
16. Ⓐ Ⓑ Ⓒ Ⓓ	36. Ⓐ Ⓑ Ⓒ Ⓓ	56. Ⓐ Ⓑ Ⓒ Ⓓ	76. Ⓐ Ⓑ Ⓒ Ⓓ	96. Ⓐ Ⓑ Ⓒ Ⓓ
17. Ⓐ Ⓑ Ⓒ Ⓓ	37. Ⓐ Ⓑ Ⓒ Ⓓ	57. Ⓐ Ⓑ Ⓒ Ⓓ	77. Ⓐ Ⓑ Ⓒ Ⓓ	97. Ⓐ Ⓑ Ⓒ Ⓓ
18. Ⓐ Ⓑ Ⓒ Ⓓ	38. Ⓐ Ⓑ Ⓒ Ⓓ	58. Ⓐ Ⓑ Ⓒ Ⓓ	78. Ⓐ Ⓑ Ⓒ Ⓓ	98. Ⓐ Ⓑ Ⓒ Ⓓ
19. Ⓐ Ⓑ Ⓒ Ⓓ	39. Ⓐ Ⓑ Ⓒ Ⓓ	59. Ⓐ Ⓑ Ⓒ Ⓓ	79. Ⓐ Ⓑ Ⓒ Ⓓ	99. Ⓐ Ⓑ Ⓒ Ⓓ
20. Ⓐ Ⓑ Ⓒ Ⓓ	40. Ⓐ Ⓑ Ⓒ Ⓓ	60. Ⓐ Ⓑ Ⓒ Ⓓ	80. Ⓐ Ⓑ Ⓒ Ⓓ	100. Ⓐ Ⓑ Ⓒ Ⓓ

answer sheet

PRACTICE TEST 1: DIAGNOSTIC

100 Questions • 3 Hours

Directions: Read each question carefully and mark the letter of the best answer on the answer sheet.

1. An express agency relationship is created
   - (A) through an agreement between a principal and a realtor.
   - (B) through the actions of a principal and a realtor.
   - (C) when a realtor does more than authorized to do, but the principal raises no objection.
   - (D) if the realtor has an interest in the property.

2. A fiduciary relationship exists
   - (A) as part of any agency.
   - (B) as part of all agencies except a buyer agency.
   - (C) in a general agency only.
   - (D) in a special agency only.

3. Master plans include assessments of all of the following EXCEPT
   - (A) infrastructure.
   - (B) land use.
   - (C) government organizational structure.
   - (D) demographics.

4. A rectangular lot with frontage of 207' feet and a depth of 317' is sold for $4.25 per square foot. If the agent's commission is 6%, how much will she receive for the sale?
   - (A) $16,732.85
   - (B) $3,937.14
   - (C) $12,539.65
   - (D) $4,826.87

5. Chris Downes is considering buying some property to hold as an investment. The property is 1 square mile. He wants to figure out how many acre lots he could subdivide the property into and then how many square feet the property is. How many acres is it and how many square feet?
   - (A) 640 acres; 20,037,600 square feet
   - (B) 640 acres; 27,878,400 square feet
   - (C) 460 acres; 27,878,400 square feet
   - (D) 460 acres; 20,037,600 square feet

6. With a graduated lease, the
   - (A) rent is a percentage of gross sales.
   - (B) rent adjusts payment amounts on a predeterminded schedule.
   - (C) rent adjusts with interest rate changes.
   - (D) term of the lease adjusts automatically.

7. Which of the following is an example of external obsolescence?
   - (A) Only having one bathroom in a three-bedroom house
   - (B) Construction of a sewage treatment plant near a residential zone
   - (C) The lack of a dishwasher
   - (D) Leaking roof

8. To be binding, a real estate contract must be
   (A) signed by both parties in the presence of the broker of either party.
   (B) witnessed by a notary.
   (C) signed by both parties to the sale.
   (D) signed by both parties to the sale and witnessed by a notary.

9. Which of the following is a violation of the Fair Housing Amendments Act?
   (A) An ad listing an age requirement for ownership
   (B) An ad indicating that a property was affordable housing
   (C) A deed restricting ownership to certain groups
   (D) An ad noting that an apartment is a fourth-floor walk-up

10. An estate of indeterminate duration is a/an
    (A) estate from period to period.
    (B) freehold estate.
    (C) leasehold estate.
    (D) estate at will.

11. Joseph Gomez died without known heirs, and his estate is turned over to the state, which is known as reversion by
    (A) escheat.
    (B) estoppel.
    (C) eminent domain.
    (D) rescission.

12. A 2,574 square foot house sells for $475,000. The broker's commission is 6% of selling price. What is the commission?
    (A) $2,850
    (B) $28,500
    (C) $285,000
    (D) $2,850,000

13. Which of the following is an example of a net listing?
    (A) A seller signs an agreement that gives a realtor the exclusive right to market the property.
    (B) A seller lists the property with a number of realtors at the same time.
    (C) A seller agrees that the property can be open to sale by any number of realtors.
    (D) A seller tells the realtor what the seller wants to make on the sale and the realtor takes anything over that amount, or the loss on anything under that amount.

14. Charlene Wood's lease has expired, and she and the landlord have not negotiated a new lease. However, the landlord accepts Charlene's rent check each month. Charlene is in which type of tenancy?
    (A) Tenancy at will
    (B) Tenancy by the entirety
    (C) Periodic tenancy
    (D) Tenancy at sufferance

15. The grantee in transferring a title is the
    (A) mortgage lender.
    (B) seller of the property.
    (C) buyer of the property.
    (D) person overseeing the transaction.

16. The datum in a legal property description is
    (A) the beginning point of a metes and bounds description.
    (B) the reference point, line, or surface used in surveying air rights.
    (C) any object used as a reference point in a monument description of property.
    (D) the corners in a rectangular survey system.

17. A real estate broker has earned his or her commission

    (A) when the sales contract is signed.

    (B) when the closing is over.

    (C) by bringing the principals to the table for the closing.

    (D) when the seller accepts the offer of the buyer.

18. What is the amount of interest paid per year on a loan of $34,050 at an interest rate of 4.38%?

    (A) $1,118.43

    (B) $1,284.33

    (C) $1,309.21

    (D) $1,491.39

19. Which of the following is considered a fixture?

    (A) Stone wall

    (B) Inflatable swimming pool

    (C) Modular bookcase

    (D) Portable dishwasher

20. The Habibs are taking over the mortgages on a condo that they are buying from the Hudsons because the mortgage rate is lower than they could otherwise get. What the Hudsons are doing is

    (A) assuming their mortgage.

    (B) converting their mortgage.

    (C) voiding their mortgage.

    (D) assigning their mortgage.

21. The purchase price is which component of a real estate sales contract?

    (A) Acknowledgement

    (B) Consideration

    (C) Earnest money

    (D) Lawful object

22. What is the rate of appreciation on Jim Christopher's house, if he bought it 12 years ago for $573,247, and sold it for $849,001?

    (A) 32.5%

    (B) 36.4%

    (C) 44.7%

    (D) 48.1%

23. A townhome owner who owns her property in fee simple

    (A) has the most complete form of legal title to her property.

    (B) has the most restrictive form of property ownership.

    (C) owns only the dwelling, not the land.

    (D) is not bound by HOA covenants.

24. The Byrons have signed an exclusive agency buyer agency agreement with Joellen Scarpa. However, the Byrons find a home to buy on their own, so

    (A) they owe Joellen her commission anyway.

    (B) they do not owe Joellen her commission.

    (C) Joellen has to collect her commission from the seller's agent.

    (D) they owe Joellen only half the agreed-upon commission.

25. Which of the following clauses may NOT be allowable according to local or state laws?

    (A) Use of premises

    (B) Occupancy limits

    (C) Right to sublet or not

    (D) Provisions for the tenant to make improvements to the premises or not

26. An unfixed leak in the bathroom ceiling has finally caused the ceiling to collapse, making it impossible to use the bathroom in the one-bathroom apartment. The tenants have moved out. They consider that theirs is a/an

(A) actual eviction.

(B) nonjudicial eviction.

(C) judicial eviction.

(D) constructive eviction.

27. A portfolio lender offers mortgages

(A) on the secondary mortgage market.

(B) on the primary mortgage market.

(C) only to residential borrowers.

(D) only to mortgage brokers to sell to residential and commercial borrowers.

28. Private mortgage insurance is required if the borrower

(A) is a veteran.

(B) does not qualify for the FHA mortgage insurance program.

(C) is borrowing more than 80 percent of the purchase price.

(D) has been foreclosed once.

29. A property manager has which type of relationship with a property owner?

(A) General agency

(B) Special agency

(C) Universal agency

(D) Exclusive agency

30. A requirement of a multiple listing service is that

(A) the seller pays each broker involved in the sale a commission.

(B) all brokers involved in the sale split the commission evenly.

(C) all brokers involved in the sale share in the commission, but the split is negotiable.

(D) only the selling broker receives a commission.

31. If a party to a real estate contract fails to perform the agreed-upon actions by the specified time, the injured party has all of the following options EXCEPT

(A) breach the contract.

(B) sue for damages.

(C) rescind the contract.

(D) sue for specific performance.

32. Joe's Sofas owns its building in downtown Metropolis, which is valued at $1.2 million. The building is in a special business incentive zone that has a tax rate of $24 per thousand dollars rather than the regular rate of $32 per thousand dollars. If the building is assessed at 48% of actual value, how much is the business saving each year in taxes?

(A) $9,600

(B) $10,800

(C) $28,800

(D) $38,400

33. The Le Roi Development Company is planning on rehabbing a block of tenements in the city. It is buying up the property from three owners and is paying them in installments. This type of installment contract is also known as a/an

(A) binder contract.

(B) option.

(C) equity contract.

(D) land contract.

34. Which of the following is typically a debit to the buyer at closing?
    (A) Title insurance
    (B) Deed preparation
    (C) Transfer tax
    (D) Down payment

35. The period of time during which an asset is anticipated to remain economically viable is called its
    (A) profitable life.
    (B) useful life.
    (C) median life.
    (D) productive life.

36. The Abbases paid their taxes of $3,564 in advance in full for the year. The Creightons bought the house on May 17. What is the portion of unused taxes owed to the Abbases?
    (A) $2,217.60
    (B) $2,207.70
    (C) $1,613.70
    (D) $1,623.60

37. The Hidalgos are considering buying a listed 3 bedroom, 2 bathroom house. A comparable 3 bedroom, 3 bathroom house in the same area just sold for $142,780. If a bathroom in that area is worth $7,500, what is the value of the house the Hidalgos are looking at?
    (A) $125,780
    (B) $127,780
    (C) $135,280
    (D) $150,280

38. A *pur autre vie* estate is one in which
    (A) a person has ownership of a property only for his or her lifetime.
    (B) the grantor has a right of reversion.
    (C) a person is given interest in a property for the duration of the life of someone else.
    (D) a syndicate owns property.

39. The highest and best use of property includes all of the following EXCEPT
    (A) conformity to the surroundings.
    (B) economically viable.
    (C) possible within the physical limits of the property.
    (D) most productive use.

40. Which of the following types of zoning would be appropriate for a developer wishing to set aside open space in the subdivision she is building?
    (A) Special permit variance
    (B) Area variance
    (C) Cluster zoning
    (D) Density zoning

41. Leach fields are used to dispose of
    (A) radon.
    (B) sanitary wastes.
    (C) nuclear wastes.
    (D) water pollution.

42. The Trungs are looking for a mortgage that doesn't have a prepayment penalty. Which mortgage type fits what they're looking for?
    (A) Blanket mortgage
    (B) Open-end mortgage
    (C) Reverse mortgage
    (D) Open mortgage

43. An overturned tanker truck leaking gasoline into a creek in a residential area would come under the oversight of
    (A) OSHA.
    (B) HMTA.
    (C) USDOT.
    (D) SARA.

44. "NW ¼ of the NE ¼ of Section 4, T6N, Range 6 West of the second principal meridian" is an example of which type of legal property description?

    (A) Metes and bounds

    (B) Rectangular survey system

    (C) Plat

    (D) Lot and block

45. The Pollins are selling their house as part of a bankruptcy proceeding. Which of the following liens must be paid off first?

    (A) Tax

    (B) Mechanic's

    (C) Judgment

    (D) Mortgage

46. The neighborhood in which a property is located is an example of which of the following economic factors affecting property value?

    (A) Conformity

    (B) Contribution

    (C) Balance

    (D) Externality

47. The Marconis have signed an exclusive agency agreement with Todd Jones. This is an example of a/an

    (A) unilateral contract.

    (B) implied contract.

    (C) express contract.

    (D) buyer's agency agreement.

48. If a lot frontage is 95' and has a depth of 225', what fraction of an acre is the lot?

    (A) 1/2

    (B) 1/4

    (C) 1/5

    (D) 2/3

49. When a title is passed from the seller to the buyer, the form used in the conveyance is the

    (A) agreement of sale.

    (B) sales contract.

    (C) deed.

    (D) *habendum* clause in the title.

50. Jake Mervin sold a parcel of land to his church to build a retreat center with the stipulation that if the center wasn't built, he would regain possession of the land. He dies and the church paves over the land for a parking lot. Jake's heirs find that the sale gave the church the property in qualified fee conditional, so they can

    (A) do nothing about it.

    (B) file a lawsuit for return of the land.

    (C) offer to buy it back from the church.

    (D) exercise their right of reentry and reversion.

51. Which of the following is NOT an example of a party wall easement?

    (A) Wall between townhouse units

    (B) Wooden fence separating two properties

    (C) Shared driveway

    (D) Boundary line between two properties

52. A deed that guarantees only that the grantor has legal title and has not placed any encumbrances on the property while holding the title is a

    (A) special warranty deed.

    (B) quitclaim deed.

    (C) general warranty deed.

    (D) deed of trust.

53. Melba Taylor is buying a timeshare. At the closing, she will own the timeshare as a
    - (A) fee simple estate.
    - (B) tenancy in common.
    - (C) joint tenancy.
    - (D) shareholder in the underlying corporation.

54. Which of the following groups is NOT protected under the Fair Housing Act and its amendments?
    - (A) Alcoholics
    - (B) Gender
    - (C) National origin
    - (D) Active drug addicts

55. Owners of condo units pay taxes
    - (A) individually.
    - (B) as part of their monthly association fees.
    - (C) quarterly as part of their association fees.
    - (D) based on the bylaws of the condo association.

56. The broker on the LaSalle-Fuentes transaction received a $5,500 commission. How much did the house sell for, if the commission rate is 5%?
    - (A) $27,500
    - (B) $275,000
    - (C) $110,000
    - (D) $1.1 million

57. After having shown the Killigans 100 homes without a sale, Pat Ogura has decided that they are too high maintenance and decides to end the agency relationship before the expiration of the agency agreement. He
    - (A) can do this by renouncing the agreement.
    - (B) can do this by revoking the agreement.
    - (C) can only do this if the Killigans agree.
    - (D) cannot end the relationship before the expiration of the agency agreement.

58. A fiduciary relationship between principal and agent includes all of the following responsibilities EXCEPT
    - (A) loyalty.
    - (B) disclosure.
    - (C) substitution.
    - (D) obedience.

59. Mattie Jeffords has taken out a home equity loan of $33,070. If the rate is 11.99%, what is her monthly payment?
    - (A) $230.42
    - (B) $330.42
    - (C) $354.92
    - (D) $376.42

60. The value of a property for tax purposes is its
    - (A) investment value.
    - (B) market value.
    - (C) assessed value.
    - (D) appraised value.

61. Which of the following is an accurate statement about the metes and bounds form of property description?
    - (A) The metes and bounds system includes sections and townships in its property descriptions.
    - (B) The metes and bounds system uses the phrase "point of beginning" as the first reference.
    - (C) A metes and bounds property description begins with reference to tiers and moves to the next level, which is ranges.
    - (D) A metes and bounds system does not use degrees, minutes, and seconds.

62. Which of the following phrases would NOT be permissible in a real estate ad?

    (A) "With mother-in-law suite"

    (B) "Female roommate for two-bedroom apartment"

    (C) "No wheelchairs"

    (D) "Within walking distance to schools"

63. At the end of a closing, who is responsible for having the deed recorded?

    (A) Seller's attorney

    (B) Buyer's attorney

    (C) Seller's broker

    (D) Buyer's broker

64. Chris Wang has been hired to do an appraisal on a single-family home. Which approach will probably provide the most accurate valuation?

    (A) Income approach

    (B) Cost approach

    (C) Replacement approach

    (D) Sales comparison approach

65. A property management company interacts with tenants and potential tenants in all of the following ways EXCEPT

    (A) deciding the rent.

    (B) advertising for tenants.

    (C) settling disputes among and with tenants.

    (D) checking references and negotiating with potential tenants.

66. Jean Forsythe is looking at condo units to buy and asks the salesperson what the age demographic of the 300-unit condo community is. The salesperson's best answer is,

    (A) "I can't tell you anything about the demographics of the owners."

    (B) "I have no idea."

    (C) "It's against the law to ask me that question."

    (D) "I would say that it's a mix of ages from young families to downsizers."

67. If your property taxes are $0.005 on the dollar and you pay $100 per year, what would your annual taxes be if the taxes were raised to 0.0065 on the dollar?

    (A) $115

    (B) $130

    (C) $145

    (D) $200

68. Which of the following is a special assessment?

    (A) Renovation of a terminal at the city airport

    (B) Construction of sidewalks along a residential road

    (C) Construction of a cloverleaf to alleviate traffic congestion

    (D) Repair to a downtown bridge

69. Which of the following would terminate an estate for years?

    (A) Expiration of the lease

    (B) Death of the landlord

    (C) Death of the tenant

    (D) Sale of the property

70. Carmen Gomez owned her home with her husband who has died. As the surviving spouse, she has written her will to leave her home to her three children. Carmen is exercising her

    (A) right to bequeath her property.

    (B) life estate.

    (C) community property rights.

    (D) right to set up an *inter vivos* trust.

QUESTIONS 71 TO 75 REFER TO THE FOLLOWING MAP.

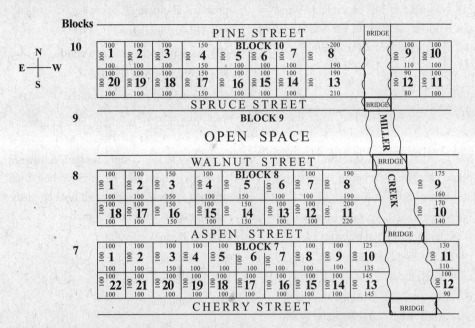

71. Which of the following lots does NOT overlook the open space?

(A) Block 10, Lot 20

(B) Block 10, Lot 13

(C) Block 8, Lot 6

(D) Block 8, Lot 13

72. Which is the largest lot?

(A) Block 10, Lot 13

(B) Block 8, Lot 8

(C) Block 8, Lot 11

(D) Block 8, Lot 14

73. Which lot is the smallest lot west of Miller Creek?

(A) Block 10, Lot 10

(B) Block 10, Lot 12

(C) Block 8, Lot 10

(D) Block 7, Lot 12

74. The smallest lot in the subdivision is

(A) Block 7, Lot 12.

(B) Block 8, Lot 18.

(C) Block 10, Lot 5.

(D) Block 10, Lot 12.

75. Driving west, to get to Lot 9 in Block 8, you would need to cross the bridge over

(A) Pine.

(B) Spruce.

(C) Walnut.

(D) Aspen.

76. A condo is sold on June 2. The condo fee of $278 was paid in full on June 1. What amount is to be credited to the seller and debited from the buyer at the closing?

    (A) $9.27
    (B) $18.54
    (C) $259.56
    (D) $268.83

77. The Morrises have prepaid the third-quarter real estate taxes on their home. The Allens are buying the house in August, so

    (A) the Morrises will lose the money that they paid for third-quarter taxes.
    (B) the taxes will be prorated and credited to the Morrises at closing.
    (C) the Allens will have to pay the taxes for part of August and September in addition to what the Morrises paid.
    (D) the taxes will be amortized and credited to the Allens at closing.

78. Jinan Allawi's mortgage is a conventional mortgage, which means that it

    (A) is not government insured or government guaranteed.
    (B) is not a conforming mortgage.
    (C) can only be a fixed-rate mortgage.
    (D) is not a straight-term mortgage.

79. A person's interest in a property that the person has agreed to buy and signed the contract to purchase, but has not closed on yet, is called

    (A) informal title.
    (B) marketable title.
    (C) abstract of title.
    (D) equitable title.

80. Which of the following costs is typically prorated at closing?

    (A) Hazard insurance
    (B) Association dues for a condo
    (C) Preparation of the deed
    (D) Flood insurance if required

81. The Weisnefski brothers have signed a lease with the Harris Street Management Company to rent a store for their hardware business. They will be paying their own utilities as well as repair and upkeep costs, which means they have signed a

    (A) net lease.
    (B) gross lease.
    (C) traditional lease.
    (D) ground lease.

82. Which of the following will always make a real estate sales contract invalid?

    (A) Lack of witnesses
    (B) Lack of a written contract
    (C) Omission of an expiration date
    (D) Coercion of one party to the contract

83. Blockbusting refers to

    (A) condemning certain properties on a block, but not others.
    (B) stirring up fear among homeowners that certain groups are moving into the neighborhood, so the homeowners will sell for low prices.
    (C) refusing to write mortgages for certain groups so they can't move into certain neighborhoods.
    (D) turning single family homes into multiple rental units.

84. Which document at a closing actually states the promise to repay the money borrowed?

    (A) Title
    (B) Deed
    (C) Note
    (D) Mortgage

85. What is the depreciation of a house that originally sold for $153,132 and just sold for $117,423 six years later?

    (A) $35,709

    (B) 23.3%

    (C) $117,423

    (D) 45.2%

86. The Good Faith Estimate is a provision of

    (A) RESPA.

    (B) the Fair Housing Act.

    (C) the Civil Rights Act.

    (D) the Statute of Frauds.

87. The Flahertys have failed to pay their property taxes for the last 4 years. When the mortgage company discovered this, it moved to have the Flahertys pay their entire mortgage. The mortgage company could do this because the mortgage contained a

    (A) default clause.

    (B) prepayment penalty clause.

    (C) escrow clause.

    (D) acceleration clause.

88. Which of the following statements defines the covenant of seisin?

    (A) It warrants that the seller has the right to transfer title to the buyer.

    (B) It grants the right to the mortgage to the mortgagee.

    (C) It states that the mortgagee will turn over to the mortgagor the title to the property when the mortgagor pays off the mortgage.

    (D) It is the requirement to preserve the value of the property by maintaining it.

89. Which of the following is NOT a federally required disclosure that a seller must make to a potential buyer, if applicable?

    (A) The property has lead paint.

    (B) The property is in a flood hazard area.

    (C) A convicted sex offender lives in the neighborhood.

    (D) The property is near three bars that are noisy on weekend nights.

90. The Lims want to be sure that the title to their new home is protected, so they ask for

    (A) a certificate of title.

    (B) title insurance.

    (C) a covenant against encumbrances.

    (D) a judicial deed.

91. Under the Federal Interstate Land Sales Full Disclosure Act, the sales contract

    (A) does not require the inclusion of a rescission clause.

    (B) must tell buyers that they have seven hours to change their minds about purchasing the property.

    (C) must give notice that violation of the terms of the contract can result in penalties to the developer.

    (D) is invalid if the buyer has not personally inspected the property to be purchased.

92. If a comparable contemporary 3,200 square foot house just sold for $298,000, what is the value of a similar house of 2,952 square feet?

    (A) $93,120

    (B) $320,000

    (C) $298,000

    (D) $274,890

93. The establishment of an adult day-care center in a home in a residential area might need which kind of variance?

    (A) Nonconforming use

    (B) Accessory use

    (C) Special use permit

    (D) Area

94. For which of the following is there no exception under antidiscrimination laws?

    (A) Age

    (B) Owner-occupied dwellings

    (C) Race

    (D) Religious organizations and facilities

95. A percolation test may be used to identify

    (A) a septic system.

    (B) asbestos insulation.

    (C) radon.

    (D) lead paint.

96. A lot that is $\frac{3}{8}$ of an acre is how many square feet?

    (A) 14,296

    (B) 15,876

    (C) 17,355

    (D) 16,335

97. What are the taxes on a $452,000 house if the tax rate is 45 mills and the rate of assessment is 72%?

    (A) $10,459

    (B) $12,453.90

    (C) $14,644.80

    (D) $20,340

98. The Bensons decide that they want to buy a larger house than the Minhs' house for which they have signed a contract of sale. The Bensons walk away and, in so doing,

    (A) forfeit the contract.

    (B) void the contract.

    (C) rescind the contract.

    (D) invalidate the contract.

QUESTIONS 99 AND 100 REFER TO THE FOLLOWING MAP.

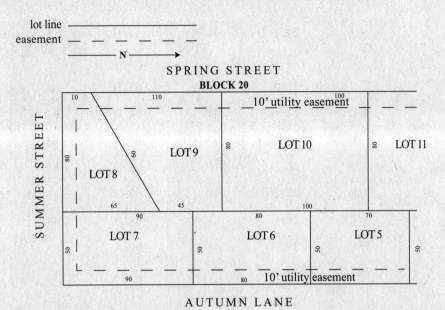

99. The owner of which lot has given the utility company the largest easement?

(A) Lot 10

(B) Lot 9

(C) Lot 7

(D) Lot 6

100. Which lot measures 4,000 square feet?

(A) Lot 5

(B) Lot 6

(C) Lot 7

(D) Lot 9

ANSWER KEY AND EXPLANATIONS

1. A	21. B	41. B	61. B	81. A
2. A	22. D	42. D	62. C	82. D
3. C	23. A	43. C	63. B	83. B
4. A	24. B	44. B	64. D	84. D
5. B	25. B	45. A	65. A	85. A
6. B	26. D	46. D	66. D	86. A
7. B	27. B	47. C	67. B	87. D
8. C	28. C	48. A	68. B	88. A
9. C	29. A	49. C	69. A	89. D
10. B	30. C	50. D	70. A	90. B
11. A	31. A	51. D	71. D	91. B
12. B	32. A	52. A	72. C	92. D
13. D	33. D	53. A	73. B	93. C
14. C	34. A	54. D	74. D	94. C
15. C	35. B	55. A	75. C	95. A
16. B	36. A	56. C	76. D	96. D
17. D	37. C	57. A	77. B	97. C
18. D	38. C	58. C	78. A	98. A
19. A	39. A	59. B	79. D	99. C
20. D	40. C	60. C	80. B	100. B

1. **The correct answer is (A).** Choice (B) is an implied agency. Choice (C) is an agency by ratification. Choice (D) is an agency coupled with an interest.

2. **The correct answer is (A).** Choices (B), (C), and (D) are incorrect. A fiduciary relationship exists in all agency relationships.

3. **The correct answer is (C).** Choice (C) is not part of a master plan analysis. Choices (A), (B), and (D) are analyzed as part of municipality's or region's master plan.

4. **The correct answer is (A).**

   $207' \times 317' = 65,619$ square feet

   $65,619 \times \$4.25 = \$278,880.75$

   $\$278,880.75 \times 0.06 = \$16,732.85$

5. **The correct answer is (B).** You only have to do one operation—if you remember how many acres there are in a square mile.

   1 square mile = 640 acres

   $640 \times 43,560 = 27,878,400$

6. **The correct answer is (B).** Choice (A) is a percentage lease. Choice (C) may seem familiar, but it's a mortgage rate that adjusts with interest rate changes, not a lease. Choice (D) may also seem familiar, but it's an adjustable-rate mortgage that adjusts automatically.

7. **The correct answer is (B).** Choices (A) and (C) are examples of functional obsolescence. Choice (D) is an example of physical deterioration.

8. **The correct answer is (C).** Choices (A), (B), and (D) are not true. The contract must be signed by both parties to the sale, but technically witnesses are not needed, nor is a notary necessary. Witnesses are standard, but go more to the "proof" of the contract or signatures than to its validity. The sales agents may be the witnesses.

9. **The correct answer is (C).** Choice (A) is not a violation of fair housing laws if the property is in an age-restricted community. Noting the cost or rent of a property is not discriminatory, and this includes noting that a property is an affordable housing unit. Choice (D) is not discriminatory against those with disabilities, but a statement of fact about the property.

10. **The correct answer is (B).** Choice (A) is a leasehold estate, known also as an estate for years. Choice (C) is the tenant's interest in a rental property. Choice (D) is also a type of leasehold estate.

11. **The correct answer is (A).** Choice (B) is a bar against making a denial or allegation that contradicts what one has previously claimed to be true. Choice (C) is the right of government to take possession of a property for a public good in exchange for payment. Choice (D) is the cancellation of a contract.

12. **The correct answer is (B).** $475,000 \times 0.06 = $28,500$

13. **The correct answer is (D).** Choice (A) is the definition of an exclusive listing. Choice (B) is the definition of an open listing. Choice (C) defines a multiple listing service approach to selling real estate.

14. **The correct answer is (C).** Choice (A) occurs when the tenant is allowed to stay by the landlord without having any end date to the arrangement. With choice (D), the landlord tacitly agrees to the arrangement by accepting the rent. Choice (B) relates to property co-owned by a married couple and has nothing to do with leases.

15. **The correct answer is (C).** Choice (A) is the mortgagee. Choice (B) is the grantor. Choice (D) is meant to confuse.

16. **The correct answer is (B).** The beginning point in choice (A) is called the point, or place, of beginning. Choice (C) has no special designation for objects used as reference points; the specific name of the object is used such as a brick wall or split rail fence. Choice (D) describes property by giving compass points, township designations, ranges, and meridians.

17. **The correct answer is (D).** When the offer is accepted, the real estate broker has earned the commission because the broker has brought a "ready, willing, and able" buyer to the seller. Choices (A) and (C) confuse the timing of the payment with when it is earned. Choice (B) is when the commission is typically paid.

18. **The correct answer is (D).** $34,050 \times 0.0438 = $1,491.39$

19. **The correct answer is (A).** Choice (B) may be there in the summer, but not in the winter, and the sellers may it take with them when they leave. Choices (C) and (D) are not permanently attached to the property, so they are not fixtures.

20. **The correct answer is (D).** Choice (A) would be the right answer if the question asked you to name the action of the Habibs. Choice (B) might be the answer if someone were changing the mortgage from an adjustable rate to a fixed rate, but that's not the question. Choice (C) is not an action related to mortgages.

21. **The correct answer is (B).** Choice (A) is the witnessing and notarizing of the title transfer for a piece of property. Choice (C) is the down payment given by the buyer to the seller at the time that the real estate sales contract is signed. Choice (D) refers to the purpose of a contract.

22. **The correct answer is (D).**

    $849,001 - $573,247 = $275,754

    $275,754 ÷ $573,247 = 0.481, or 48.1%

23. **The correct answer is (A).** A townhome owner who owns his or her property in fee simple has the most complete form of legal ownership—subject, of course, to public and private restrictions. Choice (B) is the opposite of what is true. Choice (C) is incorrect because a homeowner owns the land and the dwelling. Choice (D) is incorrect because a townhome owner is bound by HOA covenants—as long as the covenants are not illegal.

24. **The correct answer is (B).** Choice (A) would be true if the Byrons and Joellen had signed an exclusive buyer agency agreement. Choice (C) would be true if Joellen were due a commission. Choice (D) is not true.

25. **The correct answer is (B).** Choice (B) is illegal in some states and municipalities. Choices (A), (C), and (D) are all typical clauses found in rental leases.

26. **The correct answer is (D).** Choice (A) occurs when the tenant is evicted as a result of a lawsuit brought and won by the landlord to recover possession of the premises. Choices (B) and (C) are meant to confuse by mixing the word "eviction" with foreclosure terms.

27. **The correct answer is (B).** Choice (A) is incorrect because portfolio lenders are part of the primary mortgage market. Choice (C) is incorrect because portfolio lenders are more likely to sell mortgages for commercial real estate projects like subdivisions and malls than to residential borrowers. Choice (D) is incorrect because mortgage brokers don't offer mortgages but act as intermediaries.

28. **The correct answer is (C).** Choice (A) is meant to confuse; a veteran may qualify for a loan guarantee from the VA. A borrower may not qualify for a FHA-insured mortgage, choice (B), but that does not mean that the borrower must buy PMI. Choice (C) is the reason that a borrower is required by many lenders to buy PMI. Choice (D) sounds like it should be true, but whether the borrower has to buy PMI usually depends on the down payment in the current transaction. A party who has gone through a foreclosure may not even be able to get a mortgage or may have to pay a much higher rate of interest, although mortgage insurance could also be required.

29. **The correct answer is (A).** Choice (B) is an agency entered into to conduct one type of activity for the principal. Whereas choice (A) acts for a principal in a variety of activities, choice (C) adds a power of attorney to this array of duties and responsibilities. Choice (D) may seem familiar because it uses the word "exclusive," but that is meaningless in this context.

30. **The correct answer is (C).** Choice (A) is incorrect because the seller pays his or her broker who then splits the commission with the buyer's broker. Choice (B) is incorrect because the split is negotiable. Choice (D)

is incorrect because sharing the commission is a characteristic of an MLS.

31. **The correct answer is (A).** Choice (A) is what the other party has done, so it can't be the correct answer. Choices (B), (C), and (D) are all actions that either the seller or the buyer may take if the other party does not perform. The seller may also forfeit a contract, which, depending on the wording of the contract, may entitle the seller to the earnest money.

32. **The correct answer is (A).**

   $1,200,000 \times 0.032 = \$38,400$

   $1,200,000 \times 0.24 = \$28,800$

   $\$32,400 - \$28,800 = \$9,600$

33. **The correct answer is (D).** Choice (D) may have another name in your state, so be sure that you know what terms are used in your state for all unfamiliar terminology used in this book. Choice (A) may seem familiar because of the word "binder," but a binder contract doesn't exist. Choice (B) is a contract that entitles the buyer to buy property within a certain period of time and is often used by a developer assembling land for development. Choice (C) may also seem familiar because of the word "equity," but an equity contract doesn't exist.

34. **The correct answer is (A).** Choices (B) and (C) are typically debits to the seller. Choice (D) at the closing is a credit to the buyer. This may seem counterintuitive because the buyer pays the down payment, but it's already been paid at the time of the closing so it's a credit.

35. **The correct answer is (B).** Choices (A) and (D) present the right idea, but they are nonexistent terms, at least in this context. Choice (C) is incorrect because another term for useful life is mean life or economic life.

36. **The correct answer is (A).**

   $\$3,564 \div 12 = \$297$

   $\$297 \div 30 = \$9.90$

   $\$297 \times 7 = \$2,079$

   $\$9.90 \times 14 = \$138.60$

   $\$2,079 + \$138.6 = \$2,217.60$

37. **The correct answer is (C).** $\$142,780 - \$7,500 = \$135,280$

38. **The correct answer is (C).** Choice (A) is the definition of an ordinary life estate. Choice (B) is a partial definition of a qualified fee simple estate. Choice (D) is a type of business ownership of property.

39. **The correct answer is (A).** Choices (B), (C), and (D) are three of the four qualities used to determine the highest and best use of property; the missing characteristic is legal.

40. **The correct answer is (C).** Choice (A) is used when a property owner wants to introduce a use for which an area is not zoned. Choice (B) is required when a property owner wants to construct a building that will be larger than allowed under the existing zoning ordinance. This can also be called a height variance. Choice (D) refers to the number of houses that may be built on an acre of land, that is, more houses of smaller sizes.

41. **The correct answer is (B).** Concentrations of choice (A) can be reduced with ventilation. Choice (C) is stored by the federal government. Choice (D) is stopped by the addition of chemicals to the water and/or identification and eradication of the source of the pollution.

42. **The correct answer is (D).** Choice (A) is a mortgage on more than one property. Choice (B) can be borrowed against up to the original amount after it has been partially repaid.

Choice (C) enables the property owner to take equity out of a property without having to sell it.

43. **The correct answer is (C).** Choice (B) stands for Hazardous Material Transportation Act and regulates the transportation of materials such as gasoline, but enforcement under the act comes under the U.S. Department of Transportation, choice (C). Choice (D) stands for Superfund Amendments and Reauthorization Act, which deals with long-term environmental pollution such as brownfields. Choice (A) is the Occupational Safety and Health Administration and oversees worker safety, not real estate.

44. **The correct answer is (B).** Whenever you see the words "principal meridian" and "range," you know that the legal property description is based on the rectangular, or government, survey system. Choice (A) would use compass points only. Choice (C) is the name of the map that shows land divisions into sections, lots, blocks, streets, etc. Choice (D) is based on numbered divisions of land.

45. **The correct answer is (A).** Choices (B), (C), and (D) are paid off after any unpaid taxes are paid. The other liens are paid off in the order in which they were attached to the property, which is known as the order of priority.

46. **The correct answer is (D).** Choice (A) is whether a property is similar to the other properties in the neighborhood. Choice (B) is how much a characteristic of a property adds or subtracts from the value of the property. Choice (C) is the equilibrium between the value of land and the value of a building on that land.

47. **The correct answer is (C).** Once it's in writing, a contract can't be choice (B). There are two parties to the contract, so it can't

be choice (A). Choice (D) can't be verified from the information in the question, so this can't be the best answer.

48. **The correct answer is (A).**

$$95' \times 225' = 21,375'$$

$$21,375 \div 43,560 = 0.49, \text{ or } \frac{1}{2} \text{ acre}$$

49. **The correct answer is (C).** Choices (A) and (B) are the same thing, and the way that a title is conveyed. Choice (D) is incorrect for two reasons. First, the *habendum* clause is in the deed, and second, it reiterates that the seller has the right to transfer ownership to the buyer.

50. **The correct answer is (D).** Choice (D) gives the heirs the right to inspect the property and reclaim it if they find the church has violated the contract of sale. Choice (B) is qualified fee determinable. Choice (A) is incorrect because they can do choice (D). Choice (C) is unnecessary in terms of the law.

51. **The correct answer is (D).** Choices (A), (B), and (C) are all examples of party walls, so they are incorrect answers to the question. Choice (D) is not an example of a party wall, so it is the correct answer to the question.

52. **The correct answer is (A).** Choice (B) has no warranties attached to it at all and only conveys the interest that the grantor has in the property. Choice (C) conveys the fullest protection to the buyer. Choice (D) is used as security for a loan and conveys title from the trustor to the trustee.

53. **The correct answer is (A).** Choice (B) is a form of ownership between two or more parties that have an undivided interest in a property in its entirety. It sounds as though it should be the right answer, but it is not. The same is true for choice (C), which is equal ownership of a piece of property by two or more parties, but not the interest in a timeshare. Choice (D) is incorrect because

a timeshare does not involve ownership of the underlying corporation.

54. The correct answer is (D). Choice (A) is protected, but active drug addicts, choice (D), are not. Choices (B) and (C) are protected classed under the various fair housing acts and amendments.

55. The correct answer is (A). Choices (B) and (C) are not true of condo owners because unlike co-op owners, they pay their taxes individually, not as part of their association fees. Choice (D) is not true because association bylaws have nothing to do with when condo owners pay their taxes.

56. The correct answer is (C). $5,500 ÷ 0.05 = $110,000

57. The correct answer is (A). A revocation, choice (B), can only be done by the principal, not the agent. Choice (C) is incorrect because the agreement can be terminated without the other party's agreement. Choice (D) is incorrect because the agency can be terminated before it expires, which is choice (A).

58. The correct answer is (C). Choice (C) may sound familiar, but it is an economic factor that affects the value of property; it's not a duty to provide additional, similar properties. Choices (A), (B), and (D) are all aspects of the fiduciary relationship between agent and principal, so they are not the correct answer to the question.

59. The correct answer is (B).

$33,070 × 0.1199 = $3,965.09

$3,965.09 ÷ 12 = $330.42

60. The correct answer is (C). Choice (A) is the value that an investor would see in a property. Choice (B) is the highest price for a property that a buyer will pay a seller, neither of whom is under duress to offer or to accept the price. Choice (D) is the opinion of the market value of a property determined by an appraiser.

61. The correct answer is (B). Choice (A) describes the rectangular survey system of property description. Choice (C) also describes the rectangular survey system. Choice (D) is the opposite of what is true about the metes and bounds system; it does include degrees, minutes, and seconds.

62. The correct answer is (C). A better way of phrasing choice (C) would be to indicate that the premises was a walk-up. Choice (A) is a common description of the physical size and layout of a property and is not discriminatory. Choice (B) is allowable because it is implied that the living space is shared by the roommates, and limiting the roommate to the same gender as the person placing the ad (assumed) is permissible. Choice (D) is also permissible as a description of a characteristic that would appeal to a family, but does not discriminate against single persons.

63. The correct answer is (B). Choices (A), (C), and (D) are incorrect because it's the buyer's attorney who is responsible for having the deed recorded. In reality, the title company's representative can take on the responsibility for having the deed and mortgage recorded, and in a business closing, the lender often requests that the title company representative do so.

64. The correct answer is (D). Choice (D) is most often used to appraise residences. Choice (A) is used to value income-producing, or investment, property. Choice (B) is used to value property where few comparables exist, and the income approach is not appropriate. Choice (C) may seem familiar because replacement cost is one of the factors used in applying the cost approach.

65. **The correct answer is (A).** Choice (A) is incorrect because the property management company collects the rent, but doesn't set it. The property owner does. Remember that if one part of an answer choice is incorrect, the whole answer is incorrect. Choices (B), (C), and (D) are all typical activities of a property management company.

66. **The correct answer is (D).** Choice (A) is not true because the salesperson can provide some general information. Choice (B) appears to be avoiding the issue and so is not helpful to the customer. Choice (C) is not true; the customer can ask, but the salesperson can provide only a general answer.

67. **The correct answer is (B).**

    $100 ÷ 0.005 = $20,000

    $20,000 × 0.0065 = $130

68. **The correct answer is (B).** Choices (A), (C), and (D) would require large amounts of money and would benefit large numbers of people. A special assessment is used for a small project with targeted beneficiaries.

69. **The correct answer is (A).** Choices (B), (C), and (D) do not terminate an estate for years, that is, a lease. Only the ending of the lease terminates the lease. However, whether a lease continues after the death of a tenant can vary by state, so be sure you know what your state law is in regard to leases.

70. **The correct answer is (A).** Choice (A) is one of the bundle of rights that comes with property ownership. Choice (B) is limited to the lifetime of the property owner, or the lifetime of someone designated by the owner. Choice (C) are rights to property held by a married couple in some states. Choice (D) is incorrect because the question does not mention anything about a trust.

71. **The correct answer is (D).** Choices (A), (B), and (C) overlook the open space, so they are the incorrect answers. Choice (D) overlooks Aspen Street and the houses on the other side of Aspen, so it is the correct answer.

72. **The correct answer is (C).** Do the math, and you'll find that choice (C) is the largest lot.

73. **The correct answer is (B).** Do the math, and you'll find that choice (B) is 180 square feet smaller than the other choices.

74. **The correct answer is (D).** Choice (D) is the smallest lot in the subdivision.

75. **The correct answer is (C).** The way the roads are laid out, to get to Block 8, Lot 9, you would need to drive along Walnut Street, choice (C).

76. **The correct answer is (D).**

    $278 ÷ 30 = $9.27

    $9.27 × 29 = $268.83

77. **The correct answer is (B).** Choice (A) is incorrect because they owed the taxes for July and that part of August during which they owned the house. Choice (C) is incorrect because the Allens will not be paying any third-quarter taxes because the Morrises paid them on the property. Choice (D) is incorrect because mortgages, not taxes, are amortized.

78. **The correct answer is (A).** Choice (B) is incorrect because a conventional mortgage may also be a conforming mortgage. Choice (C) is incorrect because a conventional mortgage may be a fixed-rate or an adjustable-rate mortgage. Choice (D) is incorrect because a conventional mortgage may pay just the interest without paying down any principal, which is a straight-term mortgage.

79. **The correct answer is (D).** Choice (A) is meant to confuse, but no such title exists. Choice (B) is incorrect because it is what

the seller must produce at the closing—a title that the seller has the right to convey and that is free and clear of encumbrances. Choice (C) is incorrect because it is a report that details the history of ownership of a property.

80. **The correct answer is (B).** The buyer typically pays for choices (A) and (D). The seller typically bears the full cost of deed preparation, choice (C).

81. **The correct answer is (A).** Choice (B) is incorrect because the brothers would only be paying the utilities. Choice (C) is incorrect because it does not usually apply to a store. Choice (D) is incorrect because the store already exists; a ground lease is for unimproved land.

82. **The correct answer is (D).** Choice (A) is incorrect because the presence of witnesses is not one of the five factors needed to make a contract valid. Did you notice the word "always" in the question? Depending on the state, a real estate sales contract doesn't need to be in writing, so choice (B) is not the correct answer. Choice (C) may make a contract difficult to enforce, but it doesn't make it invalid.

83. **The correct answer is (B).** Choices (A) and (D) are incorrect, but they are meant to seem like plausible answers if you didn't know the correct answer. The first part of choice (C) refers to redlining, but the part about moving into neighborhoods is meant to confuse because it is similar to the correct answer.

84. **The correct answer is (D).** Choices (A) and (B) are brought to the closing by the seller, so they have nothing to do with the buyer's promise to repay the loan. Choice (C) gives the terms and conditions of the mortgage, but it is the mortgage, choice (D), which is the promise to repay the loan.

85. **The correct answer is (A).** $153,132 − $117,423 = $35,709

86. **The correct answer is (A).** Choices (B) and (C) are good guesses, but incorrect. They deal with discriminatory practices. Choice (D) is incorrect because it deals with which contracts need to be in writing.

87. **The correct answer is (D).** Choice (A) is incorrect because it is not precise enough, but this answer choice is a good distracter. Choice (B) is incorrect because it refers to a penalty that a mortgagor pays if the mortgagor pays off the loan ahead of schedule. Choice (C) is incorrect because this refers to the account into which the mortgagor pays a certain amount in advance on a regular basis to pay property taxes.

88. **The correct answer is (A).** Choice (B) is incorrect, but meant to confuse because it seems like the granting clause, but that involves the seller and buyer, not the financial institution and the buyer. Choice (C) is incorrect because it is the definition of the defeasance clause. Choice (D) is incorrect, but such a clause is typically part of the mortgage document.

89. **The correct answer is (D).** The federal government does not mandate that choice (D) be disclosed to a potential buyer. Choices (A), (B), and (C) are federally mandated disclosures.

90. **The correct answer is (B).** Choice (A) is incorrect because it does not provide the fullest protection for a property owner; it only provides an opinion about the ownership of the property. Choice (C) is incorrect because it is one covenant in a general warranty. Choice (D) is incorrect because it would apply only if the Lims were buying a home that was under a court order for disposal. It also only warrants that the entity selling the property has the right to sell it.

91. **The correct answer is (B).** Choice (A) is incorrect because it is the opposite of choice (B), the correct answer. Choice (C) is incorrect because it's not true. Choice (D) is incorrect because failure to inspect makes the contract voidable if the buyer chooses to invoke this contract term. Failure to inspect does not automatically make it invalid—or voidable.

92. **The correct answer is (D).**

    $298,000 \div 3,200 = $93.12

    $93.12 \times 2,952 = $274,890

93. **The correct answer is (C).** Choice (A) is incorrect because a nonconforming use is one that predates present zoning; it's not a variance. Choice (B) is not a variance either, but adding something—an accessory use—to further the primary function of a property is a reason to ask for a variance. Choice (D) refers to the size of a lot, not to the use to which it is put.

94. **The correct answer is (C).** Choices (A), (B), and (D) each have exceptions under anti-discrimination laws, but there are no exceptions for discrimination on the basis of race.

95. **The correct answer is (A).** Choice (B) is visible to the eye. Choice (C) is identified by a radon test kit; there is no specific name for the test. Choice (D) is done by a paint inspection test or a risk assessment.

96. **The correct answer is (D).**

    $3 \div 8 = 0.375$

    $0.375 \times 43,560 = 16,335$

97. **The correct answer is (C).**

    $452,000 \times 0.72 = $325,440

    $325,440 \times 0.045 = $14,644.80

98. **The correct answer is (A).** In forfeiting the contract, they are also subject to damages. Choice (B) is incorrect because the Bensons' refusal to buy is not a reason that voids a contract. Choice (C) is incorrect because rescission is the right of the seller in this situation, not the buyer. Choice (D) is incorrect because refusing to buy does not invalidate a valid contract.

99. **The correct answer is (C).** Choice (C) has given the largest easement to the utility company, which can be found by adding the length of the property along the two streets that the lot fronts ($50 + 90$).

100. **The correct answer is (B).** Multiply the length times the width (80×50), and the square footage of the property is 4,000 square feet.

PART III

REVIEWING REAL ESTATE EXAM CONTENT

Law of Agency

OVERVIEW

- The agent, the principal, the broker, and the third party
- The relationship between agency and client
- Types of listing agreements
- Buyer agency agreements
- Termination of agency/agreements
- Commissions
- Disclosures
- Fiduciary responsibilities of agents
- A word about puffing, misrepresentation, and fraud
- Summing it up

Someone who has never taken the basic real estate course may look at this chapter title and think it refers to laws related to running a real estate agency; however, he or she would only be half right. There are laws related to how a real estate agency is set up and operates, but as anyone who has taken that basic course knows, *law of agency* refers to the body of law that regulates the relationship between buyer or seller and his/her real estate broker/agent. It is the legal under-pinning of that relationship.

THE AGENT, THE PRINCIPAL, THE BROKER, AND THE THIRD PARTY

There are a few terms to keep in mind as you review for the exam. An *agent* is the person who has been given the authority, or power, to act for another and that "other" is the *principal* who has authorized the agent to act for him or her. In real estate terms, the principal is either the buyer or seller of property, depending on which side the agent is representing, and the agent is either a licensed salesperson working for a real estate broker, or the broker himself or herself acting as an agent.

A *real estate broker* is the licensed owner-manager of a real estate agency who hires agents, or sales associates, to work for the agency. A real estate agent must be licensed by the state and work for a real estate broker. Brokers generally have more experience selling real estate and have taken more advanced real estate courses than agents. All listings that come into a real estate brokerage are in the name of the broker, not an agent.

chapter 3

ALERT!

Be sure to get a copy of your state's licensing laws and regulations and study them as part of your exam review.

ALERT!

In some states, general agency is called universal agency. Typically, however, a universal agency means a power of attorney to conduct all real estate transactions for the principal. Check your state's laws to find out the terminology your state uses.

Consider a typical real estate transaction. It involves you, the agent, and your principal, the client who wants to sell her townhouse, and the buyer who in this case is called the *third party,* or *customer,* and her agent from another real estate agency. Hovering in the background is your boss, the real estate broker, and the broker for the other agent. All of you are regulated by a series of federal and state laws to make sure that the deal is legal. Some of these are not related to the agency relationship, that is, the relationship between principal and agent, but by federal and state fair housing and environmental laws, which you will review later in this book.

THE RELATIONSHIP BETWEEN AGENCY AND CLIENT

There is a variety of reasons why a principal contacts a real estate brokerage. The principal may wish to either buy or sell property. In some cases, the principal may be interested in renting his or her property rather than selling. A principal could also be a developer seeking to amass several parcels of land or an investor wanting to buy land, houses, or buildings. In all cases, the relationship that the agent enters into with the principal is regulated by state real estate licensing laws, rules, and regulations.

Types of Agencies

There are several types of agencies, or relationships, which can be formed between agent and buyer.

- **Special or specific agency:** The principal gives the agent authority to do one specific thing on the principal's behalf: sell property. Principal and agent (broker) enter into a contract that stipulates what that one thing is. The agreement will also list how the task will be done, for example, through multiple listings of the property, and what commission the agent will receive if successful.

- **General agency:** The principal and agent enter into a contract giving the agent (broker) the authority to conduct several activities on the principal's behalf, such as show a property to potential renters, check renters' references, and negotiate the lease.

- **Buyer agency:** Go back to the scenario mentioned before. The principal who is the buyer in this case and the real estate agent representing her have formed a buyer agency relationship. The real estate agent looks out for the buyer's interest in all negotiations.

- **Dual agency:** This occurs when the same agent in a brokerage represents both a buyer and a seller in a real estate transaction.

- **Designated agency:** The issue with a dual agency is that the agent cannot fully represent either party because of potential conflicts of interest. The designated agency was created to solve this problem. The broker designates another real estate agent in the same office to represent either the buyer or seller. Usually, it is the buyer.

The Nonagency

A number of states also have nonagency brokerages, also called transaction brokerage or facilitative brokerage. No agency relationship exists between the broker and the buyer and the seller. The broker facilitates the transaction by showing properties and assisting with paperwork and the general real estate process. Both the buyer and the seller are on their own when it comes to their interests.

TYPES OF LISTING AGREEMENTS

The listing contract, or listing agreement, is not between the agent and the seller, but between the seller and the broker (the agent's boss). There are several different kinds of listing agreements, and typically, they are in writing.

The listing contract states what the principal is authorizing the agent to try to do, such as sell or lease property, for a certain price in exchange for a certain commission earned during a certain period of time. The contract must be signed by the owners of the property and by the agent (broker).

There are four basic listing agreements: (1) exclusive right to sell, (2) exclusive agency, (3) open listing, and (4) net listing. The exclusive right to sell listing is the most common, and the net listing is the least common. Each type of listing protects the broker's commission.

Exclusive Right to Sell

The exclusive right to sell listing gives the broker the sole right to market a property. It is the most advantageous type of listing both for a broker and a principal because the broker knows he or she will be paid the commission if the property sells. It motivates the broker to work hard to find a ready, willing, and able buyer.

Even though the principal always retains the right to sell his or her own property, if the principal or anyone other than the broker—say the principal's son—sells the property, the broker still receives the commission. If another broker finds a ready, willing, and able buyer and the principal accepts that buyer, the original broker normally splits the commission with the second broker. The original broker wants the same reciprocity should the situation be reversed.

Exclusive Agency Listing

The exclusive agency listing gives the broker the right to market the property. However, if the principal sells the property, the broker is not paid a commission. The principal may not give the listing to another broker while the contract period is in force with the original broker.

Open Listing

An open listing, also called a general listing and a nonexclusive listing, gives the right to market the property to a number of brokers. There is no assurance that a broker will get a commission because the possibility of finding a ready, willing, and able buyer is spread across a number of brokers. Also, the principal may reserve the right to sell the property himself or herself. If this occurs, none of the brokers receive a commission. This form of listing is used more often in commercial real estate than in residential real estate.

ALERT!
Be sure to check your state's laws regarding the types of agencies allowed in your state and the laws related to them. Dual agency is illegal in some states.

NOTE
The National Association of Realtors (NAR) first adopted a Code of Ethics and Standards of Practice in 1913 and amends it periodically. The document contains duties to clients and customers, the public, and realtors themselves. For more information, check www.realtor.org.

Net Listing

This form of listing may be illegal in your state or be limited, so check your state's real estate laws. Under a net listing, the broker receives the difference—the net—between the selling price and the price that the owner wants. For example, if the net price—what the owner is willing to take—is $1 million, and you sell the house for $1.1 million, you keep the $100,000 as your commission. However, if the property sells for $990,000, you're out a commission. Net listings may be exclusive or nonexclusive.

Multiple Listing

Multiple listings are not listings like the four described above. Multiple listing systems or multiple listing services (MLS) are marketing tools. An MLS allows brokers to share listings—and commissions. When a broker in an MLS signs a listing agreement with a principal, the broker sends the listing to an MLS clearinghouse that posts it for all members within that MLS. This means that more brokers are looking for that ready, willing, and able buyer for the principal's property. The listing broker receives the commission and, typically, splits it 50/50 with the selling broker, the one who produces the buyer.

NOTE

Be sure to review your state's license laws related to buyer agency agreements as you study for the exam. The types allowable vary from state to state.

BUYER AGENCY AGREEMENTS

A buyer agency agreement binds the broker to look out for the best interests of the buyer. This means that the broker can advise the buyer about issues such as the best property to meet the buyer's needs and the best price for that property. With a dual agency, a broker would not be able to tell the buyer if the property that the broker is representing is overpriced or that there is another property that might better suit the buyer's needs.

There are three basic types of buyer agency agreements: exclusive buyer agency, exclusive agency buyer agency, and open buyer agency. Typically, a buyer agency agreement has the same components as a listing agreement, such as time period, fee, etc. These may be terminated in the same ways as listing agreements.

The fee is typically paid out of the seller's commission to his or her broker and is stated as such in the buyer's agreement. The agreement also covers contingencies such as a listing contract that does not allow splitting of the commission. Then the buyer will have to pay the buyer agency agreement fee. All states require that buyer agency agreements be written contracts.

Exclusive Buyer Agency Agreement

Also known as the exclusive right to represent, the exclusive buyer agency agreement gives the broker the exclusive right to help a buyer find a property to buy. The broker must be paid his or her commission even if the buyer buys a property during the time period of the agreement without the broker's help.

Exclusive Agency Buyer Agency Agreement

Similar to the exclusive agency listing, the exclusive agency buyer agency agreement does not guarantee that the buyer's agent will get a commission. The broker is given exclusivity over other agents to find a property for the buyer, but if the buyer on his or her own finds a property and buys it without the aid of the broker, the buyer does not have to pay the broker a fee.

Open Buyer Agency Agreement

The buyer enters into an agreement with a number of brokers to find a property to buy. The buyer pays only the broker who actually finds the property that the buyer ultimately purchases. If the buyer finds a property without the help of any of the brokers, no commission is paid to any of them.

TERMINATION OF AGENCY/AGREEMENTS

The fervent desire of real estate agents and brokers is that the agency terminates with a happy buyer and a happy seller at a closing, which is termination by performance. But that does not always happen. States sanction a variety of ways of terminating agencies, or agreements. Be sure to check what is legal in your state. In general, an agreement may be terminated because of issues between the principal and the agent or broker, or because of legal issues. The former includes the following:

- Expiration of the time period in the listing contract if no buyer has been found
- Mutual agreement between principal and agent
- The resignation of the agent, known as renunciation by the agent
- The principal's firing of the agent, known as revocation by the principal

Depending on the reasons for a resignation or discharge, a principal may be able to collect damages from an agent who resigns, and an agent may be able to collect damages from the principal who fires him or her.

Laws regulate the termination of agency as a result of the following:

- Destruction of the property
- Government seizure of the property through eminent domain
- Bankruptcy of either the principal or the agent
- Death of either the principal or the agent
- Declaration of incompetence of either the principal or the agent

COMMISSIONS

Generally, real estate brokers receive a commission—a percentage of the final sale price of a property—at the completion of a transaction. Based on how real estate practice has developed, the commission is paid at the closing. However, the commission is actually earned when the broker brings a ready, willing, and able buyer to the seller and the seller and buyer accept the terms of sale. However, in reality, if there is no closing for a reason that is not the fault of the principal, the principal does not expect to pay the realtor. By law, there is no standard percentage for commissions.

ALERT!
Some states have regulations regarding commission rebates to buyers, so check your state's real estate laws on commissions.

Any attempt to set standard rates among real estate brokers is considered price fixing and a violation of federal antitrust laws.

The commission rate is set by individual brokers for their own agencies. As a result, any commission is negotiable between principal and broker and the agreed-upon rate should be included in the listing or buyer agency agreement (and the contract of sale). However, there is usually a commonly accepted rate in any area.

DISCLOSURES

NOTE

Be sure to review your state's laws on property disclosures as well as federal fair housing laws.

If you were buying a house, would you want to know that the shiny new stainless steel dishwasher was really 20 years old and just had the front cover replaced? The answer is an unequivocal "yes." Is it a property defect? Probably not, but the buyer will be grateful to know that he or she may have to buy a new dishwasher at some not too distant point in the future. However, the seller would not have to volunteer the age of the dishwasher, but would have to tell the truth if asked.

A real estate agent is obliged by law to disclose material defects, also known as property defects. It is the agent's "affirmative duty to disclose." This disclosure would include, for example, leaking pipes in the basement that are not immediately apparent or a cockroach infestation that would only be apparent at night. In some states, sellers have to fill out a form disclosing property defects. Other kinds of information also need to be reported to potential buyers. For example, if the agent knows that a wooded acreage behind a development is going to be turned into a shopping mall, this would need to be disclosed to potential buyers.

NOTE

For more information on the Real Estate Settlement Procedures Act (RESPA), check the U.S. Department of Housing and Urban Development Web site at www.hud.gov. New RESPA regulations went into effect in 2010, so be sure you are up to date on what is required.

There are also laws in many states that require disclosures related to environmental hazards, financing, and agency relationships. In a number of states, the seller's broker must have a buyer sign an agency disclosure form before the broker can begin working with him or her. The form acknowledges that the broker is working for the interests of the seller and not the buyer. In states that allow dual agency, brokers must notify both the seller and the buyer if the agent is representing both parties to a transaction. Both the buyer and seller must agree to this in writing and acknowledge that the broker is stepping back from the relationship with both principals to avoid any conflicts of interest.

The Real Estate Settlement Procedures Act (RESPA), a federal law, also requires certain disclosures such as a standard Good Faith Estimate (GFE) that explains key loan terms and describes a best estimate of closing costs.

Among other mandated disclosures are

- the presence of lead paint in homes built before 1978. A seller doesn't have to test for lead paint, but must disclose the fact if known.
- that a property is in a flood hazard zone, as designated by the Federal Emergency Management Agency (FEMA).
- the need for the buyer to purchase flood disaster insurance, because the current property owner has received flood disaster insurance from the federal government.

Depending on the state, a seller may be required to tell a potential buyer about the presence of any convicted sex offenders within a certain radius of the property. This requirement results from the passage of Megan's Law, a federal statute. Interpretation of what is required under the law by the seller and the broker varies from state to state.

There is also the issue of property stigmas. The seller and seller's agent need to be honest with potential buyers about anything in the history of the property that could hinder their efforts at resale. These include criminal acts such as murder or even death by natural causes as well as long-term structural or plumbing issues.

FIDUCIARY RESPONSIBILITIES OF AGENTS

Real estate agents have certain fiduciary responsibilities to the principal. These have arisen over time and are based both in law and custom. According to the National Association of Realtors, they include (1) loyalty, (2) obedience, (3) disclosure, (4) confidentiality, (5) reasonable care and diligence, and (6) accountability.

The first two are obvious. The agent owes loyalty to his or her principal and also obedience to the instructions of that principal—so long as those instructions are legal.

As you have just read, disclosure of all known facts to the buyer is not only a responsibility, but certain disclosures are mandated by law. However, the duty of disclosure also relates to the broker-seller relationship. The agent has a fiduciary responsibility to reveal any business or personal relationship with the broker, sales associate, or co-broker for the buyer as well as any fee received from any of them or from the mortgage broker, home inspector, or attorney involved in the transaction. The agent must also disclose to the seller all offers made on the property, even if they are below the asking price or if there are any financial problems that a potential buyer may have that the agent is aware of.

An agent needs to safeguard a principal's privacy, including any reason why the principal is selling. An agent must also keep confidential information, such as the final price that a seller is willing to take or whether the agent thinks that the house is overpriced or underpriced. However, the agent may not hide any information that violates disclosure mandates.

Agents must use all the "reasonable care and diligence" possible to further the interests of the principal. This means not only advertising a property accurately and attractively, but also working with the seller so that the property shows well. For agents of nonlisting brokers, it means learning about the property so that they can show it to its best advantage.

At the completion of the relationship, that is, the successful sale or purchase of the property, the agent must account to the principal for all funds and property that are part of the deal.

NOTE

The booklet *Protect Your Family from Lead Paint in Your Home* published by the Environmental Protection Agency, the Consumer Product Safety Commission, and HUD must be given to all buyers of homes built before 1978.

A WORD ABOUT PUFFING, MISREPRESENTATION, AND FRAUD

If an agent were to tell a prospective buyer that a particular house is the best buy that he's seen in ten years, the agent would be exaggerating the benefits of the property. It's known as puffing. It's not illegal, but it's not a good practice either. It's also risky for the agent because if it turns out to be a bad deal, the principal may want to sue for false representations constituting breach of fiduciary duty, negligent misrepresentation, etc.

If an agent tells a prospective buyer that a wooded area behind a particular development is a nature sanctuary and can never be developed when the agent knows that the land is zoned for commercial development, it is misrepresentation. That's a nice name for fraud, and agents can be sued for fraud. Fraud occurs when an agent intentionally tells a lie in order to sell the property.

What if a buyer asks whether that wooded area behind the development is a nature preserve? The agent doesn't know, but says "yes" anyway. It turns out that three months after the buyer moves in, a developer begins to bulldoze the woods and stake out a shopping mall. The agent should have known and if he didn't, he should have found out the answer to the question or suggested where the buyer could find out the answer. The agent was caught in what is called negligent misrepresentation.

EXERCISES

1. That a buyer was turned down for a mortgage on a prior property
   - (A) is of no material importance in the current transaction.
   - (B) must be told to the seller.
   - (C) must be told to the agent's broker.
   - (D) cannot be revealed to the seller.

2. Which of the following guarantees a broker a commission?
   - (A) Buyer agency agreement
   - (B) Net listing agreement
   - (C) Special agency agreement
   - (D) Exclusive right to sell agreement

3. Under a multiple listing service, the property owner pays
   - (A) only the selling broker.
   - (B) the same commission to both the listing and selling broker.
   - (C) only the listing broker.
   - (D) splits the commission 50/50 between the listing and selling broker.

4. The downside to a dual agency is that
   - (A) no one is looking out for the interests of the buyer.
   - (B) the seller's agent can tell the buyer's agent what the seller will take as a final offer.
   - (C) neither party to the transaction is getting the most advice from the agent.
   - (D) the commission must be split 50/50 between the two agents.

5. Another name for a facilitative brokerage is
   - (A) special agency.
   - (B) nonagency.
   - (C) designated agency.
   - (D) general agency.

6. Which of the following is NOT a way that a listing agreement can be terminated?
   - (A) Revocation
   - (B) Resignation
   - (C) Incompetence
   - (D) Retirement

7. Which of the following is NOT a property defect that an agent is bound to disclose to a buyer?
   - (A) The presence of radon
   - (B) Leaking basement pipes
   - (C) Zoning change
   - (D) Ten-year-old water heater

8. Which of the following is true about a listing agreement?
   - (A) It establishes an agency relationship.
   - (B) A time period is included.
   - (C) The sales price is listed as a range.
   - (D) A commission rate is not included.

ANSWER KEY AND EXPLANATIONS

1. B	**3.** C	**5.** B	**7.** D
2. D	**4.** C	**6.** D	**8.** B

1. **The correct answer is (B).** If an agent knows of a financial problem of the potential buyer, the agent has a duty to tell the seller in the current transaction.

2. **The correct answer is (D).** Only exclusive right to sell and exclusive buyer agency agreements guarantee a commission. Choice (A) is the general category of buyer agency agreements, and choice (C) is not a listing agreement, but a type of agency.

3. **The correct answer is (C).** Don't be fooled by the term "50/50" in choice (D). It seems familiar because typically the listing broker will split the commission with the selling broker, but the property owner pays only the listing broker in an MLS transaction.

4. **The correct answer is (C).** In a dual agency relationship, there are two principals, not two agents. Even if you didn't know that choice (C) was correct, you could rule out the other choices as incorrect.

5. **The correct answer is (B).** A facilitative brokerage is also called a nonagency and transaction brokerage. A facilitative brokerage involves a nonagency relationship between seller and broker, so none of the other answers can be correct.

6. **The correct answer is (D).** You can retire debt, but you can't retire a listing agreement. All the other answers choices are ways that a listing agreement can be terminated.

7. **The correct answer is (D).** An agent is bound by law and the realtor's code of ethics to inform a buyer of any material defects the agent is aware of even if the seller does not want to. All of the answer choices come under the heading of material defects except choice (D). Typically, appliances need only be "in good working order" at closing.

8. **The correct answer is (B).** Choice (A) may have given you pause. The agency relationship is established prior to signing the listing agreement when the principal asks the agent to act for him or her. Choice (C) is incorrect because the sales price is stated, and choice (D) is the opposite of what is true.

SUMMING IT UP

- An agency relationship is established when a principal authorizes another to perform a certain action or actions for the principal.

- A real estate agent must work for a licensed real estate broker.

- There are a number of types of agency relationships that can be established in real estate. Among them are the following:

  - ☐ Special or specific agency
  - ☐ General agency
  - ☐ Buyer agency
  - ☐ Dual agency (Dual agency is not recognized in all states.)
  - ☐ Designation agency

- A nonagency may be called a transaction brokerage or a facilitative brokerage.

- A listing agreement, or contract, contains the following:

  - ☐ Action to perform
  - ☐ Sales or lease price
  - ☐ Commission rate
  - ☐ Time period for the agreement
  - ☐ Signature of both parties

- There are four basic types of listing agreements:

  1. Exclusive right to sell
  2. Exclusive agency
  3. Open
  4. Net

- Multiple listing service (MLS) is not a type of listing, but a marketing arrangement among brokers.

- There are three types of buyer agency agreements:

  1. Exclusive buyer agency
  2. Exclusive agency buyer agency
  3. Open buyer agency

- An agency agreement can be terminated by:

  - ☐ Performance
  - ☐ Expiration of the time period
  - ☐ Mutual agreement
  - ☐ Renunciation by the agent
  - ☐ Revocation by the principal
  - ☐ Destruction of the property
  - ☐ Eminent domain

- ☐   Bankruptcy
- ☐   Death
- ☐   Incompetence

- By law, there is no standard percentage for commissions. Any attempt to standardize commission rates among brokers is considered price fixing according to federal law.

- Both state and federal law require certain disclosures to the buyer by the seller and the seller's agent. Ethics also require disclosure of anything that affects the value or usefulness of the property.

- Agents have certain fiduciary responsibilities to their principals: (1) loyalty, (2) obedience, (3) disclosure, (4) confidentiality, (5) reasonable care and diligence, and (6) accountability.

Interests, Estates, and Ownership

chapter 4

OVERVIEW

- Real vs. personal property
- Rights of ownership
- Types of ownership
- Freehold estates
- Leasehold estates
- Private restrictions on ownership rights
- Government/public restrictions on ownership rights
- Summing it up

The right to something or to share in something is called an interest. An interest in real estate is called an estate. There are different types of interests—estates—in real estate, and each gives a person certain rights. In legal terms, property is not the house that your principal buys, but the legal right to use and enjoy that house and the land on which it sits. Remember, too, that an interest in real estate doesn't necessarily mean ownership. It can mean leasing or renting property from the owner.

REAL VS. PERSONAL PROPERTY

Property is either publicly or privately owned, and is either real property or personal property. Your state capitol building is an example of publicly owned property. Personal property, also called personalty and chattel, includes things like clothing, cars, flat-screen TVs, laptops, and so on. These are tangible things that you can unplug, pick up, carry around, and put down or drive around. Real property, also called realty, is "land, and everything that is permanently attached to it." However, the "permanently attached" things can be an issue in a real estate deal.

Fixtures

If an article is permanently attached to the property, it is considered a fixture and becomes real property like the land itself. It is easy to see that the foundation of the house, the separate garage, and the paved driveway are real property, but suppose the homeowner has installed a wine cellar in the basement that is built into the walls and floor. This has become a fixture. Landscaping that are annuals such as trees, bushes, and tulip bulbs are considered fixtures, too. What is a fixture and what is not also enters into the tenant/landlord relationship.

In order to determine whether something is a fixture and, thus, real property to be sold with the land (and all its rights) or can be removed by the owner or tenant, the following questions need to be answered:

- **How is the item attached to the property?** If removing the item will damage or destroy the underlying property, then it's probably a fixture. The method of attachment is also known as method of annexation.

- **What did the person who attached the item intend?** If the person intended it to become part of the property, then it's probably a fixture.

- **Is there a contract stating what is considered real property and what is personal property?** A tenant and a landlord may write into a lease that the tenant may add a new light in the kitchen that the tenant may remove when she leaves.

- **What is the relationship of the parties?** Improvements made by an owner are usually considered permanent and, therefore, real property to be sold. Changes made by a tenant are usually considered temporary to be removed by the tenant when vacating the premises. This particularly applies to commercial tenants who may customize a property for their business purposes. However, in many commercial leases, unless the lease demands that the tenant restore the premises to the way it was when the tenant moved in, the lease will often provide that all fixtures become the property of the landlord. As you can imagine, the specifics of these clauses are carefully negotiated.

Typically, if there is any concern about whether something is chattel or realty, the item is included in the contract. A principal may indicate in the listing contract that he or she is taking the chandelier in the dining room and not including it with the house. If the buyer makes leaving it a condition of sale and the seller agrees, then the agreement should be included in the final sales contract.

RIGHTS OF OWNERSHIP

When a person buys real estate, certain ownership rights may come with the property. These are automatically conveyed with the title of the property, and include surface, subsurface, and mineral, water, and air rights. The exceptions are condo and co-op ownership. Skip ahead a few sections for more on Owning in Common.

In the condo form of ownership, these rights may be included in ownership unless the developer has already sold them. If they have not been sold off, these rights are part of the common area, and the condo buyer will own only a fractional share of the common area. It could also be the case that the developer did not purchase these rights from the original owner. They could have been specifically excluded from the developer's purchase.

Under co-op ownership, the corporation owns these rights if they came with the land. In that case, the co-op buyer would own a share in these rights through ownership of the stock of the corporation.

Surface rights

Surface rights relate to the surface of the land. In purchasing the property, the buyer gets the right to use the land in any way that is legal. That is, the new owner can construct a detached garage as long as the local zoning laws allow it. Skip ahead a few sections for more information on government restrictions on land use.

Surface rights also give an owner the right to grant someone an easement through the property. Skip ahead a few sections for more information on easements.

Subsurface Rights and Mineral Rights

Want to dig a tunnel to China? As a landowner, you would be within your rights at least until you got to the Earth's core. In theory, an owner has subsurface rights down to the center of the Earth. In practice, there is little value in this right, unless a utility or local municipality wants to run a power, water, or sewer line under the property. Also, the use of geothermal heating is making subsurface rights more attractive to the eco-friendly.

The owner of land has the right to extract, or lease to others the right to extract, any minerals found underground. It is also possible for an owner to sell a property, but retain the mineral rights. In addition to the rights to underground minerals like gold and silver, the rights to coal, oil, and natural gas fall under the category of mineral rights.

Water Rights

State laws define water rights and may place restrictions on those rights in some circumstances, notably in areas prone to drought or with rapid population growth. In general, however, riparian and littoral water rights grant owners whose property is adjacent to bodies of water use of the body of water, but not exclusive rights to it.

- **Riparian rights:** These are the rights of property owners bordering a flowing body of water. If the waterway is navigable, the property owners own the land to the water's edge, or to the average or the mean high water mark. If the waterway is not navigable, property rights extend to the center of the waterway.

- **Littoral rights:** These are the rights of property owners whose land is adjacent to lakes, an ocean, or a sea. These rights grant ownership of the land to the water's edge or to the average or mean high water mark.

Air Rights

The owner of a property owns the air space above it. However, there are limits on this right imposed by federal aviation laws and local zoning laws. Such easements typically cover all successors and assignees once a property owner has signed it. The easement could be in the deed or in a recorded easement, and if it is supposed to continue after transfers, it is said to "run with the land."

Air rights typically come into play when a property owner wants to sell the air rights above the property to someone else, generally a developer. Local zoning laws determine how high the additional construction may be. The original property owner retains ownership of the land and his or her original building, whereas the developer owns only the additional stories. An owner could also sell air rights for an elevated pedestrian bridge over his or her land to connect from one building to another.

ALERT!

If you live in a state with water resource issues like many of the western states, be sure that you know your own state's water laws. Look for information on the doctrine of prior appropriation.

ALERT!

In a state with a coastline, riparian rights are also important because they govern where you can build (and sit) on the beach.

Bundle of Rights

The rights that owners may exercise over their property are called the bundle of rights. In totality, these are the rights to occupy, use, and enjoy their property including the land, water, air, etc. More specifically, the bundle of rights includes the rights to employ the property in productive ways such as farming or leasing, and to sell, bequeath, give, or lease the property in part or in total. The bundle of rights also means that an owner has all these rights and may do nothing with them if he or she so chooses. However, not all types of estates have the complete bundle of ownership rights attached to them.

TYPES OF OWNERSHIP

There are a variety of ways that property may be owned. Individuals, married couples, two cohabitors, trusts, corporations, and so on can buy, own, and sell property. There are also special types of property ownership such as condominiums.

Sole Owner

An individual's ownership of property is called sole ownership or tenancy in severalty. No one else has an interest in that particular property except that individual.

Joint Tenancy

Joint tenancy is an ownership arrangement for two or more individuals. Typically, the creators of a joint tenancy must fulfill four requirements, or unities as they are called:

1. **Unity of time:** All parties must acquire their interests at the same time.
2. **Unity of title:** A single deed or title conveys all parties' interests.
3. **Unity of interest:** Each party has the same percentage of ownership.
4. **Unity of possession:** All parties own the total property.

Parties to a joint tenancy have the right of survivorship, that is, if one tenant dies, the other tenants automatically take ownership of the deceased's share. The person's heirs do not inherit the interest.

Tenancy in Common

Although it does not give the tenants right of survivorship, tenancy in common is the most often used form of co- or joint ownership. This is the form of ownership that two unmarried people would probably enter into if they bought a house together.

Tenancy in common gives each person undivided interest in the property; however, the percentage of ownership may vary. It does not have to be split 50/50. Also, each tenant holds ownership in severalty, which means that each tenant may dispose of that interest as he or she chooses without the consent of the other tenant. One tenant may put a second mortgage on his interest, sell the interest, or leave it to a third party in his will.

Owning as a Married Couple

There are two special forms of property ownership by married couples: tenancy by the entirety and community property. However, community property ownership is not recognized by all or even most states. Not all states recognize tenancy by the entirety either.

- **Tenancy by the entirety:** Property is owned by the two parties in a marriage as if they were one. They each have an undivided and equal interest in the property and the right of survivorship. Neither spouse may sell, give away, will, or mortgage the property without the consent of the other. Should the marriage be dissolved by divorce, tenancy by the entirety is replaced by tenancy in common. The four unities plus unity of person must be met to be tenancy by the entirety.

- **Community property:** If a couple buys property during their marriage, it is considered jointly and equally owned by both spouses, but there is no right of survivorship in community property states. A spouse may leave his or her half to the surviving spouse, to a child, or to anyone the person wishes. Property that a spouse owned before the marriage or inherited during the marriage is not community property. It is termed separate property, and the original owner or inheriting owner may use and dispose of it as the owner determines.

NOTE

Know if your state recognizes community property ownership or tenancy by the entirety, and if so, what the law says about it.

Trusts

A trust is a legal arrangement in which the owner (trustor) conveys the ownership of the property to the trust, thus giving another (trustee) the power to manage the property/trust for the benefit of a third party (beneficiary). There are various tax advantages to trusts; however, real estate agents should direct any customers seeking answers about taxes and trusts to their lawyer and to their tax accountant, unless the person is a tax lawyer. A trust may be one of the following:

- *inter vivos,* **or living, trust:** A trustor creates the trust to be effective during his or her lifetime.

- **testamentary trust:** A trustor leaves instructions in his or her will about establishing a trust that will not be effective until after he or she dies.

NOTE

A few states allow land trusts. This type of trust conceals the identity of the owner and is useful to developers trying to buy up land. Check to see if your state allows this type of trust.

Owning in Common

There are four basic types of property ownership that don't fit precisely into the categories that you've just read about: ownership of condominiums, cooperatives, planned unit developments (planned housing developments like townhouse complexes), and timeshares, the newest wrinkle in owning.

- **Condo ownership:** When a person or couple buys a condominium unit, a deed changes hands. The buyer buys a specific unit as well as ownership of common areas such as the lobby and fitness center and the land under the building and around it. Condo owners pay a monthly fee called a maintenance fee for the management and upkeep of the condominium. A volunteer board oversees the management of the building or buildings, sets policy, and writes rules for condominium owners. Condo owners pay real estate taxes for their units and their fractional shares in the common areas.

- **Co-op ownership:** Someone who buys a co-operative apartment buys shares in the underlying corporation, and, therefore, does not get a deed to a specific unit, but a proprietary lease to that unit. Like a condominium, there is a board, a monthly fee, and a management company that takes care of the maintenance of the building or buildings. Unlike a condominium, the monthly charge in a co-op includes maintenance and property taxes. A potential buyer in a co-op must pass a board interview and review of finances in order to buy into a co-op.

- **Planned unit developments (PUD):** A townhouse may be a condominium or part of a PUD, which is defined as a combination of residential, commercial, and industrial properties in a single project designed and built by a single developer. Single family homes may also be part of a PUD, and a PUD may also contain only residential buildings. In a PUD, a property owner owns the land under and around his or her unit. The land is not owned jointly by the PUD. However, all owners in a PUD own the common areas such as parking and recreation areas. A board, typically called a homeowners association (HOA), is elected by homeowners to oversee the management company that maintains the PUD, to set policy, and to write rules for the PUD. Property owners pay their own taxes.

- **Timeshares:** A timeshare gives a person a fractional ownership share in a property, allowing that person the right to use the property for a period of time, usually one or two weeks every year. The ownership of the property, which is usually an apartment in a resort area or a hotel room in a city, belongs to another party. A timeshare is a fee simple interest in the real estate. There is an annual maintenance fee associated with timeshares.

Real Estate Ownerships by Businesses

Any form of business organization can own real estate, from the biggest Fortune 500 company that owns huge office campuses to the local pet adoption nonprofit that buys the building housing its shelter to the two friends who decide to invest in a condo to rent. As an agent, you are more likely to deal with business property ownership if you decide to work in commercial real estate.

- **Partnerships:** There are two kinds of partnerships: general and limited. A number of states have Uniform Partnership and Uniform Limited Liability Partnership Acts that regulate how partnerships investing in real estate may operate. In a general partnership, the partners must agree to all activities related to a property such as selling it or mortgaging it as well as the management of the property. All partners also share in the liability related to the actions of the partnership, and partners pay taxes in relation to the amount of their interest, which is, investment, in the partnership. A limited liability partnership limits the amount of liability of each partner to the amount of the partner's interest in the partnership. Generally, one partner assumes day-to-day management of the partnership.

- **Corporations:** Corporations may buy real estate for a variety of reasons including investment, construction of their own facilities, or to develop and sell. Even though a corporation may have thousands of shareholders and thousands of employees, before the law a corporation is considered an individual entity, and, therefore, has sole ownership, or tenancy in severalty, of its property. Liability is generally limited to the amount of the shareholders' investment in the corporation, and management of the property falls to the managers of the corporation. The corporation pays taxes on any profits and shareholders pay taxes on the distribution of any profits. Nonprofit corporations such as charities, churches, and universities may own property. They may apply for and receive tax exemption status that allows them to forego paying federal and state income taxes and real estate taxes.

- **Limited liability company (LLC):** Under federal law, an LLC may choose to be taxed as a corporation or as a partnership. Its members may be equal or not and may have an equal say

NOTE

Federal and state syndication laws regulate real estate syndicates. Unless you plan to deal in commercial real estate, you probably won't come across real estate syndicates, but know what they are for the test.

or not in how the LLC is operated. The LLC may also have a managing member. Most of the details are set forth in the formation documents for each LLC. If the documents do not specify, then the LLC defaults to whatever the state's LLC statute says. An LLC may also be a sole proprietorship.

- **Joint ventures:** Two friends decide to buy a condo and rent it out as an investment and form a joint venture for their business. Two or more business entities may also form a joint venture to buy, own, and develop property for some purpose. Joint ventures are typically project-based and entered into for a stated period of time. A joint venture may take any form of ownership. However, unless they have some recognized written agreement, the members of the joint venture will be deemed to have a general partnership and will be equally liable. In a business joint venture, the rights, responsibilities, and liabilities are spelled out for the protection of the joint venturors.

- **Syndicates:** A syndicate is a group of people or business entities that combine to invest in real estate. Rather than cooperating for a single project the way a joint venture does, a syndicate works on a number of real estate projects. Syndicators—those who set up and manage the syndicate—typically bring in a number of investors to maximize investment potential and return on investment. A syndicate is basically a big investment pool.

FREEHOLD ESTATES

In real estate, there are freehold estates and leasehold estates. A freehold estate grants ownership of a property for an indeterminate period of time, whereas a leasehold estate grants the holder of the lease possession of the property for a set period of time. In other words, a renter's interest in a property is a leasehold estate.

Fee Simple Estates

A fee simple estate is the most complete form of property ownership. The owner has all rights to use, enjoy, and dispose of the property—subject to public and private restrictions. These restrictions are described later in this chapter. Fee simple estates are also called fee absolute and indefeasible fee estates.

Estates in Qualified Fee

A qualified fee simple estate is subject to certain conditions or contingencies that the grantor puts on the property. Unlike a fee simple estate, a fee simple qualified estate has a stated endpoint—if the conditions are not met—and a limit on the interest in the property. The property reverts to a fee absolute estate if the conditions are not met and the property is returned to the grantor. Heirs of the grantor/seller may exercise the right of reversion in each case. This category is also known as fee simple defeasible estates.

- **Qualified fee conditional:** This form of fee simple qualified estate is also known as qualified fee subject to condition subsequent. A grantor/seller stipulates in the sale of a property that the buyer and his or her heirs may not use the property for a certain purpose. For example, suppose the grantor has sold the property to the county for open space, but the county in need of money sells part of the property to a developer to build homes on. The qualified fee conditional gives the grantor the right of reentry and reversion. The former is the right to inspect the property to see if the condition has been violated, and the latter is the court mechanism for reclaiming the property if the condition has been violated.

- **Qualified fee determinable:** The difference between qualified fee conditional and qualified fee determinable is that no legal process is needed to revert the property to the grantor if a condition is violated. The reversion of the property to the grantor is automatic.

Life Estates

Life estates have an endpoint. Ownership and possession of the property last only for the life of the person who is called the life tenant.

- **Ordinary life estate:** Upon the death of the life tenant, the life estate passes to someone else. If the life estate goes back to the grantor/owner, then it is an ordinary life estate with reversion. If the life estate goes to some other person such as the children of the holder of the life estate, it is an ordinary life estate with remainder. The person (or persons) who is entitled to the estate is called the remainderman.

- **Life estate *pur autre vie*:** This form of life estate designates someone, let's call him Person 1, as having interest in a property for the duration of the life of someone other than Person 1. For example, a husband gives his son and daughter-in-law (Person 1) the right to live in his home to take care of his demented wife (Person 2) while he moves to Paris. If, when the wife dies, the house reverts back to the husband of the dead woman, this is known as a life estate *pur autre vie* with reversion. However, when the wife dies, it turns out that the husband had created a life estate *pur autre vie* with remainder: He doesn't take the property back because he has already given it to his girlfriend.

LEASEHOLD ESTATES

The lessee, known familiarly as the tenant, has a leasehold estate, leasehold interest, or tenant's estate in the property to which the lessee has a lease. The landlord's interest is called leased fee interest or leased fee estate. Under a leasehold estate, the owner gives up the right of occupancy in exchange for a sum of money (rent). The owner, however, retains other rights and the tenant gains certain rights; the rights for each depend on the type of leasehold estate that is established. There are several types of leasehold estates.

- **Estate for years:** The lessee and the landlord agree to a lease for a term of years. The lease states the beginning and end dates of that term. Upon expiration of the term, the lessee must vacate the premises unless a new lease has been negotiated and signed. The lease is still in force even if the landlord or the tenant dies. Selling the property does not terminate the lease either.

- **Estate from period to period:** Also known as periodic tenancy, this form of leasehold does not have a specified end date, but is for a specified period of time such as a week or a month. The leasehold automatically renews unless the landlord or the tenant wishes not to renew. Then the nonrenewing party must give the other notice, usually the amount of time of the period of tenancy, that is, a week or a month. If the landlord sells the property and the new owner decides to end a periodic tenancy, the new owner simply stops accepting the rent check from the lessee. In the modern world, if either the landlord or the tenant dies, the estate would end at the end of the current "period."

- **Estate at will:** In this form of leasehold, the landlord allows a tenant to occupy a property without a specified end date. There may or may not be a written lease. Generally, estate at will ends if either party gives the other reasonable notice. The death of either party also terminates an estate at will as does the sale of the property by the landlord to another party.

- **Estate at sufferance:** This is also known as a holdover tenancy. Estate at sufferance occurs when a tenant stays past the end of his or her lease, and the landlord has not agreed to an extension or renewal. The lessee may or may not be trying to pay rent, but the landlord refuses it. The landlord's recourse is to start eviction proceedings.

PRIVATE RESTRICTIONS ON OWNERSHIP RIGHTS

An encumbrance is anything that limits or negatively affects the title of a property. The title is the legally recognized bundle of rights that an interest holder has in property. A mortgage is an encumbrance, as are leases, easements, liens, and deed restrictions.

Easements

An easement gives a person the right to pass through or use another's property. The local sewer company may gain easements from all the owners on a block to lay a new pipe line across their properties, or your next-door neighbor may request an easement to create a vegetable garden in part of your yard that is much sunnier than his yard. An easement is often referred to as a right of way.

There are typically two parties to an easement, the dominant estate and the servient estate. The dominant estate is the one that receives the benefit of the easement, and the servient estate is the one that bestows the benefit.

- **Appurtenant easements:** Also called easements appurtenant, these easements are permanent once negotiated, that is, each time the property with the easement and the property that granted the easement are sold, the agreement continues in force. Appurtenant easements may be overhead, surface, and underground.

- **Party wall:** A party-wall easement is a type of appurtenant easement. Townhouses and semi-detached houses have party, or a shared, wall between units. A party-wall easement gives each party an easement to the half of the wall that he or she doesn't own. The purpose of the easements is to maintain the shared wall.

- **Easements in gross:** The beneficiary of an easement in gross is not a property, but a person. No dominant estate exists with an easement in gross. The beneficiary is often a utility company wanting access over or under property to lay pipe or string wires to other properties. Other easements in gross are easements for railroads, telephone and cable companies, and sidewalks. Easements in gross to commercial entities like utility companies are transferred with the property when it is sold. In other words, they run with the land.

- **Easements by prescription:** Suppose that for 10 years you and your children always crossed your neighbor's backyard as a shortcut to the YMCA behind her property. This use of your neighbor's backyard may be an easement by prescription if your neighbor never gave you permission, you have done it in plain sight of your neighbor, you have done it without interruption, and the 10-year time period is the period of time that your state considers the prescribed statutory

NOTE

In selling a property, the seller and the real estate agent need to disclose to the buyer the presence of any easements, and these may affect the value, and thus, price, of the property.

TIP

There are a variety of kinds of easements that states allow, so be sure you know what your state allows.

time for an easement by prescription. You have established your right to use the shortcut across your neighbor's backyard.

An easement can be ended simply by agreeing to end it. It can also be terminated by merger, that is, one party buys out the other, thus ending the need for the easement. The need for the easement may end. For example, the avid gardener took up golf and told you that he no longer needs your yard. On the other hand, lack of use of the easement is considered abandonment, and that ends an easement.

Liens

A lien is a financial claim against property. The property becomes security for the payment of a debt or taxes. Liens may be voluntary or involuntary; they may also be classified as specific or general.

A voluntary lien is one that the property owner agrees to; for example, a mortgage is a voluntary lien. A lien against property because of an unpaid debt like back IRS taxes is an involuntary lien. This is also called a statutory lien.

A specific lien applies to one property, and a general lien applies to more than one. If a property owner owns a half dozen rental properties, a carpenter might put a lien against only the unit where he did work. Only that one could be seized and sold to discharge the lien. A creditor who was stuck with a large debt might decide to get a lien against all six properties. Then all six could be sold to satisfy the debt.

There are several types of liens that fit into these categories.

- **Mortgage lien:** A mortgage lien is a voluntary, specific lien that must be paid off at the time of resale.

- **Tax lien:** A tax lien is both involuntary and specific. All levels of government may place a tax lien on property for nonpayment of taxes. These include real estate taxes, state and federal income taxes, and estate and inheritance taxes. Real estate liens are specific. Other government liens such as IRS liens may be general.

- **Judgment lien:** A judgment lien is involuntary and general, applying to all the property of the person on whom the judgment was rendered. A judgment results from a decision in a legal case that directs the loser in the case to pay a certain amount called the judgement. When the person can't pay the judgment, a judgment lien is attached to the loser's property.

- **Mechanic's lien:** This is an involuntary, specific lien that a contractor attaches to a property for work done on the property for which the property owner has not paid the contractor.

When an owner is selling property, all liens against the property must be cleared up. For example, a mortgage on a home is paid off at the time of the closing. If a mechanic's lien had been placed on the property for nonpayment of a new deck, the seller must pay off that debt at the time of closing as well. A property can also be seized and sold to pay a debt or back taxes. A home foreclosure is an example of a property seizure for failure to pay agreed-upon mortgage payments.

The priority of liens determines the order in which multiple liens on one property are to be paid off. First is payment of any general real estate taxes that are owed. Second is payment of any taxes for special assessments. Third is payment of the outstanding mortgage. After that, payment is made to lien holders in the order in which they recorded their liens with the local government's office of public records.

Deed Restrictions

Deed restrictions are also called restrictive covenants and covenants, conditions, and restrictions (CCRs). These are private restrictions on what a property owner is allowed to do with his or her property as opposed to public restrictions on what a property owner can do. Both types of restrictions are legally binding. However, a private restriction such as a restrictive covenant in a homeowners' association cannot be illegal, such as refusing to allow property to be sold to African Americans. A deed restriction "runs with the land"—goes with title to the property—so that anyone who buys the property after the deed restriction is placed on the property must abide by the restriction.

CCRs are typically placed on subdivisions by the developer, but townhome, condo, and neighborhood associations as well as developers of PUDs also place CCRs on property owners. A typical list of builder CCRs might include a restriction on subdividing a lot to build a second house on it or on the architectural style of a home that may be built in the development. Typical homeowner association CCRs relate to the types of window and door replacements that may be used or the color of the paint for trim. The list of restrictions is called a declaration of restrictions.

Laches is the failure to enforce or exercise a right that then causes the right to be lost. Laches doesn't specifically deal with deed restrictions, but a deed restriction can be lost in effect by the failure to enforce it by the person or entity that has the right to enforce it. With real estate, it would usually be the previous owner who put the restriction on the property in the first place. The time limit for enforcement is set by a state's case law, that is, judicial decisions in such cases, and will vary from state to state.

Encroachments

An encroachment is something that intrudes on another person's property such as a tree that has grown over and under a fence or the fence itself that was built over the neighbor's property line. It may be accidental or deliberate, but it is still an encumbrance on the neighbor's property. One hopes that accidental encroachments can be corrected without recourse to the law courts once the offending neighbor has been apprised of the situation. Unfortunately, this is not always true. However, in this case, the offending neighbor is not claiming ownership of the area in dispute, just use of the extra few feet that the fence gives him or her.

Suppose there is no fence between two properties and Property Owner A builds a garden shed on what he knows is his neighbor's property, but he doesn't care because his neighbor has more land than he does. The owner on whose land the shed is built, Property Owner B, knows that it's his property, but doesn't want to get into a fight about it. When Property Owner B goes to sell, the deed clearly shows that the neighbor's shed is on Property Owner B's property. When Property Owner B tells his neighbor this and asks him to move or tear down the shed, Property Owner A refuses and claims adverse possession of the land under the shed and between his property line and the shed by nature of his having used the area for 10 years, or whatever the time requirement in the state.

NOTE
Deed restrictions could impact the intended use of a property by a buyer, so it's important that a buyer be made aware of any restrictions.

GOVERNMENT/PUBLIC RESTRICTIONS ON OWNERSHIP RIGHTS

Major restrictions on ownership rights are fair housing laws that ban discrimination in housing and land use laws. Other government restrictions include the following:

- **Eminent domain:** A government may condemn and take possession of private property that the government wants to use for the public good such as building a new bridge. Each state and the federal government have certain regulations and procedures that must be followed in claiming the right of eminent domain, and the owner must be compensated for the property at a fair price. Eminent domain is typically the last resort and used when a property owner will not negotiate or will not accept the government's offer.

- **Escheat:** If you own property and die without a will and without relatives, the state will take that property by escheat. Even the most secluded piece of forest is owned by someone or by a government entity. There is no free land in this country anymore.

- **Taxation:** All levels of government tax U.S. residents. If taxes aren't paid, a person's property—real and personal—can be seized and sold for payment of back taxes.

EXERCISES

1. Suppose a tenant's estate for years ends, but the tenant is buying a house and the closing is delayed. The tenant and landlord agree to a month-to-month lease. This is known as
   (A) tenancy by the entirety.
   (B) estate at will.
   (C) periodic tenancy.
   (D) estate at sufferance.

2. Which of the following is NOT included in the bundle of rights?
   (A) Right to leave property to another
   (B) Right to transfer title of a property
   (C) Right of occupancy
   (D) Right of eminent domain

3. In buying a co-op, a buyer buys
   (A) the land under the co-op building as well as the unit.
   (B) air and water rights as well as the unit.
   (C) shares in the corporation.
   (D) a fee simple estate in the co-op unit.

4. Ownership in severalty is the same as
   (A) joint tenancy.
   (B) sole ownership.
   (C) ownership by a corporation.
   (D) tenancy in common.

5. A lien is a form of
   (A) encroachment.
   (B) easement.
   (C) escheat.
   (D) encumbrance.

6. Someone who buys a timeshare owns it as
   (A) a share in a fee simple estate.
   (B) community property.
   (C) a partnership.
   (D) a qualified fee conditional.

7. The order in which multiple liens must be paid is
   (A) general real estate taxes, special assessments, mortgage, order in which a lien was recorded.
   (B) order in which a lien was recorded, special assessments, general real estate taxes, mortgage.
   (C) mortgage, order in which a lien was recorded, general real estate taxes, special assessment.
   (D) order in which a lien was recorded, mortgage, special assessments, general real estate taxes.

8. A fee simple estate is one that
   (A) is a leasehold category.
   (B) is for a determinate period of time.
   (C) is the most common form of partnership.
   (D) is the most complete form of property ownership.

9. Which of the following would be considered a fixture?
   (A) Clothes washer
   (B) Built-in bookcase
   (C) Bunk beds
   (D) Above-ground pool

10. Laches is
    (A) a type of deed restriction.
    (B) the loss of the right to evict a tenant.
    (C) the loss of the right because of a failure to enforce it within the proper amount of time.
    (D) the court order to enforce an eviction.

ANSWER KEY AND EXPLANATIONS

1. C	3. C	5. D	7. A	9. B
2. D	4. B	6. A	8. D	10. C

1. **The correct answer is (C).** A periodic tenancy is also known as an estate from period to period. Choice (A) is ownership by a married couple and is a freehold estate. Choice (B) is a leasehold estate, but refers to a situation in which the landlord allows a tenant to occupy a property without a specific end date. Choice (D) is also a leasehold estate, but the tenant is staying without the landlord's permission after the expiration of a lease.

2. **The correct answer is (D).** Choice (D) is the right of a level of government to seize private property under certain circumstances. Choices (A), (B), and (C) are all part of a property owner's bundle of rights.

3. **The correct answer is (C).** A buyer of a co-op actually buys shares in the corporation and with those the right to occupy, use, and bequeath a particular unit (though the heir may still have to go before the co-op board to occupy the unit and the board might insist on buying out the heir). Choices (A), (B), and (D) do not apply to a co-op.

4. **The correct answer is (B).** Ownership by severalty is ownership by an individual. Choices (A) and (D) are incorrect because they refer to property ownership by two or more people, but don't be fooled because of the word *tenancy. Tenancy* in these two forms of ownership refers to freehold estates, not leaseholds. Choice (C) is a form of business ownership.

5. **The correct answer is (D).** A lien places an encumbrance on a property. Choice (A) is some element of one property that intrudes

on another. Choice (B) is a right of way given to another party by a property owner. Choice (C) occurs when a government takes title to property that had been owned by someone who dies without a will and without heirs.

6. **The correct answer is (A).** A timeshare is owned as a fee simple estate. Choice (B) refers to property ownership by a married couple in some states. Choice (C) is a form of business ownership. Choice (D) is a form of qualified fee ownership that puts certain conditions on ownership.

7. **The correct answer is (A).** The order in which multiple liens must be paid, choice (A), is called the priority of payments or priority of liens. Choices (B), (C), and (D) are incorrect.

8. **The correct answer is (D).** Choice (D) affords to the property owner all the rights of possession, use, and enjoyment of his or her property to the limit of any private or public restrictions. Choice (A) is incorrect because a fee simple estate is a category under freehold estates. Choice (B) describes a leasehold. Choice (C) may have confused you because a partnership is the most common form of business organization.

9. **The correct answer is (B).** Choice (B) is affixed to the property unlike choices (C) and (D). Choice (A) can be unplugged and taken away if the buyer doesn't want it.

10. **The correct answer is (C).** Choices (A), (B), and (D) are incorrect.

SUMMING IT UP

- A fixture is any article that is permanently attached to the property and, thus, becomes part of the real property. To determine if something is a fixture, you need to ask and answer four questions:

  1. How is the item attached?
  2. What did the person who attached the item intend?
  3. Is there a contract stating what is considered real property and what is personal property?
  4. What is the relationship of the parties?

- Rights of ownership include surface, subsurface and mineral rights, water rights, and air rights.

- Property owners have what is known as a bundle of rights that entitles them to occupy, use, and enjoy their property, but not all types of ownership entitle owners to the complete bundle.

- There are a variety of types of ownership:

  - [ ] Sole ownership or tenancy in severalty
  - [ ] Joint tenancy that requires that the four unities (of time, title, interest, and possession) be met
  - [ ] Tenancy in common
  - [ ] Ownership by a married couple that may be tenancy by the entirety or, in some states, as community property
  - [ ] Trusts: *inter vivos,* testamentary trust
  - [ ] Common ownership: condominium, co-operative, planned unit development (PUD), timeshare
  - [ ] Business ownerships of real estate: partnerships, either general or limited; limited liability partnership; corporation; limited liability company (LLC); joint venture; syndicate

- Freehold estates grant ownership of a property for an indeterminate period of time and include:

  - [ ] Fee simple estates
  - [ ] Qualified fee estates: qualified fee conditional, qualified fee determinable
  - [ ] Life estates: ordinary life estate with reversion, ordinary life estate with remainder, life estate *pur autre vie* with reversion, life estate *pur autre vie* with remainder

- Under a leasehold estate, the owner gives up occupancy in return for the rent. Leasehold estates include:

  - [ ] Estate for years
  - [ ] Estate from period to period
  - [ ] Estate at will
  - [ ] Estate at sufferance

- Private restriction on ownership rights are called encumbrances and include:
  - ☐ Easements: appurtenant easements, party wall, easements in gross, easements by prescription
  - ☐ Liens that may be voluntary or involuntary and specific or general and include mortgages, tax liens, judgment liens, and mechanic's liens
  - ☐ Deed restrictions: restrictive covenants; covenants, conditions, and restrictions (CCRs)
  - ☐ Encroachments: adverse possession
- Multiples liens are paid off in a specific order known as priority of payments or priority of liens.
- Government or public restrictions on ownership rights include:
  - ☐ Eminent domain
  - ☐ Escheat
  - ☐ Taxation
  - ☐ Land use laws

Fair Housing Laws

OVERVIEW

- The purpose of fair housing laws
- A brief history of federal fair housing laws
- Americans with Disabilities Act
- What can you not do?
- What do you have to do as a realtor?
- What is the penalty for discrimination?
- State and local housing laws
- Summing it up

Federal, state, and local fair housing laws can be summed up in a simple sentence: You cannot discriminate in selling or leasing property. The "you" is you, the realtor, and you, the property owner, whether selling or renting property. The goal of fair housing laws is to provide a level playing field for every person when they choose housing. The limit should be the potential buyer's or renter's finances and housing wish list, not the seller's or landlord's biases. The enforcement of fair housing laws operates as a major public restriction on private property owners. Enforcement of fair housing laws is also the mission of HUD, the federal Department of Housing and Urban Development.

THE PURPOSE OF FAIR HOUSING LAWS

The basic law regulating fairness in housing is the Fair Housing Act of 1968 and the Fair Housing Amendments Act of 1988. Under these acts:

> It is the policy of the United States to provide, within constitutional limitations, for fair housing throughout the United States. No person shall be subjected to the discrimination because of race, color, religion, sex, handicap, familial status, or national origin in the sale, rental, or advertising of dwellings, in the provision of brokerage services, or in the availability of residential real estate-related transactions.
>
> —Title 24. Part 100. Discriminatory Conduct Under the Fairing Housing Act, Subpart A—General, 100.5 Scope

The categories listed in the above paragraph are referred to as protected classes. For the most part, the definitions of the classes are self-explanatory. However, there are two that are worth further explanation: familial status and handicap. Familial status refers to a household with existing or prospective children. Under the Fair Housing Act, a seller or landlord may not deny property to parents or legal guardians who have a person younger than 18 living with them. The law specifically covers pregnant women and adults in the process of gaining custody of children under 18.

chapter 5

Section 100.201 of Title 24 of the Fair Housing Act makes it illegal to discriminate against a person with "a physical or mental disability which substantially limits one or more major life activities." This category does not include current use of or addiction to controlled substances. It does include the following disabilities:

- Mental retardation
- Hearing and visual impairments
- Mobility impairments such as cerebral palsy and muscular sclerosis
- Cancer, diabetes, heart disease, epilepsy, and similar physical diseases
- Chronic mental illness
- AIDS and AIDS-related illnesses
- Drug addiction from past illegal use of drugs
- Alcoholism

A BRIEF HISTORY OF FEDERAL FAIR HOUSING LAWS

The Federal Fair Housing Act applies to most housing. See the exceptions listed below.

ACT	MAJOR PROVISIONS
Civil Rights Act of 1866	Prohibits racial discrimination, which by extension includes the sale or purchase of property
Civil Rights Act of 1964: Title VI	Prohibits discrimination on the basis of race, color, or national origin in programs and activities that receive federal funding
Civil Rights Act of 1968: Title VIII (Fair Housing Act of 1968)	• Prohibits discrimination in housing on the basis of race, color, or national origin (for specific prohibitions see below) • Provides for certain exemptions (listed below)
Rehabilitation Act of 1973: Section 504	Prohibits discrimination based on disability in any program or activity receiving federal funding
Civil Rights Amendments Act of 1974	Amends Title VIII to include sex (gender) as a protected class
Housing and Community Development Act of 1974: Section 109	Prohibits discrimination on the basis of race, color, national origin, sex, or religion in programs receiving federal funding from HUD's Community Development and Block Grant Program
Housing and Community Amendments Act of 1981	Amends 1974 Act and extends coverage to include age and those with handicaps, ensuring that new multifamily construction (property of more than 4 units) be handicap accessible
Fair Housing Amendments Act of 1988	• Assigns enforcement responsibility to HUD • Increases penalties for violations • Expands coverage to include those with disabilities and families with children

Under the Fair Housing Act, persons with disabilities who rent property may make "reasonable modifications" to the property to enable them to live there. When the tenant's lease is up and he or she leaves, the property must be restored to how it was before the modification was made. However, this is negotiable if the modification "will not interfere with the . . . [future] use and enjoyment" of the property.

Federal Executive Orders

There are also several federal executive orders that relate to housing. Federal executive orders are signed by the President of the United States and have the force of law.

FEDERAL EXECUTIVE ORDERS	PROVISIONS
11063 John F. Kennedy	Prohibits discrimination in the sale, leasing, rental, or other disposition of properties and facilities owned or operated by the federal government or provided with federal funds
12892 William J. Clinton	• Requires federal agencies to further fair housing in all their programs and activities • Establishes the President's Fair Housing Council
13166 William J. Clinton	Eliminates limited English proficiency as a barrier to full and meaningful participation by beneficiaries in all federally assisted and federally conducted programs and activities, including housing
13217 George W. Bush	Requires federal agencies to evaluate their policies and programs to determine if any can be revised or modified to improve the availability of community-based living arrangements (CLAs) for persons with disabilities

Exemptions to the Fair Housing Act

The Fair Housing Act of 1968 provides for the following exemptions to what is prohibited:

• Owner-occupied buildings with no more than four units

• Single-family homes sold or rented without the use of a broker

• Housing operated by religious organizations that limit occupancy to members (if the organization does not otherwise discriminate in whom it accepts as members)

• Housing operated by private clubs that limit occupancy to members

• Over-55 housing

However, there are no exemptions that allow racial discrimination, which is universally prohibited under the Civil Rights Act of 1866. Unlike lawsuits over housing discrimination brought under other statutes, lawsuits filed under the Civil Rights Act of 1866 are always heard in federal court.

AMERICANS WITH DISABILITIES ACT

In 1992, Congress passed the Americans with Disabilities Act (ADA) to protect those with disabilities against discrimination. While the Fair Housing Act prohibits discrimination in housing, the ADA prohibits discrimination in a variety of environments such as employment. In terms of property, the ADA protects the right of access to public spaces for those with disabilities and also requires the elimination of architectural barriers in new construction. Title III of the ADA incorporates the ADA Accessibility Guidelines that deal with the identification and elimination of architectural barriers in old and new construction. If some barrier cannot be removed in an old building, then alternatives are required.

WHAT CAN YOU NOT DO?

Here it is direct from HUD:

In the sale and rental of housing, no one may take any of the following actions:

- Refuse to rent or sell housing
- Refuse to negotiate for housing
- Make housing unavailable
- Set different terms, conditions, or privileges for sale or rental of a dwelling
- Provide different housing services or facilities
- Falsely deny that housing is available for inspection, sale, or rental
- For profit, persuade owners to sell or rent (blockbusting)
- Deny anyone [realtors who are members of minorities] access to or membership in a facility or service (such as a multiple listing service) related to the sale or rental of housing

In addition, it is illegal for anyone to

- threaten, coerce, intimidate, or interfere with anyone exercising a fair housing right or assisting others who exercise that right.
- advertise or make any statement that indicates a limitation or preference based on race, color, national origin, religion, sex, familial status, or handicap. This prohibition against discriminatory advertising applies to single-family and owner-occupied housing that is otherwise exempt from the Fair Housing Act.

Blockbusting, Steering, and Redlining

There are three terms that you should know regarding prohibited practices: blockbusting, steering, and redlining.

1. **Blockbusting:** As noted in the list of banned activities, blockbusting is persuading owners to sell or rent by playing on people's fears and with the intention of making a profit. A realtor or investor doesn't just persuade Joe Smith to sell up and move. The realtor uses scare tactics in persuading homeowners to sell because "those people" are moving into the neighborhood. "Those people" may be members of another religion, race, or ethnic group. Blockbusting is a cynical practice that feeds on people's biases and fear in order to generate real estate listings and commissions for a real estate agent and/or investor. It also drives prices down, which may accelerate sales.

2. **Steering:** A real-estate agent maneuvers, or steers, a buyer or renter who is a member of a protected class away from a particular neighborhood. It was a favored tactic of the housing industry during the civil rights era (as was blockbusting) to keep African Americans from moving into all-white neighborhoods. It is also used to keep members of other ethnic and religious groups and families with young children out of particular neighborhoods or residential buildings. However, there is a reverse aspect to steering. A potential buyer may ask to be shown property only in certain neighborhoods based on race, religion, or ethnic group. A realtor who complies with this request is participating in steering and acting illegally. Properties that are selected for showing need to be based on a nondiscriminatory wish list from the buyer.

3. **Redlining:** This practice is related to lending. It is the practice of banks to refuse to give loans and mortgages or limit the amount of them to people in certain neighborhoods. Typically, those neighborhoods are in an inner city.

Discriminatory Advertising

The list of discriminatory practices from HUD includes advertising because that is, after all, how most property is marketed and sold or rented. The Fair Housing Act, Part 109 describes what constitutes discriminatory advertising practices for property. The guidelines apply both to those placing the advertisement and to the advertising media running the ad. Placing an ad in any media where only certain groups are likely to see them can also be considered discriminatory.

HUD's guidelines list certain categories of words, phrases, symbols, and forms that appear most frequently to "convey either overt or tacit discriminatory preferences or limitations." The presence of such words and phrases could be considered evidence of possible discrimination and grounds for further investigation of any complaint. These include:

- **Words used to describe dwelling, landlord, and tenants:** Examples in the HUD list include "white private home," "Hispanic residence," and "adult building." These are overt, but other phrases such as "upscale neighborhood" can be used to mean all-white.

- **Words that refer to race, color, religion, sex, handicap, familial status, or national origin:** These are self-evident except for the following three:

  1. *Sex:* Using words in ads that state or suggest that the rental property "is available to persons of only one sex and not the other, except where the sharing of living areas is involved." The latter means that if you are a male advertising for a roommate to share an apartment, you may advertise for a male roommate. However, a landlord advertising for a tenant may not advertise "men only."

  2. *Handicap:* A seller or renter cannot write ads in such a way as to deter a person with a disability, but may include the information that the property is handicap accessible.

  3. *Familial status:* This prohibition doesn't preclude the owner of a property in a legitimate over-55 community or program recognized as such by law from advertising that the property is for over-55s.

- **Catch words:** These include words and phrase such as "exclusive," "private," "integrated," and "board approval."

- **Symbols or logos:** The use of symbols or logos that imply or suggest any of the protected classes.

- **Colloquialisms:** These are defined by HUD as words that have a regional or local use to suggest any of the protected classes.

- **Directions to a property:** References to certain kinds of sites used as landmarks in directions to a property can signal a racial, national origin, or religious preference. For example, citing a synagogue as a landmark on the way to a house can signal that the area is Jewish. Noting as a landmark the presence of the African Methodist Episcopal Church on the corner rather than simply saying a church may cue African Americans to the neighborhood.

- **Area (location) description:** Using the names of facilities that cater to particular racial, national origin, or religious groups in an ad is prohibited. For example, a realtor writing an ad could not note that the condo is near the Fairhaven Country Club or that the apartment is close by the Buena Vida Social Club for the intention of signaling to prospective buyers or renters that only members of a certain group will be welcome.

In addition to the wording in an ad, the illustrations may also be suspect. The Fair Housing Act prohibits the use of models in media directed to one racial or national origin group without a similar campaign directed to other groups. Also prohibited is the use of models to suggest that only adults are welcome in a particular property, or that only one sex is welcome.

The location where an ad is placed also comes under the HUD guidelines. For example, billboards, brochures, and newspaper ads that are intended to be seen by only particular segments of the community are prohibited. Sending property announcements and displays to only selected brokers is also banned.

The use of the fair housing logo on selective advertising pieces only is prohibited. Not putting the logo on an ad and then steering a customer to that property in violation of the fair housing law won't keep a lawsuit from the realtor's doorstep.

EQUAL HOUSING OPPORTUNITY

We Do Business in Accordance With the Federal Fair Housing Law

(The Fair Housing Amendments Act of 1988)

It is illegal to Discriminate Against Any Person Because of Race, Color, Religion, Sex, Handicap, Familial Status, or National Origin

---

- ◼ In the sale or rental of housing or residential lots
- ◼ In advertising the sale or rental of housing
- ◼ In the financing of housing

- ◼ In the provision of real estate brokerage services
- ◼ In the appraisal of housing
- ◼ Blockbusting is also illegal

Anyone who feels he or she has been discriminated against may file a complaint of housing discrimination:

    1-800-669-9777 (Toll Free)
    1-800-927-9275 (TTY)

U.S. Department of Housing and Urban Development
Assistant Secretary for Fair Housing and Equal Opportunity
Washington, D.C. 20410

Previous editions are obsolete

form HUD-928.1 (2/2003)

Check out the Fair
Housing Declaration of
the National Association
of Realtors at
www.realtor.org.

WHAT DO YOU HAVE TO DO AS A REALTOR?

By law, realtors must post the Fair Housing poster on their premises. Failure to post it may be considered a discriminatory housing practice if a lawsuit is filed against the realtor. Realtors must also live up to the code of ethics of their profession, and this includes not agreeing to noncompliance with any aspect of the law.

WHAT IS THE PENALTY FOR DISCRIMINATION?

A person who believes that he or she was discriminated against in the selling, buying, or renting of property may file a complaint with HUD. HUD may refer the complaint to your state or local agency if either has the same fair housing powers as HUD. If not, HUD will investigate the complaint.

If the investigation turns up reasonable evidence of discrimination, HUD will assign an administrative law judge (ALA) to hear the case. The complainant (person who lodged the complaint) may have a lawyer to represent his or her interests at the hearing. If the ALA finds in the favor of the complainant, also called the aggrieved person, penalties against the respondent may include:

- payment of damages, which include humiliation, pain, and suffering.
- injunctive or other forms of relief such as making the property available.
- payment of a civil penalty (fine) to the federal government.
- payment of reasonable attorney's fees and costs.

The maximum penalty for the first violation is up to $11,000. If there has been only one other violation within the past five years, the maximum penalty is $27,500. If two or more violations have occurred within the past seven years, the maximum fine is $55,000.

STATE AND LOCAL HOUSING LAWS

States and local government units have their own sets of laws to enforce fair housing practices. These laws may be more strict or less strict than federal law in terms of protected classes and prohibited actions, and in a court case, the law that is stricter would be applied. However, no state or local law may be in conflict with federal law. That means, for example, that no local law that allows redlining would be found to be constitutional.

It is important for the exam that you research and learn the provisions of your state and local fair housing laws. You can use the federal laws as your baseline for comparison.

EXERCISES

1. Which of the following phrases would NOT be considered discriminatory?

   (A) Upper-class neighborhood

   (B) Family-oriented neighborhood

   (C) Strong church-going neighborhood

   (D) Close to schools

2. There are no exceptions to which of the following classes?

   (A) Race

   (B) Gender

   (C) Religion

   (D) Familial status

3. The Fair Housing Amendments Act of 1988 expanded coverage to which of the following classes?

   (A) National origin

   (B) Religion

   (C) Persons with disabilities

   (D) Sex

4. A multi-unit property of four or fewer units is exempt from the provisions of the Fair Housing Act if

   (A) the building owner occupies one of the units.

   (B) a unit is sold without the help of a broker.

   (C) a unit is rented without the help of a broker.

   (D) it is over-55 housing.

5. The maximum penalty for a first-time violation of the Fair Housing Act is

   (A) $5,000.

   (B) $11,000.

   (C) $27,500.

   (D) $55,000.

6. If a potential co-op buyer is denied approval by the co-op board because the owner works on commission, the potential buyer can

   (A) lodge a complaint with HUD.

   (B) file a lawsuit in federal court.

   (C) has no legal recourse.

   (D) must file a complaint within two years of the alleged violation.

7. Blockbusting is

   (A) maneuvering people into certain neighborhoods.

   (B) refusing to give mortgages to buyers in certain neighborhoods.

   (C) scaring people into selling their homes.

   (D) buying up and tearing down single-family homes in order to build high-rises.

8. The category of familial status protects

   (A) children over 18 living at home.

   (B) a childless couple seeking adoption of an infant.

   (C) children regardless of age living with parents in an over-55 community.

   (D) a gay childless couple.

ANSWER KEY AND EXPLANATIONS

1. D	**3.** C	**5.** B	**7.** C
2. A	**4.** A	**6.** C	**8.** B

1. **The correct answer is (D).** Choice (D) is a straightforward statement of fact. Choices (A), (B), and (C) could be considered code words or signals to certain types of potential buyers or renters. Choice (A) could signal a white neighborhood. Choice (B) could signal that a single man or woman or a gay couple would not be welcome. Choice (C) could signal that non-Christian buyers or renters would not be welcome.

2. **The correct answer is (A).** Under certain conditions, there are exceptions to all protected classes except race.

3. **The correct answer is (C).** The amendments that were added in 1988 to the Fair Housing Act of 1968 added those with disabilities and familial status to the classes protected under the housing law.

4. **The correct answer is (A).** A property of no more than four units is exempt from the Fair Housing Act if one of the units is owner-occupied. Choices (B) and (C) both relate to single-family dwellings.

5. **The correct answer is (B).** The maximum penalty for a first-time violation is $11,000. Choice (C) is the maximum for a second violation within five years. Choice (D) is the maximum for a third-time violation within seven years.

6. **The correct answer is (C).** The potential buyer has no legal recourse. Refusing a potential buyer because of concerns over the person's financial stability is not considered discriminatory. Choices (A), (B), and (D) would be possible actions if the potential buyer had been discriminated against.

7. **The correct answer is (C).** Choice (A) is steering. Choice (B) is redlining. Choice (D) may be the purpose of blockbusting, but it is not blockbusting.

8. **The correct answer is (B).** A parent or parents with children under 18 or an adult seeking custody of a child under 18 is protected under the category of familial status. Choices (A) and (C) are incorrect. There are provisions about children living with parents in an over-55 community but they are not covered under familial status. Choice (D) does not apply because there is no child under 18.

SUMMING IT UP

- The basic law regulating fairness in housing is the Fair Housing Act of 1968 and the Fair Housing Amendments Act of 1988.

- The protected classes are race, color, religion, sex, handicap, familial status, and national origin.

- There are exemptions to the Fair Housing Act, but they do not include any exceptions based on race.

- The Americans with Disabilities Act protects the right to access to public spaces for those with disabilities and requires the elimination of architectural barriers in new and existing construction.

- HUD has specific guidelines about what is prohibited when selling or renting property. Three specific forms of discrimination in housing are blockbusting, steering, and redlining.

- The ban on discriminatory practices includes a ban on discriminatory advertising, which includes the placement of advertising and the use of certain words, phrases, symbols and logos, and human models in some situations.

- HUD has a process for filing a formal complaint if a person believes he or she has been discriminated against in housing. If found guilty, the respondent may have to pay damages, attorney's fees and costs, and a fine of up to $55,000, depending on the number of violations and the space of time involved.

- It is important to learn state and local fair housing laws because they can vary from state to state and locale to locale. However, they cannot be in conflict with federal law.

Public Land Use Laws

OVERVIEW

- **A word about the different boards**
- **Zoning ordinances**
- **The right of eminent domain**
- **Interstate land sales**
- **Summing it up**

The right of government to regulate the use of private property is one of the police powers that the U.S. Constitution grants to government. "Police powers" sounds ominous—big brother looking over your shoulder all the time—but the purpose of police powers is to regulate the conduct of its citizens for the common good, that is, the public's general welfare, order, and safety. For example, a state building code may mandate that a bedroom must have a window, but a slumlord might violate that by permitting tenants to put up illegal partitions and locks in order to collect more rent from desperate people. Not only does this violate the state building code, but also the state fire code that specifies a safe number of occupants for a building.

A WORD ABOUT THE DIFFERENT BOARDS

There are two boards that are involved in real estate, namely, the zoning board and the planning board. The zoning board, also known as the Zoning Board of Adjustments and Zoning Board of Appeals,

- hears applications for relief from zoning ordinances.

- provides an annual report to the planning board of the variances granted.

The planning board

- adopts the master plan.

- reviews and decides subdivision and site plan applications (and may grant ancillary variances in connection with these).

- reviews and decides conditional-use applications.

- recommends changes to the official map.

- recommends changes to the zoning code to the governing body (city council, for example) after reviewing the zoning report.

Sometimes, jurisdiction overlaps between the two boards. In the course of an application, one board may have the power to exercise some powers of the other. So, in a site plan review, or subdivision application, the planning board may grant a certain type of variance. With some applications, the applicant must also apply to a county or regional board for additional approval. An example of this would be the expansion of a shopping center that is on a county road.

ZONING ORDINANCES

Except for Houston, Texas, every major city and most municipalities have zoning laws. These regulate how private property owners may use their land. The most common form of zoning divides a city or town into geographic areas, and each area is designated for a certain use.

For example, a city may have two categories of residential zones (single-family and multifamily), commercial zones, and industrial zones. Within those zones, only certain types of buildings may be constructed, and thus, only certain types of uses may be allowed. However, a city may also have a zone called a "mixed-use zone" that might include convenience stores, dry cleaners, and the like, as well as offices and housing.

In addition to use, zoning ordinances may also regulate lot size, setbacks, the square footage of buildings, and the height of buildings. Depending on the strictness of the zoning code, a property owner might not be allowed to build a shed to house tools, or the size and placement of the shed might be regulated.

Zoning Variances

Zoning variances provide some flexibility. For example, if a developer is denied a building permit because of a zoning ordinance, the applicant can seek relief by applying for a variance from the local Zoning Board of Adjustment. The developer would appear before the zoning board in a public hearing to state his or her case. The zoning board, like the planning board, is a quasi-judicial body.

The applicant may present witnesses, some of whom are usually experts. Each of these experts may be examined by members of the public. If there are objectors who have hired an attorney, the attorney may also cross-examine the witnesses. The objectors and the general public may present evidence, including the testimony of witnesses, who are then subject to cross-examination by the applicant or applicant's attorney. After both sides conclude, the general public may make statements under oath that also become part of the record of the proceedings, that is, the zoning board meeting.

According to the evidence presented and the local zoning ordinances, state land use law, and judicial case law, the zoning board either grants the variance or rejects the applicant's request for the variance. There are both positive and negative criteria that must be met to be granted a variance.

Area Variance

An area variance is an exception from a zoning law that involves yard or lot size, floor area ratio, or building height. For example, consider a homeowner who wants to build an addition for a garage. Because of the shape of the lot, the addition would be closer to the street than allowed by zoning. There are both positive and negative criteria the property owner must meet to qualify for an area variance.

The applicant must satisfy the positive criteria that peculiar practical difficulties or exceptional hardship arises from the shape of the property, or that an exceptional situation exists that affects the specific property. In terms of negative criteria, the applicant must show that the grant of the variance would not be substantially detrimental to the public good, nor would it substantially impair the intent and purpose of the zoning plan and zoning ordinance.

For a different kind of zoning, the applicant must show that the application relates to a specific piece of property and that the purposes of the land use laws would be advanced by the grant of the variance. On the negative side, the applicant must show that there would be no substantial detriment to the public good, that the benefits would substantially outweigh any detriment, and that the grant of the variance would not substantially impair the intent and purpose of the zone plan and zoning ordinance.

Use Variance

Use variance is an exception based on a use that is not permitted in the zone in question. One example would be a property owner who requests a variance to turn an empty space over the garage into a rental apartment. The use must be considered inherently beneficial or peculiarly fitted to the particular property. If one of these positive criteria is proven, then the negative criteria must be met, that is, the variance must be shown not to cause substantial detriment to the public good and not to substantially impair the zoning plan and zoning ordinance.

Special Use Permit

An applicant for a special use permit is requesting a variance in order to introduce a use for which an area is not zoned. For example, a charter school wants to turn a mansion into a school. The zoning board would consider such factors as compatibility with the neighborhood, the public's testimonial or other evidence given in response to the request, and the consistency of the proposed use with the general intent of the zoning code. A special use permit is also called a conditional use application, conditional use permit, or a special use variance.

Other Use Variances

There are also some other variations that may require use variances if a property owner wishes to make changes.

- **Nonconforming use:** A nonconforming use is a use or structure that is out of character with the surrounding neighborhood, and it predates the zoning. A variance is only required if the owner wants to expand the nonconforming use or structure. For example, the owner of a gas station that predates the zoning code and is in a residential area decides to add an area to service cars with mechanical problems. In doing this, the owner would be expanding his nonconforming use, and therefore, needs a use variance.

- **Accessory building:** Suppose a property owner was prohibited by a zoning ordinance from putting up a garden shed. The property owner could apply for a zoning variance, and appear before the zoning board at a public hearing to plead his or her case. The criteria would be the same as for a use variance.

- **Accessory use:** A dry cleaner wishes to open a drive-thru window for customers to drop off and pick up their cleaning without having to park their cars and go into the store. This is an accessory use. It is not the typical way that customers interact with a dry cleaner, but it supports the dry cleaner's business. The dry cleaner would first need to go before the planning board for

NOTE

If a buyer plans to run a business out of a property in a residential area, the customer should check with the local government department that deals with zoning to find out what's permissible. For example, a tutoring business may be allowed, but a beauty salon may not be.

NOTE

Even the criteria used to evaluate variance requests may vary from state to state. Be sure that you know not only the names of the variances used in your state, but also their definitions and how applications are evaluated.

a site plan review and might not need a variance. However, if the accessory use is forbidden by the zoning ordinance, then the dry cleaner would have to seek a use variance from the zoning board based on the criteria for that type of variance.

The Master Plan

Historically, cities just grew up and out. It was not until the early twentieth century that municipalities began to adopt zoning ordinances. Then came the master plans. A master plan is a long-range plan for the land that forms a particular governmental unit such as a city, town, or region. The master plan is developed and then reviewed periodically with a single purpose: to describe what the government unit, in consultation with the public, considers the most desirable development for the future of the town, city, or region. The plan considers a variety of factors such as housing, transportation networks, public utilities, open spaces, and economic development. A locality puts into practice its master plan by writing and enforcing zoning ordinances that conform to the recommendations of the plan.

Specific Types of Zoning Ordinances

Density zoning, downzoning, inclusionary zoning, and cluster zoning are being used in some states and communities to address specific issues of growth and affordable housing.

- **Density zoning** refers to the number of houses that may be built on an acre of land. It is being used in rural areas where farmers are selling off their land to developers. By introducing this type of zoning, communities can control growth in these rural areas while also supporting farmers. Farmers can maximize their land assets by selling some of their farmland to a developer who can build more houses on smaller lots and make as much money—hypothetically at least—as selling larger lots with bigger houses. In turn, the farmer can keep some of the land to farm.

- **Downzoning** typically reduces the amount of density or use that is allowed on a property. For example, an area could be zoned for apartment buildings with 400 units, but the government body (not the zoning board), concerned with density in the area, could change the zoning to buildings with 250 units.

- **Inclusionary zoning** seeks to provide low- and moderate-income housing in new housing construction, including apartment buildings and subdivisions. It is also called affordable housing. A ratio of affordable housing units to market rate units is established, and developers must follow this ratio.

- A **planned unit development (PUD)** may be zoned for a mix of types of land use: residential as well as commercial and even industrial. A portion is also set aside for open space. The different types of land use are clustered, or grouped, in certain areas, which is known as *cluster zoning*.

Subdivisions

A subdivision is a large piece of land that has been divided into smaller parcels on which homes will be built. Like most aspects of real estate, zoning laws related to subdivisions vary from state to state, but in general, the owner of the tract must file a plat, which is a map indicating the size and placement of individual lots, streets, power lines, and any common buildings or features, such as a clubhouse or swimming pool.

Developers of subdivisions must obey all zoning ordinances in establishing lot sizes and constructing buildings in the subdivision. If the original developer sells lots to other homebuilders or to individual homebuyers, they too must obey all applicable zoning laws. For example, the developer would have to submit the plan to subdivide the land to the appropriate planning board for review and approval. Even a homeowner who wants to subdivide a lot into two lots must go through this process.

THE RIGHT OF EMINENT DOMAIN

Eminent domain is the taking of property by a unit of government—federal, state, and local—for public use. There are a variety of uses that come under this category, such as highways, open space, urban renewal, and public housing. Public utilities like electric companies may also claim the right of eminent domain. The purposes for which property may be taken are regulated by states and localities, and property owners must be paid the fair market value of the property. The value is arrived at after an appraisal of the property.

For example, a city negotiates with property owners to purchase land for a new approach to a bridge. Those property owners who believe that the appraised value is the fair market value accept the city's offer and move.

A few property owners refuse the offer. The city can take their property through a legal process known as condemnation. If the city is successful, the property owners still receive payment for their land—the original fair market price that the city offered.

Suppose the approach will occupy 2 ½ blocks. The property owners on the remaining half block may demand that the city buy their properties as well because of the adverse effects that the additional traffic and noise will have on their quality of life. This is known as inverse condemnation.

INTERSTATE LAND SALES

Interstate land sales are regulated by the Interstate Land Sales Full Disclosure Act (ILS), a federal law. The act applies to certain categories of subdivisions and is enforced by HUD. Under the law, land developers must register with HUD and provide each potential buyer with a property report before the contract of sale is signed. The purpose of the law is to protect consumers from fraudulent practices in interstate land sales and leasing. Often, these transactions involve vacation homes and condos. State laws also regulate these types of sales.

The property report must include information such as a legal description of the subdivision, including a map, a statement of the condition of the title to the land in the subdivision, and a statement of the general terms and conditions for selling or leasing lots in the subdivision. As part of the property report, the developer must provide copies of the articles of incorporation, the trust papers, or partnership agreement depending on the developer's type of business entity. Also included in the report must be copies of the deed to the subdivision and any easements or restrictions. The information must be included in the property report, but not the documents. They are on file with HUD and may be obtained for a small fee. These and additional documents are listed in the law and are part of the registration that the developer must file with HUD. The additional documents include information

NOTE

Zoning ordinances and building codes apply not just to mansions on 4 acres, but to mobile home subdivisions too.

NOTE

Complying with ILS has become a hot potato in some states with a large market in condominium sales like Florida. Be sure you understand what constitutes compliance if you become a sales agent for a developer building and selling condominiums or subdivisions.

such as the distances to nearby communities over paved or unpaved roads, the existence of mortgages or other liens, availability of recreational facilities, and similar information.

A number of exemptions for developers exist under the law, depending on when and how lots in a subdivision are sold or leased. However, in general, subdivisions with fewer than 25 lots being sold in one offering are exempt, as are subdivisions with lots that are more than 20 acres in size. Subdivisions with fewer than 100 lots may also be exempt.

There are also a number of consumer protections built into the law. A buyer who received a property report may cancel a contract and receive a refund within seven days of signing. A buyer who did not receive a property report before signing, as required by law, may cancel the contract and receive a refund up to two years from the date of signing. Depending on the circumstances, a buyer who received a property report may also cancel the contract and receive a refund within a two-year period.

Buyers who believe that they are victims of fraud can file a complaint with the Office of Real Estate Settlements Procedures Act (RESPA) and Interstate Land Sales, which begins an investigation. Penalties for violation of the law can be both criminal and civil. If convicted of fraud, the developer may be fined up to $10,000 or be sentenced to up to five years in prison, or both. HUD may also impose civil penalties, which may not exceed $1,000 for each violation or $1 million in any one year. In the case of a continuing violation, each day would be a separate violation. The law is aimed at developers' falsifying information, but a realtor could be liable as well, depending on the facts in the case.

EXERCISES

1. Which of the following would be considered an accessory use for a car rental agency near an airport?

    (A) Running a limousine service

    (B) Operating a commercial car wash

    (C) Running a shuttle service to and from area hotels

    (D) Running a long-term parking lot for fliers

2. A buyer is entitled to a refund in interstate land sales if the buyer decides it was a bad idea within

    (A) forty-eight hours.

    (B) seventy-two hours.

    (C) seven days.

    (D) ten days.

3. Which of the following is required under the Interstate Land Sales Full Disclosure Act?

    (A) The developer must be bonded.

    (B) The buyer must receive a property report before signing the contract.

    (C) The buyer must inspect the property before signing the contract.

    (D) The developer must sign a declaimer that all measures have been taken to secure title to the property.

4. A neighbor who parks her car on your property for years without you complaining about it could claim that area under

    (A) adverse possession.

    (B) the right of eminent domain.

    (C) inverse condemnation.

    (D) rescission.

5. A deli owner who lives behind his store decides to convert the entire property into a restaurant. The owner will need to apply for

    (A) an area variance.

    (B) an accessory use variance.

    (C) a nonconforming use variance.

    (D) a use variance.

6. A plat is a

    (A) master plan for a city, town, or region.

    (B) property report for an interstate land sale.

    (C) different name for a building lot.

    (D) map showing the location of lots and features in a proposed subdivision.

7. Building 10 affordable housing units in a 30-unit condo development is an example of

    (A) downzoning.

    (B) inclusionary zoning.

    (C) density zoning.

    (D) exclusionary zoning.

8. An exemption under the Interstate Land Sales Full Disclosure Act is granted developments

    (A) with more than 100 lots.

    (B) with more than 20 lots.

    (C) in which each lot is less than 5 acres.

    (D) in which each lot is more than 20 acres.

ANSWER KEY AND EXPLANATIONS

1. C	3. B	5. D	7. B
2. C	4. A	6. D	8. D

1. **The correct answer is (C).** An accessory use furthers the primary use of a property. While choices (A), (B), and (C) might provide additional money to the car rental agency, only choice (C) supports the business use of the agency: to provide easy access to the agency's rental cars. In reality, it would depend on the zoning ordinance.

2. **The correct answer is (C).** The Interstate Land Sales Full Disclosure Act gives a buyer the right to a refund within seven days of signing.

3. **The correct answer is (B).** If the buyer does not receive a property report before contract signing, the buyer is entitled to a refund. Choice (C) is a recommendation from HUD that buyers actually see the property before signing a contract. Choices (A) and (D) do not relate to ILS.

4. **The correct answer is (A).** If you don't complain and, thereby, don't take measures to stop the use of your property by another, you could lose it through adverse possession. Choice (B) can only be exercised by a government unit. Choice (C) refers to a process under the right of eminent domain. Choice (D) ends a contract as though it had never existed in the first place.

5. **The correct answer is (D).** Choice (A) would deal with the physical aspect of the property. Choices (B) and (C) are not variances, but types of use in and of themselves.

6. **The correct answer is (D).** Only choice (D) accurately defines a plat.

7. **The correct answer is (B).** Choices (A) and (C) refer to ways to limit density or use, not to the types of property built. Choice (D) is the opposite of inclusionary zoning and is illegal unless related to housing for those over a certain age.

8. **The correct answer is (D).** Choice (A) is incorrect because the exemption is for developments with less than 100 lots. Choice (B) is meant to confuse you because the number 20 sounds familiar, but it's lots in a subdivision that are 20 acres, not 20 lots.

SUMMING IT UP

- Zoning ordinances regulate how private property owners may use their property.

- Typically, cities are zoned residential (single-family and multifamily), commercial, and industrial.

- A zoning variance enables a property owner to use his or her property for something other than what is possible under the existing zoning designation.

- Typically, property owners may request an area, use, or special use permit zoning variance. If a property owner wishes to expand or change a nonconforming use, accessory building, or accessory use, the owner may also have to request a use variance.

- A city, town, or region may draw up a master plan to describe what the government unit and public consider the most desirable development for the future of the city, town, or region.

- There are several types of special zoning ordinances:
  - ☐ Density zoning
  - ☐ Downzoning
  - ☐ Inclusionary zoning
  - ☐ Cluster zoning

- Developers and homeowners must abide by all zoning ordinances in building homes in subdivisions.

- The right of eminent domain gives a unit of government—federal, state, and local—the right to take private property for public use. The owner must be offered the fair market value arrived at through an appraisal. If a property owner refuses to sell, the government may seize the property, paying the owner for the property. This is known as condemnation.

- A property owner may claim inverse condemnation if the public use for a neighbor's property diminishes the claimant's use and enjoyment of his or her property.

Environmental Laws

chapter 7

OVERVIEW

- What are hazardous materials?
- Hazardous materials in the air
- Hazardous materials in the water supply
- Hazardous waste
- Electromagnetic fields
- A word to the wise: environmental site assessment
- The environment and construction
- Summing it up

A quick search for "environmental hazards" on the National Association of Realtors' Web site (www.realtor.org) turns up 260 hits. As scientists learn more about the potential health-related dangers associated with environmental hazards and people become more attuned to "green" issues, knowing what constitutes an environmental hazard becomes more and more important for real estate agents. Lawsuits have been filed against agents for not disclosing information about hazards. There is the risk not just of intentional misrepresentation, but also of negligent misrepresentation. It is important to learn the federal, state, and local laws and regulations about environmental hazards relevant to real estate.

Realtors need to be aware of any potential health hazards when they list a property or, if they are not the listing agent, before they show a property to prospective buyers. It is the duty of real estate agents to inform sellers of their responsibilities under various laws—such as the Lead Paint Disclosure Act—and buyers of their rights under any laws related to hazardous materials. Realtors also have a responsibility to know about any past or present environmental hazards in the area, such as a polluted stream from runoff at a chemical plant higher up the river (even if it has been cleaned up) or the presence of a nuclear plant in the area.

WHAT ARE HAZARDOUS MATERIALS?

How a "hazardous material," or "hazmat," is defined depends on which federal agency's definition you read. Four federal agencies regulate hazardous materials: the Environmental Protection Agency (EPA), the Occupational Safety and Health Administration (OSHA), the Department of Transportation (DOT), and the Nuclear Regulatory Agency (NRC).

The DOT regulates the transport of hazardous materials, and the NRC regulates nuclear materials and their by-products. These two agencies don't concern us here—unless a hazardous materials spill has occurred on or near a property or a nuclear plant is located near a property.

The EPA's definition of hazardous materials combines OSHA's definition of what hazardous materials can do with how hazardous materials enter the environment. According to the Institute of Hazardous Materials Management, hazardous materials are described as any health or physical hazard that is carcinogenic, toxic, corrosive, an irritant, or a sensitizer that acts on various parts of the body—human, animal, or plant—and that may get into the environment, "through spilling, leaking, pumping, pouring, emitting, emptying, discharging, injecting, escaping, leaching, dumping, or disposing." The EPA lists more than 350 such hazmats, which may be in the form of "dusts, gases, fumes, vapors, mists, or smoke."

HAZARDOUS MATERIALS IN THE AIR

A prospective buyer will be able to identify smoke belching from a nearby manufacturing plant as a health hazard and tell the realtor to keep on driving, but other potential health hazards are less easily identifiable. Lead, asbestos, radon, and mold may not be visible, though mold can be detectable by smell. You may find questions about the following on the exam.

Lead

Lead was once a common ingredient in paint. In 1978, its use was banned because of its toxicity, especially to children under the age of six. The lead in the paint is typically breathed in as lead dust and may damage the nervous system, the kidneys, and reproductive organs. Studies have shown that lead poisoning can also cause attention deficit disorder (ADD) and attention deficit hyperactivity disorder (ADHD).

In 1992, Congress passed the Residential Lead-Based Paint Hazard Reduction Act that requires property owners whose homes were built before 1978 to disclose to potential buyers or renters the presence of lead paint in the home or apartment. The owner must also provide the buyer or renter with a copy of the federal pamphlet *Protect Your Family from Lead in Your Home* upon contract signing. The buyer then has ten days to have testing conducted to determine the presence of lead in the property. The testing is voluntary, but the EPA recommends it, especially if there are young children involved. The testing may take the form of a lead-based paint inspection, a risk assessment, or a lead hazard screen.

Asbestos

Asbestos is a mineral fiber that was once added to certain materials to provide better heat absorption and fire resistance. It was routinely used in producing siding and roofing, insulation for pipes and furnace ducts, and soundproofing material. Beginning in 1989, the EPA began banning the use of asbestos in certain materials because asbestos can cause lung cancer and asbestosis, which is also a lung disease. The ban has grown to include a variety of materials used in construction and other industries.

Asbestos itself is not the problem. Its friability, or ability to crumble, is the problem. If the asbestos begins to break down or is disturbed during building renovation, small particles are released into the air and can be breathed in by humans and animals. As long as the asbestos is in good condition, it doesn't need to be removed. If a property owner decides to have it removed, it should be done by a professional trained in correct removal procedures. If a property owner is having repair work done that involves asbestos, it should be done by a trained professional as well.

Rather than removing the asbestos, it may be enough to have the asbestos encapsulated or enclosed. The former treats the asbestos with a sealant that binds the fibers together or coats them. Enclosure covers the asbestos.

Radon

This is a colorless, odorless, tasteless, and radioactive gas that is the second-leading cause of lung cancer in the United States. It occurs naturally in rocks and soil and is a product of their decay. Radon is found all over the country (and the world). Usually, it is found in lower levels like a basement. That is why radon testing should be done in the lowest level that will be used as a living space.

The EPA and the Surgeon General recommend that sellers have their homes tested before putting them on the market. They also recommend that all buyers ask if radon testing has been done and, if so, for a copy of the test results. If a seller has not had a radon test conducted, then the EPA and the Surgeon General recommend that the buyer have it done. If the buyer has the radon test conducted, the buyer may have it done before the contract is signed, or after. However, if it is done afterward, the contract must state the sale of the house is dependent on the buyer's satisfaction with the test results, which may be set by statute.

There are several ways to check for radon. The simplest is a charcoal canister that is placed in a home for a certain period of time and then analyzed in a lab. The other methods include some kind of device or detector that monitors radon levels for a period of time. The EPA does not require radon remediation, but some states and localities do. Radon levels can be lowered by increasing ventilation in the problem areas.

NOTE

If a client is planning on having asbestos corrective action done, the property owner should get a written contract, which, according to the EPA, should describe "the work plan, clean-up, and applicable federal, state, and local regulations." State and local regulations, as well as EPA and OSHA regulations, may apply.

NOTE

The EPA does not require radon testing, but some states and localities may. Check the National Radon Information Line at 800-767-7236 or online at www.epa.gov/radon.

Mold

Mold is an increasing problem for many people with severe allergies. Mold is a microscopic fungus that produces spores that can cause allergic reactions in humans. Mold is found in damp areas. For example, if there has been a leak from a bathroom on one floor to the ceiling of a closet on the floor below, mold might grow there.'

The EPA acknowledges that there is "no practical way to eliminate all mold and mold spores in the indoor environment" and there are currently no EPA regulations or standards for mold. The EPA does recommend that "the way to control indoor mold growth is to control moisture." The EPA suggests several things that homeowners can do such as fixing plumbing leaks and seepage into basements from the ground, using dehumidifiers and air conditioners to remove moisture from the air, and using insulation on storm windows to keep moisture from forming. However, any smart seller will eliminate any traces of mold.

HAZARDOUS MATERIALS IN THE WATER SUPPLY

Most people get their water from a privately owned water company or a publicly owned water utility. Neither of these is immune from spreading water-borne diseases, but the federal Safe Drinking Water Act (SDWA) of 1974 requires periodic testing to ensure that the public's water supply is safe. The greater danger is from private wells that serve fewer than 25 people. These are not regulated by the SDWA. In addition to the presence of a private well, a buyer should also be made aware of whether wastes are disposed of by sewer, septic system, or cesspool.

- **Private well:** Unless you deal in rural properties, you will find few private wells anymore. Only about 10 percent of the population still gets their drinking water from private wells. The EPA recommends testing well water once a year. Wells can be tested for lead, radon, the presence of chemicals from fertilizer and pesticide runoff, and other hazardous materials.

- **Septic system and cesspool:** These are systems for disposing sanitary wastes where there is no sewer system to speed it off to a central sewage treatment plant. A septic system consists of a large tank that collects the sewage from the house and a leaching field. Bacteria in the tank treat the wastes, and the liquid portion is then released through a series of below-ground pipes into a leach field, or absorption field, where it is absorbed into the ground. It is wise for a prospective buyer to ask for a percolation, or perc, test to check the viability of the septic system as well as the costs associated with maintaining one. Depending on how much sludge has accumulated, a buyer may ask that, as a condition of sale, the seller have the tank pumped. A cesspool works like a septic system, but instead of a leaching field, the treated liquid flows directly from the tank into the ground around the tank. A prospective buyer should find out the same information about a cesspool as a septic tank.

As you can see, both a septic system and a cesspool are potential polluters of well water—and soil—if not placed strategically and cleaned regularly. Another source of groundwater pollution is leaking underground storage tanks (USTs). See below for more information on USTs.

HAZARDOUS WASTE

A realtor should be aware of—and could be tested on the exam about—environmental issues related to brownfields, underground storage tanks, and landfills. Realtors should be aware of the presence of any of these in relation to the property they are listing and/or showing.

In addition to the hazardous wastes that may leak into the water supply, be released into the air, or seep into the soil, another danger is lead contamination of the soil. This may occur when lead paint on the exterior of the house is scraped off during repainting.

Brownfields

According to the EPA, brownfields are "abandoned or underutilized properties where redevelopment or expansion may be complicated by possible environmental contamination." Typically, these areas were once commercial or industrial facilities. The EPA estimates that there are between 500,000 and 1 million brownfields in the United States.

Revitalization of the brownfields is regulated by the Comprehensive Environmental Response, Compensation, and Liability Act of 1980 (CERCLA), also known as Superfund, the Superfund Amendments and Reauthorization Act of 1986 (SARA), and the Small Business Liability Relief and Brownfields Revitalization Act of 2002 (SBLRBRA).

CERCLA established a tax on the chemical and petroleum industries to pay for cleanup of brownfields, which became the basis of the Superfund; established requirements for dealing with closed and abandoned hazardous waste sites; and provided for the liability of those responsible for releases of hazardous wastes at these sites. Liability is defined under CERCLA as both strict and joint and several. Under strict liability, the property owner is held responsible regardless of any "fault" on the part of the owner. Joint and several liability means that any and all owners are liable, which includes past owners. All can be sued. If liability is found and only one, for example, has money, the money to satisfy the judgment will come from that party, although the judgment is against all the owners. (This is why contracts for commercial real estate, including mortgages, always have environmental indemnification clauses.)

SARA increased the amount of money in the Superfund from $1.6 billion to $8.5 billion plus $500 million for cleaning up leaking underground oil tanks. Among other provisions, the act stresses the importance of permanent remedies and the use of new technologies to clean up hazardous waste sites, increases the involvement of the states in Superfund programs, establishes the public's right to know about the use and release of chemicals into the environment, and encourages greater community participation in decisions about site cleanup.

In addition, the act creates what is known as innocent landowner immunity. Under CERCLA, the current owner of the property was held responsible and had to pay for cleaning up the site, even if this owner had nothing to do with the past creation or dumping of hazardous wastes. Under SARA, if the current owner, at the time of the sale, had a Phase I environmental study conducted and no hazardous materials were detected (though present), this owner would not have to pay for site cleanup. SBLRBRA enlarges the classes protected from liability to include those engaged in certain real estate transactions and further clarifies the innocent landowner immunity. The act also enhances state brownfields programs and provides financial assistance for brownfield revitalization.

NOTE
Check the responsibility of brokers and agents under your state's brownfield laws and regulations.

The Brownfields Program, which is administered under these acts, gives states and communities, as well as other stakeholders, the power to work together to "prevent, inventory, assess, safely cleanup, and sustainably reuse brownfields" in order to reduce the risks to humans and the environment.

Underground Storage Tanks

The EPA estimates that the United States has approximately 617,000 underground storage tanks, known as USTs, which store petroleum or hazardous wastes. Leaking USTs constitute a danger to groundwater and, thus, the water supply for more than half the U.S. population. USTs are regulated under the Resource Conservation and Recovery Act (RCRA) of 1984 and 1986. Under the federal regulations, USTs must be protected from spills, overfills, and corrosion, and any leaks must be cleaned up. The 1986 RCRA set up the Leaking Underground Storage Tank (LUST) Trust Fund to oversee cleanups and to pay for cleanups where the responsible party is "unknown, unwilling, or unable" to pay for cleanup. The Energy Policy Act of 2005 expands the use of the trust fund and includes additional provisions related to inspections, containment, financial responsibility of owners and operators of USTs, and cleanup of oxygenated fuel additives.

Landfills

Landfills can be the dumping grounds of municipal solid wastes (MSWLF); wastes from factories, such as coal ash, which are hazardous wastes; or radioactive wastes. The danger, of course, is the potential for waste products to leak into the environment. The EPA regulates and sets standards for MSWLFs and other types of landfills, and the NRC regulates radioactive waste disposal.

Under federal regulations, MSWLF may take only nonhazardous household and industrial wastes and construction and demolition debris. The regulations include restrictions on the location of landfills; requirements on liners for the landfills, leachate collection and removal systems, and groundwater monitoring; and closure and post-closure care requirements. In addition to the federal rules and regulations, states and localities also regulate landfills.

ELECTROMAGNETIC FIELDS

Research studies have been inconclusive about the effects of electromagnetic fields on health. Some studies have indicated that there is a link between cancer and electromagnetic fields, and others have not. However, many people choose to be safe rather than sorry and don't want to live near overhead power lines, utility transformers, or cell phone towers. The presence of any of these can affect the price and saleability of property. (Of course, the aesthetics of a cell phone tower "disguised" by 10 feet of fake branches at top can also dissuade a homebuyer from even a great deal.)

NOTE

The primary responsibility for ensuring compliance with UST regulations falls to the states, and while federal regulations exempt certain tanks, state and local agencies may not exempt them, so find out what your state and locality mandates.

A WORD TO THE WISE: ENVIRONMENTAL SITE ASSESSMENT

Until your state requires an environmental site assessment (ESA) of all properties before sale, it is wise to recommend such an inspection to your buyer. (One expects that someone buying commercial property such as a warehouse would insist on one.) The following descriptions are typical actions in each phase of an environmental site assessment.

A Phase I inspection is a general assessment of the property and costs between $200 and $4,000, depending on the size and type of property. The inspector researches the history of the property in terms of possible contaminants, the present use of the property, and the identification of potential and existing problems. The inspector looks at when the house was built, whether there is paint under the layers of latex, what materials were used for insulation, and so on.

If the inspector finds evidence of contamination of some kind, the inspector will recommend a Phase II inspection. This costs from $3,500 to $10,000 and up. This level of inspection involves taking samples and analyzing them in a lab to confirm that contamination exists.

A Phase III assessment seeks to pinpoint the type, source, and extent of contamination through more extensive testing. A plan for cleaning up the site is developed and the cleanup is undertaken by professionals trained to remove hazardous materials.

If the contamination cannot be removed, the inspector develops a site management plan as Phase IV. The plan provides steps for containing the contamination and then managing the site over time.

If your state does not require an environmental inspection and the property buyer objects to the cost and decides to forego the inspection, it is best to get in writing that you recommended one and that the buyer chose not to have one. This will give you some protection. Of course, if you know that there is an environmental hazard present, you are both ethically and legally bound to disclose that. Otherwise, you can be accused of fraud!

NOTE

If you live in an area with wetlands, check the federal Clean Water Act and other applicable federal laws and regulations related to wetlands, as well as your state's laws and regulations.

THE ENVIRONMENT AND CONSTRUCTION

Construction, especially the building of a subdivision, industrial park, or shopping mall, can have a huge impact on the environment. Depending on state regulations, a developer will be required to file an environmental impact statement (EIS) before getting any permits for construction. The environmental study and concluding report are completed by experts on the environment.

The study analyzes how the proposed project will affect the environment in all phases of construction and after completion. In addition to a description of the project and the reasons for it, the report describes the area to be affected and presents a range of alternatives to sections of the proposed project, such as moving mall entrances and corresponding parking lots. Each alternative and its impact on the environment are explored in the report.

EISs are required under the National Environmental Policy Act (NEPA) for federal agencies undertaking construction projects that would alter the environment in significant ways.

NOTE

There are also special concerns applicable to seacoasts. If you live in a coastal state, check federal and state laws related to the beaches and coastline.

EXERCISES

1. A Phase I environmental inspection includes
   (A) sampling and analysis.
   (B) a history of the property.
   (C) testing for pesticides and solvents.
   (D) recommendations for cleanup of contaminants.

2. A brownfield is
   (A) so contaminated it can't be used for any purpose.
   (B) another name for a leach field.
   (C) an abandoned or underused commercial or industrial site.
   (D) agricultural land poisoned by pesticides and overuse of chemical fertilizers.

3. Which of the following is a provision of SARA?
   (A) Requirement to disclose lead paint in a property
   (B) Creation of the Superfund
   (C) Establishment of innocent landowner immunity
   (D) Protection of additional classes from liability

4. Federal regulations require that a seller do which of the following before selling a property?
   (A) Drain a septic system
   (B) Test for radon
   (C) Remove or encapsulate asbestos
   (D) Notify the buyer that lead paint is present

5. Which of the following terms is associated with brownfields?
   (A) Revitalization
   (B) Friability
   (C) Perc test
   (D) EIS

6. Which of the following phases of environmental assessment provides a site management report?
   (A) Phase I
   (B) Phase II
   (C) Phase III
   (D) Phase IV

7. Radon is
   (A) nonhazardous.
   (B) a radioactive gas.
   (C) a mineral fiber.
   (D) a by-product of the breakdown of sewage.

8. The main federal agency that regulates hazardous materials relevant to real estate is the
   (A) HUD.
   (B) EPA.
   (C) NRC.
   (D) OSHA.

ANSWER KEY AND EXPLANATIONS

1. B	**3.** C	**5.** A	**7.** B
2. C	**4.** D	**6.** D	**8.** B

1. **The correct answer is (B).** Choice (A) is part of a Phase II environmental site assessment. Choice (C) is part of Phase II. Choice (D) is part of Phase IV.

2. **The correct answer is (C).** Choice (A) is incorrect because turning brownfields into useful acreage is the purpose of the Brownfields Program. Another name for a leach field, choice (B), is absorption field. Choice (D) sounds very convincing, but it isn't a real answer.

3. **The correct answer is (C).** Choice (A) is a provision of the Lead-Based Paint Hazard Reduction Act. Choice (B) is a provision of CERCLA. Choice (D) is a provision of SBLRBRA.

4. **The correct answer is (D).** Choice (A) is incorrect because no such federal regulation or rule exists. Choice (B) is a recommendation only. Asbestos removal, encapsulating, or covering is not a federal regulation or rule. Asbestos does not have to be removed if it is not deteriorating.

5. **The correct answer is (A).** Choice (B) is associated with asbestos. Choice (C) is the test used for septic systems among other things. Choice (D) is the acronym for environmental impact statement and is related to construction.

6. **The correct answer is (D).** A site management report is part of a Phase IV assessment if the contamination cannot be remediated, but must be contained over time. Choice (A) is a review of the history of the property and a site inspection. Choice (B) is sampling and testing, and choice (C) is remediation of the site.

7. **The correct answer is (B).** Choice (A) is incorrect because radon is hazardous. Choice (C) describes asbestos. Choice (D) is incorrect because radon is result of the decay of rocks and soil.

8. **The correct answer is (B).** The main duty of choice (A) is housing, not the environment. Choice (C) regulates nuclear hazardous wastes and those do not typically affect real estate unless there is seepage or a spill. The main duty of choice (D) is overseeing worker health and safety.

SUMMING IT UP

- Realtors need to ask sellers about environmental hazards on their property so that potential buyers can be informed.

- Realtors also need to be knowledgeable about environmental hazards in the areas in which they work.

- In addition to learning about federal laws, regulations, and rules relevant to hazardous materials and real estate, realtors also need to know what their state and local laws are in regard to environmental hazards and real estate.

- Hazardous materials in the air include lead, asbestos, radon, and mold. Sellers must inform buyers of the presence of lead paint, but the federal government does not require removal of lead paint. The federal government recommends that all housing be tested for radon. Asbestos does not need to be removed, encapsulated, or covered unless it is deteriorating or a renovation will displace it.

- Public water supplies and private wells can be contaminated by lead, septic systems, and cesspools.

- Another form of potential contamination is hazardous wastes that may leak into the air, soil, or water supply from brownfields, underground storage tanks (UST), and landfills.

- Brownfields are regulated by federal laws, rules, and regulations under the Comprehensive Environmental Response, Compensation, and Liability Act of 1980 (CERCLA), also known as Superfund, the Superfund Amendments and Reauthorization Act of 1986 (SARA), and the Small Business Liability Relief and Brownfields Revitalization Act of 2002 (SBLRBRA).

- CERCLA set up the Superfund, created requirements for dealing with closed and abandoned hazardous waste sites, and provided for the liability of those responsible for releases of hazardous wastes at these sites. Liability under CERCLA is both strict and joint and several.

- SARA increased the amount of money in the Superfund, stresses the importance of permanent remedies and the use of new technologies to clean up hazardous waste sites, increases the involvement of the states in Superfund programs, establishes the public's right to know, encourages greater community participation in decisions about site cleanup, and creates innocent landowner immunity.

- SBLRBRA enlarges the classes protected from liability to include those engaged in certain real estate transactions, further clarifies the innocent landowner immunity, enhances state brownfields programs, and provides financial assistance for brownfields revitalization.

- Underground storage tanks (USTs) store petroleum or hazardous materials. Remediating leaking USTs is under the supervision of the EPA's LUST Program. A LUST Trust Fund oversees cleanups and pays for cleanups where the property owner is unknown or unwilling or unable to pay for the cleanup.

- Landfills are a potential danger to groundwater and are regulated by the federal government and state and local governments.

- The research on the relationship between health problems, especially cancer, and electromagnetic fields is controversial and the presence of overhead power lines and similar emitters of radio frequency waves devalues nearby properties.

- Environmental site assessments (ESAs) are particularly important in commercial and industrial real estate transactions and may require four phases of testing and remediation.

- Developers of large sites may be required to file environmental impact statements (EISs) before they can begin clearing a site for building. EISs typically contain a description of the project and the reasons for it, a description of the area to be affected, a range of alternatives, and the impact of each alternative on the environment.

Contracts and Deeds

chapter 8

OVERVIEW

- Basic requirements for a valid contract
- Types of contracts
- Real estate sales contracts
- Sales contracts and negotiating the deal
- Breach of contract: when the deal falls apart
- Other real estate contracts
- Basic requirements for a valid deed
- Types of deeds
- Summing it up

A contract is an agreement between two or more parties to do or not to do something and is enforceable by law. Agency agreements, whether a listing agreement or a buyer agency agreement, are contracts. A deed is also a legal document and conveys, and is evidence of, a person's legal right to possess property. This right of possession, or ownership, is the title to the property.

Contracts begin the selling and buying process, and transferring the title of the property by signing over the deed ends it. It is important that realtors understand contracts and deeds. There are undoubtedly a number of questions on the exam about them. You also need to understand this information because as a realtor you will be negotiating contracts—including your commission.

BASIC REQUIREMENTS FOR A VALID CONTRACT

All valid contracts have the following characteristics in common:

- **Competent parties:** All parties to a contract must be legally competent, that is, know what they are entering into. They must be of legal age, as determined by the state in which the contract is being drawn; neither mentally challenged nor mentally ill; not under undue influence, duress, or misrepresentation by another; and not under the influence of alcohol or drugs. (However, if a property is owned by tenants in common, one party can sell his or her half, even if the other party is incompetent or unwilling.)

- **Mutual agreement:** All parties to a contract must agree to the terms and conditions of the contract. This requirement is also called offer and acceptance, reality of consent, mutual assent, mutual consent, and meeting of the minds. This requirement also means that the wording of a contract must be easily understood. A party who decides to back out of a contract could try to use ambiguous wording in a contract to claim that he or she didn't understand it.

- **Legal purpose:** The purpose for entering into the contract must be legal. A contract with an illegal purpose would be void, that is, as though it never existed. For example, if a person applies for and gets a mortgage on one property but intends to use it to finance the purchase of another property, the mortgage contract is void.

- **Consideration:** There must be an exchange of benefits (something of value) between the parties to the contract. In a real estate sales transaction, this occurs at the closing with the transfer of money (the selling price) from the buyer to the seller in exchange for property. The payment of commissions executes (completes) the contracts between real estate agents and principals. A lease is also a type of contract, and the consideration for a lease is the payment of rent (money) by the renter to the landlord in exchange for possession of the rental unit.

- **Written agreement:** Whether a contract for a real estate sales transaction needs to be in writing depends on the state, but in general such contracts do need to be in written form. Whether a state requires a written contract or not, it is a good idea to have one so all parties know exactly what they are agreeing to. It is also easier to negotiate terms when all parties are clear about the agreement. Listings must be in writing in all states. These are agreements of employment and are covered by real estate licensing laws, not the Statute of Frauds.

Contracts: Valid, Void, Voidable, Enforceable, and Unenforceable

To help you unravel these seemingly similar, but actually different, legal concepts about contracts, here are a few examples.

- A valid contract has the five characteristics mentioned above. A contract may have additional characteristics based on the reason for the contract, but those five are always part of a valid contract.

- A valid contract is enforceable. If a seller signs a contract to sell his or her property and then decides not to, the buyer can sue the seller to force him or her to sell the property. Depending on the circumstances, a court would probably uphold the buyer; in reality, however, the buyer would probably settle for monetary damages. The point is that a valid contract is enforceable by the courts.

- Typically, a valid contract can be unenforceable because of the statute of limitations, laches, or estoppel. The statute of limitations is a law limiting the time period during which legal action may be brought against another. The time period begins when the action occurred. For example, a state law may set a time limit of two years for suing a seller who breaches a contract by refusing to sell once the contract has been signed. The buyer then has two years to file a lawsuit against the seller. If the buyer waits longer than that, the contract becomes unenforceable, that is, a lawsuit will fail. Time also plays a role in determining whether a contract is enforceable under the doctrine of laches. Laches requires that a person file a claim without undue delay. Laches is relevant when there is no statute of limitation establishing a time limit on action to enforce one's rights. Estoppel is a legal rule of evidence that prevents a person from making an allegation or denial that contradicts what the person has previously said was true. As a legal principle, a person cannot state something in a contract, or promise something in a contract, and then try to take the opposite position. The person will be "estopped" from doing so by the person's own words or actions.

- A contract based on a mistake of fact is a void contract and unenforceable. As mentioned above, a valid contract must be for a lawful purpose. If it is not, it is void. If a person enters into a contract with the intent to defraud, then the contract is void. For example, a homeowner colludes with an appraiser to overvalue his or her property in order to get a bigger mortgage from the bank. The contract with the appraiser is void because both parties entered into it for illegal purposes.

- The property owner's mortgage contract with the bank in the above example is a voidable contract because the owner misrepresented information about the property (its value). Misrepresentation is one circumstance that will cause a contract to be voidable by the victim, in this case the bank, but it is binding on the other party. Another example includes a nondisclosure of material facts and undue influence on one or both parties. Initially, a voidable contract is one that is legal and enforceable, but any one of the above problems, if proven, will cause a contract to be voidable.

TYPES OF CONTRACTS

There are various types of contracts. They vary in the ways that they are entered into and they may also overlap. For example, an express contract may also be a bilateral contract if both parties have exchanged promises to perform certain actions. A net listing, which must be in writing because it is a listing agreement, is, therefore, an express contract, but it is also a bilateral contract because both the seller and the broker have agreed to a certain performance. The seller has agreed to have the broker sell the property, and the broker has agreed to accept a fee based on the difference between the selling price and the price that the seller wants.

- **Express contract:** The parties to the contract clearly, or expressly, state and agree to the actions to be taken or not taken by each party. Express contracts may be express written contracts or express oral contracts. An exclusive right to sell an agency agreement that a seller and a broker sign is an example of an express contract. Generally, contracts involving real estate are express contracts.

- **Implied contract:** Parties to an implied contract, which is always an oral contract, act as though a contract exists. A seller asks a real estate agent to view her property and to make recommendations about what needs to be done to sell the property. The agent suggests painting and new carpet among other things and the owner follows the recommendations. The agent then begins to bring buyers to view the house. The seller and the agent never sign an agreement, but because the seller never objects to the agent's actions, an implied contract exists between them. The question here is: What's the agent's commission?

- **Unilateral contract:** One party promises to do something if the other party does something. The first person's promise to act is based on the second person's actually doing something. In real estate, an option to buy and an open listing agreement are both types of unilateral contracts. For example, one party (the seller) promises to do something (pay the broker a commission) if the other party (realtor) finds a willing and able buyer, which the realtor may or may not be able to do, but has not promised to do.

- **Bilateral contract:** Both parties in a bilateral contract exchange promises to perform some action. For example, a buyer promises to buy a property at a price that the seller and the buyer have negotiated, and the seller has agreed to sell it at that price to the buyer. The buyer turns over the agreed-upon price, and the seller turns over the title to the property.

- **Executed contract:** An executed contract is one for which the parties have fulfilled the terms and conditions of the contract. The example of the buyer turning over the selling price and the seller relinquishing the title is an example of an executed contract.

- **Executory contract:** This is a contract that is still in process. In this case, some, or perhaps even none, of the terms have yet been completed. A buyer agency is an executory contract until the title to a property that the buyer wishes to buy is handed over to the buyer at the closing.

REAL ESTATE SALES CONTRACTS

NOTE

Be sure you know what your state law says about who can draw up a contract and whether an attorney must participate in real estate transactions. It is always best to remind clients that real estate agents do not practice law and that they should have an attorney review their sales contract.

A real estate sales contract, or agreement of sale, has certain other characteristics besides the ones needed to make it a valid contract. It should include

- who the parties are.
- the street address and a legal description of the property
- the selling price.
- the amount of the deposit (also called earnest money).
- the closing date.
- who the brokers are and how the commission will be paid and by whom.
- signatures of the parties.
- signatures of witnesses.

Conditions

In addition, a real estate sales contract may have certain conditions and contingencies added to the standard contract form by either the buyer and/or the seller. A condition is something that must be done or accomplished by one or the other party, or it may state something about the property. For example, a condition of sale may be that the appliances be in working order at the moment of closing. Another condition of sale could be that the premises must be turned over "empty of seller's possession and in broom clean condition." These are generally contract provisions that must be met by closing. If the seller has not complied, closing can be adjourned until the seller does. Or, for something like a nonworking air conditioning system that the seller failed to have repaired as required in the contract, the parties usually agree to take something off the selling price.

Contingencies

A contingency is a statement—a clause—that describes some action that must be met in order for the contract to be valid. Inspecting a home, obtaining a mortgage, and selling a present home are typical contingencies for residential sales contracts. A contingency usually refers to a material term in the contract so important to the buyer that the contract can/will be canceled if the contingency is not met. Contingencies are usually (but not always) met early in the contract. For example, there are usually one or more inspection contingencies. A buyer will have "x" days after the contract is signed to have the premises inspected by a pest control inspector. If a pest problem is found, the seller must eliminate the problem and produce a certificate from the professional within a certain amount of time. If the seller does not, and the time expires, the buyer may/will cancel the contract without penalty to the buyer, and the seller must return the deposit.

A contingency that will often end a sale, for example, is if a property is found to be in a flood zone and the contract provides that the sale is contingent on the property not being in a flood zone. On the other hand, a contingency in a contract (and also a condition) may be waived by the party who was to benefit from it.

Exclusions and Inclusions

A sales contract may also include exclusions and inclusions. A seller may list the dining room chandelier and the rosebush her Aunt Mildred gave her as exclusions. A buyer may request that the seller leave the refrigerator, which is not typically considered a fixture in that area. With both exclusions and inclusions, both parties must agree in order for the items to be included in the final sales contract. By signing the contract, both the buyer and the seller accept any exclusions and inclusions.

Additional Items in a Real Estate Sales Contract

Any disclosures about the property are also included in the sales contract. A real estate sales contract may also contain the following, depending on the state and the custom of an area:

- A time period during which the buyer may change his or her mind, that is, the right to contract recision (a state law may dictate the time period)
- Who is responsible for paying for inspections
- Who is paying closing costs
- Title searches and title insurance
- Proration of insurance, taxes, rent, etc.
- Inclusion of a "time is of the essence" clause, if delay of the closing will result in a hardship for either party

- What happens if the property is damaged or destroyed between contract signing and sale (see the section on Equitable Title below)
- The type of deed the buyer will accept
- The exact form of payment required by the seller
- Any warranties by the seller
- Right to a walk-through by the buyer before closing

SALES CONTRACTS AND NEGOTIATING THE DEAL

The previous section describes the information and clauses that must and might appear in a real estate sales contract, also known as an agreement of sale and contract of sale. However, getting to the acceptance/contract stage can be a long, drawn-out affair of offer and counteroffer. During this period of negotiating, a buyer may sign several successive offers. Each one is binding on the buyer until the seller makes a counteroffer. Then the offer no long exists, and the counteroffer is binding on the seller. If the buyer rejects the seller's counteroffer, it no longer exists.

An offer or counteroffer, when accepted, becomes a contract when the offeror is notified. Until then, no contract exists between buyer and seller. Typically, the offeree's agent notifies the offeror's agent, who immediately notifies the offeror. At any time in this process, the buyer or seller can walk away from the potential deal because no contract exists. Either buyer or seller can also withdraw the offer or counteroffer because no contract exists. This is a very important principle: No party is obligated to negotiate with another.

Offers and counteroffers typically have a stated time limit by which the other party must respond with acceptance or rejection of the offer. During that period, say 24 hours, the offeror may withdraw the offer/counteroffer from the offeree at any time. The offeror is not obligated to keep the offer/counteroffer on the table.

Binder

A contract exists with the acceptance of the offer or counteroffer, but the formal sales contract may still need to be negotiated. Certain items, for example, exclusions or inclusions, may need to be worked out. In some states and markets, a binder is used at this point. Both the buyer and seller sign the binder, which lists the key terms of the acceptance and "binds" them to continue working toward the final sales contract. There may also be a "good faith" payment, usually $1,000, by the buyer.

Review Period

There may also be a three-day review period once the contract is signed by the parties. During this time, the attorneys for the buyer and seller review the contract, and at that point, either party, but typically the buyer, may reject the contract for any reason on the advice of his or her attorney.

If the contract is accepted, the good faith money, along with the rest of the deposit, is turned over to the seller's attorney to be held in escrow until the closing.

Rider

Once the final sales contract has been signed, any changes are made by the addition of riders. A rider is an amendment to a contract. The addition of riders typically occurs during the three-day review period. Riders are signed by all parties and witnessed. At the beginning of the rider, there is usually language incorporating it into the contract. A rider might state that the dining room chandelier will, after all, not be excluded from the sale.

Equitable Title

At the time of the final contract signing, the buyer is said to receive equitable title in the property. Legal title still resides with the seller, and it will until closing. Because of the contract, if the property is damaged or destroyed, the buyer may be at risk for the loss. In some states, state law dictates whether the buyer or seller is at risk. Because of the potential loss involved, the sales contract should indicate which party will bear the loss and also which party will pay for insurance on the property until the closing. However, in reality, an insurance company will say that the buyer has no insurable interest in the property. For this reason, the seller usually pays the insurance.

BREACH OF CONTRACT: WHEN THE DEAL FALLS APART

Up until the time that the offeree accepts the deal and the offeror is notified, the offeree or the offeror can walk away. Once the offer/counteroffer is accepted, walking away has consequences if there is no valid reason. Suppose the buyer is doing the walk-through 2 hours before the closing and finds a massive leak from a second-floor bathroom into the kitchen. When the ceiling fell, it revealed flaking asbestos on the pipes. The buyer decides that asbestos removal will cost too much and calls the realtor to announce he or she is not buying the property. Is this a valid reason? The seller can agree, and the two parties can bilaterally rescind the contract, or the seller can disagree and take the buyer to court.

The following are possible options if one or both parties breach, or default on, the contract of sale:

- **Rescind the contract:** Suppose the seller decides not to sell. He or she rescinds the contract and returns the money to the buyer. This is a unilateral recision. Suppose the seller decides not to sell and at the same time, the buyer gets a better job offer in another city. Both parties decide on a mutual, or bilateral, recision, and the seller gives the buyer back the earnest money.

- **Forfeit the contract:** In the above example, the seller still wants to sell, but the buyer decides to take the job offer in another city. The buyer forfeits the contract and probably the earnest money.

- **File for compensatory damages:** The injured party in the contract may file a lawsuit asking for compensatory damages from the other party. Compensatory damages are monetary damages that the plaintiff claims to have lost as a result of the breach of contract. Suppose that the seller removed an in-ground pool at the request of the buyer as part of the contract. Now the buyer has decided not to buy. The seller can sue for reasonable replacement costs to reinstall the pool claiming that the pool removal was done solely at the request of this buyer. The seller might also sue for lost profits while under contract because the market has since fallen, for attorney's fees, and to keep the deposit because of the buyer's breach of contract.

- **File for specific performance:** The injured party brings a lawsuit to force the other party to execute the contract. If the seller has changed his or her mind, the buyer may go to court to force the seller to sell, or vice versa. For example, a buyer wants a particular house because of the excellence of the school district, and houses large enough for the couple's five children rarely come on the market in this area. Conversely, a seller may go to court to force a buyer to go through with the purchase. However, in reality, specific performance is available only when money cannot provide the remedy. This might be the case for the family wanting to buy the house in this example. Most likely, a seller will have to be content with money damages.

OTHER REAL ESTATE CONTRACTS

Most of what you just read deals with straight-forward real estate sales contracts, mostly for housing. However, there are several other types of real estate contracts you should know about for the exam and possibly for your job. One type is the lease for rental property.

Buying and Selling Land

Buying and selling land is done under a land contract, also known as a land sales contract, installment sales contract, installment contract, and contract for deed. In this form of real estate sales transaction, the vendee pays the vendor only part of the purchase price initially and the rest in regular payments, or installments, over time. The vendee gets equitable title with the down payment, but not full title. The seller keeps full title and ownership of the land until the vendee pays either a certain number of payments or the complete purchase price. The terms of payment are stated in the contract. Typically, the vendee takes control of the property in the meantime, but may not alter it without the agreement of the vendor.

This form of contract is used when it is difficult for the buyer to get financing. For example, a builder wants to finance the purchase of a large tract of land from a real estate developer for a subdivision, but can't get a good rate on a business loan, so he approaches the developer with a proposal to enter into a land contract. The downside for the developer is that if the builder defaults on the contract, say because of bankruptcy, it may be difficult for the owner to sell the property because of the previously recorded contract. In legal terms, this is known as a cloud on the title. (See quitclaim deeds bullet below for more information.)

Optioning Property

An option gives a person the right to buy a property within a stated period of time for a stated price. The buyer doesn't have to buy the property, but if he or she does, then the seller must sell it at the agreed-upon price. For agreeing to the optioning, the seller receives a payment from the potential buyer. This money may count toward the purchase price or it may not, depending on what the option contract says that both parties sign.

ALERT!

Here are two more terms to know: *grantor* (seller) and *grantee* (buyer).

BASIC REQUIREMENTS FOR A VALID DEED

A deed is a written legal document that conveys, and is evidence of, a person's legal right to ownership of a particular property. It is delivered by the seller to the buyer at the closing. Delivery is an important element of conveying title, that is, ownership. To be valid, a deed must be

- a written document.
- signed and witnessed.
- delivered and accepted.

It must include

- a grantor who is competent.
- a consideration (something of value).
- a granting clause specifying the type of deed and type of title (ownership).
- a *habendum* clause reiterating the ownership in the granting clause.
- a legal description of property.
- any exceptions and reservations such as covenants and restrictions.

In some states, deeds are required to include an acknowledgement in order to be recorded. An acknowledgement attests to the fact that the grantor is the person who he or she claims to be and is not under duress or undue influence to complete the transaction. It may also attest to the consideration. The acknowledgment is usually given before a notary public.

NOTE

Check what your state requires as the consideration in a deed. It may be the full purchase price or some nominal consideration.

TYPES OF DEEDS

Like sales contracts, there are a number of different types of deeds. The specific deed for a transfer of property depends on the purpose, that is, the type of guarantee that is accompanying ownership of the property.

- **General warranty deed:** These are also called full covenant and warranty deeds and, by the name, you can figure out that they provide the fullest protection to the buyer, or grantee. A deed warranty works like any other warranty, except that there is no expiration date. A general warranty deed provides a number of warranties, or covenants:

  - ☐ *Covenant of seisin:* This guarantees that the grantor owns the property and has the right to transfer the ownership.

  - ☐ *Covenant of quiet enjoyment:* This warrants that the title to the property will not be claimed by a third party. If, at some future point, a third party provides a better claim to the property, the grantor will make good on any losses that the grantee suffers as a result of the third party's claim.

  - ☐ *Covenant against encumbrances:* The grantor guarantees that there are no encumbrances such as liens or easements against the property other than the easements stated in the deed.

  - ☐ *Covenant of further assurance:* The grantor promises to provide any documents or perform any actions needed to clear up any errors or problems with the deed.

- **Special warranty deed:** Unlike a general warranty deed, a special warranty deed guarantees only the actions of the person conveying the title, not the complete history of the property. A

NOTE

Be sure to check the types, titles, and the description of deeds used in your state.

special warranty deed guarantees only that the grantor has legal title and has not placed any encumbrances on the property while holding the title. The most common use of the special warranty deed is for sales of properties that have been seized and sold, such as foreclosures or in payment of delinquent taxes. Executors of estates and trustees may also use this form of deed.

- **Grant deed:** This form of deed is the most common form of deed used in California, and it is also used in a few other states. A grant deed limits the warranties to the period that the grantor owned the property. There are also fewer warranties in a grant deed. The grantor warrants only that he or she

  ☐ has not conveyed the property to anyone else.

  ☐ has encumbered the property only as noted in the deed.

  ☐ will convey to the grantee any interest that the grantor may acquire in the property at some later time.

- **Quitclaim deed:** This form of deed has no warranties attached to it. All it does is convey the interest that the grantor has in the property. Quitclaim deeds can be used to clear up the cloud on the title when the buyer in a land contract defaults and the seller wants to resell the land.

- **Deed of trust:** Also known as a deed in trust and trust deed, this form of deed is used as security for a loan and conveys title from the trustor to a trustee for the beneficiary. The trustor is the borrower, the beneficiary is the originator of the financing, and the trustee is the third party. When the trustor repays the loan, the title passes from the trustee to the trustor. Should the trustor default on the loan, the beneficiary may take back the property or the trustee may sell the property and give the beneficiary the proceeds. In either case, the process begins with a foreclosure.

- **Deed of reconveyance:** When the deed of trust is conveyed from the trustee to the trustor at the time of repayment of the loan, a deed of reconveyance is used.

- **Deed of release:** This is used when a mortgage is paid in full and conveys the title from the financial institution to the buyer.

- **Judicial deeds:** A number of different kinds of deeds fall into the category of judicial, or court-ordered deeds, which are established and regulated under state laws. Some examples include:

  ☐ *Sheriff's deeds:* given to buyers of government-seized property

  ☐ *Commissioner's or referee's deed in foreclosure:* given to buyers of property foreclosed by financial institutions; name of entity authorized to sell the property depends on the state

  ☐ *Tax deed:* given to buyers of property seized and sold for nonpayment of taxes

The list goes on and on, and covers a variety of possible ways to give a buyer title to a property that somehow involves the courts. The one thing to remember about judicial deeds is that the only warranty that they may contain is that the entity selling the property has the right to sell it.

- **Bargain and sale deed:** Executors, trustees, and officers of the court (for example, a referee in a foreclosure) may use this form of deed rather than one of the judicial deeds or a special warranty deed. No warranties are included in this type of deed. That the grantor has an interest in the property is implied.

NOTE

In some states, the buyer gets a satisfaction of mortgage instead of a deed of release, or the buyer gets the mortgage back endorsed for cancelation. Both documents can be recorded. The note is also returned to the buyer and can be destroyed. Be sure you know how your state handles mortgages paid in full.

EXERCISES

1. A contract would be judged invalid if which of the following was present?

   (A) Encumbrance

   (B) Misrepresentation

   (C) Laches

   (D) Omission of consideration

2. A contract to sell real estate is

   (A) an express contract only.

   (B) a bilateral contract only.

   (C) a unilateral and an express contract.

   (D) an express and a bilateral contract.

3. The Patels make an offer on the Browns' house. The Browns reject it and come back with a counteroffer. The Patels reject it as too expensive, but make no counteroffer. The Browns decide to take the Patels' first offer. Can they do this?

   (A) Yes, because the Patels' counteroffer is still on the table.

   (B) Yes, because the Browns' acceptance takes precedence over their earlier rejection.

   (C) No, because the Patels' offer is superseded by the Browns' counteroffer.

   (D) No, because the Browns waited until the time had expired to get back to the Patels.

4. Which type of deed grants the highest and most complete form of ownership?

   (A) General warranty deed

   (B) Quitclaim deed

   (C) Deed of trust

   (D) Judicial deed

5. Deeds must have which of the following to be valid?

   (A) Meeting of the minds

   (B) Consideration

   (C) Habeas corpus clause

   (D) Warranty

6. A satisfaction of mortgage is similar to

   (A) deed of trust.

   (B) deed of release.

   (C) deed of conveyance.

   (D) grant deed.

7. An option is a

   (A) unilateral, express contract.

   (B) bilateral, express contract.

   (C) bilateral, implied contract.

   (D) unilateral, implied contract.

8. A joint tenancy signed a contract to buy a property. One of the joint tenants dies before the closing. The transaction was to take place in a state that recognizes the right of survivorship in a joint tenancy. Which of the following statements is true in this situation?

   (A) The contract is valid, but unenforceable.

   (B) The contract is voidable.

   (C) The contract is invalid and unenforceable.

   (D) The contract is valid and enforceable.

ANSWER KEY AND EXPLANATIONS

1. D	3. C	5. B	7. A
2. D	4. A	6. B	8. D

1. **The correct answer is (D).** Consideration is a necessary characteristic for a contract to be valid. Choice (A) is irrelevant. Choice (B) would result in a voidable contract. Choice (C) is a reason a valid contract would be unenforceable.

2. **The correct answer is (D).** A real estate contract must be in writing, so it is an express contract, and it also requires the action of two parties, so it is bilateral. Choices (A), (B), and (C) do not fulfill these characteristics, and so they are incorrect.

3. **The correct answer is (C).** Once an offer or counteroffer is replaced by a new counteroffer, the previous one ceases to exist. For this reason, choice (A) is incorrect. Choice (B) is not true. Choice (D) is irrelevant.

4. **The correct answer is (A).** Choice (B) has no warranties. Choice (D) has no warranty. Choice (D) has limited warranties.

5. **The correct answer is (B).** Choice (A) is a requirement of a valid contract. Choice (C) sounds familiar, but it's a *habendum* clause that is required for a deed to be valid. Choice (D) is not true.

6. **The correct answer is (B).** Choice (A) is used as security for a loan. Choice (C) is a distracter; it seems correct, but the term is "reconveyance," not "conveyance." Choice (D) is incorrect because it is a deed that limits warranties to the period during which the grantor owned the property.

7. **The correct answer is (A).** An option is in writing, but only one party is required to perform an action, that is, sell the property, so choices (B), (C), and (D) do not satisfy this definition and are incorrect.

8. **The correct answer is (D).** Choice (A) is incorrect because all the characteristics that make a contract valid were present when the contract was signed. Choice (B) is incorrect because none of the circumstances that make a contract voidable are present. Choice (C) is incorrect because the characteristics that make a contract valid were present when the contract was signed.

SUMMING IT UP

- For a contract to sell real property to be valid, it must have the following characteristics: competent parties, mutual agreement, legal purpose, consideration, and be in writing.

- Contracts may be judged valid, void, voidable, enforceable, and unenforceable.

- A valid contract may be enforceable or void and unenforceable, depending on the statute of limitations, laches, and estoppel.

- A contract may be voidable because of misrepresentation, nondisclosure of material facts, mutual acknowledgement that the contract was a mistake, undue influence, and breach of contract.

- Contracts may be express or implied, unilateral or bilateral, and executory or executed.

- Real estate sales contracts should include the parties; street address and legal property description; selling price; amount of deposit or earnest money; closing date; brokers, their commissions, and the party paying them; signatures of the parties; and signatures of the witnesses.

- There are a number of other items that may be listed in a real estate sales contract including conditions, contingencies, disclosures, exclusions, and inclusions.

- In the process of negotiating a real estate contract, once a counteroffer has been made, the previous offer/counteroffer no longer exists. Later changes to a signed contract are made by adding riders.

- On signing the contract, the buyer receives equitable title to the property.

- If both parties decide to walk away from a signed contract, they would rescind the contract. If the buyer decides to walk away, he or she could forfeit the contract. In the case of a breach of contract, the injured party could file for compensatory damages or specific performance.

- Other real estate contracts include land contracts and options.

- For a deed to be valid, it must be a written document, be signed and witnessed, and be delivered and accepted. It must also include a grantor who is competent, consideration, a granting clause, a *habendum* clause, a legal description of the property, and any exceptions, reservations, and restrictions.

- Among the types of deeds are a general warranty deed, special warranty deed, grant deed, quitclaim deed, deed of trust, deed of reconveyance, deed of release, judicial deed, and bargain and sale deed.

- The general warranty deed is the fullest form of deed and contains covenants of seisin, of quiet enjoyment, against encumbrances, and of further assurance.

Leasing

OVERVIEW

- **Requirements for a valid lease**
- **Additional provisions in a lease**
- **Types of leases**
- **Rent control laws**
- **Breaking a lease**
- **Managing property**
- **Summing it up**

A lease is the way that a leasehold estate is established. It is a contract between a lessor (landlord) and a lessee (tenant), usually for a specific period of time and a specific consideration (rent), and usually in writing. In most states, a lease that will run for a year or more must be in writing; this is regulated under a state's Statute of Frauds.

In addition, states and some municipalities have other laws, rules, and regulations that govern the landlord-tenant relationship. Rent control laws are explained below. In 1972, the National Conference of Commissioners on Uniform State Laws created the Uniform Residential Landlord and Tenant Act as a model for the states. Many states have adopted its provisions in full or in part.

Remember that a lease survives the sale of a property. If you buy an apartment building with tenants, the tenants have the right to remain during the term of their existing leases and under the provisions of those leases, including the amount of rent. (There may be exceptions with commercial leases.)

REQUIREMENTS FOR A VALID LEASE

A lease is a contract, and like all contracts, a lease must have the following requirements to be valid:

- Competent parties
- Mutual agreement
- Legal purpose (rental)
- Consideration (amount of rent)
- Be in writing (as noted above, the length of time may not require a written lease; however, having the agreement in writing, including sufficient identification or description of the exact premises leased is always safest)

ADDITIONAL PROVISIONS IN A LEASE

A rental lease has many more provisions than those that make it a valid contract. Typically, a lease has the following provisions:

- Description of the premises, including address
- Names of the parties to the lease
- Term of the lease (time period)
- The amount of rent and due date for payment of the rent
- Any rent increase over the term of the lease (a two-year lease, for example, might have one amount for year 1 and another amount, due to an increase, for year 2)
- The amount of a late charge, if the rent is not paid on time, and details on when the late charge kicks in
- The amount of the security deposit, where it is deposited, when it must be returned to the renter, and how much could be kept by the landlord and under what circumstances
- How the premises may be used (limits the premises to specific purposes, such as use as a residence; the tenant would then not be allowed to open a retail outlet in the living room or to change a clothing boutique to a restaurant)
- Whether the landlord or the tenant pays the utilities
- Whether the landlord or tenant is responsible for liability insurance and in what amount
- The services the landlord will provide (such as snow removal and trash collection)
- Which party makes which type of repairs (this relates to other items that may appear in a lease: the circumstances under which a landlord may enter the premises and the tenant's right of quiet enjoyment)
- Whether the tenant may make alterations and improvements (typically the tenant, if allowed to make changes, must return the place to the condition in which the tenant received it)
- The obligations of tenant and landlord if the premises are destroyed
- Information about lease renewal (nonrenewable, automatic renewal, or renewal with notice to the landlord)
- The condition of the premises at the time of the surrender of the premises (in the same condition in which it was received or with "normal wear and tear")

Additional provisions may include no pets or a limit on pets. The courts have also found that tenants have the right of quiet enjoyment (the premises are free of claims of others), whether stated in the lease or not.

Sublet and Assignment

Some leases may allow a tenant to sublease the premises or to assign them to another person with landlord approval. Under a sublease, the original tenant retains the right to retake possession of the premises at the end of a specific period of time. Under an assignment, the original tenant gives up all rights to the premises. Under neither arrangement does the original tenant give up his or her obligations under the lease. The original tenant, not the sublessee or assignee, is ultimately responsible to the landlord for the rent and for all other tenant obligations and responsibilities under the lease.

The sublease also specifies that the sublessee is obligated to observe all the terms of the tenant's lease and will not violate those terms. The sublease also makes the sublessee subject to the tenant's lease so that if the tenant is evicted, the sublessee must go, too.

Option to Purchase

An option to purchase is also called a lease option or lease purchase option. It gives the tenant the right to purchase the premises at some point during the term of the lease. The price is stated in the lease. A portion of each month's rent may be applied to the purchase price. In addition, the tenant pays a nonrefundable option deposit that is also put toward the purchase price. An option must be exercised in strict compliance with its terms.

There is also what is known as "right of first refusal," which is popular with long-term tenants, especially those who intend to invest substantial money in improvements to the premises. The lease provision would provide that the property first be offered to the tenant when the landlord decides to sell, or if the landlord receives a good faith offer to buy from someone else, the tenant will have the right to purchase if the tenant meets that offer.

TYPES OF LEASES

The type of lease that a landlord uses generally depends on one of two factors: the type of property that the landlord is renting and the way the rent is calculated. The following are the common types of real estate leases:

- **Gross lease:** A gross lease is the typical apartment lease. The tenant agrees to pay the same amount of rent each month for a specified time, the term of the lease. In exchange, the landlord assumes responsibility for paying real estate taxes, taking care of maintenance and repairs, making improvements, and buying liability insurance. Either the tenant or the landlord pays the utilities, depending on what is negotiated in the lease. An office lease may work the same way.

- **Net lease:** A net lease is typically used for commercial real estate rentals. The tenant pays the base rent and some or all of the expenses of the property, not just the utilities. Depending on how much of the expenses the tenant picks up, a net lease may be called a double net lease, triple net lease, or an absolute net lease. For example, with an absolute net lease, the tenant pays utilities, all repair and maintenance costs, and real estate taxes. If the building needs a new roof, the tenant pays for that, too.

- **Percentage lease:** Like a net lease, the tenant pays a base rent under a percentage lease. However, the tenant also pays a percentage of the gross sales of his or her business to the landlord. This type of lease is used primarily for retail rentals such as stores in malls and shopping centers. In some percentage leases, the base rent is credited toward the percentage.

A retail lease may be either a gross or a net lease in addition to being a percentage lease, that is, the tenant may or may not pay some or all of the operating expenses of the premises.

- **Ground lease:** Also called a land lease, a ground lease is the rental of a parcel of unimproved land with the intention that the tenant will build on it within the term of the lease. Ground leases are typically multiyear long-term leases. For example, a developer might enter into a 99-year lease with a real estate holding company to build a shopping center on the holding company's

NOTE

Like sales contracts, leases have different names in different areas. Find out what name is generally used in your state and area.

land. When the lease is up, the holding company (landlord) will take possession of the buildings as well as the land. In the meantime, the tenant pays all costs associated with the shopping center, such as real estate taxes, water and sewer fees, maintenance, and so on. The amount of rent may be fixed or a percentage of the sales of the business.

- **Graduated lease:** A graduated lease is also a multiyear, long-term lease. Unlike the rent for a ground lease, though, the rent for a graduated lease varies. There are two methods of determining rent. It may be adjusted from time to time to reflect the changes in the appraised value of the premises, or it may be changed based on a benchmark rate such as the consumer price index.

RENT CONTROL LAWS

States, counties, and municipalities may pass laws regulating the amount of rent that landlords may charge tenants. Certain categories of apartments may not be included under rent control laws, like two-family houses and new construction. Typically, rent laws also include landlords' responsibilities with providing heat and hot water and making repairs and tenant eviction procedures.

Landlords obviously oppose rent controls and have been able to lobby governments to change or end the laws. The chief beneficiaries of rent control are long-time renters of the same apartment. They may be paying as little as $400 for an apartment in a prime location while apartments in the same building, which are no longer under rent control, lease for $1,500 a month. The difference in rent is legal due to vacancy decontrol. Under vacancy decontrol, when a tenant who was living under rent control moves out, rent control for the apartment ends and the landlord may charge the going market rate.

Some states and municipalities also have separate rent stabilization laws. Generally, a rent stabilized apartment means that the landlord can raise the rent only a certain percentage a year, and the tenant has the right to renew the lease when it expires. Like rent control, certain categories of rentals may be excluded from regulation under rent stabilization laws.

BREAKING A LEASE

A tenant gets a new job and has to relocate, but has eight months left on the lease. If the lease allows it, the tenant can try to get a sublessee or an assignee, but there is a good chance the lease does not allow this remedy. The only option is to break the lease. Hopefully, the tenant and landlord can come to an amicable agreement, but at the least, the tenant will most likely lose the security deposit in lieu of a month's rent. If the landlord and the tenant are unable to enter into a termination of lease, the tenant is said to have abandoned the lease and will forfeit the security deposit. In addition, the landlord may sue for damages, including lost rent.

There are other non-amicable partings between tenant and landlord: actual eviction, constructive eviction, and retaliatory eviction. Eviction is the removal of a tenant and the return of the possession of the premises to the landlord.

- **Actual eviction:** The usual problems that result in an actual eviction are nonpayment of the rent by a tenant, a tenant's refusal to move when the lease expires (holdover tenant), and repetitive disregard of other terms of the lease. Damaging the premises is also an issue that may merit eviction. An actual eviction includes filing a complaint with the court for an eviction notice, serving the tenant with the notice, and holding a hearing to gather evidence from both sides in the dispute. If the landlord's case is upheld, the tenant is served with a warrant to dispossess and must surrender the premises. This is the actual eviction, or expulsion, of the tenant from the premises.

- **Constructive eviction:** A constructive eviction is caused by a landlord's neglect of the premises so that they become uninhabitable. The tenant in this case has the right to vacate the premises and break the lease. For example, the landlord refuses to fix a plumbing leak between floors that damages the kitchen appliances in the lower apartment so that they are unusable and, therefore, the tenant cannot cook or refrigerate food. More typical causes of constructive eviction are lack of heat or water and poor or no maintenance.

- **Retaliatory eviction:** This is an illegal expulsion of a tenant from a property. Suppose that, in the previous example, the tenant reports the landlord's unwillingness to repair the leaking plumbing to the appropriate municipal department. In retaliation, the landlord turns off all water to the apartment, and unable to get help from the local government, the tenant moves. This is a retaliatory eviction and can subject the landlord to criminal action.

MANAGING PROPERTY

In addition to finding tenants for landlords, some real estate brokers and agents also serve as property managers for landlords. Property managers, with the exception of apartment building resident managers, must have a valid real estate license, regardless of state regulations.

To manage a property, the realtor and the landlord enter into a contract that specifies the services that the realtor as property manager may handle. These may include:

- Finding suitable tenants, including advertising for tenants and checking references
- Negotiating leases
- Collecting rents
- Hiring/overseeing individuals and companies for property maintenance, janitorial services, landscaping, trash removal, security, bookkeeping, and other services
- Appearing in court on behalf of the landlord in eviction proceedings
- Paying the bills

The property manager may receive a percentage of the rents as payment for services or a fixed fee. If it is a percentage, the amount depends on the services that the manager provides.

NOTE

For more information about property management of non-commercial properties, check out the National Association of Residential Property Managers at www.narpm.org.

EXERCISES

1. Which of the following is NOT required for either a real estate sales contract or a lease?

   (A) Consideration

   (B) Competent parties

   (C) Mutual agreement

   (D) Legal description of the property

2. Which of the following guarantees the right of a tenant to exclude people from their premises?

   (A) Vacancy decontrol

   (B) Right of quiet enjoyment

   (C) Constructive eviction

   (D) Retaliatory eviction

3. Which of the following is true?

   (A) A landlord may enter a tenant's apartment whenever the landlord wants.

   (B) A landlord may enter a tenant's apartment only when the tenant is home.

   (C) A landlord may enter a tenant's apartment at any time to make repairs.

   (D) Barring an emergency, a landlord may enter a tenant's apartment dependent on what the lease says.

4. Which of the following is NOT a typical lease provision?

   (A) That no pets are allowed

   (B) That a security deposit is required

   (C) That the tenant may use the common washers and dryers only on Thursday nights

   (D) That the tenant may make improvements, but they must be removed on surrender of the premises

5. If a tenant subleases his or her apartment,

   (A) the original tenant retains all obligations under the lease.

   (B) the original tenant assigns all obligations under the lease to the sublessee.

   (C) the original tenant need not obtain permission from the landlord.

   (D) the sublessee is responsible only for the rent.

6. Which of the following would most likely hold a gross lease that is also a percentage lease?

   (A) Individual apartment

   (B) Clothing boutique

   (C) Doctor's office

   (D) Department store in a mall

7. An absolute net lease requires that a tenant pay

   (A) no operating expenses of the premises.

   (B) all operating expenses of the premises.

   (C) some operating expenses of the premises.

   (D) a percentage of operating expenses based on the rate of use.

8. A property manager may do all of the following EXCEPT

   (A) advertise for tenants.

   (B) evict a holdover tenant at the direction and in the name of the landlord.

   (C) fire a low-performing maintenance company.

   (D) enter into a contract to sell the premises.

ANSWER KEY AND EXPLANATIONS

1. D	**3.** D	**5.** A	**7.** B
2. B	**4.** C	**6.** B	**8.** D

1. **The correct answer is (D).** To be valid, neither a real estate sales contract nor a lease needs a property description, so choice (D) is the correct answer. Choices (A), (B), and (C), in addition to a legal purpose and a written document, are needed.

2. **The correct answer is (B).** Choice (A) occurs when an apartment under rent control becomes vacant and the landlord can charge the market rate. Choice (C) occurs when a tenant must leave premises that are no longer habitable. Choice (D) is an illegal action of a landlord against a tenant.

3. **The correct answer is (D).** Without seeing the lease, we can't tell when the landlord may enter a tenant's apartment, so choice (D) is the best answer.

4. **The correct answer is (C).** Choices (A), (B), and (D) are typical provisions of leases, which doesn't meant that they will always appear in a lease. But more often than not, they will be included.

5. **The correct answer is (A).** Subleasing does not absolve the tenant (lessee) from any of the obligations under the lease, but the lessee does give up the right of possession for a period of time. Choice (B) is the opposite of choice (A), and so, it is incorrect. Choice (C) is not true; the lessee must have permission of the landlord for a legal sublet. Choice (D) is incorrect because the sublessee presumably signed a sublet lease with the lessee that obligated the sublessee to certain additional obligations.

6. **The correct answer is (B).** A clothing boutique is a small retail outlet and would most likely have negotiated to pay only utilities, not all building expenses. Choice (A) would have no sales on which to pay a percentage. Choice (C) is a professional office, not a retail space. Choice (D) would most likely have a net lease, not a gross lease.

7. **The correct answer is (B).** Choice (A) describes a gross lease. Choice (C) is a form of a net lease, but not an absolute net lease. Choice (D) may sound familiar because it mixes words from several concepts, but it is incorrect.

8. **The correct answer is (D).** Choices (A), (B), and (C) are actions that a property manager may take, so they are incorrect answers to the question. Choice (D) is not part of a property manager's job, so it is the correct answer to the question.

SUMMING IT UP

- The federal government as well as states and municipalities regulate fair housing laws, but states and municipalities alone regulate tenant-landlord relations.

- To be valid, a lease must be in writing and have competent parties, mutual agreement among parties, a legal purpose, and consideration.

- A lease has any number of provisions including description of the premises, names of the parties, terms of the lease, the amount of rent, the date rent is due, the amount of the security deposit, the use of the premises, services rendered by the landlord, alterations and improvements, the surrender of the premises, and landlord-tenant responsibilities in case of the destruction of the premises, among other provisions.

- A tenant may sublet or assign a lease only with the landlord's permission. A tenant who subleases gives up the right of possession for a certain period of time, whereas a tenant who assigns a property gives up right of possession completely. However, the tenant retains the obligations of the lease under both arrangements.

- An option to purchase gives the tenant the right to purchase the premises during the term of the lease for a certain price. A nonrefundable option deposit and a portion of the rent may be counted toward the purchase price.

- There are five common types of leases:

    1. Gross lease

    2. Net lease

    3. Percentage lease

    4. Ground lease

    5. Graduated lease

- Rent control laws limit the amount of rent that landlords can charge. A landlord of rent-stabilized premises is limited by law in the amount of rent that he or she may charge a tenant.

- There are three types of eviction:

    1. Actual eviction

    2. Constructive eviction

    3. Retaliatory eviction

Describing Property and Appraising It

chapter 10

OVERVIEW

- **What is a legal description of a property?**
- **Metes and bounds system**
- **Lot and block system**
- **Rectangular survey system**
- **Describing thin air**
- **What is the purpose of a real estate appraisal?**
- **Categories of value**
- **Principles of appraising value**
- **Factors that influence value**
- **Sales comparison approach to valuing property**
- **Cost approach to valuing property**
- **Income approach to valuing property**
- **Reconciliation: arriving at the final number**
- **Summing it up**

A legal description of a property is a necessary component of both a real estate sales contract and a lease. A tenant needs to know exactly which unit at what address the tenant is renting. Buyers need to know exactly what they are purchasing. Does their purchase include that tree in the unfenced yard behind the house or is the tree on the adjoining neighbor's property? The tree and the additional 40 square feet in the backyard will add to the price but also the value of the property.

Determining the value of a property is the job of a licensed real estate appraiser; however, real estate agents need to have a familiarity with the work of appraisers both to do their own jobs well and because they may find questions on their exam about how property is valued. The same is true about the methods of surveying and describing property. You do not have to know the ins and outs of surveying, but for the exam you should know the basics of the different systems.

WHAT IS A LEGAL DESCRIPTION OF A PROPERTY?

The tree in the above example would not be part of the legal description of a property, but the boundary line that encloses the tree in the property would be. A legal description of property lists only the boundary lines of a property. Any structures or physical features like a pond or trees are not mentioned. The legal description is the description that appears on the deed to the property.

The word *legal* is important in the sentence above. It indicates that the description meets certain requirements under law. Specifically, the description must be made in accordance with accepted legal standards, is legally sufficient to identify the property, and shows that this identity is unique and separate from all other real property. Without a legal description, it would be much more difficult to buy and sell property.

Typically, a legal description is arrived at by using one of following three methods: metes and bounds, lot and block system, and rectangular survey system. All three systems are used throughout the country, though the rectangular survey system is used less often in the Northeast and Middle Atlantic states, North and South Carolina, and Georgia, the states originally settled by English colonists. The metes and bounds system is the typical system in those areas, whereas most of the rest of the country uses the rectangular survey system. However, the lot and block system is used for subdivisions throughout the country. It may also be used for creating tax maps.

METES AND BOUNDS SYSTEM

> Beginning at a point on the Northeast corner of the intersection of Main Street and Oak Road, and running thence 300 feet East 90°0'0" along Oak to a point; thence North 90°0'0" 300 feet to a point; thence West 90 °0'0" 300 feet to a point; thence South 90 °0'0" 300 feet along Main to the point and place of beginning.

As you probably can tell from this description, the surveyor who uses the metes and bounds system divides the area into the points of a compass and moves clockwise around the circle giving both compass points (direction) and measurement (distance). Note also that the description begins with a "point of beginning." This is the main reference point and the point to which the boundary line must return.

Monument Description

The monument system is a variant of the metes and bounds system. Instead of using distances and directions, the monument system lists the boundary lines using monuments, or landmarks, as the reference points. These may be either natural or artificial, that is, made by humans.

> Beginning at the intersection of Main Street and Oak Street; thence along Oak Street to the creek bed; then along the creek bed to the fence; thence along the fence to Main Street; and thence along Main Street to the point of beginning.

Suppose the creek is rerouted or dries up, or the neighbor removes the fence? That is the downside to a description based on monuments. They can change or be removed.

LOT AND BLOCK SYSTEM

The lot and block system is also called the recorded plat—not plot—system, recorded map system, or lot block tract system. A plat is the map of the lots in a subdivision. The subdivision is divided into blocks and each block is divided into lots. Each lot has both a lot and a block number, for example, Block 10, Lot 56. The map also shows streets and physical features such as a lake.

To write a description of the lots, the surveyor uses the metes and bounds system. Otherwise, no one would know exactly where Lot 56 ends and the surrounding lots begin.

RECTANGULAR SURVEY SYSTEM

The rectangular survey system is also called the government survey system and the public land survey system. It is the primary method by which property in the United States is surveyed and described. The system uses a series of principal meridians and baselines. The 37 principal meridians run north and south and are parallel, and the baselines run east and west and are parallel.

The area enclosed by the intersection of two prime meridians and two baselines is called a quadrangle. The distance between the two prime meridians is 24 miles, and the area of the quadrangle is 576 square miles. (Distances and areas are approximations.)

A quadrangle is subdivided into 16 townships. Each township is 6 miles on a side and 36 square miles in area.

A township is subdivided into 36 sections. Each section is 1 square mile or 640 acres.

The next level of subdivision is called a quarter. Each section is divided into four parts, or quarters, of 160 acres each. The divisions continue as the area is subdivided into smaller and smaller parcels of land until a suburban homebuyer buys his or her dream house on one acre of land (or a half acre or a quarter acre).

There are two other terms to remember: guide meridians and standard parallels. Unlike a grid pattern, the Earth is not flat, so the principal meridians are not equidistant. To correct for this, the government has shifted each fourth meridian 24 miles from where it is on the globe. These adjusted meridians are called guide meridians, and the original meridians are called the standard meridians.

Describing Property Under the Rectangular Survey System

Each column of townships in a section is called a range, and each row of townships is called a tier. The townships are numbered in a zigzag pattern from the upper right corner to the bottom right corner, that is, from the upper northeast corner to the bottom southeast corner.

6	5	4	3	2	1
7	8	9	10	11	12
18	17	16	15	14	13
19	20	21	22	23	24
30	29	28	27	26	25
31	32	33	34	35	36

A legal property description will cite the tier and range of the section. Suppose section 10 in the grid is in township 16 north of the baseline in tier 5 north and range 3 east of principal meridian 5. The notation would read Sec.10, T5N, R3E.

As you have just read, sections can be subdivided and subdivided, so a deed to a suburban property might read: The SE 1/8 of NE 1/8 of NW 1/8 of Sec.10, T5N, R3E of the Fourth Principal Meridian.

You can determine the size of the property by multiplying how often the land has been subdivided to reach the present size ($\frac{1}{8} \times \frac{1}{8} \times \frac{1}{8} \times 640 = 1.25$ acres).

Sometimes more than one method of surveying a piece of property is needed because of irregular boundary lines in the real world. In that case, a designation from one of the other systems may be used, for example, a boulder as a turning point.

DESCRIBING THIN AIR

The information you just read deals with describing physical land, or land and water if the land contains a waterway, lake, or pond. However, legal descriptions of property may also include air rights. A five-story private school in a city decides to sell its air rights to a developer to a build a 20-story condominium. The air space above the school would be surveyed and the space divided into individual condo units for the purposes of sale (also for designing and construction).

The point, line, or surface used as a reference in surveying is called the *datum*. It is the Latin word from which we get the word *data*. The datum for measuring elevations anywhere in the United States is set at the mean sea level in New York Harbor.

BECOMING A REAL ESTATE APPRAISER

Becoming a real estate appraiser—like becoming a realtor—requires taking [and] passing licensing exams. In 1989, the U.S. Congress passed the Financial In[stitutions] Recovery, and Enforcement Act (FIRREA) that requires all appraisers valuing [what] are called federally related transactions (FRT), for example, Fannie Mae and Freddie M[ac] gages, be licensed or certified. The Act also gives the states the responsibility for licensing and certifying appraisers. Many states have also enacted their own laws requiring licensure or certification of real estate appraisers. Licensing is the first level, and certification recognizes higher levels of experience and education.

Founded in 1986, The Appraisal Foundation (TAF) established standards, criteria, and qualifications for the appraisal profession. It is a nonprofit organization that today numbers more than 100 organizations and government agencies related to real estate. TAF's Appraisal Standards Board and Appraiser Qualifications Board does the bulk of the Foundation's work. In addition to TAF's coursework requirements and federal requirements, states have their own requirements for licensure and certification.

The appraisal process itself has eight steps:

1. Define the appraisal problem: What property and when, why, and how is the property to be appraised?

2. Conduct a preliminary analysis: Determine the data necessary to appraise the property, the sources of the data and where they are available, for example, market trend data. This is also the step in which the appraiser sets the fee and submits a contract for the work.

3. Collect, verify, and analyze the data.

4. Determine the highest and best use of the property.

5. Estimate the value.

6. Apply the cost, sales income, and comparable approaches to valuing property.

7. Reconcile the three approaches to reach a final number.

8. Write up and deliver the appraisal report.

Appraisers conducting a valuation of a home whose mortgage will be underwritten by Fannie Mae or Freddie Mac must use the Universal Residential Appraisal Report (URAR).

For more information about becoming an appraiser and the work of appraisers, check out these links:

- The Appraisal Foundation: www.appraisalfoundation.org
- American Society of Appraisers: www.appraisers.org
- Appraisal Institute: www.appraisalinstitute.org
- National Association of Independent Fee Appraisers: www.naifa.com

WHAT IS THE PURPOSE OF A REAL ESTATE APPRAISAL?

The purpose of a real estate appraisal is to estimate the value of a property. Owners may need to know the current value of their property to refinance the mortgage or to set a price for selling it. A potential buyer needs an appraisal in order to qualify for a mortgage. Other reasons to have property appraised often involve government proceedings in some way. Before the government can take property through its right of eminent domain, the property must be appraised to reach a fair market value for the owner. Determining a property's value for the payment of estate taxes when someone dies or the payment of gift taxes when a person gives or receives real property as a gift also require appraisals. An appraisal also helps to establish a tax basis, so the gain can be calculated if the property is later sold.

CATEGORIES OF VALUE

Value is defined as the relative worth of a thing expressed in monetary terms. In real estate, this means what buyers and sellers believe real property is worth in dollars and cents. There are four characteristics that determine value in real estate or any commodity:

1. Utility (ability to satisfy a buyer's want or need)
2. Scarcity (see supply and demand)
3. Transferability (ability to convey title by selling, leasing, bequeathing, or giving away the property)
4. Effective demand (ability to pay for what is wanted or needed)

To have value, a property must have the four characteristics noted above. However, there are different kinds of value. The following types of value are important to know for real estate:

- **Market value:** The *Code of Federal Regulations* defines market value "as the most reasonable price which a property should bring in a competitive and open market under all conditions requisite to a fair sale." Market value is not the same as price. The final price (what a buyer is willing to pay and a seller is willing to accept) for a property may be higher or lower than the market value. Market value also fluctuates over time. Typically, a real estate appraiser estimates the market value of a property.

- **Value in use:** Value in use estimates the value of a property based on a particular use of, or purpose for, the property. For example, a restaurant has a value as a restaurant. Someone wishing to buy property and open a retail outlet would have less use for the restaurant because of the amount of renovation needed, whereas someone wishing to open a restaurant would find it very useful.

- **Investment value:** Investment value is the value of a property to someone (investor) who wishes to use the property for a specific purpose. In the example above, a restaurateur might be willing to pay a certain amount for the restaurant property because it suits his or her use. However, someone wanting to start a store selling men's clothing would see potential in the site if it were completely remodeled. In other words, the future store owner would see the building's investment value, but would also be willing to pay less (value) than the restaurateur.

- **Assessed value:** Assessed value is the value placed on property by a government official known as a tax assessor. The assessed value of property is used as the basis for calculating property taxes. The tax is calculated *ad valorem,* that is, in proportion to the value of the property.

PRINCIPLES OF APPRAISING VALUE

It is a cliché, but buying a home is typically the most expensive decision that an individual or couple will ever make. Whether or not people realize it, their behavior in purchasing a home is influenced by certain economic principles. This is also true for buyers of commercial properties and for renters. In valuing property, appraisers need to be aware of the following economic principles that influence value:

- **Supply and demand:** Supply and demand are two basic principles of economics. The greater the supply, the smaller the demand. The smaller the demand while the supply increases or remains the same, the less something will cost. The greater the demand while the supply decreases or remains the same, the more something will cost. This works in real estate, too. A housing surplus reduces home prices (value decreases) because there are fewer buyers; a shortage of homes in a desirable neighborhood enables a seller to ask a higher selling price (value increases—if the buyer can find a seller willing to pay).

- **Competition:** In a so-called buyers' market, sellers need to compete to attract buyers, and in a sellers' market, buyers need to compete to buy the property they really want. A buyers' market represents a surplus of properties and a sellers' market represents a shortage of properties. Competition works to bring the imbalance between supply and demand back into balance. However, competition can also drive the market to the other extreme, from a shortage of properties, which raises prices, to a shortage of buyers, which lowers prices.

- **Substitution:** Buyers including renters will look for the least expensive alternative to satisfy their wants and needs. Equivalent value is the key here. The appraiser must be able to figure out what the market considers "equivalent."

- **Change:** Change is a constant in the operation of supply and demand and, therefore, must be taken into consideration in valuing property. Because a comparable house sold for $300,000 a month ago doesn't mean that the same house will sell for $300,000 today. It could be more or could be less. (The housing crisis of the recession that began in 2007 was a dramatic illustration of this principle as housing values in some parts of the country dropped weekly.)

- **Anticipation:** For many years, buyers purchased homes with the expectation that the value of the home would increase while they enjoyed the benefits of living in the home. The twin expectations of gain and use (utility) are the benefits that people anticipate when buying a home. These factors working in the marketplace can act to raise or lower the value of property. Anticipation of the closing of a local factory with the resulting decrease in economic activity will lower property values. Anticipation of a company's opening a factory with the resulting increase in economic activity will raise property values.

- **Balance:** Another word for balance in this instance is proportionality. If you remember from your economics classes, there are four factors of production: land, labor, capital, and entrepreneurship. Maximal value is realized when the factors are in balance, or in proportion. Suppose all the properties in a neighborhood are valued at between $200,000 and $300,000. A buyer purchases

TIP

You might find some questions on the test that ask you to identify examples of the principles, the principles represented by examples, and definitions of the principles.

one of these homes, tears it down, and builds a McMansion that is valued at $600,000. This is an overimprovement of the land; too many resources were expended for the relative value in the neighborhood. The McMansion throws the values in the neighborhood out of balance.

- **Surplus productivity:** Surplus productivity measures the value of improved land. To find the amount of the surplus productivity, subtract the cost of the factors of production from the total net income. Suppose a developer builds a strip mall and rents all the stores. The properties bring in $1.2 million a year for the owner in rent, and the expenses for operating the mall are $750,000, so the surplus productivity is $450,000.

- **Contribution:** This principle states that the value of something is not in its cost, but in the value that it adds or subtracts from the property as a whole. This is an important factor in applying the sales comparison approach to valuing property. An appraiser needs to consider, for example, how much a parkside view adds to the value of one condo and how much the view of an airshaft detracts from the value of another condo, all else being equal.

- **Increasing and decreasing (diminishing) returns:** Up to a point, adding features to a property will increase its value more than the cost of the additional feature. But at a certain point, additional features return less value than they cost. That point is the point of diminishing returns. Suppose in readying a house for sale, a seller adds a half bath to the first floor where none existed. It costs the seller $6,500, but adds $8,500 to the selling price for a return to the seller of an additional $2,000. However, the seller also paints the interior and replaces the carpet. It costs the seller $5,000, but adds only $4,000 to the sale price. The return to the seller is $1,000 less than the cost.

- **Highest and best use:** The highest and best use is the most profitable and legally permissible use for a property. Determining highest and best use is the first step in determining market value. "Legally permissible" in the definition means whether the use anticipated for the property fits within zoning ordinances. In addition to being legally permissible, there are three other criteria that are considered in analyzing highest and best use: physically possible, financially feasible, and maximally productive. The first three determine what enterprise will be most productive, that is, most profitable, for the property. When an appraisal is being conducted on improved land, rather than vacant land, the appraiser considers the viability of the structures on the land in relation to the highest and best use. The appraiser may recommend that they be torn down, renovated in some way, or left as is. For example, an abandoned gas station on land to be developed for a mall would be demolished.

- **Conformity, progression, and regression:** In a subdivision, conformity—even to the color that owners can paint their front doors—is maintained through restrictive covenants and association rules. An owner might not like that much conformity, but it eliminates one potential problem in appraising property: how the neighbors affect the value of your house. In towns and cities, zoning ordinances seek to maintain conformity to a degree by regulating lot size and general architectural style, but within those limits, people can still show originality and creativity in what they build. However, a nonconforming house—a mid-century modern in a neighborhood of colonials—could well result in a lower valuation. When properties in an area are similar (conform), they enhance the value of one another. That similarity may be in use—such as all single-family homes or all semi-detached homes—or in architectural style—such as all mid-century modern or all colonial. Related to conformity are the principles of progression and regression. Progression refers to a rise in price, and regression refers to a decline in price. It is similar to guilt by association. A small colonial in a neighborhood of mid-century modern homes will experience a rise in its value as the value of the mid-century moderns increase with increasing buyer interest. Conversely, a McMansion in the midst of Cape Cods will experience a decline in value as interest in Cape Cods declines.

FACTORS THAT INFLUENCE VALUE

There are a variety of factors—social, economic, political, and environmental—which affect valuation in the housing market.

Social Factors

Social factors include prestige, recreation, culture, family orientation, and homeowner restrictions. Prestige relates to the desirability of living in certain areas and not others. How close a property is to certain types of recreational or cultural attractions such as tennis courts and museums can be factors that influence value.

Family orientation refers to how family-friendly a place is. How does the school district fare on state tests? What's the high school graduation rate? Are there playing fields for sponsored sports teams? Are there after-school programs?

Typically, these four factors would be seen generally as increasing the value of a property, though any specific buyer may not care about any or all of them. Restrictive covenants of a homeowners association may add value or be a value detractor, depending on what they are and how a buyer feels about being limited in how he or she uses the property.

Economic Factors

Economic factors that affect the value of property include the local economy, interest rates, vacancies, rents, parking, corner influence, and plottage. Notice how many of these factors are affected by the principles of supply and demand.

If the local economy is not doing well, the housing and commercial real estate markets will not be doing well. A contraction of the local economy will mean problems with defaults on rents and mortgage payments, foreclosures, and a glut of property on the market with a resulting decline in property values.

Interest rates also affect value. If interest rates are high, housing construction will slow because it costs too much to borrow money to finance construction projects. It also means that mortgage rates will rise. On the one hand, fewer new homes mean that older homes become more attractive to buyers, but on the other hand, high interest rates mean fewer buyers. However, when interest rates are low, more people will be interested in buying homes.

Interest rates can also affect vacancy rates. When interest rates are low, developers may build more properties in an area than there are tenants. The result is a glut on the market and a high rate of vacancies. This can occur in residential buildings as well as retail and industrial sites. Any appraisal of a commercial building takes into consideration the vacancy rate and may result in a lower valuation than if the building had a lower vacancy rate.

NOTE Understanding the principle of contribution can help you as a realtor, too. If a seller has only so much to spend to touch up a property before listing it, what will add the most value? Replacing the carpet or the appliances? Adding landscaping for curb appeal or a fresh coat of neutral paint to the bedrooms?

High rents result in more people looking to buy property, whereas low rents result in fewer people interested in becoming property owners. The former would increase valuations, and the latter would decrease valuations.

Whether there is parking and where it is affects a property's value. A townhouse with a garage is valued higher than a townhouse without a garage. An appraisal of a townhouse that is an end unit, or corner unit, will be higher than the appraisal of an interior unit all things being equal. However, a free-standing home at an intersection of two streets would be appraised at a lesser value than a house in the middle of the block, because of the traffic, noise, and loss of privacy.

Combining properties, known as plottage, results in a total value that is greater than the sum of the values of the individual parcels.

Political Factors

The political factors that affect property valuation are straightforward: taxes, zoning, rent control, limits on growth, environmental restrictions, and building and health codes. These factors can have negative effects on valuation by imposing restrictions, usually monetary, either directly (taxation) or indirectly (through compliance). However, they can also influence valuations positively.

Low taxes can mean more demand for property and higher valuations. A property zoned for a commercial use will bring in more tax revenue than residential zoned areas and have higher valuation. In addition, the taxes raised from commercial zoning can offset residential taxes, so that residential property owners pay lower taxes, which increase their valuations. Smart growth limits can mean a greater demand for homes or rental properties and, thus, higher valuations.

Environmental Factors

Location! That may be the most important factor to a buyer or renter. How close is a property to what the person wants: recreational sites, museums, the subway, and so on.

Other environmental factors that typically add to value are climate; water supply, especially for commercial and industrial enterprises; transportation network; view; size and shape of the property, that is, regularly shaped property versus a pie-shaped parcel; exposure, that is, direction in relation to the rising and setting sun; environmental hazards; and the physical layout of the land, that is, a stream running through a suburban property would add value, whereas rocky outcroppings on farmland would decrease the value.

SALES COMPARISON APPROACH TO VALUING PROPERTY

There are three ways that appraisers use to value property: the sales comparison approach, the cost approach, and the income approach. The one used most often for single-family homes is the sales comparison approach. This approach compares the subject property (property being appraised) to similar properties, either recently sold or currently on the market. Also called the market comparison approach, it is based on sales price.

In this approach, the appraiser reviews the physical property, looking at such things as interior and exterior condition, foundation, age, HVAC, roof, gutters and downspouts, porch, number of rooms, flooring, trim and finish, walls, and so on. Then the appraiser collects data on homes with the same or close to the same attributes as the subject's property that have recently been sold or are currently for sale in the same market, that is, the same area. "Recently" is usually no longer than six months ago.

The price of the comps are adjusted to reflect differences between the comps and the subject property. The appraiser has a checklist of elements of comparison that he or she analyzes, and these include such things as financing terms, market conditions, location, real property rights, and highest and best use. Adjustments can be made based on different factors, such as numbers of bedrooms and bathrooms, square footage, level of finish, location, finished basement, and similar items. Adjustments are made by adding or subtracting percentages that represent money values for the elements of comparison. For example, the comp may have a wood exterior and the subject house, a vinyl exterior. What is a positive for the subject is a negative for the comp, and a negative for the subject is a positive for the comp, so, in this case, the appraiser would add to the comp because the vinyl siding on the subject is considered a negative.

Once the appraiser has adjusted the value of all the comps either upward (worse than the house being appraised) or downward (better than the house being appraised), the appraiser reviews the data again and determines a value for the subject property. Because the comps will not all arrive at the same value, the appraiser suggests a value within the range of the value of the comps.

COST APPROACH TO VALUING PROPERTY

The cost approach analyzes the replacement or reproduction cost of improvements on a piece of land plus the depreciation of those improvements to arrive at the value of the property in total. The formula for computing the cost approach is the following:

Value = Replacement or Reproduction Costs – Depreciation + Land Value

The replacement or reproduction costs are figured in today's dollars. A reproduction is exactly the same as the original structure. A replacement is the same in its usefulness to the owner, but will be built with modern materials and according to current building methods.

Four Methods to Determining Costs

To apply the cost approach, the appraiser first determines the cost of replacing or reproducing the improvements on the land. The following are the four ways to determine costs:

1. **Comparative unit method:** Also called the square foot method, the costs are arrived at by multiplying the square footage of the structure by the cost of building that type of structure. For example, the cost of building a two-bedroom Cape Cod would be substantially different than building a 7-unit block of townhouses.

2. **Unit-in-place method:** The appraiser measures the number and, in some cases, the area of various elements in a building and multiplies each by its unit cost. For example, that two-bedroom Cape might have four interior doors that cost $300 apiece and 1,500 square feet of flooring at $10 a square foot for a total cost of $15,000 installed.

3. **Quantity survey:** This approach to determining cost is most useful to builders and contractors because of its reliability. This method is similar to the unit-in-place method, but is

more detailed. The cost of the materials of each component and the cost to install each is listed separately, whereas the costs are combined in the unit-in-place method.

4. **Index method:** The index method is the least reliable of the four methods, but it is useful as a quick way to estimate costs in today's dollars if the original construction costs are known. Like the consumer price index that tracks the relative change in costs for certain consumer goods over time, there are construction cost indexes that track the relative change in the costs of construction over time. Suppose the original cost of a ranch house built in 1954 was $30,000. The construction cost index for that type of house in 1954 was at 80, and today it is at 180 for that type of house.

   a. Divide today's construction cost index of 180 by 80; you will get 2.25.

   b. Multiply the cost in 1954 ($30,000) times the construction cost index today (2.25) to find the cost in today's dollars.

   c. $30,000 × 2.25 = $67,500

Remember that is this cost of the improvements only, not the cost of the underlying land.

The Depreciation Step

Once the appraiser has determined the cost, he or she has to figure out the depreciation on the improvements. Depreciation is the difference in value between the improvements (structures) on the land if they were brand new and their current value because of a variety of factors that have reduced that value:

- **Physical deterioration:** This results from wear and tear on the structure, and can be curable or incurable. An incurable physical deterioration would be one that costs more to fix than it adds to the value of the structure. Replacing water-damaged hardwood flooring would be a curable deterioration because the value that it add to the overall value would outweigh the cost of the new flooring.

- **Functional obsolescence:** A functional obsolescence is a design defect and can be either curable or incurable depending on the cost to correct the defect versus the amount of value it will add. Adding a half bathroom in a closet under the stairs in a Victorian house because there is no bathroom on the first floor may not be worth the cost.

- **External obsolescence:** Once the neighborhood was close to stores, an elementary school, and restaurants, but now most of the shops and restaurants have closed because of a mall on the outskirts of town and the school has been converted into an office building with a lot of foot traffic from a nearby garage. This is a picture of external obsolescence. The houses may still be well maintained, but the neighborhood has changed. External obsolescence is considered incurable.

Now that the appraiser has decided which type of depreciation to use, he or she has to actually figure out what the depreciation factor is. A typical method is the economic age-life method, also known as the straight-line method. This method assumes that an improvement loses value at a steady rate over the period of its economic life, and when the improvement ceases to be at the highest value for the property, the economic life of the improvement ends. Economic life is defined as the length of time during which the improvement contributes to the value of the property.

To find depreciation in the straight-line method, the appraiser would use the following formula substituting a number from a prepared age-life table for the operation in the parentheses:

Depreciation = (Effective Age ÷ Economic Life) × Cost

Suppose the improvement had an age-life of 15 percent (effective age of 3 years and economic life of 20 years) and the replacement cost was $500,000.

Depreciation = 0.15 × 500,000 = 75,000

So, the depreciated value of the property is $500,000 − $75,000 = $425,000.

The final step in the cost approach is valuing the land. The sales comparison approach is typically used to determine land value, and the environmental factors that affect value play a role in this process.

INCOME APPROACH TO VALUING PROPERTY

The income approach, or income capitalization approach, is used to appraise investment properties and estimates value based on the amount of income that a property produces. However, the estimate includes not just the current income (value), but also the future benefit (value) that the investor can expect to receive. To calculate this value, the appraiser must determine net operating income and then the rate of capitalization.

Estimating Net Operating Income

An appraiser begins by estimating the net operating income (NOI), which involves four steps. First, the appraiser combines information about the income and expenses of the property obtained from a number of sources such as the current owner's accounting firm and the property manager.

Second, once the information has been obtained, the appraiser estimates potential gross income (PGI). This is the total amount of revenue that the property could generate if there were no vacancies. The amount is based not on contract rent—actual rents being charged—but market rent, the rents that could be charged based on market conditions. Properties can also generate income from other revenue streams besides rent, for example, charging for parking in a building's underground parking garage or a parking lot. This income is also added in when calculating PGI.

Third, from the PGI, the appraiser subtracts an allowance for vacancies and an allowance for nonpayment of rents, or a bad debt collection loss. The new amount is the effective gross income (EGI).

Fourth, the property's operating expenses (both fixed and variable expenses) and reserves for replacement are deducted from the EGI. Property taxes are an example of fixed expenses, and leasing commissions are an example of a variable expense. Over time, certain items need to be replaced such as carpet and paint, and the cost of these items are included under reserves.

Determining the Capitalization Rate

Once the appraiser has the NOI, the appraiser determines the capitalization rate, which is the percentage that is used to convert the income into value. The capitalization rate represents the relationship between income and value. In any textbook on appraising, pages and pages are devoted to the process of finding the capitalization rate because the process can be very complex, depending on the property being appraised and the number of comps. The following formula for the overall capitalization rate is a simple way to look at the problem:

Capitalization Rate = NOI ÷ Sales Price

With this information, the appraiser can estimate the value of the property using the formula:

Value = NOI ÷ Capitalization Rate

Suppose the NOI is $100,000 and the capitalization rate is 0.5, the equation would look like this:

Value = $100,000 ÷ 0.5 = $200,000

RECONCILIATION: ARRIVING AT THE FINAL NUMBER

To value a property, appraisers use all three approaches: sales comparison, cost, and income. If you read the above feature on becoming an appraiser, you'll remember that the step before writing the appraisal report is the reconciliation. This is the process by which the appraiser analyzes the results of the different approaches and determines a single value or range of values that is best supported by the data that has been collected and analyzed. In working through the process, the appraiser will give more weight to some data than others, based on the amount, accuracy, relevance, and reliability of the findings. Reconciliation is also the final judgment that the appraiser makes about the value of the property.

EXERCISES

1. A legal property description lists
   (A) boundary lines only.
   (B) boundary lines and topographical features.
   (C) boundary lines, topographical features, and structures.
   (D) boundary lines and structures.

2. Block 51, Lot 12, is an example of which of the following systems of property description?
   (A) Metes and bounds
   (B) Monument
   (C) Recorded plat
   (D) Rectangular survey system

3. If a buyer wanted an appraisal of a house, the appraiser would most likely conduct an appraisal for
   (A) market value.
   (B) value in use.
   (C) investment value.
   (D) assessed value.

4. A social factor that affects value is
   (A) parking.
   (B) corner influence.
   (C) building and health codes.
   (D) whether the school district has all-day kindergarten.

5. Which of the following describes external obsolescence?
   (A) A type of depreciation that results from a built-in design problem
   (B) A type of depreciation that results from a locational factor
   (C) A curable problem related to depreciation
   (D) Another name for straight-line depreciation

6. Which of the following is an example of functional obsolescence?
   (A) Lack of a garage
   (B) Lack of a closet in the third bedroom
   (C) Lack of an eat-in kitchen
   (D) An unfinished basement

7. Which of the following is not used in finding the NOI?
   (A) PGI
   (B) EGI
   (C) Vacancy allowance
   (D) Capitalization rate

exercises

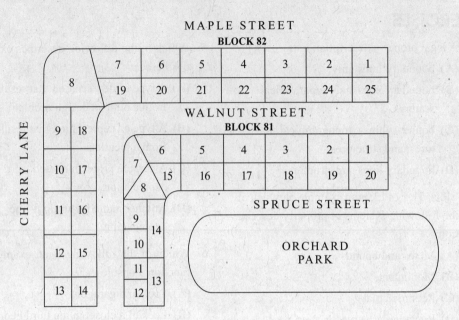

8. On what street is Block 81, Lot 12?

   (A) Maple

   (B) Cherry

   (C) Walnut

   (D) Spruce

ANSWER KEY AND EXPLANATIONS

1. A	3. A	5. B	7. D
2. C	4. D	6. A	8. C

1. **The correct answer is (A).** Choices (B), (C), and (D) are incorrect definitions of all the types of legal property description.

2. **The correct answer is (C).** Another name for the recorded plat system is the lot and block system. Choice (A) uses compass directions. Choice (B) uses objects and/or street names. Choice (D) uses section, tier, and range numbers as well as compass directions.

3. **The correct answer is (A).** Choice (B) is used when a property is being appraised based on its particular use. Choice (C) is used to appraise a property for a specific purpose. Choice (D) is the value assigned to a property for tax purposes.

4. **The correct answer is (D).** Choice (D) is in the subcategory of family orientation under social factors. Choice (A) could be an economic factor. Choice (B) is an environmental factor. Choice (C) is a political factor.

5. **The correct answer is (B).** Choice (A) is an example of functional obsolescence. Choice (C) applies to obsolescence factors, but it is not one in itself. Choice (D) is incorrect; another name for straight-line depreciation is economic age-life method.

6. **The correct answer is (A).** Choices (B), (C), and (D) may be necessities to some people, but they are not examples of functional obsolescence.

7. **The correct answer is (D).** The NOI is used to find the capitalization rate as in choice (D); the capitalization rate is not used to find the NOI as in choices (A), (B), and (C) are used to find the NOI.

8. **The correct answer is (C).** Choice (C) is the only street that fronts Block 81, Lot 12.

SUMMING IT UP

- The legal description of a property lists only the boundary lines.

- There are three systems used for a legal description of a property:

  1. Metes and bounds
  2. Lot and block
  3. Rectangular survey

- A real estate appraisal estimates the value of property, which is different from the price. Value is the relative worth of a property expressed in monetary terms.

- There are four categories of value:

  1. Market value
  2. Value in use
  3. Investment value
  4. Assessed value

- A number of economic principles influence value:

  - ☐ Supply and demand
  - ☐ Competition
  - ☐ Substitution
  - ☐ Change
  - ☐ Anticipation
  - ☐ Balance
  - ☐ Surplus productivity
  - ☐ Contribution
  - ☐ Increasing and decreasing returns
  - ☐ Highest and best use
  - ☐ Conformity, progression, and regression

- Other factors that influence value are social, economic, political, and environmental.

- There are three approaches to valuing property:

  1. Sales comparison approach
  2. Cost approach
  3. Income approach

Mortgages

OVERVIEW

- Mortgages, notes, and trust deeds
- Requirements of mortgages and notes
- Assignments, assumptions, and "subject to the mortgage"
- Mortgage markets
- Mortgage insurance programs
- Categories of mortgages
- Mortgage terms and rates
- Federal laws related to mortgage financing
- Foreclosure
- Summing it up

A mortgage is the promise to repay a loan for the purchase of real property. The lender (mortgagee) provides the financing, and the borrower (mortgagor) provides the property as security for the loan. In states that work under the lien theory, the mortgage creates a lien on the title of the property. When the mortgage is paid off, the lien is removed. During the term of the mortgage, the mortgagor keeps both the equitable title and the legal title to the property. If a state uses the title theory, only the legal title transfers to the mortgagee. When the mortgage is paid off, the mortgagee receives legal title to the property.

MORTGAGES, NOTES, AND TRUST DEEDS

Whereas a mortgage is the promise to repay the loan on the property, the note, or promissory note, that accompanies it states the amount, terms, and conditions under which the mortgage will be repaid.

In some states, when a government-sponsored agency such as Freddie Mac provides the loan to purchase property, a trust deed is used instead of a mortgage. However, like a mortgage, the trust deed requires a promissory note.

A trust deed conveys title from the trustor to a trustee for the beneficiary. The trustor is the borrower, the beneficiary is the originator of the financing, and the trustee would be a third party. When the trustor repays the loan, the title passes from the trustee to the trustor by means of a release deed.

chapter 11

REQUIREMENTS OF MORTGAGES AND NOTES

Like any other contract, a mortgage must contain certain elements. Typically, a mortgage will include information on the following:

- Loan amount
- Legal description of the property
- Granting clause that gives the right to the mortgage to the mortgagee
- *Habendum* clause that reiterates the ownership specified in the granting clause
- Covenant of seisin that guarantees the mortgagor has the right to transfer title to the mortgagee
- Defeasance clause that states the mortgagee will turn over to the mortgagor the title to the property when the loan has been paid off
- Proration of property taxes and assessment
- Insurance clauses that relate to the type and amount of insurance such as flood insurance and any requirement for title insurance
- Escrow, or reserve, account into which the mortgagor will pay a certain amount in advance on a regular basis to pay property taxes
- Acceleration clause that provides for full repayment of the loan should the mortgagor default on any aspect of the mortgage
- Prepayment clause listing the penalty that will be charged the mortgagor if the mortgagor pays off the loan ahead of schedule (this is different from the acceleration clause; prepayment is voluntary on the part of the mortgagor, whereas acceleration is demanded by the mortgagee because of some lack of performance by the mortgagor)
- Requirement to preserve the value of the property over time by maintaining it
- Requirement to get the approval of the mortgagee before any large-scale renovation is done
- Copy of the note

A note typically contains the loan amount and interest rate, schedule of payments, and amount of each payment as well as an acceleration clause and the amount of late charges. (See Variable-Rate Mortgages below for information about what to look for with adjustable-rate mortgages (ARMs).) The note also contains the mortgagor's explicit promise to pay back the loan. A promissory note may also include co-signers if the mortgagee requires an additional guarantee of payment. For example, a person recently out of college who wants to buy a condo may be required to have his or her parents co-sign the note.

Both the mortgage and the note must be in writing and be signed and acknowledged. The mortgage is then recorded by the municipal government as a lien on the property.

ASSIGNMENTS, ASSUMPTIONS, AND "SUBJECT TO THE MORTGAGE"

By the time a mortgage is repaid, neither the original mortgagee nor mortgagor may be a party to the process because of assignments and assumptions. Both are typically covered in a mortgage.

In an assignment, another lender buys, or, in the case of a bank merger, takes over the mortgage from the original lender. The right of assignment by the lender is a standard part of a mortgage.

In an assumption, another party takes over the mortgage from the original mortgagor. For example, a mother sells her house to her son who takes over the mortgage on the house. If the son "assumes" the mortgage, he will be responsible for the entire unpaid portion of the mortgage. His mother has no liability should he default on the mortgage. However, the lender must agree to this. (If the lender doesn't agree, then the mother has to pay off her mortgage with the money from the sale, and the son has to apply for his own mortgage.)

However, a purchaser may also assume a mortgage under a "subject to the mortgage" clause. The original purchaser will be responsible for the entire balance should the purchaser to whom the mortgage was transferred default on the mortgage. Suppose the mother (while still living) sells the house to her son who assumes the mortgage under this clause. If the son defaults on the mortgage payments, his mother is still responsible for whatever is left on the mortgage.

In both types of assumptions, the mortgagee must approve the transfer of the mortgage from one person to another.

MORTGAGE MARKETS

There are two "markets" for financing real property: the primary mortgage market and the secondary mortgage market. The primary market originates, that is, writes, mortgages and the secondary market buys mortgages from the primary market, bundles them, and sells them as investments. These are called mortgage-backed securities (MBS) and the process is known as securitization. It raises capital to enable the primary market to continue offering mortgages.

The financial crisis that precipitated the recession of 2007 through 2009 began in the housing market as interest rates for risky mortgages began to adjust higher and higher and homeowners began to default on their loans. The crisis soon spread to the secondary mortgage market as waves of defaults hit the mortgages that underlay the securitized mortgages.

Primary Mortgage Market

The principal players in the primary mortgage market include:
- Commercial banks
- Savings and loan associations
- Credit unions
- Mutual savings banks
- Mortgage companies (mortgage bankers)
- Portfolio lenders like REITs (Real Estate Investment Trusts), insurance companies, and pension funds.

The first five types of financial institutions listed above typically offer mortgages directly to potential buyers of residential property, that is, a buyer interested in purchasing a home or condo. Portfolio lenders offer loans for large-scale projects such as malls and housing developments.

NOTE
Be sure you know what the requirements for mortgage brokers are in your state.

Mortgage brokers are also included in the primary mortgage market, but do not be confused by the term. The job of mortgage brokers is to find the best rate and terms for the borrower, but mortgage brokers don't originate loans themselves. They act as intermediaries between potential buyers, especially in commercial real estate transactions, and lenders.

Secondary Mortgage Market

The most important players in the secondary mortgage market include:

- **Fannie Mae:** Chartered by Congress in 1938, Fannie Mae is a government-sponsored entity (GSE), but not a government-backed entity. It is a corporation owned by its stockholders. It works with mortgage originators in the primary mortgage market by buying their mortgages, bundling them, and selling the resulting securities to investors. The money that Fannie Mae gets in return is used to buy more mortgages, bundle them, etc. Fannie Mae was created and continues to provide capital to the primary mortgage market "to make homeownership and rental housing more available and affordable."

- **Freddie Mac:** Like Fannie Mae, Freddie Mac is also a GSE owned by its stockholders. It was established by Congress in 1970 to expand the amount of money available for housing and thus to provide additional "liquidity, stability and affordability to the U.S. housing market." It operates in a similar way to Fannie Mae.

- **Ginnie Mae (Government National Mortgage Association):** Unlike the other two GSEs, Ginnie Mae is a government-backed corporation within the Department of Housing and Urban Development. It does not buy, sell, or securitize mortgages, but rather "guarantees mortgage-backed securities backed by federally insured or guaranteed loans," those insured by the Federal Housing Administration (FHA) or guaranteed by the Department of Veterans Affairs (VA). (See Mortgage Insurance Programs below.) Ginnie Mae issues what are known as pass-through securities that guarantee investors of mortgage-backed securities (MBS) the regular payment of principal and interest on their investment.

In addition to Fannie Mae and Freddie Mac, private mortgage companies also buy, bundle, and sell mortgages to investors. However, Fannie and Freddie are the largest entities in the secondary mortgage market.

To whom do players in the secondary mortgage sell their MBS? The typical purchasers are large pension funds, insurance companies, and hedge funds, which are investment companies for small numbers of very wealthy clients. They typically specialize in high-risk investing.

MORTGAGE INSURANCE PROGRAMS

Depending on how much money a buyer has to put down for a property, the buyer may need mortgage insurance. There are two types, government and private. The purpose of the insurance is to guarantee that the lender will not lose money if the mortgagor defaults on the mortgage. It's important to note that the FHA and the VA do not actually *lend* money even though we typically refer to the loans as "FHA mortgages" and "VA mortgages." The agencies only insure the mortgages; private lenders like credit unions actually provide the mortgages.

Federal Housing Administration

The FHA offers mortgage insurance to purchasers who meet certain requirements. The purchaser

- must be using an FHA-approved lender.
- must be buying single-family or multifamily housing of no more than 4 units, one of which will be owner occupied.
- has less than 20 percent for the down payment on the property.
- must use an FHA-approved appraiser.
- meets the FHA debt-to-income ratio (29 percent mortgage payment expense to effective income and 41 percent total fixed payment to effective income).

There are lending limits based on the value of the property, and these vary by state and county.

The FHA charges an upfront fee of 2.25 percent of the loan amount, called the mortgage insurance premium (MIP). The borrower then pays an annual premium until certain conditions are met. At that point, the mortgagor no longer pays the insurance premium.

Department of Veterans Affairs

VA-insured mortgages are part of the GI Bill of Rights passed after World War II. More than 25.5 million veterans have bought homes since then using the VA program. Up to 25 percent of a home loan, or $104,250, can be guaranteed by the VA. This means that the home may not cost more than $417,000. Here are some of the benefits of the VA programs:

- Generally, a down payment is not required.
- There is no monthly mortgage insurance payment.
- A limit is placed on the buyer's closing costs.
- The mortgage is assumable, but must be approved by the VA.
- No prepayment penalty.

Veterans are not automatically eligible. They have to qualify by completing a form that includes their length of service and type of discharge. The property must also be appraised by a VA-approved appraiser.

Private Mortgage Insurance

If a home buyer has less than 20 percent to put down on a property, the lender may require that the buyer purchase private mortgage insurance (PMI) from a private mortgage insurance company. PMI ensures that the lender will be paid if the mortgagor defaults. The mortgagor pays the PMI as part of the regular mortgage payment.

The federal Homeowners Protection Act of 1998 requires that PMI be cancelled automatically when the equity in the home rises above 22 percent for mortgages signed on or after July 29, 1999. However, the law does not apply if the mortgagor is not current with payments, and it applies only to PMI, not VA- or FHA-insured mortgages. Some states also have their own laws related to PMI.

NOTE

For more information about how the FHA program works, check the Web site www.fha.com/important_facts.cfm. The site clearly explains the program and offers a checklist that clients can use to prepare their applications and to calculate a debt ratio for eligibility. The site also has information on the loan limits by geographical area of the country.

NOTE

For more information on the VA program, see www.valoans.com/geninfo-01b.cfm. This site includes information on how a client can apply for eligibility for the VA Loan Program.

CATEGORIES OF MORTGAGES

Both Fannie Mae and Freddie Mac deal in conventional mortgages, which is one of three types of mortgages:

1. **Conventional mortgage:** This is a mortgage that is secured by real property and is not insured or guaranteed by a government agency. Many home mortgages and all nonresidential mortgages, for example, a construction mortgage, are conventional mortgages.

2. **Conforming mortgage:** A conventional mortgage that is eligible for sale to Freddie Mac or Fannie Mae is called a conforming mortgage. The mortgage amount cannot be above their annually adjusted dollar threshold for any given year. In 2009, the limit was $417,000 for a single-family home. The mortgage must also have certain uniform provisions required by Fannie Mae and Freddie Mac.

3. **Nonconforming mortgage:** A nonconforming mortgage cannot be sold to Fannie Mae or Freddie Mac for a variety of reasons: the mortgage is over the loan threshold, the mortgagor has a poor credit rating, sufficient documentation does not exist, and the mortgage does not include the standard provisions required by Fannie Mae and Freddie Mac.

MORTGAGE TERMS AND RATES

The fixed-rate, 30-year mortgage was once a standard home mortgage, but as the banking industry was deregulated, bankers found new ways to make money by lending money. There are now a variety of mortgages available for homebuyers, depending on their credit rating and the size of their wallets.

Fixed-Rate Mortgages

A fixed-rate mortgage has an interest rate and, therefore, a payment amount that remains the same for the life of the mortgage. The term of a fixed-rate mortgage is typically 15, 20, or 30 years. This is sometimes referred to as a conventional mortgage.

Variable-Rate Mortgages

Variable-rate mortgages, also known as adjustable-rate mortgages (ARMs), have interest rates that fluctuate. The rate is affected by changes in the Treasury Bill or the prime rate. You do not need to know the ins and outs of the policy behind these changes; it is enough to know that the Fed's policies can cause a rise or fall in short-term interest rates and, thus, the mortgage rates that your buyers will pay. In determining whether to get an ARM and what type of ARM, a buyer should consider

*   the index used to compute changes in interest rate (1-year Treasury rates, London Interbank Offered Rate (LIBOR), or Costs of Funds Index (COFI)).

*   the margin—a percentage—added to the index as the lender's revenue.

*   caps on the interest rate, that is, a ceiling on the amount a lender can raise interest rates:

    ○   annual cap (typically by no more than 2 percentage points).

    ○   life-of-the loan cap (typically by no more than 6 percentage points overall).

- the frequency of the rate adjustment, which can be monthly, semiannually, or annually.

- a payment cap, which can result in a mortgagor paying less than the full amount of interest necessary in each payment to pay off the mortgage at the end of the term of the mortgage.

ARMs come in a variety of forms:

- **Standard ARM:** The interest rate adjusts monthly, semiannually, or annually for the life of the mortgage depending on the terms of the mortgage. The loan amount is amortized over the life of the mortgage and is paid off at the end of the term of the mortgage.

- **5/1 ARM:** The monthly payment is fixed for the first 5 years. After that, the rate and the payments adjust for the remaining 25 years. Variations on this are the 3/1 ARM and the 2/1 ARM. The rate and payment amount are set for the first 3 years or 2 years and then adjust for the remaining years on the mortgage. These are known as hybrid mortgages because they contain elements of both fixed-rate mortgages and ARMs. They are also called two-step mortgages.

- **Balloon ARM:** This mortgage is also a hybrid mortgage because it has elements of both a balloon mortgage with a fixed rate and an ARM. The rate adjusts so that the payments vary over the life of the mortgage. However, the mortgagor is only paying the interest with each payment, not the principal. At the end of the term of the mortgage, the borrower must repay the entire principal in a single payment.

- **Convertible ARM:** This type of ARM allows the mortgagor to convert from an ARM to a fixed-rate mortgage after a certain period of time. The determination of the new interest rate is set in the original ARM mortgage. The mortgagor pays a fee at the time of the conversion.

- **Interest-only ARM:** This type of ARM has an initial period in which only the interest on the mortgage is paid. Then the mortgage is amortized over the shorter repayment period, and the payment amount increases, often substantially, in order to ensure that the entire mortgage is paid off at the end of the term of the mortgage.

Other Financing Options

While there are two basic types of mortgages—fixed and ARM—there are a variety of features that show up in mortgages that may fit some borrowers better than the straight fixed mortgages and ARMs. These include:

- **Balloon loan:** The mortgagor pays a fixed amount each month for the term of the mortgage, usually 5 or 7 years, and at the end of that time, must pay the full amount remaining on the mortgage. The difference with a balloon ARM is that the monthly payments are fixed. (Any loan that doesn't self-amortize, i.e., pay the amount in full, results in a balloon payment at the end.)

- **Biweekly loan:** The mortgagor pays off the loan every two weeks instead of monthly. The payments are half what a monthly payment would be, but the mortgagor pays an interest payment each year (26 payments versus 12 payments).

- **Straight-term mortgage:** Familiarly known as an interest-only mortgage, the mortgagor pays only the interest during the term of the mortgage and at the end of the term, the entire principal is due.

- **Open mortgage:** The mortgage can be paid off early without the mortgagor having to pay a prepayment penalty.

NOTE

If buyers ask about ARMs, suggest that they download and read *Consumer Handbook on Adjustable Rate Mortgages* published by the Federal Reserve Board and the Federal Home Loan Bank Board.

- **Open-end mortgage:** This is a mortgage that permits the mortgagor to borrow additional money under the same mortgage under certain conditions, usually having to do with the assets of the mortgagor.

- **Package mortgage:** This is used when the buyer is buying not only the real property, but also personal property in the home such as furniture.

- **Purchase-money mortgage:** This is also known as seller financing or owner financing. The buyer borrows from the seller rather than from a financial institution or in addition to the financial institution. A buyer unable to quality for the full mortgage might use this type of mortgage.

- **Shared equity:** To finance the purchase of a property, the potential buyer borrows money for the down payment and in return, the lender gets a partial share in the property. When the property is sold, the lender gets part of the profit in proportion to the amount the lender provided. Parents helping an adult child or newlyweds to buy a home could be an example of using shared equity for the purchase. Depending on the state, the parents would have to qualify for the mortgage, too, and be on the mortgage and the deed.

- **Graduated payment mortgage (GPM):** The rate is fixed, but the payments start low and increase over time. Initial payments do not cover the interest. The difference in payment is added to the loan balance. A GPM may be used for borrowers who qualify using the initial payment amount.

- **Growing equity mortgage (GEM):** The rate remains fixed with both options, but the amount of payments increases over time according to a schedule of increases. With the GEM, the increases are applied to the principal only. People starting out who expect to see their incomes increase over time may choose this mortgage option.

- **Wraparound mortgage:** The buyer takes out a mortgage that includes the remaining amount on the seller's mortgage and makes payments to his or her lender that include payments on the original mortgage. This lender then pays the original seller's mortgagee. It is usually a method of refinancing in which the new loan is second to the original debt, but it is considered an obligation of the borrower.

- **Temporary loan:** This is also known as a bridge loan or a swing loan and is used when the buyer doesn't have the funds immediately available to close on the sale. A bridge loan is used, for example, when a buyer must sell his or her home in order to finance the purchase of the new home, but the closing on the current home has been delayed.

Some types of mortgages and property financing are used more often by businesses than by individual buyers.

- **Blanket mortgage:** A blanket mortgage covers more than one piece of property and is widely used in developing subdivisions. If the mortgage has a partial release provision, it allows a builder to develop and sell lots separately, paying off part of the mortgage with each sale.

- **Construction mortgage:** This type of mortgage provides funding for a construction project at different stages in the project. It may be taken out to build a single-family home or to build a housing development.

- **Sale-and-leaseback:** This is a type of financing for commercial enterprises, and not a mortgage as such. The owner of a property sells it and agrees to remain as a tenant of the new owner. The original owner gains the value of the property to use and the new owner is assured of rent for a period of time.

- **Mortgage rate buydown:** This, too, is not a mortgage but a form of financing usually offered by developers to help buyers purchase their new construction. It is similar to a subsidy by helping the purchaser pay a percentage of the monthly mortgage payment for the first year or two.

A Word About Subprime Mortgages

The financial crisis that rocked the world's economies beginning in 2007 began with defaults in the subprime mortgage market. Subprime mortgages are a type of loan offered to people with low credit ratings who would not otherwise qualify for a mortgage. Lenders charge high rates of interest for these mortgages because of the high probability of loan defaults with this class of borrowers. Many of the more exotic mortgages such as ARMs that adjust monthly or that have low teaser rates (initial rates) are offered as subprime mortgages. Some of the companies that provided subprime loans during the peak of subprime lending were accused of predatory lending practices by the government. Some have closed their doors, but there are still subprime mortgages available. Buyers who wait until their credit has improved before trying to get a mortgage will save themselves a lot of money in interest payments.

A Word About Liens

A mortgagor may also get mortgages on top of mortgages—if the first mortgage does not prohibit it. A second mortgage is known as a junior mortgage, and the first mortgage is known as the senior loan. If a buyer eventually defaults on the senior mortgage, the original mortgagee has precedence in being paid back over any later (junior) mortgages.

FEDERAL LAWS RELATED TO MORTGAGE FINANCING

Oversight of the mortgage industry is a responsibility of the Federal Reserve Board. In addition, the U.S. Congress has passed laws that protect consumers of mortgage credit, and the Department of Housing and Urban Development and other federal agencies have rules and regulations related to mortgage originators and their duties to borrowers.

- **Real Estate Settlement Procedures Act (RESPA):** The current rules and regulations that implement RESPA were phased in between January 2009 and January 2010 and relate to all housing purchases for which the residential purchaser takes out a mortgage loan and also for residential refinancing transactions. (The form is also sometimes used to a degree in small commercial real estate transactions as a convenient way to keep track of the costs of the loan.) Among other items, it requires "that loan originators provide borrowers with a standard Good Faith Estimate that clearly discloses key loan terms and closing costs and that closing agents provide borrowers with a new HUD-1 settlement statement."

- **Consumer Credit Protection Act:** This law is also known as the Truth-in-Lending Act and regulates certain disclosures for mortgage loans including fees, charges, advertisements for mortgage financing, and information about variable rate mortgages. It is the law that requires certain information be given buyers applying for an ARM. (See Variable-Rate Mortgages above.)

- **Community Reinvestment Act:** Passed in 1977 and amended as recently as 2005, this law is intended to encourage banks and other depository institutions "to help meet the credit needs of

NOTE
Check the Real Estate Settlement Procedures Act (RESPA) at www.hud.gov.

NOTE
Be sure to check your state's laws to see how they impact mortgage financing.

NOTE

To help owners in danger of losing their homes during the financial crisis that began in 2007, the federal government instituted the "Making Home Affordable" programs. For more information, check out www.makinghomeaffordable.gov.

NOTE

Find out your state's provisions for foreclosure. Some states may have different processes based on their statutes regulating foreclosures.

the communities in which they operate, including low- and moderate-income neighborhoods." This includes originating mortgages for qualified buyers.

- **Equal Credit Opportunity Act:** This law prohibits discrimination in any credit transaction, including shopping for a mortgage.

- **The Fair Housing Act:** This law prohibits discrimination in housing sales and loans.

FORECLOSURE

As many Americans unfortunately learned during the recession of 2007–09, if you don't make your mortgage payments regularly, you can lose your home through foreclosure. There are three types of foreclosure:

- **Judicial foreclosure:** When the mortgagee asks the court for a foreclosure order, the court sets a date for the mortgagor to pay off the mortgage. If the mortgagor is unable to meet the deadline, the court orders the property be sold at public auction. If the sale nets (after payment of court costs and allied costs) less than the amount needed to pay off the mortgage (and other liens), the lien holders can seek a deficiency judgment against the mortgagor for payment of the outstanding sums.

- **Strict foreclosure:** In this process, the mortgagee goes to court for an order demanding payment of the mortgage and setting a time period for payment. If the mortgagor is unable to pay, the mortgagor loses all rights to the property and the mortgagee gains title to the property. The mortgagee may retain the property rather than sell it to satisfy the lien on the property. Not all states allow strict foreclosures.

- **Nonjudicial foreclosure:** The mortgagee may sell a property when the mortgagee is in default without having to go to court. The mortgagee must serve notice on the defaulting homeowner first, however. If the person cannot pay off the mortgage, the mortgagee can then sell the property to satisfy the mortgage.

EXERCISES

1. Which of the following is NOT typically contained in the note with a mortgage?

    (A) Loan amount

    (B) Acceleration clause

    (C) *Habendum* clause

    (D) Amount of any late charge

2. The right of assignment by the lender

    (A) is a standard part of a mortgage.

    (B) is part of a lease, but not a mortgage.

    (C) is another name for the right of assumption.

    (D) eliminates the original buyer's liability for the mortgage.

3. Which of the following does business in the secondary mortgage market?

    (A) Commercial bank

    (B) Portfolio lender

    (C) Credit unions

    (D) Private mortgage company

4. Which of the following programs allows homebuyers to buy a home without paying mortgage insurance even if the down payment is less than a certain percentage?

    (A) FHA

    (B) VA mortgage

    (C) Fannie Mae

    (D) Freddie Mac

5. Who of the following people would obtain a conforming mortgage?

    (A) Person building a home

    (B) Person buying a home for $529,000

    (C) Person buying a home for $259,000

    (D) Veteran buying a home for $447,000

6. Not paying off the principal by the end of the term of an ARM is a risk that results from

    (A) the index used to compute the rate.

    (B) the rate itself.

    (C) the annual cap.

    (D) the payment cap.

7. Seller financing of the loan secured by the buyer's mortgage is a

    (A) purchase-money mortgage.

    (B) graduated payment mortgage.

    (C) swing loan.

    (D) package mortgage.

8. Ginnie Mae

    (A) insures mortgages.

    (B) provides mortgages directly to homebuyers.

    (C) guarantees mortgages insured by the FHA.

    (D) guarantees mortgages issued by GSEs.

ANSWER KEY AND EXPLANATIONS

1. C	3. D	5. C	7. A
2. A	4. B	6. D	8. C

1. **The correct answer is (C).** Choice (C) is typically found in a mortgage document (or in a lease), but not in the promissory note that accompanies the mortgage. Choices (A), (B), and (D) are typically found in a promissory note, so they are incorrect answers to the question.

2. **The correct answer is (A).** Choice (B) is not true; it can be a clause in both a lease and a mortgage. Choice (C) is incorrect because the assumption of a mortgage is different from the assignment of a mortgage. Choice (D) is incorrect. It uses the explanation of the "subject to the mortgage" clause used in some rights of assumption, but choice (D) misstates the clause.

3. **The correct answer is (D).** Choices (A), (B), and (C) do business in the primary mortgage market.

4. **The correct answer is (B).** Choice (A) insures mortgages that have low down payments. Choices (C) and (D) do not deal directly with homebuyers.

5. **The correct answer is (C).** Choice (A) would get a conventional mortgage. Choices (B) and (D) would need nonconforming mortgages.

6. **The correct answer is (D).** All four choices are elements of an ARM that a person shopping for an ARM should check, but only choice (D) can result in a mortgagor not having paid the entire principal off by the end of the term of the mortgage.

7. **The correct answer is (A).** Choice (B) has increasing payments over the time of the mortgage according to a set schedule. Choice (C) is also called a bridge loan and is used to enable the buyer to purchase the new home while waiting for his/her own home to sell. Choice (D) is used when the buyer is purchasing both real and personal property from the seller.

8. **The correct answer is (C).** Choice (A) is incorrect because Ginnie Mae does not insure, buy, or securitize mortgages. Choice (B) is incorrect because Ginnie Mae operates in the secondary mortgage market. Choice (D) is incorrect because the GSEs do not issue mortgages; they insure them.

SUMMING IT UP

- A mortgage is a promise to repay a loan for the purchase of real property. It includes a promissory note. Some states use trust deeds and notes rather than mortgages and notes.

- A mortgage must contain certain elements, including the loan amount, legal property description, granting clause, *habendum* clause, covenant of seisen, defeasance clause, property taxes and assessments, insurance clauses, information on escrow, acceleration clause, prepayment clause, clause to preserve the value of the property, and clause requiring approval of the mortgagee before large-scale renovation is done.

- A note includes elements like the loan amount, interest rate, schedule of payments, amount of each payment, acceleration clause, amount of late charges, and the mortgagor's explicit promise to repay the loan.

- Mortgages may be assigned by one lender to another, and mortgages, if the terms permit, may be assumed by one borrower from another. Assumptions must be approved by the lender, and some assumptions include a "subject to mortgage" provision.

- The primary mortgage market offers mortgages directly to buyers, whereas the secondary mortgage market buys, bundles, and sells mortgages to investors. The most important players in the secondary mortgage market are Fannie Mae and Freddie Mac.

- Ginnie Mae guarantees the mortgage-backed securities insured by the Federal Housing Administration and guaranteed by the Department of Veteran Affairs.

- The Federal Housing Authority insures home loans for buyers who have less than 20 percent to put down and whose homes fall below the lending threshold. The Department of Veterans Affairs insures home loans for veterans who meet certain qualifications. There is also private mortgage insurance sold by companies.

- Mortgages may be conventional, conforming, or nonconforming.

- Mortgage rates may be fixed or variable and the terms of mortgages vary widely. The standard residential mortgage is a fixed-rate, 30-year mortgage.

- The federal government has passed several laws that relate to mortgage financing, including the Real Estate Settlement Procedures Act, the Consumer Credit Protection Act, the Community Reinvestment Act, the Equal Credit Opportunity Act, and the Fair Housing Act.

- Foreclosures are governed by statutes and, depending on the terms of the applicable statute, may be a judicial, nonjudicial, or strict foreclosure.

Taxes and Assessment

chapter 12

OVERVIEW

- Property taxes
- Property tax exemptions
- Special assessments
- Additional taxes
- Summing it up

The major source of revenue that fuels the operation of all levels of government is taxes. The taxes that affect real estate are property taxes, which are local taxes as opposed to state or federal taxes. The good news is that property taxes (and any state income tax) are deductible from your federal tax bill.

Local municipalities use property tax revenue to fund things such as employee salaries, regular road and bridge repair and maintenance, and equipment and materials for the police and fire departments. Large-ticket items such as school construction and bridge replacement are funded through the sale of bonds to investors, and the dividends are paid with taxpayers' dollars.

In addition to municipal governments such as towns and cities, counties and special districts, also called special-purpose districts, have taxing authority as well. Depending on the state, special-purpose districts may be school districts, water and sewer districts, irrigation districts, and metropolitan transportation districts. Their operating revenues come from taxes and appear as part of the property tax bills collected by the local municipality. The tax revenue is then distributed to the special districts in proportion to the special districts' tax rates. For example, an irrigation district's portion of a property tax bill for real estate assessed at $256,000 may be $154.

PROPERTY TAXES

For the most part, municipalities do not borrow money for their recurring operating expenses like salaries, only for large unusual expenses such as the purchase of open space for a public park. In order to fund their operations, they make a budget and then determine how to pay for what is in the budget. If the tax revenue does not cover all budget items, the municipality has to make cuts. If cuts are not enough, the municipality may increase property taxes.

Property taxes are *ad valorem* taxes, that is, they are paid according to the value of property. The value may be computed as a rate of mills per dollar (for example, 50 mills per dollar), with a mill being one-tenth of a cent. The value may also be computed as a certain tax amount per

$100 or $1,000 of assessed value (for example, $3 per $100 written as $3/$100, or $30 per $1,000 written as $30/$1,000).

Determining Property Taxes

NOTE

Find out how your municipality calculates tax rates.

Every few years, as mandated by a state's tax laws, a municipality must have all the property within its boundaries appraised. The usual time frame is every 10 years. Improving a property, for example, by adding a garage, and selling a property may also trigger an appraisal. The municipal tax assessor's department may conduct the appraisals, or an outside firm may be hired to do it if the entire municipality is being appraised at one time.

The appraisers visit the properties within the municipality, taking notes and measurements, and write up their findings. They use assessors' standard tables to determine a value for each property based on what they have observed.

NOTE

Find out how often your state requires municipalities to conduct property assessments. This can help a buyer make a decision about the value of a property.

The tax assessor applies a formula (millage or unit of taxes per $100 of value) to the assessed value for each property and calculates the property tax for that property for the upcoming fiscal year. The tax assessor does this each year, even if it is not a year when tax appraisals are being conducted. The tax rate has to be assessed annually because the municipal budget changes annually as a result of increases or decreases in anticipated needs and/or increases or decreases in inflation. Homeowners receive a tax bill each year stating what they have to pay in property taxes for the upcoming year.

Assessed Value and Market Value

The assessed value of a property may or may not be a reliable indicator of the market value of a property. An unusual occurrence can affect home values between tax assessments. For example, a sudden drop in home values can occur as it did during the recession of 2007–09, when home prices fell from week to week in some areas of the country. More typically, market values may rise above or fall below tax assessments when assessments are only conducted every 10 years. The value of property in a particular township may increase because of a new company moving into the area and bringing with it many new jobs and employees. Conversely, property values may fall when a company shuts down. In addition, the assessed value of a house for which no improvements have been made for a long time may be well below market value by the end of the 10-year period.

Appealing Property Tax Assessments

NOTE

Property tax reviews are handled differently in different states. Find out how the procedure works in your state and municipality.

Municipalities may assess property at 100 percent of value or at some lesser amount, such as 80 percent of value. The rate is set by state law. To find the assessed value of a property, multiply the market value by the assessment's percentage rate, known as the assessment ratio. Suppose the market value is $268,000 and the assessment ratio is 80 percent, then the assessed value is $268,000 × 0.80 = $214,400.

Suppose the homeowner believes the property is worth less than the assessed value. Say, it is year 8 of the 10 years between assessments, the local economy has not recovered from the latest recession, two big manufacturing plants have closed, and many people have moved away. The homeowner—and all property owners—can appeal property tax assessments. Generally, the property owner begins by registering a complaint with the tax assessor who may be able to solve the problem. If not, the property owner can complain to the tax review board if there is one. The last resort is a tax appeal lawsuit.

PROPERTY TAX EXEMPTIONS

Property tax exemptions vary from state to state and from time to time. The following is a general discussion of why not every property owner pays property taxes. Government-owned real estate is tax-exempt, that is, federal, state, and local governments pay no property taxes on their property. Other tax-exempt properties may include educational facilities, which include public and private schools, colleges, and universities; and property owned by religious organizations such as churches, synagogues, mosques, temples, schools, rectories, and convents.

There are also classes of persons who by reason of some characteristic may be granted tax exemptions. These include people over a certain age (such as over 65) with income below a certain level, those with disabilities, and veterans. Unlike owners of properties that are tax exempt, those with a partial tax exemption pay some property tax, but less than those without the partial tax exemption.

NOTE

In some states, the partial tax exemption is called a homestead exemption. Find out what your state calls partial property tax exemptions.

SPECIAL ASSESSMENTS

A municipality or a special district may levy a tax called a special assessment on property owners for a particular improvement and for a certain period of time. The special assessment may be on all taxpayers in a municipality, or only on those who will benefit from the project. For example, a municipality may decide to add sidewalks to the property on both sides of a road and recoup the cost by imposing a special assessment on all property owners on the street. Or, the sewer authority may impose a tax on property owners on a particular street in order to lay sewer lines to serve the properties on that street. Note that in each case the property owner benefits from the improvement, not just in convenience, but in an increase in property value.

All property owners are assessed at a flat rate regardless of the value of individual properties.

Homeowner associations, co-ops, and condos may impose special assessments on property owners from time to time for things such as new roofs or a renovated building lobby. These assessments are not taxes in the sense that they are being raised by and paid to a government entity, although these groups are legally constituted entities. If an owner doesn't pay the special assessment, the board can fine the owner and even place a lien on the property for nonpayment.

If a buyer is buying into an association, co-op, or condo with a current assessment, the buyer will have to assume the payments are going forward unless the buyer negotiates at the time of the contract for the seller to pick up the remaining payments. A seller and a real estate agent must inform potential buyers about an assessment.

NOTE

A condo, co-op, or townhome development may have a special assessment that has nothing to do with the local government. Who pays for this assessment needs to be negotiated while the contract of sale is being negotiated. The apportionment between buyer and seller usually depends on when it is effective.

ADDITIONAL TAXES

Fees are a form of taxation when they are paid to a government entity. In a real estate transaction, usually the seller pays a transfer fee, or transfer tax, to the county at the time of the transfer of the property's title from the seller to the buyer.

The buyer also pays a recording fee to the county at the time of the closing. This fee covers all the documentation necessary to enter the change of title from the seller to the buyer into the public record, record the new mortgage, and cancel the old mortgage of record or record a satisfaction of mortgage. This fee is a line item in the Good Faith Estimate for closing costs and is in the final closing statement. While the buyer pays this tax, it is usually charged back to the seller.

In some places where co-ops are popular, especially New York City, a co-op's bylaws may require the payment of a flip tax when a unit is sold. Depending on the bylaws, either the buyer or the seller pays the amount. Although it is called a "flip tax," it's not a tax. It is a payment demanded by the co-op for the privilege of buying or selling one of its units. It's a way for the co-op to raise money without increasing monthly co-op fees.

EXERCISES

1. A special assessment might be levied to
   (A) build a new school.
   (B) add a new terminal to the municipal airport.
   (C) build a loop road around a city.
   (D) add sidewalks to certain streets.

2. Which of the following types of property is NOT exempt from property taxes?
   (A) Private university
   (B) Church
   (C) Mosque
   (D) Private hospital

3. The Wilson-Johns have appealed to the tax review board for a decrease in their property taxes and have been denied. The next step for the Wilson-Johns is
   (A) to appeal to the tax assessor.
   (B) to appear before the planning board for a review.
   (C) to file a lawsuit.
   (D) There is no next step because the tax review board has the final word.

4. An assessment ratio is
   (A) the percentage rate used to determine assessed value of a property.
   (B) the percentage rate used to determine the market value of a property.
   (C) another name for the range between assessed value and market value.
   (D) always described in millage.

5. Assessed value
   (A) is always the same as the market value.
   (B) may or may not be a good indicator of market value.
   (C) is never a good indicator of market value.
   (D) is used as the basis of computing market value.

ANSWER KEY AND EXPLANATIONS

1. D	**3.** C	**5.** B
2. D	**4.** A	

1. **The correct answer is (D).** Choices (A), (B), and (C) would be funded by some other method such as bond issues rather than by a special assessment, which has a more narrow focus.

2. **The correct answer is (D).** Choice (D) by virtue of being a private, and therefore, for-profit business would not be tax exempt, but a public hospital would be. Choices (A), (B), and (C) are all tax-exempt properties.

3. **The correct answer is (C).** Choice (A) would be the first step for a property owner seeking to appeal an assessment, which is the basis of a property tax appeal. Choice (B) has no authority over property tax issues. Choice (D) is incorrect because a lawsuit is the next—and last—step in a property tax appeal.

4. **The correct answer is (A).** Choice (B) is incorrect because that is not how market value is determined. Choice (C) is a distracter; it does not mean anything, but seems authoritative. Choice (D) is incorrect because assessment ratio may be described as dollars/tax rate per hundred or dollars/tax rate per thousands.

5. **The correct answer is (B).** Be wary of answers that use absolutes such as "always" and "never," as in choices (A) and (C). Choice (D) is incorrect.

SUMMING IT UP

- Municipalities, counties, and special-purpose districts levy taxes on property owners.

- Property taxes are *as valorem* taxes, and the value may be expressed as mills per dollar, tax rate per $100, or tax rate per $1,000, depending on how the taxing authority expresses the assessment ratio, or percentage of assessment.

- Assessments for the purpose of taxing properties are done on a regular schedule, often every 10 years, but tax bills are prepared every year because a municipality's budget changes each year.

- Assessed value is not necessarily the same as market value.

- A property owner may appeal a tax assessment and the resulting property taxes by consulting the tax assessor and then the tax review board, if the situation has not been remedied to the property owner's satisfaction. The final step is a tax appeal lawsuit against the municipality or special district.

- Property tax exemptions are available to governmental entities and usually to educational and religious organizations. Partial tax exemptions are available to the elderly below a certain income level, those with disabilities, and veterans.

- Special assessments are taxes levied by a unit of government on property owners for a certain period of time and for a particular improvement.

- At closings, two special taxes related to the transfer of title to property are paid: a transfer tax and a recording fee.

Closings

OVERVIEW

- **Types of closing**
- **Documents for the closing**
- **What the buyer produces at the closing**
- **The seller's costs at closing**
- **Credits, debits, and proration**
- **It's not over 'til it's over**
- **Summing it up**

The buyer has found the perfect house, the seller is relieved, and the closing date is set. What now? This chapter explains the steps that must be taken prior to the closing, the closing itself, and what happens after the closing. While the seller gets ready for the closing, the buyer orders a home inspection and the lending institution orders an appraisal of the property. A problem with either can derail or at least delay the closing.

TYPES OF CLOSING

There are two types of closings. The type depends on a state's real estate laws: traditional closings and escrow closings.

1. **Traditional closings:** This form of closing is also called the settlement and is used in much of the United States. The buyer and seller and their attorneys attend. Representatives of both the buyer's and seller's lenders and an agent from the title insurance company, may or may not attend. In that case, the buyer's attorney acts as a fiduciary for the absent entities. Realtors often attend to pick up their commission checks. The closing may be conducted by any one of the nonprincipals. Often, it is the buyer's attorney, but in some states, the agent of the title company runs it. In the simplest explanation, the closing consists of signing documents and handing over checks to transfer the title of the property from the seller to the buyer. Later in this chapter, we discuss how many and what documents are signed and what the checks are for.

2. **Escrow closings:** With this form of closing, the buyer and seller turn over the documents that each is responsible for before the day of closing to an escrow agent whom they have agreed will act in this capacity. Usually, the person is an attorney, an agent of the title company, or an agent of an escrow company. The buyer, seller, and lender

agree on a closing date, and the principals submit their completed documents to the escrow agent by this date. All aspects of the contract of sale must be completed prior to the closing date, and documents are not submitted until all terms and conditions have been met. The actual closing is called the "closing of escrow." The seller gives the escrow agent the deed, title, and paperwork from the current lender indicating the payoff on the current mortgage. The seller is also responsible for providing proof that the title to the property is free of all encumbrances, which may require actions on the part of the seller. The buyer gives the escrow agent a certified check for the purchase price and all documents related to the new mortgage. The buyer also turns over proof that the buyer has taken out the required insurance policies on the property.

DOCUMENTS FOR THE CLOSING

A variety of documents need to be gathered before a closing. Some are the responsibility of the seller, and others are the responsibility of the buyer.

The Title

The major document that the seller must produce is a marketable title to the property. The seller has to show evidence that the title is the seller's to convey and is free and clear of encumbrances. This can be done in one of four ways:

1. **Abstract of title:** This is a report that details the history of ownership of a property and is obtained through a title search. The buyer's attorney reviews the report and, if the attorney finds the title is good, the attorney issues what is called an attorney's opinion of title. It does not warrant ownership of the property.

2. **Certificate of title:** This is a written opinion issued by a title company or an attorney about the status of ownership of a property. Like the abstract of title, it is obtained by a review of public records and also does not warrant ownership of the property.

3. **Title insurance:** This protects the buyer in case someone claims an interest in the property in the future. The buyer purchases it, and often the lender also buys title insurance, which the borrower pays for, to protect his (the buyer's) investment in the property. Title insurance may be purchased after an abstract of title or certificate of title is issued, or it can be purchased after a title search has been conducted.

4. **Certificate of Torrens:** Some states use the Torrens Systems, which is a land title registration system guaranteed by the state. The state keeps a register, or record, of all land titles. When a transfer of title is to be made, the buyer asks the registrar of the county in which the land is located for a certificate of Torrens title. The court reviews the documents affecting the change, and if satisfied that all is in order, the court orders the registrar to change the register to reflect the new ownership and to issue the certificate. The title is indefeasible, that is, no one can void or annul the ownership of the title/property.

Clearing the Title

In the process of providing a marketable title, the seller must clear the title of any liens and other encumbrances that impact the title. The mortgage is a lien on the title that is typically paid off at the time of the closing from the proceeds of the sale. Other liens may include unpaid taxes. These may be paid off from the proceeds at the time of the closing, or before the closing, if the seller is able.

In addition to liens, a title may be encumbered by easements and deed restrictions. If the title search finds any, they are reviewed by the buyer and the buyer's attorney before closing and must be resolved with the seller. Some easements and restrictions "run with the land," and the lender's title policy will provide that they will not cause a forfeiture of title. Usually, buyers are willing to buy property with easements if the easement will not interfere with their use of the property, and if it does not affect the marketability of title.

The Deed

A deed is the written legal document that conveys and is evidence of a person's legal right to ownership of a particular piece of real property. At the closing, a new deed passes from seller to buyer, and the title is transferred at this time. The deed and the mortgage will be recorded, and the lender will get back the recorded mortgage and the note. The buyer will get the recorded deed and a copy of the recorded mortgage.

WHAT THE BUYER PRODUCES AT THE CLOSING

Money! That's the major responsibility of the buyer: to have qualified for a mortgage, completed all the paperwork, and arrive at the closing with the check for the purchase price. In addition, the buyer may be paying other costs at the closing, including the

- loan origination fee.
- credit report for the lender.
- title search.
- title insurance.
- hazard insurance.
- survey, if one was required.
- appraisal fee for the bank-ordered appraisal.
- home inspection.
- portion of taxes as prorated between seller and buyer.
- recording fee (usually charged back to the seller).
- the buyer's attorney's fee.

NOTE

Check with your state and your locality to see what fees are typically paid by the seller and the buyer because laws and customs vary.

NOTE

Laws differ from state to state on the way income and expenses are prorated. Check with your state to find out if the proration is done on a monthly or annual basis and what date is used for the calculation: the day of or the day before the closing.

THE SELLER'S COSTS AT CLOSING

The seller pays a number of costs at the closing as well. Typically, these are

- the unpaid balance on the mortgage and any prepayment penalties.
- any other unpaid liens, such as back taxes that have not already been cleared.
- the commission to the broker.
- a transfer fee.
- a portion of taxes as prorated between seller and buyer.
- the deed.
- the seller's attorney's fee.

The buyer may have negotiated with the seller to pay some or all of the discount points on the mortgage. The points are a fee paid to a lender to lower the interest rate on the mortgage. Otherwise, the buyer pays the points.

CREDITS, DEBITS, AND PRORATION

The various costs related to the closing are figured ahead of time. According to HUD guidelines, the buyer of a property that is being purchased with an FHA-insured loan is entitled to see the closing costs one day before the closing. In the statement of closing costs, certain moneys will be shown as credits to the seller or the buyer, and certain moneys will be shown as debits to the seller or the buyer. Income and expenses may also be prorated before being credited or debited.

Credits and Debits

A credit is money paid by one party to the other, and a debit is the money that is owed by one person to the other. For example, the buyer is credited for the down payment, so at the closing, the amount of the down payment is deducted from the purchase price:

$$\$425,000 - \$85,000 = \$340,000$$

If this were the only adjustment, then the buyer would have to arrive at the closing with a check for $340,000. The seller credits the buyer for the entire $425,000. At the same time, the seller is debited the broker's commission. However, adjustments are never so simple. For the typical credits and debits of buyers and sellers, see the sections What the Buyer Produces at the Closing and Seller's Costs at Closing above.

Proration

A variety of income and expenses are prorated at the closing, such as

- property taxes, including municipal, county, and special-purpose districts.
- hazard insurance.
- association dues if the property is a condo, co-op, or other form of homeowner association.
- rents if the property is commercial.

- utilities (including the number of gallons left in the tank for oil heat; water and sewer; current electric and gas bills).

- flood insurance if required.

Who pays what—the buyer or the seller—and how much (the percentage) is determined when the sales contract is negotiated.

IT'S NOT OVER 'TIL IT'S OVER

After the documents have been signed and the seller hands the buyer the keys, there is still work to be done. The following still must be completed:

- The final closing statement must be prepared by one of the attorneys or the title company.

- The mortgage, deed, liens, and easements must be filed with the appropriate county office, which serves as constructive notice to the public that this transaction has taken place.

- The recording fees and transfer tax, if applicable, must be paid.

Some sellers may also need to file Form 1099-S when preparing their income taxes for the year. The exceptions are those who sell a residential property that is less than $250,000 for an individual and $500,000 for a couple.

EXERCISES

1. The word "escrow" is used for all of the following EXCEPT
   - (A) a form of closing.
   - (B) a reserve account from which taxes and mortgage insurance are paid.
   - (C) a credit to the buyer or the seller.
   - (D) an account into which a down payment is deposited and kept until closing.

2. A title that has been cleared of all encumbrances is called a
   - (A) marketable title.
   - (B) free title.
   - (C) certificate of title.
   - (D) certificate of Torrens.

3. The seller pays for the
   - (A) preparation of the deed.
   - (B) broker's commission.
   - (C) pest inspection.
   - (D) taxes to the day before or of closing.

4. Which of the following is a buyer debit at closing on a commercial property?
   - (A) Prepayment penalty
   - (B) Earnest money
   - (C) Prorated rent
   - (D) Transfer fee

5. An expense that is typically prorated at closing is
   - (A) mortgage insurance.
   - (B) association dues.
   - (C) survey cost.
   - (D) discount points.

6. Which of the following is NOT a cost related to the loan?
   - (A) Origination fee
   - (B) Appraisal fee
   - (C) Assumption fee
   - (D) Recording fee

ANSWER KEY AND EXPLANATIONS

1. C	3. C	5. B
2. A	4. D	6. D

1. **The correct answer is (C).** Choices (A), (B), and (D) are all different meanings of the word "escrow" related to real estate. Choice (C) is incorrect; a credit to the buyer or seller is just called a credit.

2. **The correct answer is (A).** Choice (B) is meant to confuse because it sounds right; it describes a marketable title, but is not a term. Choice (C) is a written opinion about the status of ownership of a property, but it is only part of the process of clearing a title. In some states, choice (D) is part of the land registration system.

3. **The correct answer is (C).** Choice (C) is the responsibility of the buyer and part of the suggested home inspections. The payment of choices (A), (B), and (D) are the seller's responsibility.

4. **The correct answer is (D).** Choice (A) is a debit against the seller. Choice (B) is a credit to the buyer; earnest money is another name for a down payment. Choice (C) is a credit.

5. **The correct answer is (B).** Choices (A) and (C) list a cost to the buyer alone. Choice (D) is paid by the borrower unless the buyer has negotiated with the seller to pay some of the discount points.

6. **The correct answer is (D).** Choices (A), (B), and (C) are related to procuring a mortgage. Choice (C) is present only if the buyer is assuming the seller's mortgage. Choice (D) is the buyer's responsibility, but is not related to the mortgage.

answers exercises

SUMMING IT UP

- There are two types of closings used in the United States: traditional closing and escrow closing.

- A seller must present a marketable title at closing that establishes that the seller has the right to convey the title and that the title is free and clear of liens and encumbrances.

- Part of establishing a marketable title includes obtaining one of the following: abstract of title, certificate of title, title insurance, or certificate of Torrens.

- At the closing, the buyer receives a new deed from the seller.

- The buyer must arrive at the closing with financing for the mortgage in-hand and ready to pay the other costs typically assigned to buyers, while the seller must appear at the closing with marketable title prepared to pay costs typically assigned to the seller.

- Certain expenses and income are prorated between seller and buyer.

- The closing statement lists payments as credits or debits to the buyer and seller.

- After the closing, the final closing statement is prepared, the mortgage and deed are recorded, and the recording and transfer fees must be paid.

Review of Real Estate Math

OVERVIEW

- **Commissions**
- **Interest**
- **Taxes and Assessments**
- **Proration**
- **Appreciation and Depreciation**
- **Appraisal**
- **Measurement and Area**
- **Math Test-Taking Tips**

The math that you will need to know for the real estate exam is basic math. You will need to know how to add, subtract, multiply, and divide. The most advanced math that you will need is the ability to multiply and divide with percentages. The examiners are trying to determine if you have a basic understanding of math and the ability to use it in your everyday dealings within the field of real estate. You will be asked to solve problems involving:

- commissions.
- interest, taxes, and assessments.
- proration.
- amounts and rates of appreciation and/or depreciation.
- value of a property by using one of three appraisal methods.
- area and conversion from one measurement to another.

Check with your state to find out if you can use a calculator during the exam. Also, find out if there are any restrictions on the type of calculator that can be used. Take along an extra battery for it to the exam.

Depending on the state in which you take your licensing exam, you may find that 10 percent or fewer of the questions involve math. The Diagnostic and Practice Tests in this book may have more math questions than your state's exam will actually have, but working out questions in a simulated test environment will help you become comfortable with the type of questions you will encounter.

COMMISSIONS

Commissions are a dollar value based on gross selling price and the rate of commission. A commission can either be split between two or more brokers or go only to one broker depending on the transaction.

- Gross selling price is the actual selling price of the property.
- Rate of commission is the agreed-upon rate to be paid once the sale has been completed.

There are three simple formulas for figuring commission:

    1. Commission = Gross Selling Price × Rate of Commission

    2. Rate of Commission = Commission ÷ Gross Selling Price

    3. Gross Selling Price = Commission ÷ Rate of Commission

To solve commission problems, you will need to decide which formula to use and then fill in the values that you know.

The easiest types of questions will provide you with only the information that you need in order to solve the question. They will also provide two of the three pieces of information in the formulas.

EXAMPLE 1:

An agent sells a property for $80,000 at a commission rate of 6%. How much is the commission?

We are looking for the commission, so we will need to use:

    Commission = Gross Selling Price × Rate of Commission

What we know from the question:

    Gross selling price = $80,000

    Rate of commission = 6%, or 0.06 (We get this number by moving the decimal point 2 places to the left.)

Enter what we know:

    Commission = Gross Selling Price × Rate of Commission

    Commission = $80,000 × 0.06

               = $4,800

EXAMPLE 2:

An agent sells a house for the listing price of $1,567,000 and receives a commission of $117,525. What is the commission rate?

We are looking for the rate of commission, so we will need to use:

Rate of Commission = Commission ÷ Gross Selling Price

What we know from the question:

Gross Selling Price = $1,567,000

Commission = $117,525

Enter what we know:

Rate of Commission = Commission ÷ Gross Selling Price

Rate of Commission = $117,525 ÷ $1,567,000

= 0.075, or 7.5%

EXAMPLE 3:

A broker receives a commission check for $7,200 and wonders what house sale it is for. The broker knows that she receives a 5.5% commission on every house the brokerage lists, so how much did the house for which she received the commission sell for?

We are looking for gross selling price, so will need to use:

Gross Selling Price = Commission ÷ Rate of Commission

What we know from the question:

Commission = $7,200

Rate of Commission = 5.5%

Enter what we know:

Gross Selling Price = Commission ÷ Rate of Commission

Gross Selling Price = $7,200 ÷ 5.5%, or 0.055

= $130,909.09

EXAMPLE 4:

A house is listed for $250,000, with an agreed-upon 6.5% rate for the commission. The owner receives an offer for $225,000 and, after negotiations, sells for $235,000. How much commission will the selling broker and the listing broker each receive?

This is a two-part question. First, we must find the overall commission and then divide it by 2 to find the answer to the question.

When looking for commission, use:

Commission = Gross Selling Price × Rate of Commission

Add what we know from the question:

Commission = $235,000 × 6.5%, or 0.065

Answer:

Commission = $15,275

Split the commission so that each will receive an equal share:

$15,275 ÷ 2 = $7,637.5

EXAMPLE 5:

Which of the following sales will yield the seller exactly $162,550?

	Sales Price	Broker's Fee	Other Expenses
(A)	$175,500	6%	$375
(B)	$170,000	7%	$225
(C)	$180,000	6.5%	$700
(D)	$175,000	7%	$200

This is another two-part question. We must find the broker's fee first, and then subtract that and the other expenses to find the net selling price.

If we do this for all of the choices, we will find that choice (D) is the correct answer.

$175,000 × 0.07 = $12,250

$175,000 − $12,250 − $200 = $162,550

An easy way to check your answer is to multiply the sales price by (100% − broker's fee) and then subtract the other expenses from this.

$175,000 × 0.93 (100% − 7% = 93%) − $200 = 162,550

EXAMPLE 6:

An agent who sells units in a condominium building receives a 6% commission on the first $150,000 of sales per month and a 2% commission on all sales exceeding that. If in July, she sold condos for $95,000, $105,000 and $87,000, what is her total commission for the month?

First, find the total of all sales:

$95,000 + $105,000 + $87,000 = $287,000

Second, subtract the commission kicker from the total:

$287,000 − $150,000 = $137,000

Third, multiple the commission rates of both numbers and add them together:

$150,000 × 0.06 = $ 9,000

$137,000 × 0.02 =   + $ 2,740

                      $11,740

EXERCISES

1. Broker Sharon Eisen lists a property for $75,000, with an agreed-upon commission rate of 6.5%. An offer is made through another broker for $73,000 and is accepted. What is Sharon's commission as the listing broker?

    (A) $4,745.00

    (B) $2,372.50

    (C) $4,875.00

    (D) $2,437.50

2. After paying a commission of 8% and additional expenses of $700, the seller's netted $229,300. What was the seller's gross selling price?

    (A) $248,344

    (B) $248,400

    (C) $250,000

    (D) None of the above

3. After settlement, the seller nets $61,350 and pays additional expenses of $425 and a commission of $3,250. What was the rate of commission?

    (A) 4%

    (B) 5%

    (C) 6%

    (D) 7%

4. How much commission will the seller pay on the sale of $111,000 house if the listing agent gets 40% of the commission and the rate of commission is 7%?

    (A) $7,770

    (B) $1,154

    (C) $4,662

    (D) $3,108

5. Sammy Smith receives a commission check for a house he listed. The check is for $68,295, and he always works for a 5% commission. How much did the house sell for, rounded to the nearest dollar?

    (A) $3,415

    (B) $136,590

    (C) $64,880

    (D) $1,365,900

ANSWER KEY AND EXPLANATIONS

1. B	3. B	5. D
2. C	4. A	

1. **The correct answer is (B).**

   $73,000 \times 0.065 = \$4,745$

   $\$4,745 \div 2 = \$2,372.50$

2. **The correct answer is (C).**

   Gross selling price = ($229,300 + $700) ÷ (1.00 − 0.08)

   = $230,000 ÷ 0.92

   = $250,000

3. **The correct answer is (B).**

   Rate of commission = $3,250 ÷ ($61,350 + $425 + $ 3,250)

   = $3,250 ÷ $65,000

   = 0.05, or 5%

4. **The correct answer is (A).**

   $111,000 \times 0.07 = \$7,770$

5. **The correct answer is (D).**

   $\$68,295 \div 0.05 = \$1,365,900$

INTEREST

Interest is the amount of money made or paid on an amount of principal over time.

Interest can be expressed in the formula $I = P \times R \times T$, where I is interest, P is principal, R is Rate, and T is time, and where time is usually based on 1 year. With this formula, we can answer questions that ask about interest, rate, principal, or time simply by solving for the unknown amount.

$$P = I \div (R \times T)$$

$$R = I \div (P \times T)$$

$$T = I \div (P \times R)$$

EXAMPLE 1:

How much interest would you pay on a $20,000 loan at 10% for 30 months?

We are looking for interest paid, so we would use:

$$I = P \times R \times T$$

What we know we know from the question:

Principal = $20,000

Rate = 10%

Time = 30 months, or 2.5 years

Enter what we know:

$$I = \$20,000 \times 0.10 \times 2.5$$

Answer:

$$I = \$5,000$$

EXAMPLE 2:

If you took out a loan for $50,000 and paid $6,000 a year in interest, what is the interest rate?

We are looking for rate:

$$R = I \div (P \times T)$$

What we know from the question:

I = $6,000

P = $50,000

T = 1

Enter what we know:

$$R = \$6,000 \div (\$50,000 \times 1)$$

R = $6,000 ÷ $50,000

R = 0.12, or 12%

TIP

Most questions are based on 1 year to provide an annual percentage rate. To figure out the amount per month, divide the answer by 12.

EXAMPLE 3:

What is the second month's interest on a $5,000 loan at 6% interest with a monthly payment of $500?

This is a complex problem with multiple steps. First, we must find the interest for the first month, so we use the formula:

$I = P \times R \times T$

$I = \$5,000 \times 0.06 \times 1/12$

$I = \$300 \div 12$

$I = \$25$ for the first month

Now we need to figure out how much principal was paid off in the first month, so that we can determine how much principal is left for the next month's interest calculation.

Subtract the first month's interest from the regular monthly payment:

$500 (monthly payment) – $25 (first month's interest) = $475

So, in the first month, $475 of principal was paid off.

Subtract the first month's payment of principal from the total principal to find the principal after the first month's payment:

$5,000 (principal) – $475 (first month's principal payment) = $4,525 (principal after first month's payment)

Now we start the process over again to find the interest for the second month, which is what the question is asking for. The formula we need to use:

$I = P \times R \times T$

We enter what we know is the remaining principal into the formula:

$I = \$4,525$ (principal after first payment) $\times 0.06 \times 1/12$

$I = \$271.5 \div 12$

$I = \$22.625$, or rounded to $22.63

If the question had asked for the fourth month's interest, you would repeat the process two more times.

Sample Questions

1. What is the total interest paid on a $200,000 thirty-year mortgage with an interest rate of 8% and a $1,467.53 monthly payment?

   (A) $328,310.80

   (B) $528,310.80

   (C) $428,310.80

   (D) $228,310.80

The correct answer is (A). This question is easier than it may first appear. All we need to do is figure out the total value of the loan and subtract out the principal, so we need to use:

Monthly payment × 12 × length of loan = total value of loan

What we know from the question:

Monthly payment = $1,467.53

Length of loan = 30 years

Principal = $200,000

The 8% interest rate is extra information that is not needed to work out the answer.

Enter what we know:

$1,467.53 × 12 × 30 = $528,310.80

$528,310.80 − $200,000 = $328,310.80

2. Joe Bianco has taken out a loan for 70% of the home purchase price of $365,000. The loan is for a term of 15 years with an interest rate of 4.375% and a monthly payment of $1,934.48. How much interest will Joe pay in the first month?

   (A) $11,156.25

   (B) $111,562.5

   (C) $929.69

   (D) $1,330.73

The correct answer is (C). We are looking for interest for the first month, so we would use:

$I = P \times R \times T$

What we know from the question:

Principal   = 0.70 × $365,000

              = $255,000

Rate = 0.04375

Time = 1 month, or 1/12

The monthly payment is extra information that's not needed to answer the question.

Enter what we know:

I = \$255,000 (principal borrowed) × 0.04375 × 1/12

I = \$11,156.25 / 12

I = \$929.69

3. Using the information from the previous problem, determine the amount of principal still to be paid after the first month?

(A) \$363,995.21

(B) \$254,070.31

(C) \$364,070.31

(D) \$253,995.21

The correct answer is (D). We are looking for principal after the first payment, so we manipulate the formula:

Remaining Principal = Initial Principal – First Payment Principal

First Payment Principal = Monthly Payment – First Payment Interest

What we know from the question:

Monthly payment = \$1,934.48

Initial principal = \$255,000

First payment interest = \$929.69

Enter what we know:

First payment principal = \$1,934.48 – \$929.69

= \$1,004.79

Remaining principal = \$255,000 – \$1,004.79

= \$253,995.21

EXERCISES

1. What is the interest on 80% of a $400,000 loan with a 10% interest rate for the first year?

   (A) $40,000

   (B) $32,000

   (C) $3,200

   (D) $4,000

2. The Baranskis take out a $20,000 loan to remodel their house. The loan is for 15 years at 6.5% with a monthly payment of $174. How much will they still owe in principal after their third payment?

   (A) $19,868.31

   (B) $19,801.93

   (C) $19,478.00

   (D) $19,642.00

3. Using the information from Question 2, how much interest will the Baranskis pay over the course of the loan?

   (A) $2,035.8

   (B) $11,000

   (C) $11,524.65

   (D) $11,320

4. What is the principal on a mortgage loan, if the monthly interest payment is $5,768 and the interest rate is 7.25%?

   (A) $7,955.80

   (B) $95,470.34

   (C) $79,558.00

   (D) $954,703.45

5. Using the information from Question 4, how much interest will be paid for the first year?

   (A) $69,216

   (B) $73, 874

   (C) $64,927

   (D) $66,745

6. What is the total amount of interest paid on a $265,000 thirty-year loan with a monthly payment of $1,323.89?

   (A) $207,987.40

   (B) $15,886.68

   (C) $476,600.40

   (D) $211,600.40

ANSWER KEY AND EXPLANATIONS

1. B	**3.** D	**5.** A
2. B	**4.** D	**6.** D

1. **The correct answer is (B).**

   $400,000 \times 0.8 = \$320,000$

   $320,000 \times 0.1 = \$32,000$

2. **The correct answer is (B).**

   $20,000 \times 0.065 \div 12 = \$108.33$

   $174 - \$108.33 = \$65.67$

   $(\$20,000 - \$65.67) \times 0.065 \div 12 = \$107.98$

   $174 - 107.98 = \$66.02$

   $(20,000 - \$65.67 - \$66.02) \times 0.065 \div 12 = 107.62$

   $174 - \$107.62 = \$66.38$

   $20,000 - \$65.67 - \$66.02 - \$66.38 = \$19,801.93$

3. **The correct answer is (D).**

   $174 \times 12 \times 15 - \$20,000 = \$11,320$

4. **The correct answer is (D).**

   $5,768 \times 12 \div 0.0725 = \$954,703.45$

5. **The correct answer is (A).**

   $5,768 \times 12 = \$69,216$

6. **The correct answer is (D).**

   $1,322.89 \times 12 \times 30 = \$476,600.40$

   $476,600.40 - \$265,000 = \$211,600.40$

TAXES AND ASSESSMENTS

To calculate taxes you must know how the taxes are defined. Are they calculated using an assessed value of the property? Are the taxes based on tenths of a penny, or mills? Or are they based on dollars per hundred, or dollars per thousand? They can be defined in any of the following ways:

1. Assessed Value = Actual Value × Rate of Assessment

2. Mills are based on so many tenths of a penny (mills) per each dollar of assessed value.

3. Dollars per hundred/thousand is based upon so many dollars of tax per hundred/thousand dollars of assessed value.

EXAMPLE 1:

For tax purposes John Stephens' $230,000 house is assessed at 63%. What is the assessed value of his house?

We are looking for assessed value and need to use:

Assessed Value = Actual Value × Rate of Assessment

What we know from the question:

Actual Value = $230,000

Rate of Assessment = 63%

Enter what we know:

Assessed Value = $230,000 × 0.63

Answer:

Assessed Value = $144,900

EXAMPLE 2:

Using the information from Example 1, what are John's taxes, if he is taxed at 27 mills?

We need to find the taxes owed:

Taxes Owed = Assessed Value × Millage

What we know from the question:

Assessed Value = $144,900

Millage = 27 mills, or $0.027

Enter what we know:

Taxes Owed = $144,900 × $0.027

          = $3,912.30

TIP

Tax questions do not have to be relevant to where you live, or to anywhere. Their purpose is to see if you understand the principles of figuring taxes.

Sample Questions

1. Joan Schmidt owns a parcel of land that is valued at $60,000. Taxes in her community are based on 55% of actual value. What is her total tax bill, including special assessments, if the school tax is 62 mills, the town tax rate is 3.20 per thousand, and the special assessment for upgrading public utilities is $0.21 per hundred?

   (A) $3,171.30

   (B) $2,220.90

   (C) $2,844.60

   (D) $3,795.00

The correct answer is (B). We are looking for total taxes owed, so we need to use:

Assessed Value = Actual Value × Rate of Assessment

Taxes Owed = Assessed Value × Tax Rate

What we know from the question:

Rate of Assessment = 55%, or 0.55

School tax rate = 62 mills, or 0.062

Town tax rate = 3.20 per thousand, or 0.0032

Special assessment = $0.21 per $100, or 0.0021

Enter what we know:

Assessed Value = $60,000 × 0.55

= $33,000

Now we need to work the taxes-owed equation for each different tax or special assessment, and then add them together to find a total:

Taxes owed = $33,000 × 0.062 = $2,046.00

Taxes owed = $33,000 × 0.0032 = $ 105.60

Taxes owed = $33,000 × 0.0021 = + $ 69.30

$2,220.90

2. The Acme Company owns a parcel of land that has an assessed value of $93,000, and all property in town is assessed at a rate of 58%. What is the actual value of the land?

(A) $53,940.00

(B) $154,982.45

(C) $132,345.96

(D) $160,344.83

The correct answer is (D). We are looking for actual value, so we need to use:

Actual Value = Assessed Value ÷ Rate

What we know from the question:

Assessed Value = $93,000

Rate = 58%, or 0.58

Enter what we know:

Actual Value = $93,000 ÷ 0.58

= $160,344.83

3. Ali's Sofas owns its building, which that it is valued at $1.2 million. The building is in a special business incentive zone that has a tax rate of $24 per thousand dollars, as opposed to the regular rate of $32 per thousand. If the building is assessed at 48% of actual value, how much is the business saving each year in taxes?

(A) $4,608.00

(B) $46,080.00

(C) $460.80

(D) $4, 800.00

The correct answer is (A). We are looking for the difference in dollars of taxes owed, so we need to use:

Taxes Owed = Assessed Value × Tax Rate (1)

Taxes Owed = Assessed Value × Tax Rate (2)

Then, find the difference between the two numbers.

OR

We can take the difference in the rates and multiply the difference times the value of the property to find the savings. Then the formulas would be:

(Tax Rate (1) − Tax Rate (2)) × Assessed Value

Assessed Value = Actual Value × Rate of Assessment

What we know from the question:

Rate of Assessment = 48%, or 0.48

Tax Rate 1 = $32 per thousand, or 0.032

Tax Rate 2 = $24 per thousand, or 0.024

Enter what we know:

Actual Value = $1,200,000

Assessed Value = $1,200,000 × 0.48

= $576,000

Savings = (0.032 − 0.024) × $576,000

= 0.008 × $576,000

= $4,608

EXERCISES

1. A local business owns three parcels of vacant land on Main Street that are valued at $56,000, $34,000, and $42,000. All three properties are assessed at the same rate of 57%. What is their total assessed value?

   (A) $7,524

   (B) $132,000

   (C) $231,579

   (D) $75,240

2. The Lauders have combined two building lots to build their new home. If the combined assessed value of the lots is $150,000, and the rate of assessment is 62%, how much is the new lot worth, rounded to the nearest dollar?

   (A) $241,935

   (B) $270,943

   (C) $200,912

   (D) $239,847

3. If the local tax rate is 33 mills and the rate of assessment is 48%, what would be the taxes owed on a house worth $365,095?

   (A) $57,831.05

   (B) $12,048.13

   (C) $5,783.10

   (D) $1,204.81

4. The Stavros are allowed to pay the taxes on their $576,000 home in one of four ways: annually, semi-annually, quarterly, or monthly. What is their monthly payment if the rate of assessment is 54.5% and the tax rate is $2.99 per hundred, rounded to the nearest dollar?

   (A) $9,386

   (B) $1,435

   (C) $782

   (D) $821

5. Which of the following are equivalent?

   (A) 32 mills, 32 per hundred, 320 per thousand

   (B) 32 mills, 3.20 per hundred, 32 per thousand

   (C) 3.2 mills, 3.20 per hundred, 3.20 per thousand

   (D) 32 mills, 32 per hundred, 32 per thousand

ANSWER KEY AND EXPLANATIONS

1. D	**3.** C	**5.** B
2. A	**4.** C	

1. **The correct answer is (D).**

   $56,000 + $34,000 + $42,000 = $132,000

   $132,000 × 0.57 = $75,240

2. **The correct answer is (A).**

   $150,000 ÷ 0.62 = $241,935

3. **The correct answer is (C).**

   $365,095 × 0.48 = $175,245.60

   $175,246 × 0.033 = $5,783.10

4. **The correct answer is (C).**

   $576,000 × 0.545 = $313,920

   $313,920 × 0.0299 = $9,386

   $9,386 ÷ 12 = $782

5. **The correct answer is (B).**

   32 mills = 0.032

   3.20 per hundred = 0.032

   32 per thousand = 0.032

PRORATION

Proration is the process of determining the pro rata (proportional) portions on a sale. Prorations are frequently used at closings to figure out the amounts of money owed the seller and the buyer. Property taxes and homeowner association dues are two examples of charges that are prorated, although anything that one party pays for that the other has the benefit of a part can be prorated.

EXAMPLE 1:

Jerry Pollan purchases a property on July 1. Calvin Little has paid the year's real estate taxes of $6,000 in advance. How much is Calvin owed by the buyer?

We need to find money owed. To do this, we first need to find how much is a month's worth of taxes:

Taxes ÷ 12 months = taxes per month

$6,000 ÷ 12 = $500

Next, we need to find out the number of months owed to the seller. The seller used the property from January 1 to July 1, which is 6 months, so subtract the number of months used from one year:

12 – 6 = 6

What we now know:

Number of months the seller is owed = 6 months

Taxes per month = $500

To find the taxes owed the seller, multiply the number of months times the monthly taxes:

6 × $500 = $3,000

So, the seller is owed $3,000 by the buyer for taxes paid in advance.

EXAMPLE 2:

Tim Jarvis settles on his new house in the Tanglewood Estates on September 28. Tanglewood Estates has a homeowner's association fee of $225 per month. If Elizabeth Haskins, the seller, paid her fees for the month on September 1, how much money does Tim owe Elizabeth for his share of the fee for the month?

We are looking for money owed Elizabeth. Using a 30-day month, we need to find the daily rate:

Assessment ÷ Number of Days in a Month = Daily Rate

$225 ÷ 30 = $7.50

What we know from the question:

Out of a 30-day month Tim owns the house for 3 days.

Enter what we know:

Number of Days ÷ Daily Rate = Amount Owed by the Buyer

3 × $7.50 = $22.00

Elizabeth is owed $22.00 by Tim for unused fees.

Sample Questions

1. On July 6, a property sold. The water bill of $95 and the yearly tax bill of $5,200 will be paid by the buyer for the current year. When prorated at closing, what amount does the seller owe the buyer? Round your final answer to the nearest dollar.

    (A) $3,154

    (B) $2,721

    (C) $3,201

    (D) $2,768

The correct answer is (A). We are looking for the dollar amount owed the buyer and will use 30 days to a month.

First, we'll calculate the water bill:

Annual Charge ÷ Months in a Year = Cost per Month:

$95 ÷ 12 = $7.91666, or rounded to $8 per month

Charge per Month ÷ Number of Days in a Month = Charge per Day:

$8 ÷ 30 = $0.266, or rounded to $0.27 per day

A settlement on July 6 means that the seller used the property for 6 months and 5 days. So, Charge per Month × Number of Months + Cost per Day × Number of Days = Charge Owed Buyer:

($8 × 6) + ($.027 × 5) = $48 + $1.35 = $49.35, or rounded to $49

Next, we'll calculate the taxes:

Total Tax ÷ Number of Months in a Year = Tax per Month:

$5,200 ÷ 12 = $433.33333, or rounded to $433 per month

Tax per Month ÷ Number of Days in a Month = Tax per Day:

$433 ÷ 30 = $14.43333, or rounded to $14.44 per day

A settlement on July 6 means that the seller used the property for 6 months and 5 days. So, Tax per Month × Number of Months + Tax per Day × Number of Days = Amount Owed Buyer:

($433 × 6) + ($14.44 × 5) = $2,600 + $72.2 = $2,672.20, or rounded to $2,672

To find the total amount, add the two answers together:

$49 + $2,672 = $2,721

2. A property sold on November 10. The condo fees are $255 a month and are paid for the current month. The taxes for the year are $1,152 and are paid in arrears. Who is owed how much at closing?

    (A) $906.30 to the buyer

    (B) $810.30 to the seller

    (C) $803.20 to the seller

    (D) $810.30 to the buyer

The correct answer is (D). We are looking for who is owed how much at closing, so we need to think not just about the amount, but also about who paid the amount.

Now start with the condo fee. We know that the fee is $255 per month paid typically at the beginning of the month, and we have to find out how much it is a day:

Condo Fee ÷ 30 Days = Fee per Day

$255 ÷ 30 = $8.50 per day

Because the fee was paid for the current month, the seller is owed for the days the seller did not own the condo:

(30 − 9) × $8.50 =

21 × $8.50 = $178.50 owed to the seller

Next calculate the taxes. We know that the taxes are $1,152 per year and are paid in arrears. To find the monthly and then the daily amount of the taxes:

Annual Tax ÷ 12 Months in a Year = Tax Amount per Month:

$1,152 ÷ 12 = $96

Monthly Tax ÷ 30 = Tax Amount per Day:

$96 ÷ 30 = $3.20

Since the taxes are paid in arrears, we need to figure out how much is owed to the buyer. The seller used the house for 10 months and 9 days, so Monthly Tax Amount × Number of Months + Daily Tax Rate × Number of Days = Amount of Taxes Owed to Buyer:

($96 × 10) + ($3.20 × 9) = $960 + $28.80 = $988.80

We have two amounts and each owed to a different person. To find the final amount and to whom it is owed, subtract the smaller number from the larger number:

$988.80 (owed to buyer) − $178.50 (owed to seller) = $810.30 (owed to buyer)

TIP

You can state the information in any question in terms of what you know about the problem, what you have to find, and how the pieces of information relate to one another—or don't because some information may be irrelevant. Then decide what operations (add, subtract, multiply, divide) you will need to find the answer. State what you need to do in terms of these operations just the way the sample answers go through a problem.

3. Jack Romero buys a house from Barb Hopper and assumes the unpaid mortgage amount of $23,000 with a 6% interest rate. If the loan was paid on September 9 and closing was on September 22, what was the amount of accrued interest?

   (A) $115

   (B) $49.79

   (C) $53.62

   (D) $17,940

The correct answer is (B). We need to find the accrued interest amount from September 9 to September 22. To do that, we first have to figure out the amount of the daily interest:

$P \times R \times T = I$:

$23,000 \times 0.06 \times 1$ (year) = $1,380 Interest per Year

Annual Interest ÷ 12 months = Interest per Month:

$1,380 ÷ 12 = $115 Interest per Month

Monthly Interest ÷ 30 Days in a Month = Interest per Day:

$115 ÷ 30 = $3.8333, or rounded to $3.83 interest per day

September 9 to September 22 is 13 days, therefore:

Interest per Day × Number of Days = Accrued Interest

$3.83 × 13 = $49.79 accrued interest

EXERCISES

1. Jenny pays $3,600 in taxes in arrears on December 31. She bought her house on September 5. How much does the seller owe her?

   (A) $2,750

   (B) $150

   (C) $2,400

   (D) $2,450

2. A list on expenses is presented to be paid by the buyer and the seller. The list includes title insurance for $374, appraisal fees at $425, and a home inspection fee of $525. The seller agrees to pay for 65% of all costs. How much does the buyer owe?

   (A) $373.80

   (B) $463.40

   (C) $564.30

   (D) $860.60

3. A 1-year insurance policy, dated November 1, 2008, is assumed on the closing date of January 10, 2009. The full premium of $356.40 was paid when the policy was bought. If this policy is prorated, how much of this policy did the seller use?

   (A) $98.01

   (B) $69.30

   (C) $68.31

   (D) $75.90

4. Homeowners association fees of $234.60 a month are due on the first of every month for that month. Taxes of $5,754.72 for the same property are paid in arrears on December 31. The property went to closing on July 15. Who owes what to whom?

   (A) Seller owes $125.12; buyer owes $3,101.22.

   (B) Seller owes $3,101.22; buyer owes $125.12.

   (C) Seller owes $109.48; buyer owes $2,653.50.

   (D) Seller owes $2,653.50; buyer owes $109.48.

5. Sandy Grier's lakefront property has a rental cottage. Rent for the cottage is $1,200 per month, payable in advance on the tenth of the month. Settlement on the property is June 20th. How much does Sandy owe the buyer?

   (A) $800

   (B) $700

   (C) $600

   (D) $400

6. Lehka Patel paid $864 for a 3-year homeowner's insurance policy on January 1 of last year. If closing date on her house is March 3, who owes what to whom?

   (A) $236.90 to the buyer

   (B) $357.60 to the seller

   (C) $357.60 to the buyer

   (D) $236.90 to the seller

ANSWER KEY AND EXPLANATIONS

1. D	**3.** C	**5.** A
2. B	**4.** B	**6.** B

1. **The correct answer is (D).**

   $3,600 ÷ 12 = $300 per month

   $300 ÷ 30 = $10 per day

   $300 × 8 = $2,400

   $10 × 5 = $50

   $2,400 + $50 = $2,450

2. **The correct answer is (B).**

   $374 + $425 + $525 = $1,324

   $1,324 × 0.35 = $463.40

3. **The correct answer is (C).**

   $356.40 ÷ 12 = $29.70

   $29.70 ÷ 30 = $0.99

   $29.70 × 2 = $59.40

   $0.99 × 9 = $8.91

   $59.40 + $8.91 = $68.31

4. **The correct answer is (B).**

   $234.60 ÷ 30 = $7.82

   $7.82 × 16 = $125.12 buyer owes

   $5,754.72 ÷ 12 = $479.56

   $479.56 ÷ 30 = $15.99

   $479.56 × 6 = $2,877.36

   $15.99 × 14 = $223.86

   $2,877.36 + $223.86 = $3,101.22 seller owes

5. **The correct answer is (A).**

   $1,200 ÷ 30 = $40

   30 − 10 = 20

   $40 × 20 = $800

6. **The correct answer is (B).**

   $864 ÷ 3 = $288

   $288 ÷ 12 = $24

   $24 ÷ 30 = $0.80

   $288 × 1 = $288

   $24 × 2 = $48

   $0.80 × 27 = $21.60

   $288 + $48 + $21.60 = $357.60 to the seller because the policy was paid in full.

CASH RECEIPT

Date _____ 8/23/11 _____

Fine _____ $ _____ .60 _____

Card Fee $ _____

Non Resident

Fee $ _____

Contribution $ _____

Other $ _____

#4272 _____

MJ

Washington Township
FREE PUBLIC LIBRARY
Long Valley, NJ 07853

APPRECIATION AND DEPRECIATION

Appreciation is the increase in a property's value. Appreciation can be caused by improvements in the property, inflation, or increasing demand.

Depreciation is the decrease in a property's value. Depreciation can be caused by, but is not limited to, deterioration, deflation, decreasing demand, or an external obsolescence. Depreciation can also come in the form of a tax benefit on real estate investments. A third type of depreciation takes into account the economic, or useful, life of a property. This last form is usually calculated in a straight-line depreciation, in which a property depreciates in an equal amount each year.

EXAMPLE 1:

Joe Chen sells his property for $443,208. He bought the property 9 years ago for $375,600. What is the rate of appreciation per year?

We are looking for rate of appreciation per year:

Appreciation ÷ Original Price ÷ Number of Years Owned = Appreciation per Year as Percentage

To find the appreciation per year, we first have to find the dollar value of the appreciation:

Current Value − Original Price = Appreciation in Dollars

$443,208 − $375,600 = $67,608 appreciation

Then apply the formula:

$67,608 ÷ $375,600 = 0.18

0.18 ÷ 9 = 0.02, or 2%

So, the rate of appreciation per year is 2%.

EXAMPLE 2:

If an unimproved $272,000 property depreciates at a rate of 3% a year, what is the property worth after 5 years?

We are looking for property value after 5 years:

Value × Rate × Number of Years = Value Over That Time

$272,000 × 0.03 = $8,160 × 5 = $40,800

$272,000 − $40,800 = $231,200

So, the property is worth $231,200 after 5 years.

Sample Questions

1. If a house depreciates at a rate of 2.25% a year for 4 years and was worth $132,800 at the beginning of that period, what is it worth today?

   (A) $118,096

   (B) $156,708

   (C) $144,752

   (D) $120,848

The correct answer is (D). We are looking for current value:

Value Now = Original Price – Depreciation

But to get there, we must first find the rate of depreciation at the end of 4 years:

Value × Rate for One Year × Period of Years = Rate of Depreciation

$0.0225 \times 4 = 0.09$

$132,800 \times 0.09 = \$11,952$ depreciation over 4 years

Next use the formula to find the value now:

Value Now = $132,800 – $11,952

Value Now = $120,848

2. Angie Talbot owns a $20,000 lakeside condo that she depreciates using straight-line depreciation for 10 years. What is the dollar amount of depreciation each year?

   (A) $2,000

   (B) $2,200

   (C) $2,900

   (D) $3,000

The correct answer is (A). We are looking for the dollar amount of depreciation per year. Straight-line is an equal amount that makes the value 0 after the given period.

Value ÷ Period of Time = Amount of Depreciation per Year:

$20,000 ÷ 10 years = $2,000

$2,000 is the dollar amount of depreciation per year.

3. Mickey Siano bought his twin for $70,000. Seventeen years later, it is now valued at $315,000. What are the amount of appreciation and the rate of appreciation?

   (A) $385,000; 550%

   (B) $245,000; 28%

   (C) $245,000; 350%

   (D) $385,000; 18%

The correct answer is (C). We are looking for two things: the amount of appreciation and the rate of appreciation. It may seem as though finding them will be complicated, but both are simple one-step processes.

To find the amount of appreciation:

Value Now – Original Price = Amount of Appreciation

$315,000 – $70,000 = $245,000 amount of appreciation

To find the rate of appreciation:

Amount of Appreciation ÷ Original Price = Rate of Appreciation

$245,000 ÷ $70,000 = 3.5, or 350% rate of appreciation

EXERCISES

1. If a $233,000 house depreciates at a rate of 3% a year for 6 years under straight-line depreciation, what is it worth today?

   (A) $41,940

   (B) $109,106

   (C) $180,000

   (D) $191,060

2. The Elm Street Bocce Club recently sold its property for $2,345,320. If the property was purchased 20 years ago for $509,870, what is the annual rate of appreciation?

   (A) 18%

   (B) 22%

   (C) 360%

   (D) 460%

3. DeLuca's Auto Body Shop was bought 5 years ago for $180,000. The property was just sold for $153,000. What was the depreciation per year?

   (A) 2%

   (B) 3%

   (C) 14%

   (D) 15%

4. A house sold for 155% of its original value. If it sold for $755,649.80, what was its original value?

   (A) $897,009.76

   (B) $1,171,257.19

   (C) $487,516.00

   (D) $506,897.98

5. Eight years ago, it cost $70,000 to build a home on a $15,000 lot. If the home depreciates at 4% per year, and the lot appreciates at 5% per year, what is the total value now of the property, including improvements?

   (A) $68,600

   (B) $101,400

   (C) $113,400

   (D) $56,600

6. Using straight-line depreciation, a house that is valued at $789,300 and has a useful life of 35 years, is worth what after 7 years?

   (A) $542,761.01

   (B) $763,971.99

   (C) $947,160.01

   (D) $631,439.99

ANSWER KEY AND EXPLANATIONS

1. D	**3.** B	**5.** A
2. A	**4.** C	**6.** D

1. **The correct answer is (D).**

   $233,000 \times 0.03 = \$6,990$

   $\$6,990 \times 6 = \$41,940$

   $\$233,000 - \$41,940 = 191,060$

2. **The correct answer is (A).**

   $\$2,345,320 - \$509,870 = \$1,835,450$

   $\$1,835,450 \div \$509,870 = 3.6$

   $3.6 \div 20 = 0.18$, or 18%

3. **The correct answer is (B).**

   $\$180,000 - 153,000 = \$27,000$

   $\$27,000 \div \$180,000 = 0.15$

   $0.15 \div 5 = 0.03$, or 3%

4. **The correct answer is (C).**

   $\$755,649.80 \div 1.55 = \$487,516$

5. **The correct answer is (A).**

   $\$70,000 \times 0.04 = \$2,800$

   $\$2,800 \times 8 = \$22,400$

   $\$70,000 - \$22,800 = \$47,600$

   $\$15,000 \times 0.05 = \$750$

   $\$750 \times 8 = \$6,000$

   $\$15,000 + \$6,000 = \$21,000$

   $\$47,600 + \$21,000 = \$68,600$

6. **The correct answer is (D).**

   $\$789,300 \div 35 = \$22,551.43$

   $\$22,551.43 \times 7 = \$157,860.01$

   $\$789,300 - \$157,860.01 = \$631,439.99$

APPRAISAL

Appraisal questions deal with finding the value of a piece of real property is worth. There are three ways to determine value: cost approach; sales comparison approach, also known as the market approach; and income approach.

Cost Approach

The cost approach to value is based upon the value of the land, the value of replacement, and the value of depreciation. The basic formula:

> Replacement Cost + Land Value – Depreciation = Value

To find elements of this formula use:

> Square Feet × Replacement Cost per Square Foot = Replacement Cost

> Replacement Cost × Depreciation Rate = Depreciation per Year

Square footage is the typical measurement for a structure, but it could be any measurement.

TIP

Remember in the cost approach that depreciation is only taken on replacement cost.

EXAMPLE 1:

What is the value of a 3-year-old property that is 2,465 square feet and has a replacement cost of $55 per square foot, a land value of $45,000, and a depreciation rate of 4% a year?

We are looking for total value, but first we must find the replacement cost:

> Square Feet × Replacement Cost per Square Foot = Replacement Cost

> 2,465 × $55 = $135,575

Next, we need to find the depreciation. This is taken only on structure value and not on land value:

> Replacement Cost × Depreciation Rate = Depreciation per Year

> $135,575 × 0.04 = $5,423 per year

To find the depreciation over a period of years, multiply the years times the annual depreciation:

> 3 × $5,423 = $16,269 over 3 years

Now put it all together:

> Replacement Cost + Land Value – Depreciation = Total Value

> $135,575 + $45,000 – $16,269 = $164,306

So, the value of the property is $164,306.

Market Approach or Sales Comparison Approach

The market approach to value is based upon comparisons between one real property and others, typically six. The property being appraised is called the subject property.

EXAMPLE 2:

The Triggs are looking to buy a 5-bedroom house on Elm Street. A similar house on the same street with 6 bedrooms just sold for $75,000. What is the value of the house that the Triggs want to buy?

We are looking for value based upon the number of bedrooms. So, if the 6-bedroom house sold for $75,000, a bedroom is worth:

Value ÷ Number of Bedrooms = Value of 1 Bedroom

$75,000 ÷ 6 = $12,500

A 5-bedroom house is worth:

Number of Bedrooms × Value of 1 Bedroom = Value

5 × $12,500 = $60,000

So, the value of the property is $60,000.

Income Approach

The income approach is based on the income that can be generated from a real property. These questions are similar to the interest problems from earlier in the chapter in that they have a formula that can be solved for whatever value is missing.

The basic formula is I = V × R, where I is income, V is value, and R is rate/percentage of return.

From this formula we can answer questions that ask about value and rate simply by solving for the unknown amount:

V = I ÷ R

R = I ÷ V

EXAMPLE 3:

The Stacey brothers bought a building knowing that the yearly income is $90,000. They expected that would give them a 15% return on investment. What did the building cost?

We are looking for cost of the building, so using the formula:

I = V × R

$90,000 = V × 0.15

V = $90,000 ÷ 0.15

V = $600,000

So, the value of the property is $600,000.

Sample Questions

1. What monthly income should a building costing $770,000 produce, if the annual rate of return is to be 12%?

   (A) $92,400

   (B) $7,700

   (C) $9,240

   (D) $77,000

The correct answer is (B). This question is using the income approach and we are looking for income per month. So, first we need to find yearly income using the formula:

$$I = V \times R$$

$$I = \$770,000 \times 0.12$$

$$I = \$92,400$$

To find income per month, we need to divide by 12:

$$I \text{ per month} = \$92,000 \div 12$$

$$I \text{ per month} = \$7,700$$

2. What is the value of a Cape-Cod-style house of 1,500 square feet, if a similar Cape Cod sold for $136,990 and had 1,750 square feet?

   (A) $117,420

   (B) $119,420

   (C) $116,420

   (D) $118,420

The correct answer is (A). We are looking for value using the market approach, and square footage is the basis of the comparison. We must first find the cost per square foot of the sold house:

Value of Sold House ÷ Square Footage = Cost per Square Foot

$$\$136,990 \div 1,750 = \$78.28 \text{ per square foot}$$

Next, we must find a value using the per square foot number and the subject house:

Cost per Square Foot of Sold House × Square Foot of Subject House = Value of Subject House

$$\$78.28 \times 1,500 = \$117,420$$

3. It has been determined that the replacement cost of a 2-year-old building is $435,790. What is the value for the total property if the land is worth $125,000 and the rate of depreciation is 5%?

   (A) $560,790

   (B) $504,711

   (C) $517,211

   (D) $545,619

The correct answer is (C). We are looking for a value using the cost approach:

Replacement Cost × Rate of Depreciation = Depreciation

$435,790 × 0.05 = $21,789.50

For 2 years:

Depreciation × Period = Depreciation for the Period

$21,790 × 2 = $43,579

Plug in the correct numbers into the basic cost approach formula:

Replacement Cost + Land Value − Depreciation = Value

$435,790 + $125,000 − $43,579 = $517,211

EXERCISES

1. An apartment building with 24 apartments renting at $1,100 each has just sold. If the buyers were told to expect a rate of return of 12.5%, what was the selling price of the building?

    (A) $211,200

    (B) $253,440

    (C) $2,534,400

    (D) $3,545,660

2. A duplex sold for $200,000. It has a yearly rental income of $15,000. What is the rate of return?

    (A) 12 %

    (B) 7.5%

    (C) 10%

    (D) 75%

3. What is the value of a property containing a 4-year-old building that has a replacement cost of $79,000, a land value of $17,500, and a rate of depreciation of 3%?

    (A) $94,130

    (B) $87,020

    (C) $93,605

    (D) $84,920

4. How much income must be generated from a $1,357,500 building if a 12% return on investment is desired?

    (A) $120,000

    (B) $12,000

    (C) $170,000

    (D) $162,900

5. What is the replacement cost of a building if the final value is $120,900, the land value is $11,300, and depreciation is $4,352?

    (A) $109,564

    (B) $104,348

    (C) $113,052

    (D) $135,652

ANSWER KEY AND EXPLANATIONS

1. C	**3.** B	**5.** C
2. B	**4.** D	

1. **The correct answer is (C).**

   24 × $1,100 = $26,400

   $26,400 × 12 = $316,800

   $316,800 ÷ 0.125 = $2,534,400

2. **The correct answer is (B).**

   $15,000 ÷ $200,000 = 0.075, or 7.5%

3. **The correct answer is (B).**

   $79,000 × 0.03 = $2,370

   $2,370 × 4 = $9,480

   $79,000 + $17,500 − $9840 = $87,020

4. **The correct answer is (D).**

   $1,357,500 × 0.12 = $162,900

5. **The correct answer is (C).**

   $120,000 − $11,300 + $4,352 = $113,052

MEASUREMENT AND AREA

The ability to convert and to calculate measurement and area is a basic skill both for the exam and for the real world.

Measurement is defined by units of measure such as inches, feet, yards, miles, and acres. Exam questions and real-world situations may ask you to convert one to the other and back. Usually, you will be determining one of three things: perimeter, area, or frontage.

1. Perimeter is the total distance in units of the boundary of a piece of real property or a structure.

2. Area is the total surface within the boundaries of a piece of real property or a structure expressed in square units.

3. Frontage is the distance in units along a street or streets. It is the full length of a property or building that fronts (runs along) a street or road.

UNITS OF MEASUREMENT

Some units of measurements that you should remember are:

1 foot = 12 inches

1 yard = 3 feet = 36 inches

1 mile = 1,760 yards = 5,280 feet

1 square foot = 144 square inches

1 square yard = 9 square feet

1 square mile = 640 acres

1 acre = 43,560 square feet

FORMULAS FOR AREA

Some formulas for area that you should remember:

Area of a rectangle:

Area = length × width

Area of a triangle:

Area = 1/2 × base × height

You can break down almost any straight-sided shape into a group of triangles and rectangles.

EXAMPLE 1:

Spencer Binondo has a 5-acre property that he wants to subdivide into as many 1,000-square foot lots as he can. How many lots can he sell?

We need to find out how many 1,000 square foot lots are in 5 acres. Knowing that there are 43,560 square feet in an acre, we can determine the total number of square feet:

$43,560 \times 5 = 217,800$

To find the number of 1,000 square foot lots, divide the total by 1,000:

$217,800 \div 1000 = 217.8$

So, Spencer Binondo is able to sell 217 lots and is left with 0.8 of a lot.

EXAMPLE 2:

Using the diagram below, determine the total acreage of Lot C and its frontage.

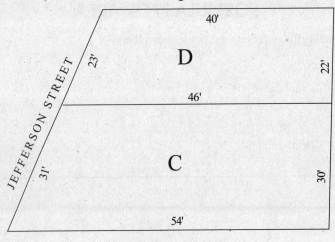

CHERRY DRIVE

Because we have to find two things, area (total acreage) and frontage, we need to break the solution into two parts. First, we'll find the frontage.

Lot C has frontage on both Cherry Drive and Jefferson Street, so by taking the measurements from the diagram, we get 54' + 31' = 85' of frontage.

Next, we'll find the acreage. However, what we know is the length and width in feet of the lot, so we will have to find the square footage and then convert the square footage into acres. There is another "however" though. The lot is a not a square, so we will get the acreage by dividing the plot into a rectangle and a triangle (shown below).

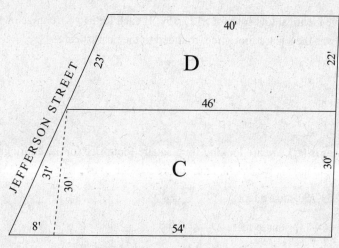

CHERRY DRIVE

The rectangle is 46' × 30' = 1,380 square feet.

The triangle is 30' × 8' × 1½ = 120 square feet.

Add the numbers together 1,380 + 120 = 1,500 square feet.

Now we need to divide this by the square feet in an acre to find what part of an acre Lot C is:

Acre = 43,560 square feet

1,500 ÷ 43,560 = 0.034 of an acre

So, the lot has a total frontage of 85' and is 0.034 of an acre.

Sample Questions

1. Jane Wing is buying a property that is 3/4 of an acre. How many square feet is the lot?
   (A) 32,670
   (B) 5,808
   (C) 58,080
   (D) 3,267,000

The correct answer is (A). We are looking for the number of square feet in an acre, and we know that an acre has 43,560 square feet.

To find 3/4 of an acre, multiply the total by 0.75:

43,560 × 0.75 = 32,670

TIP

Make sure when figuring out areas that you use the same units of measure.

2. A group of five identical lots sold for $127,550. If each lot had a frontage of 150' and a depth of 225', what was the square foot price, rounded to the nearest cent?

    (A) $1.32

    (B) $3.78

    (C) $0.76

    (D) $0.26

The correct answer is (C). We are looking for a square foot price for the entire group of five lots. Because the lots are identical, we can find the square footage of one lot and then multiply that by 5:

    150' × 225' = 33,750 square feet

    33,750 × 5 = 168,750 square feet

To find the price per square foot, divide the price by the total square footage:

    $127,550 ÷ 168,750 = $0.7558

Round to the nearest cent: $0.76

3. The township wants to install brick sidewalks in the downtown area. If it costs $23 a square foot to install the sidewalks, and the township has $345,000 to spend, how many square feet of sidewalk can the township install?

    (A) 7,935,000

    (B) 1,500

    (C) 23

    (D) 2,000

The correct answer is (B). We are looking for how many square feet of sidewalk the township can afford on its budget, so we need to divide the budget by the price per square foot:

    $345,000 ÷ $23 = 1,500 square feet

EXERCISES

1. What is the listing price for a subdivideable 225-acre lot if the asking price is $0.52 per square foot?

   (A) $5,096,520

   (B) $509,652,000

   (C) $100.67

   (D) $5,096.52

2. If land in a development sells for $25,595 an acre, how much would it cost to purchase a lot that measures 239,580 square feet?

   (A) $407,739.98

   (B) $1,407,725.00

   (C) $140,772.50

   (D) $142,774.50

3. What is the area of a triangular lot with a depth of 324' and a frontage of 223'?

   (A) 162

   (B) 72,252

   (C) 144,504

   (D) 36,126

4. It costs $12.00 per square foot for labor and $23.00 per square foot for materials to put a stone façade on a new construction home. How much would it cost to put a 4-foot tall band of stone on the front of a house that is 73 feet long?

   (A) $10,220

   (B) $1,679

   (C) $2,555

   (D) $6,716

5. The Colstons bought a beachfront property that is $\frac{3}{4}$ of an acre, and the beach frontage is 110'. Assuming that the property is rectangular, what is the depth of the property?

   (A) 296

   (B) 332

   (C) 298

   (D) 297

6. How many yards of 3/4" crushed stone is needed to fill a hole that measures 12' by 90' by 3"?

   (A) 9

   (B) 10

   (C) 11

   (D) 12

ANSWER KEY AND EXPLANATIONS

1. A	3. D	5. D
2. C	4. A	6. B

1. **The correct answer is (A).**

   $43,560 \times \$0.52 = \$22,651.20$ price per acre

   $\$22,651.20 \times 225$ acres $= \$5,096,520$

2. **The correct answer is (C).**

   $239,580' \div 43,560'$ per acre $= 5.5$ acres

   $5.5 \times \$25,595$ price per acre $= \$140,772.50$

3. **The correct answer is (D).**

   $1/2 \times 324 \times 223 = 36,126$

4. **The correct answer is (A).**

   $12 per square foot + $23 per square foot
   = $35 per square foot

   $73' \times 4' = 292$ square feet

   $292 \times \$35$ per square foot $= \$10,220$

5. **The correct answer is (D).**

   $43,560$ square feet per acre $\times 3/4 = 32,670$

   $32,670$ square feet $\div 110' = 297'$

6. **The correct answer is (B).**

   $12' \times 90' \times 1/4' = 270$

   $270 \div 27 = 10$

MATH TEST-TAKING TIPS

- In this chapter, we have covered the different types of calculations that you may be asked to use when you take a real estate licensing exam: addition, subtraction, division, and multiplication. No matter how complex the questions may seem, they all come down to using these four basic operations.

- Both commission and interest rate questions involve percents. Using percents means using multiplication and division operations.

  ☐ To find what percentage one number is of another, divide the numbers and multiply by 100.

    What percent of $50 is $5?

    $5 \div 50 = 10 \times 100 = 10\%$

  ☐ To find x percent of a number, change the percent to a decimal, multiply the number by the decimal, and then move the decimal point in the answer two places to the left.

    What is a 4% commission on a $40,000 sale?

    $40,000 \times 0.04 = 160,000$

    $\qquad\qquad = \$1,600.00$

- Percentages can be changed to decimals by moving the decimal point two places to the left. Decimals can be converted to percentages by moving the decimal point two places to the right.

- Read carefully. Questions appear complex when you are asked to figure out multiple answers, and then use those answers to come to the conclusion that the question is asking for. With all word problems, the toughest part is figuring out what the question is asking and then determining how the values you are given fit the question and what you still need to find.

- To help you work through a problem, state

  ☐ what the question asks you to find.

  ☐ what information you know from the question.

  ☐ how that information fits into a formula or make up your own formula, which is just stating what each piece of information represents (square foot, commission rate, income, etc.) and what operation you need (addition, subtraction, multiplication, division).

- Remember that not every piece of information in a question may be relevant to working out the solution.

- If the answer that you arrive at is not among the answers given, check your work, which is why it's good to work on scratch paper if you can. If you use a calculator, you won't be able to find your error easily.

- If, after rechecking your answer you still can't find the error, use the process of elimination method. Eliminate obviously wrong answers until you have one or two left; choose the one that seems the most likely to be correct.

- The biggest point to remember is that the real estate exam is designed to test your knowledge of real estate, not your knowledge of complex math. So, all the problems that involve math can, with a little patience and problem solving, be answered with basic math.

- And one final thought: You do not need to score 100 percent to pass the test.

PART IV
FIVE PRACTICE TESTS

ANSWER SHEET PRACTICE TEST 2

1. Ⓐ Ⓑ Ⓒ Ⓓ	21. Ⓐ Ⓑ Ⓒ Ⓓ	41. Ⓐ Ⓑ Ⓒ Ⓓ	61. Ⓐ Ⓑ Ⓒ Ⓓ	81. Ⓐ Ⓑ Ⓒ Ⓓ
2. Ⓐ Ⓑ Ⓒ Ⓓ	22. Ⓐ Ⓑ Ⓒ Ⓓ	42. Ⓐ Ⓑ Ⓒ Ⓓ	62. Ⓐ Ⓑ Ⓒ Ⓓ	82. Ⓐ Ⓑ Ⓒ Ⓓ
3. Ⓐ Ⓑ Ⓒ Ⓓ	23. Ⓐ Ⓑ Ⓒ Ⓓ	43. Ⓐ Ⓑ Ⓒ Ⓓ	63. Ⓐ Ⓑ Ⓒ Ⓓ	83. Ⓐ Ⓑ Ⓒ Ⓓ
4. Ⓐ Ⓑ Ⓒ Ⓓ	24. Ⓐ Ⓑ Ⓒ Ⓓ	44. Ⓐ Ⓑ Ⓒ Ⓓ	64. Ⓐ Ⓑ Ⓒ Ⓓ	84. Ⓐ Ⓑ Ⓒ Ⓓ
5. Ⓐ Ⓑ Ⓒ Ⓓ	25. Ⓐ Ⓑ Ⓒ Ⓓ	45. Ⓐ Ⓑ Ⓒ Ⓓ	65. Ⓐ Ⓑ Ⓒ Ⓓ	85. Ⓐ Ⓑ Ⓒ Ⓓ
6. Ⓐ Ⓑ Ⓒ Ⓓ	26. Ⓐ Ⓑ Ⓒ Ⓓ	46. Ⓐ Ⓑ Ⓒ Ⓓ	66. Ⓐ Ⓑ Ⓒ Ⓓ	86. Ⓐ Ⓑ Ⓒ Ⓓ
7. Ⓐ Ⓑ Ⓒ Ⓓ	27. Ⓐ Ⓑ Ⓒ Ⓓ	47. Ⓐ Ⓑ Ⓒ Ⓓ	67. Ⓐ Ⓑ Ⓒ Ⓓ	87. Ⓐ Ⓑ Ⓒ Ⓓ
8. Ⓐ Ⓑ Ⓒ Ⓓ	28. Ⓐ Ⓑ Ⓒ Ⓓ	48. Ⓐ Ⓑ Ⓒ Ⓓ	68. Ⓐ Ⓑ Ⓒ Ⓓ	88. Ⓐ Ⓑ Ⓒ Ⓓ
9. Ⓐ Ⓑ Ⓒ Ⓓ	29. Ⓐ Ⓑ Ⓒ Ⓓ	49. Ⓐ Ⓑ Ⓒ Ⓓ	69. Ⓐ Ⓑ Ⓒ Ⓓ	89. Ⓐ Ⓑ Ⓒ Ⓓ
10. Ⓐ Ⓑ Ⓒ Ⓓ	30. Ⓐ Ⓑ Ⓒ Ⓓ	50. Ⓐ Ⓑ Ⓒ Ⓓ	70. Ⓐ Ⓑ Ⓒ Ⓓ	90. Ⓐ Ⓑ Ⓒ Ⓓ
11. Ⓐ Ⓑ Ⓒ Ⓓ	31. Ⓐ Ⓑ Ⓒ Ⓓ	51. Ⓐ Ⓑ Ⓒ Ⓓ	71. Ⓐ Ⓑ Ⓒ Ⓓ	91. Ⓐ Ⓑ Ⓒ Ⓓ
12. Ⓐ Ⓑ Ⓒ Ⓓ	32. Ⓐ Ⓑ Ⓒ Ⓓ	52. Ⓐ Ⓑ Ⓒ Ⓓ	72. Ⓐ Ⓑ Ⓒ Ⓓ	92. Ⓐ Ⓑ Ⓒ Ⓓ
13. Ⓐ Ⓑ Ⓒ Ⓓ	33. Ⓐ Ⓑ Ⓒ Ⓓ	53. Ⓐ Ⓑ Ⓒ Ⓓ	73. Ⓐ Ⓑ Ⓒ Ⓓ	93. Ⓐ Ⓑ Ⓒ Ⓓ
14. Ⓐ Ⓑ Ⓒ Ⓓ	34. Ⓐ Ⓑ Ⓒ Ⓓ	54. Ⓐ Ⓑ Ⓒ Ⓓ	74. Ⓐ Ⓑ Ⓒ Ⓓ	94. Ⓐ Ⓑ Ⓒ Ⓓ
15. Ⓐ Ⓑ Ⓒ Ⓓ	35. Ⓐ Ⓑ Ⓒ Ⓓ	55. Ⓐ Ⓑ Ⓒ Ⓓ	75. Ⓐ Ⓑ Ⓒ Ⓓ	95. Ⓐ Ⓑ Ⓒ Ⓓ
16. Ⓐ Ⓑ Ⓒ Ⓓ	36. Ⓐ Ⓑ Ⓒ Ⓓ	56. Ⓐ Ⓑ Ⓒ Ⓓ	76. Ⓐ Ⓑ Ⓒ Ⓓ	96. Ⓐ Ⓑ Ⓒ Ⓓ
17. Ⓐ Ⓑ Ⓒ Ⓓ	37. Ⓐ Ⓑ Ⓒ Ⓓ	57. Ⓐ Ⓑ Ⓒ Ⓓ	77. Ⓐ Ⓑ Ⓒ Ⓓ	97. Ⓐ Ⓑ Ⓒ Ⓓ
18. Ⓐ Ⓑ Ⓒ Ⓓ	38. Ⓐ Ⓑ Ⓒ Ⓓ	58. Ⓐ Ⓑ Ⓒ Ⓓ	78. Ⓐ Ⓑ Ⓒ Ⓓ	98. Ⓐ Ⓑ Ⓒ Ⓓ
19. Ⓐ Ⓑ Ⓒ Ⓓ	39. Ⓐ Ⓑ Ⓒ Ⓓ	59. Ⓐ Ⓑ Ⓒ Ⓓ	79. Ⓐ Ⓑ Ⓒ Ⓓ	99. Ⓐ Ⓑ Ⓒ Ⓓ
20. Ⓐ Ⓑ Ⓒ Ⓓ	40. Ⓐ Ⓑ Ⓒ Ⓓ	60. Ⓐ Ⓑ Ⓒ Ⓓ	80. Ⓐ Ⓑ Ⓒ Ⓓ	100. Ⓐ Ⓑ Ⓒ Ⓓ

answer sheet

Practice Test 2

100 Questions • 3 Hours

Directions: Read each question carefully and mark the letter of the best answer on the answer sheet.

1. The four unities that must be fulfilled in a joint tenancy are unity of time, title, possession, and
   (A) place.
   (B) balance.
   (C) purpose.
   (D) interest.

2. All of the following are ways that the Truth-in-Lending Act is implemented EXCEPT
   (A) RESPA.
   (B) Good Faith Estimate.
   (C) Regulation Z.
   (D) Statute of Frauds.

3. Bob Kiley has been living in a shack in the woods on the Allens' property for 15 years with their consent, but without paying rent. When both Allens die, their heirs want to evict Kiley. He claims the property is his because of
   (A) assumption.
   (B) assignment.
   (C) escheat.
   (D) adverse possession.

4. Sam Lawrence recommends that his clients use Premier Painting Company whenever a property needs painting before putting it on the market. Lawrence receives a fee from the painting company for each job that he refers. This is known as a
   (A) transfer fee.
   (B) kickback.
   (C) logrolling.
   (D) bandwagon.

5. A utility company might have which kind of encumbrance on a property?
   (A) Easement by prescription
   (B) Easement in gross
   (C) Mechanic's lien
   (D) Easement by necessity

6. A contract made with someone who is mentally ill is a
   (A) voidable contract.
   (B) valid, but unenforceable contract.
   (C) void contract.
   (D) voidable, but enforceable contract.

7. The commission on a property that sells for $435,000 is $19,575. What is the rate of commission?
   (A) 0.035
   (B) 0.045
   (C) 0.055
   (D) 0.065

8. How much is the interest on a 10-year loan of $55,000 at 12.25%?

   (A) $673.75

   (B) $67,375

   (C) $6,737.50

   (D) $673,750

9. Which of the following is NOT part of a metes and bounds legal property description?

   (A) Distance

   (B) Baseline

   (C) Point of beginning

   (D) Direction

10. Sharon Macy and Ben Porter are buying a house together before they get married and ask their realtor what type of ownership they should agree to. The realtor should tell them

   (A) to check their state's real estate laws to see if they can use tenancy in entirety.

   (B) that the best option is to be listed as domestic partners.

   (C) to check with an attorney.

   (D) that the best option is to be listed as a partnership.

11. Lisa Thuc signed listing agreements with both the Tyler Real Estate Agency and Booth Realtors to sell her co-op. Sutton has what kind of listing with the brokers?

   (A) MLS

   (B) Net listing

   (C) Dual agency

   (D) Open listing

12. The option to purchase gives the buyer

   (A) the right to purchase a particular property.

   (B) the obligation to a purchase a particular property.

   (C) the right and the obligation to purchase a particular property.

   (D) a specified time during which the buyer and seller can work out terms to purchase a particular property.

13. The basis of the income approach in valuing a property is the principle of

   (A) conformity.

   (B) contribution.

   (C) anticipation.

   (D) substitution.

14. At closing who pays the discount points on the mortgage loan?

   (A) Buyer

   (B) Seller

   (C) Buyer or seller, depending on how the sale contract is negotiated

   (D) No points are paid at closing; they wrap into the mortgage

15. The liquidation of a debt is known as

   (A) amortization.

   (B) depreciation.

   (C) rescission.

   (D) seisin.

16. Which of the following types of mortgages have priority in order of repayment?

   (A) 20 percent loan in an 80/20 mortgage

   (B) Largest mortgage amount

   (C) First mortgage to be recorded

   (D) Back taxes

17. Which of the following statements is true about tenancy in common?

    (A) Tenancy in common requires that ownership be split 50/50.

    (B) Tenancy in common is the most frequent form of joint ownership.

    (C) A person who owns property in tenancy in common may not mortgage his or her interest without the consent of the other party or parties.

    (D) Tenancy in common confers the right of survivorship.

18. An example of functional obsolescence is

    (A) one bathroom in a three-bedroom house.

    (B) a crack in the basement floor.

    (C) the lack of a built-in barbecue in the backyard.

    (D) white wall paint in all the rooms.

19. The URAR is used to appraise a

    (A) single-family residence.

    (B) condominium.

    (C) co-op unit.

    (D) commercial property other than residential rentals.

20. Which of the following is NOT part of a legal description of real property?

    (A) Monument description of the property

    (B) Street address of the property

    (C) Lot and block system

    (D) Metes and bounds system

21. The Krasners have just bought a home for $550,000. This is the home's

    (A) market value.

    (B) appraised value.

    (C) value in use.

    (D) assessed value.

22. If the tax rate is 22 mills for the township and 29 mills for the school district, what are the taxes on a property worth $75,000 assessed at 67% of value?

    (A) $351.75

    (B) $1,105.50

    (C) $1,457.25

    (D) $2,562.75

23. To manage property, a person

    (A) must be a certified property manager.

    (B) must be a licensed real estate agent or broker.

    (C) need not be licensed.

    (D) must at the least be working toward a license.

24. Which of the following questions is one of the tests of whether something is a fixture?

    (A) How is the item attached?

    (B) Who attached the item?

    (C) Can the item be removed?

    (D) How long has the item been attached?

25. Why are deeds recorded after closings?

    (A) As the final step in filing title insurance

    (B) As part of the mortgage process

    (C) To give public notice that the title has passed

    (D) As the final step in passing title from seller to buyer

26. Sarah Mayfield, the owner of the Sally Mae Shop, signs a lease with Shepherd Realty to rent a storefront. Sarah must pay utilities and real estate taxes. She has probably signed a

    (A) percentage lease.

    (B) net lease.

    (C) double net lease.

    (D) gross lease.

27. The Thomases are selling their condo. They have been going back and forth in negotiations with Brad Morse. Brad has rejected the latest counteroffer and decided to walk away. The Thomases

    (A) can attempt to restart the negotiations by making a new, lower offer.

    (B) can accept the last counteroffer from Brad prior to their counteroffer.

    (C) can take their counteroffer off the table.

    (D) have no action they can take.

28. The local barbershop sold on March 12. If the quarterly taxes of $456.84 have not yet been paid, how much is the buyer owed by the seller?

    (A) $153.28

    (B) $304.56

    (C) $360.40

    (D) $456.84

29. A valid deed has which of the following characteristics?

    (A) *Habendum* clause

    (B) Mutual agreement

    (C) Warranty

    (D) Legal purpose

30. A listing agreement can be terminated by all of the following EXCEPT

    (A) revocation.

    (B) bankruptcy.

    (C) remainderment.

    (D) eminent domain.

31. A Phase II environmental inspection includes

    (A) history of the property.

    (B) actual cleanup of primary contaminants.

    (C) sampling and analysis of the site.

    (D) site management plan.

32. The federal government wants to build a dam on the Sawtooth River. Before the Army Corps of Engineers can proceed, what must they file?

    (A) List of endangered species on the site

    (B) Two alternative building plans

    (C) Environmental impact statement

    (D) Environmental rehabilitation plan

33. Which of the following is discrimination on the basis of familial status?

    (A) Refusal to rent to a husband and wife over 60

    (B) Refusal to rent to a Korean husband and wife

    (C) Refusal to rent to an African American husband and wife and the man's mother

    (D) Refusal to rent to a gay couple with two-year-old twins

34. First National Bank provides the Jamars with a mortgage to buy their house. At the closing, the Jamars sign the mortgage and the

    (A) note.

    (B) title.

    (C) deed.

    (D) commission check to the broker.

35. The straight-line method of measuring depreciation is best used to measure

    (A) physical deterioration.

    (B) functional obsolescence.

    (C) economic obsolescence.

    (D) external obsolescence.

36. The Hamids have bought several plots of land from different owners in order to create a lot large enough for the 10,000 square foot home they intend to build. The process of combining lots is known as

    (A) best use.

    (B) plottage.

    (C) plat.

    (D) special use.

37. Which of the following is NOT required in a listing agreement?

    (A) Price

    (B) Signature of the broker

    (C) Commission

    (D) Form of termination

38. The use of a property that predates zoning that would make the use illegal is known as

    (A) conditional use.

    (B) nonconforming use.

    (C) nonconventional use.

    (D) accessory use.

39. Gus Gryzinski bought his house in 1989 for $84,927, and sold it in 2009 for $113,908. Did the house appreciate or depreciate and by how much?

    (A) Depreciate by $198,835

    (B) Depreciate by $28,981

    (C) Appreciate by $28,981

    (D) Appreciate by $198,835

40. The distinguishing characteristic of fraud is

    (A) unknowing ignorance of the facts.

    (B) failure to learn about the property being shown.

    (C) intent to deceive.

    (D) imparting mistaken information.

41. The effective rate of a loan including costs and fees is its

    (A) APR.

    (B) APY.

    (C) API.

    (D) APAR.

42. Which of the following statements is NOT true about dual agency?

    (A) Conflict of interest is inherent in a dual agency arrangement.

    (B) In a dual agency, one broker or agent represents both parties in a real estate sale.

    (C) Dual agency is legal in all 50 states.

    (D) Dual agency must be disclosed to both parties in a real estate sale.

43. Obedience, loyalty, confidentiality, and honest accounting are known as what kind of duties of the agent to the principal?

    (A) Fiduciary

    (B) Agency

    (C) Transactional

    (D) Bundle

44. Julie Handser is interested in a Cape-Cod-style house that is comparable in every way to a Cape Cod that sold up the street last month, except that the comparable has a full finished basement, and the one she is interested in has a 25% finished basement. If a full finished basement is worth $17,900 and the comp sold for $231,000, what is the value of the house Julie is considering buying?

    (A) $217,575

    (B) $213,100

    (C) $247,575

    (D) $244,425

45. Marty Chu signs an exclusive agency listing with Morgan Realty. Marty then sells his property himself to someone who did not learn about it through Morgan Realty. Does Marty have to pay a commission to Morgan Realty?

(A) Yes, because he listed the property with Morgan Realty.

(B) Yes, but it's only 50 percent of the agreed-upon commission.

(C) No, because under an exclusive agreement, the realtor only gets a commission if the realtor sells the property.

(D) Only if Marty sold the property for more than he listed it with Morgan.

46. The cost approach to property appraisal includes

(A) the value of the land plus the cost to build the improvements (new), less depreciation of the improvements.

(B) the value of the land plus the cost to build the improvements (new), less appreciation of the improvements.

(C) the value of the land, less depreciation of the improvements.

(D) the value of the land plus the cost to build the improvements (originally), less depreciation.

47. An appraiser is valuing a townhouse with a new tile kitchen floor and all new stainless steel appliances. It has two bedrooms, a loft, and a fireplace. He found a comp that has the same floor plan, but the kitchen floor is 20-year-old linoleum and the appliances are also 20 years old. The appraiser will need to

(A) discard this comp and find one with the same value as the subject property.

(B) adjust the value of the comp upward.

(C) adjust the value of the subject house downward.

(D) adjust the value of the subject house downward and the value of the comp upward to fall within a certain range.

48. Olive's Organic Food Store is moving to a new site. Olive wants to take her shelving and counters with her. Her landlord has told her that she can't. Who is right?

(A) Olive, because she paid for the improvements

(B) The landlord, because these are now attached to the property and are, therefore, fixtures

(C) Olive, because she signed a commercial lease and under the lease, the fixtures can be removed and the premises returned to the original condition

(D) The landlord, because removing them will increase the wear and tear on the property

49. The typical relationship between a listing agent and a seller is a/an

(A) universal agency.

(B) agency with interest.

(C) special agency.

(D) general agency.

50. Tony Willow owns a triangular plot of land across the street from the park. He paid $324,000 for his lot. If it has frontage of 173' and a depth of 86', how much did he pay per square foot and how many acres does he own?

(A) $45.97 per square foot; $\frac{1}{3}$ of an acre

(B) $7.44 per square foot; $\frac{1}{3}$ of an acre

(C) $7.44 per square foot; $\frac{1}{6}$ of an acre

(D) $45.97 per square foot; $\frac{1}{6}$ of an acre

51. The Hamers, an African American couple who are interested in buying their first home, are being shown predominantly African American neighborhoods by their realtor. This practice is known as

    (A) blockbusting.

    (B) steering.

    (C) redlining.

    (D) curtailment.

52. A cloud on a title can be removed by

    (A) a quitclaim deed.

    (B) title insurance.

    (C) a special warranty.

    (D) judicial warranty.

53. An executory contract is a/an

    (A) sales contract used by an executor in selling an estate.

    (B) contract in which the obligation is in the future.

    (C) contract used in an eminent domain proceeding.

    (D) employment contract between a property management company and a real estate holding company.

54. The assessed value of the Reynolds' home is $340,000, or 85 percent of the market value. Their yearly property taxes are approximately $4,760. How much does this add to their monthly mortgage payment?

    (A) $3.96

    (B) $39.96

    (C) $396.67

    (D) There is not enough information to answer the question.

55. What is the market value of the Reynolds' home if the assessed value, $340,000, is 85 percent of the value?

    (A) $289,000

    (B) $391,000

    (C) $400,000

    (D) $629,000

56. An ARM may have all of the following features EXCEPT

    (A) interest rate adjustment cap.

    (B) life of loan interest rate adjustment cap.

    (C) periodic interest rate change.

    (D) recalculation of the principal periodically.

57. On the sale of Jon Restive's farmhouse, the saleswoman and the broker split the commission. If the house sold for $239,700 with a 5.75% commission and the broker receives 60% of the commission, how much is the saleswoman's commission?

    (A) $549.70

    (B) $5,497

    (C) $8,245.50

    (D) $13,742.50

58. The loss of real property as a result of the breach of a sales contract by a buyer is known as

    (A) foreclosure.

    (B) forfeiture.

    (C) default.

    (D) renunciation.

59. The process that uses an abstract of title ends with

    (A) the issuance of a deed.

    (B) a certificate of title being issued.

    (C) an attorney's opinion of title.

    (D) issuance of a certificate of Torrens.

60. Which of the following deed restrictions in a mixed-use PUD would be unenforceable?

    (A) Building height

    (B) Type of business

    (C) Religious affiliation

    (D) Lot size

61. Mark Neri is an experienced realtor and always qualifies potential buyers, which means that he asks

    (A) about their educational background and jobs.

    (B) about their financial situation.

    (C) why they want to buy.

    (D) where they want to buy and for how much.

62. Which of the following gives a property owner shares in the underlying corporation?

    (A) Townhome

    (B) Condo

    (C) PUD

    (D) Co-op

63. If the interest for 3 months on a loan of $92,000 was $2,300, what is the rate of interest on the loan per year?

    (A) 12%

    (B) 1%

    (C) 10%

    (D) 8%

64. Which of the following is a leasehold estate?

    (A) Estate for years

    (B) Life estate *pur autre vie*

    (C) Qualified fee determinable

    (D) Defeasible estate

65. Riparian rights refer to the rights of

    (A) those who own property along rivers and streams.

    (B) those who own beachfront and lake-front property.

    (C) commercial fishermen to fish within the 12-mile offshore limit.

    (D) shore communities to zone beach-front property.

66. Zoning ordinances typically deal with all of the following elements EXCEPT

    (A) number of rooms.

    (B) setback.

    (C) number of floors.

    (D) square footage.

67. The contract of sale may include a clause that the seller will remedy any pest infestation should an inspection find one and provide proof to the buyer, or the buyer may end the contract and receive the deposit money back. This is known as a/an

    (A) inclusion.

    (B) contingency.

    (C) condition of sale.

    (D) restriction.

68. An 80% of value loan was made on a house with an appraised value of $132,000. The annual rate of interest is 4.38%. How much interest will be paid in 6 months?

    (A) $2,312.64

    (B) $23,126.40

    (C) $4,625.28

    (D) $2,890.80

69. Which of the following is a social factor that influences housing values?

    (A) Corner influence

    (B) Local economy

    (C) Proximity to the subway

    (D) Type of restaurants and shops

70. Which of the following statements is NOT true about an ordinary life estate?

    (A) Death can terminate an ordinary life estate.

    (B) An ordinary life estate can be leased to another party.

    (C) An ordinary life estate can be sold, but not mortgaged.

    (D) An ordinary life estate cannot be willed to another person.

71. The Good Faith Estimate must contain the amount of all of the following EXCEPT

    (A) loan discount points.

    (B) property taxes—city and county.

    (C) appraisal fee.

    (D) realtor's commission.

72. PMI is not necessary if the buyer

    (A) puts down 10 percent of the purchase price and has a fixed rate mortgage.

    (B) finances no more than 80 percent of the purchase price.

    (C) is making monthly payments that are less than 28 percent of the buyer's income.

    (D) has a credit score of at least 700.

73. If a property on Main Street is valued at $1,342,900, and is assessed at 73% for tax purposes, what is its taxable value?

    (A) $98,031.70

    (B) $980,317

    (C) $9,803 170

    (D) $9,803.17

74. With a straight-term mortgage, the mortgagor pays

    (A) the loan off in regular installments over the term of the mortgage.

    (B) interest only on the mortgage over the term of the mortgage.

    (C) the mortgage off early without incurring a prepayment penalty.

    (D) a fixed monthly payment for a period of years and then adjusted rates for a period of years.

75. The Dinhs bought a home 20 years ago. The value of the property has increased from $152,000 to $312,000. The difference between the purchase price and the current price less the remaining mortgage is known as

    (A) equitable title.

    (B) dividend.

    (C) equity.

    (D) investment value.

76. Which of the following people is NOT part of a protected class under the Fair Housing Act?

    (A) A person with an IQ of 65

    (B) A person with cerebral palsy

    (C) An active heroin addict

    (D) An active alcoholic

77. Some states require that real estate sales contracts be in writing because of the state's

    (A) Statute of Frauds.

    (B) Statute of Delivery.

    (C) Real Estate Commission regulations.

    (D) Statute of Liability.

78. According to the Truth in Lending Act, all of the following must be disclosed to a borrower EXCEPT

    (A) annual percentage rate.

    (B) amount of finance charges.

    (C) prepayment penalties.

    (D) credit score.

79. Which of the following is true about VA-guaranteed mortgages?

(A) The mortgagor must be on active duty.

(B) The mortgagor will not have to pay monthly mortgage insurance.

(C) The mortgagor must put down at least 10 percent.

(D) The mortgagor will have to pay a prepayment penalty if the mortgage is paid off early.

80. A townhouse sold on August 10 for $123,000. A 3-year insurance policy premium of $751 was paid on June 1 of the previous year. What money, if any, is owed to the seller?

(A) $451.87

(B) $0.00

(C) $299.13

(D) $345.91

QUESTIONS 81 TO 83 REFER TO THE FOLLOWING MAP.

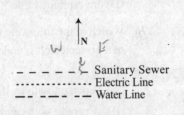

- - - - - - Sanitary Sewer
················· Electric Line
— - —- - — Water Line

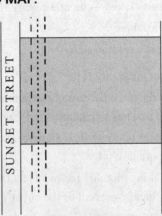

81. Which of the following describes the highlighted property on the map?

(A) A parcel that fronts Sunset Drive and is 150 feet on the west, 92 feet on the north, 150 feet on the east, and 82 feet on the south.

(B) A parcel located on Sunset Drive at the point of beginning, thence N 0°0'0" W 150 feet, thence N 90°0'0" E 92 feet, thence S 15°30'4" W 150 feet, to the point of beginning.

(C) A parcel located on Sunset Drive at the point of beginning, thence N 0°0'0" W 150 feet, thence N 90°0'0" E 92 feet, thence S 15°30'4" W 150 feet, thence N 90°0'0" W 82 feet to the point of beginning.

(D) A parcel located on Sunset Drive at the point of beginning, thence N 0°0'0" W 150 feet, thence S 90°0'0" E 92 feet, thence S 15°30'4" W 150 feet, thence N 90°0'0" E 82 feet to the point of beginning.

82. Which of the following is shown as an easement on the map?

(A) Cable line

(B) Gas line

(C) Storm sewer

(D) Sanitary sewer

83. The type of property description used in Question 81 is
   (A) monument.
   (B) lot and block.
   (C) rectangular survey system.
   (D) metes and bounds.

84. The Wibles' lot is 82 feet wide. The side yard setbacks must be a minimum of 10 feet on each side and must total at least 25 feet for both side yards. What is the maximum width that the Wibles' planned house can be before they need to request a variance?
   (A) 57 feet
   (B) 62 feet
   (C) 67 feet
   (D) 72 feet

85. What kind of variance would the Wibles need to apply for if their side yard setbacks are too narrow?
   (A) Use
   (B) Special permit
   (C) Conforming
   (D) Area

86. If Bernadette Capelli sold her house for $748,231, and she bought it for $347,295 fifteen years ago, what is the rate of appreciation per year?
   (A) $400,936
   (B) $40,936
   (C) 8%
   (D) 1.15

87. The Merwins and the Lloyds buy several townhouses together as rental properties with tenancy in common as the form of ownership. The Lloyds divorce, and Sara Lloyd sells her interest in the townhouses to a third party. Can she do this?
   (A) Yes, because tenancy in common allows a co-owner to sell his or her interest.
   (B) Yes, if she made it a provision of her divorce settlement.
   (C) Yes, but only if she lived in a community property state.
   (D) Yes, if she obtained the agreement of her ex-husband and the Merwins.

88. Constructive eviction occurs when
   (A) a landlord removes a tenant who refuses to leave the premises at the expiration of the lease.
   (B) a landlord neglects the premises so badly that it becomes uninhabitable.
   (C) a landlord expels a tenant who has complained to the authorities about the landlord's neglect of the premises.
   (D) a building has been damaged through no fault of the tenant or landlord and the tenant has to move because of renovation or rebuilding.

89. Builders are the best source of which kind of data that appraisers need?
   (A) Costs
   (B) Taxes
   (C) Market value
   (D) Real estate closings

90. Gerald and Shirley Basile have donated their property to the Bronx Zoo so long as the Zoo uses the property as a wildlife center. The Bronx Zoo has what kind of interest in the Basiles' property?

    (A) Estate at will

    (B) Testate

    (C) Estate at sufferance

    (D) Determinable

91. A colonial style house in Newmarket just sold for $465,380. It has 5 bedrooms and 3.5 bathrooms and is 2,740 square feet. A similar colonial is for sale in Newmarket with 5 bedrooms and 3.5 bathrooms and 2,846 square feet in size. What is its value?

    (A) $465,380

    (B) $483,393

    (C) $465,549

    (D) $479,424

92. In using the sales comparison approach to valuing a property in a typical market, an appraiser would not consider the sale of a comparable property a reliable market indicator if it took place more than a

    (A) month ago.

    (B) sixty days ago.

    (C) ninety days ago.

    (D) six months ago.

93. Insurable value of a property is the same as its

    (A) assessed value.

    (B) appraised value.

    (C) reimbursement value.

    (D) market value.

94. A jumbo mortgage is

    (A) another name for an 80/20 mortgage.

    (B) a mortgage that is larger than the limit to qualify for a government-insured low-interest loan.

    (C) a package of loans sold on the secondary mortgage market.

    (D) another name for a wraparound mortgage.

95. Calculate the taxes on a 90' by 363' property that sells for $17,500 an acre, if the assessed value is 63% and the tax rate is $4.30 per hundred of value?

    (A) $394.82

    (B) $463.89

    (C) $564.37

    (D) $355.56

96. Which of the following situations would be exempt under the provisions of the Fair Housing Act?

    (A) A landlord renting an apartment in a four-unit building

    (B) A FSBO property

    (C) A developer selling townhouses in a PUD

    (D) Nuns who run an assisted living facility for the elderly and accept public funding

97. The Forman father-and-son clothing business needs to sell its storefront property to satisfy its creditors. This is known as a

    (A) forfeiture sale.

    (B) liquidation sale.

    (C) tax sale.

    (D) foreclosure.

98. Why is the Truth-in-Lending Act important to homebuyers?

    (A) It details how the Good Faith Estimate is to be calculated.

    (B) It specifies how the amortization rate on a mortgage should be calculated.

    (C) It spells out how the annual percentage rate of a loan should be calculated and stated in loan documents.

    (D) It established an agency to supervise mortgage lenders.

99. A deed that has no warranty included in it is a

(A) unencumbered deed.

(B) quitclaim deed.

(C) sheriff's deed.

(D) referee's deed in foreclosure.

100. Worn, dirty carpet would be considered in an appraisal as

(A) an incurable functional obsolescence.

(B) a curable physical deterioration.

(C) an incurable economic obsolescence.

(D) a curable functional obsolescence.

practice test

ANSWER KEY AND EXPLANATIONS

1. D	21. A	41. A	61. B	81. C
2. D	22. D	42. C	62. D	82. D
3. D	23. B	43. A	63. C	83. D
4. B	24. A	44. A	64. A	84. C
5. B	25. C	45. C	65. A	85. D
6. C	26. B	46. A	66. A	86. C
7. B	27. A	47. B	67. B	87. A
8. B	28. C	48. C	68. A	88. B
9. B	29. A	49. C	69. D	89. A
10. C	30. C	50. D	70. C	90. D
11. D	31. C	51. B	71. D	91. B
12. A	32. C	52. A	72. B	92. D
13. C	33. D	53. B	73. B	93. C
14. C	34. A	54. C	74. B	94. B
15. A	35. A	55. C	75. C	95. D
16. C	36. B	56. D	76. C	96. B
17. B	37. D	57. B	77. A	97. B
18. A	38. B	58. B	78. D	98. C
19. A	39. C	59. C	79. B	99. B
20. B	40. C	60. C	80. A	100. B

1. **The correct answer is (D).** Because each joint tenant owns the whole thing at the same time, each has exactly the same interest. Choice (A) is incorrect, but place may seem correct considering the subject is real estate. Choice (B) may also seem correct because a joint tenancy sets up a balance among partners, but it's not one of the four unities. Choice (C) is probably implied when two or more individuals establish a joint tenancy, but sameness of purpose is not one of the four unities.

2. **The correct answer is (D).** Choice (A) stands for Real Estate Settlement Procedures Act. In 2009, a new RESPA form was published that mandates and implements truth-in-lending disclosures right on the form and dictates by how much the estimates may be off. Choice (B) is mandated by Regulation Z, choice (C), which is the major implementer of the Truth-in-Lending Act. RESPA mandates that the GFE be given to buyers who are purchasing homes under FHA guidelines. Choice (D) is a state law and varies from state to state, but deals with contracts.

3. **The correct answer is (D).** Choice (A) is incorrect because it refers to taking over the interest in something like a lease or a mortgage with the permission of the landlord in the first instance and the mortgagee in the second instance. The same is true of choice (B). The person who assumes the lease or mortgage or to whom the lease or mortgage is assigned agrees to abide by all requirements of the original document. Choice (C) is incorrect because it occurs when a person dies without a will or heirs, and the state takes over the property.

4. **The correct answer is (B).** Kickbacks are illegal. Choice (A) is incorrect because this is a fee that the seller pays at closing to record the transfer of the title and deed to the buyer. Choice (C) is incorrect because it is the trading of favors by politicians. Choice (D) is incorrect because it refers to a propaganda technique.

5. **The correct answer is (B).** Choice (A) is an easement that is created from an open use of another's property over a period of time without the person's consent or dissent. Choice (C) is a lien against a property by someone who did work for the owner and was not paid. Choice (D) is a court-ordered right-of-way through a neighbor's property.

6. **The correct answer is (C).** A person who is mentally ill cannot enter into a valid, enforceable contract. It is void. Choices (A), (B), and (D) are incorrect.

7. **The correct answer is (B).** $19,575 ÷ $435,000 = 0.045

8. **The correct answer is (B).** $55,000 × 0.1225 × 10 = $67,375

9. **The correct answer is (B).** Choices (A), (C), and (D) are used in metes and bounds descriptions, so they are not the correct answer to the question. Choice (B) is a point of reference in the rectangular survey system, so it is the correct answer to the question.

10. **The correct answer is (C).** Choice (C) is the best answer because it protects both the realtor and the clients. Only lawyers can practice law in any state.

11. **The correct answer is (D).** Choice (A) is a service shared by a group of brokers in an area, but it is not an agreement between a seller and a broker. Choice (B) is a listing in which the amount of the broker's commission, if there is one, depends on how much the property sells for over the price that the seller wants. Choice (C) occurs when a salesperson represents both the seller and the buyer.

12. **The correct answer is (A).** Choice (B) is incorrect because an option to purchase does not confer an obligation on the buyer according to the terms of the option. Choice (C) is incorrect because it includes the incorrect answer, an obligation to purchase. Choice (D) is incorrect because the terms of the purchase are already worked out and part of the option to purchase.

13. **The correct answer is (C).** How much future benefit may come to the owner, choice (C), is the basis of the income approach. Choice (A) is the principle that states that the value of a property is impacted by its similarities to its neighbors. Choice (B) is incorrect because it states that value is determined by the market, not by the cost. Choice (D) is incorrect because this principle states that a buyer will not pay more for a property than the cheapest of all possibilities that meet the buyer's requirements.

14. **The correct answer is (C).** Who pays the points, which must be paid in cash at the closing, is determined when the sales contract is negotiated; therefore, choices (A), (B), and (D) are incorrect. Note that, typically,

it's the buyer who pays them because it's the buyer's mortgage.

15. **The correct answer is (A).** Choice (B) is incorrect because it is a reduction in value. Choice (C) is incorrect because it is the unwinding of a transaction, which isn't the same as retiring a debt. Choice (D) is incorrect because the actual term is "covenant of seisin," which guarantees that the grantor has the right to convey the property that is being transferred.

16. **The correct answer is (C).** Choice (D) is a distracter because it is paid before any other lien on a property, but the question asks about types of mortgages, not about all liens. Choices (A) and (B) are incorrect because amount has no bearing on the order of priority for repayment of liens.

17. **The correct answer is (B).** Choices (A), (C), and (D) are incorrect because they are the opposite of what is true about the rights conferred by tenancy in common.

18. **The correct answer is (A).** Choice (B) is incorrect because it is an example of economic obsolescence. Choice (C) may be someone's wish, but wouldn't qualify as functional obsolescence. The same is true for choice (D).

19. **The correct answer is (A).** URAR stands for Uniform Residential Appraisal Report and is required for FHA loan guarantees. Choices (B) and (C) are incorrect because other forms are used for applying for FHA-insured loans for these types of residences. The report also doesn't apply for choice (D).

20. **The correct answer is (B).** Choices (A), (C), and (D) provide legal descriptions of property, so they are incorrect answers to the question. Choice (B) does not provide a legal description, so it is the correct answer to the question.

21. **The correct answer is (A).** Choice (B) may or may not be the same as the market value, but the sale price reflects a property's market value. Choice (C) is incorrect because this is the value of a property used for a particular purpose for a business. It is the opposite of market value, which is based on all possible uses for a property. Choice (D) is incorrect because this is the value put on a property by a unit of government for purposes of taxation.

22. **The correct answer is (D).**

    $75,000 \times 0.67 = $50,250$

    $22 + 29 = 51$ mils

    $50,250 \times 0.051 = $2,565.75$

23. **The correct answer is (B).** Property managers with the exception of resident property managers must be licensed. Choice (A) doesn't exist. Choice (C) is incorrect because it is the opposite of what is true. Choice (D) is incorrect because a property manager must already be licensed as a real estate agent or broker.

24. **The correct answer is (A).** Choices (B), (C), and (D) all seem like logical questions that might be asked, but they are incorrect. The other three questions are: What did the person who attached the item intend? Is there a contract stating what is considered real property and what is personal property? What is the relationship of parties?

25. **The correct answer is (C).** Choice (A) is incorrect because payment of the fee for title insurance is the final step in buying title insurance. Choice (B) is incorrect because recording the deed is not part of the mortgage process. Choice (D) is incorrect because the title is passed at the closing when the deed is signed over by the seller.

26. **The correct answer is (B).** Choice (C) would include more than just utilities and

real estate taxes; it might also include repair and maintenance to the building. Choice (A) is incorrect because Sarah would pay the utilities and a percentage of the gross sales of her business. Choice (D) is incorrect because Sarah would pay only the utilities, if even those.

27. **The correct answer is (A).** Once a counteroffer is on the table, it takes precedence over any earlier offer or counteroffer. It is as if the earlier offer did not exist; the transaction is legally dead. This makes choices (B) and (C) incorrect. However, they can take some action, choice (A), so choice (D) is incorrect. Remember that as long as offers and counteroffers are going back and forth, either side can compel the other to act by saying, "yes." If the buyer says "yes," the seller would have to sell to the buyer at that price. If the seller says "yes" to the buyer's counteroffer, the buyer would have to buy at that price. Once Brad rejects without making a counteroffer, there is no acceptance or offer, and the transaction is over. The Thomases can sell to someone else, or start the process over again with Brad by making another offer at a lower price. Brad doesn't have to do anything. He can say nothing to the offer or "yes" or "no," or make a counteroffer.

28. **The correct answer is (C).**

    $456.84 ÷ 3 = $152.28

    $152.28 ÷ 30 = $5.07

    $152.28 × 2 = $304.56

    $5.07 × 11 = $55.84

    $304.56 + $55.84 = $360.40

29. **The correct answer is (A).** Choices (B) and (D) are incorrect because they are characteristics of a valid contract. Choice (C) is incorrect because while warranties of various types are found in deeds, a warranty is not necessary in order to make a deed valid.

30. **The correct answer is (C).** Choices (A), (B), and (D) can all result in termination of a listing agreement, so they can't be the correct answer. Choice (C) is not a method for terminating a listing agreement, but is related to life estates, so it is the correct answer to the question.

31. **The correct answer is (C).** Choice (A) is incorrect because it is completed in Phase I. Choice (B) sounds very impressive but the actual cleanup of all contaminants—not just primary ones—occurs in Phase III, if possible. If cleanup is not possible, then Phase IV commences and the environmental experts write a site management plan to control the contaminants.

32. **The correct answer is (C).** You're looking for the best answer, and here it is choice (C). An EIS may list the endangered species on the site, choice (A), but that's not all that it discusses. Choice (B) is going in the right direction by talking about alternatives, but the EIS discusses alternatives that were considered and discarded and the why. Choice (D) may be part of an EIS, but it's not the best answer to the question. Only choice (C) is the most complete answer.

33. **The correct answer is (D).** Choice (D) may also be discrimination based on sex, but refusal to rent to a couple with children under 18 is discrimination on the basis of familial status. Choice (A) is age discrimination. Choices (B) and (C) are discrimination on the basis of national origin.

34. **The correct answer is (A).** Choices (B), (C), and (D) are incorrect because the seller signs the note and the deed, and the buyer's attorney typically signs the checks. Remember that a title to real property is a concept, not a document like a car title.

35. **The correct answer is (A).** Straight-line depreciation is considered most reliable

in measuring physical deterioration. This method is also called economic age-life. Choice (C) is a distracter; it's meant to sound familiar. Choices (B) and (D) are incorrect.

36. **The correct answer is (B).** Choice (A) is part of the phrase "highest and best use" and refers to an economic factor considered in appraising property. Choice (C) is a distracter; plat is a lot or plot of land as well as a map or plan. Choice (D) is incorrect because it's part of the phrase "special use permit," a type of zoning variance.

37. **The correct answer is (D).** Choices (A), (B), and (C) are required on a listing agreement, but choice (D) is not, so it is the correct answer to the question.

38. **The correct answer is (B).** Choice (A) is incorrect because it is the same as a special use permit, which requests a variance in order to introduce a use for which an area is not zoned. Choice (C) is a distracter; it sounds like a good idea, but it is meant to confuse. Choice (D) is a use that is incidental or subordinate to the primary use of the property.

39. **The correct answer is (C).** The house appreciates by $113,908 – $84,927 = $28,981

40. **The correct answer is (C).** Intent to deceive is the distinguishing characteristic of fraud. Choice (A) is innocent misrepresentation. Choice (B) may be simply a realtor's lack of compliance with the reasonable care and diligence fiduciary duty or a realtor's innocent misrepresentation. Choice (D) is negligent misrepresentation. Remember, however, that if a realtor commits any of these with the intent to deceive, it's fraud.

41. **The correct answer is (A).** Choice (A) stands for annual percentage rate, which is the true cost of the loan, containing all the charges and fees. Choice (B) stands for annual percentage yield, which is the total

interest earned on an investment. Choices (C) and (D) are distracters.

42. **The correct answer is (C).** Choices (A), (B), and (D) are true statements about dual agency, so they are incorrect answers to the question. Only choice (C) is not true, so it is the correct answer to the question. Dual agency is actually illegal in some states.

43. **The correct answer is (A).** The full list of fiduciary responsibilities are (1) loyalty, (2) obedience, (3) disclosure, (4) confidentiality, (5) reasonable care and diligence, and (6) accountability (honest accounting). Choices (B), (C), and (D) are distracters because each in some form is related to real estate. Choice (B) is the relationship between broker/agent and principal. Choice (C) is a form of brokerage. Choice (D) refers to the bundle of rights conferred with ownership or tenancy of property.

44. **The correct answer is (A).**

    $17,900 × 0.75 = $13,425

    $231,000 – $13,425 = $217,575

45. **The correct answer is (C).** Choice (A) is incorrect. Choice (B) may seem familiar because of the 50 percent, but it's incorrect. Choice (D) may also seem familiar because it describes a net listing, but that's not what Marty and Morgan Realty signed, so it's incorrect.

46. **The correct answer is (A).** Choice (B) is incorrect because improvements depreciate; everything but commodities and fine art depreciates. Choice (C) omits part of the process—estimating the reproduction or replacement cost of building the improvements. Choice (D) is incorrect because the appraiser must estimate the reproduction or replacement cost, not the original cost of the improvements.

47. **The correct answer is (B).** Choice (A) is incorrect because it would be impossible for an appraiser to find six comps in the right location and having sold within the last six months all at the same price. That's why appraisers come up with a range of prices for the six comps. Choice (C) is incorrect because the value of the subject property is never adjusted; that's the unknown that the appraiser is looking for—and another reason that choice (A) is incorrect. The appraiser doesn't know the value of the subject property until the appraisal is done. Choice (D) is incorrect because the value of the subject price isn't adjusted.

48. **The correct answer is (C).** Olive may have paid for the improvements, choice (A), but this does not give her a legal right in this instance for taking the shelving and counters. The type of lease that she signed, choice (C), does. Choice (B) might have given the landlord a case if he hadn't signed a commercial lease. Choice (D) is a distracter because of the "wear and tear" clause typically in leases—and after Olive removes the shelving and counters, she must return the premises to its original condition, which means repairing any damage that the counters and shelves caused while standing and while being removed.

49. **The correct answer is (C).** Choice (A) is incorrect because a listing agreement does not give the agent the broadest powers to act for the seller; the power is limited to listing and selling the property. Choice (B) is incorrect because this is an agency in which the agent has an interest in the property covered by the agreement. Choice (D) is incorrect because the listing agreement doesn't give the agent the power to act in a variety of activities for the seller; the powers of general agency are more limited than those of a universal agency, but broader than a special agency.

50. **The correct answer is (D).**

$$\frac{1}{2} \times 173' \times 86' = 7,439$$

$$7,439 \div 43,560 = 0.17, \text{ or } 1/6 \text{ of an acre}$$

$$\$342,000 \div 7,439 = \$45.97$$

51. **The correct answer is (B).** Choice (A) is urging people to sell their property by scaring them into thinking that certain groups are moving into the neighborhood; it is illegal. Choice (C) is also illegal; it is the refusal by mortgage underwriters to give mortgages to people in certain neighborhoods. Choice (D) is part of the phrase "principal curtailment," which is paying down the principal on a mortgage by making larger payments than required under the mortgage.

52. **The correct answer is (A).** A release and a court order can also remove the cloud on a title, which are conditions that negatively affect the title to property and that are found during the title search. Choice (B) protects the buyer in case someone claims an interest in the property in the future, but it doesn't remove a cloud on the title, which has to happen before the sale. Choice (C) is actually a special warranty deed and guarantees only the actions of the person conveying the title, but it doesn't clear a cloud on a title. Choice (D) may be a court-ordered deed, but it doesn't clear a cloud on a title. A lawsuit called a quiet title action can be filed to clear a title.

53. **The correct answer is (B).** Choices (A), (C), and (D) are all distracters meant to confuse.

54. **The correct answer is (C).** $4,760 ÷ 12 = $396.67

55. **The correct answer is (C).** $340,000 ÷ 0.85 = $400,000

56. **The correct answer is (D).** Choices (A), (B), and (C) are all features of adjustable-rate mortgages, so they are incorrect answers to the question. Choice (D) is incorrect because

it is the interest rate that is recalculated periodically, not the principal, so it's the correct answer to the question.

57. **The correct answer is (B).**

$239,000 \times 0.0575 = \$13,742.5$

$100\% - 60\% = 40\%$

$13,742.5 \times 0.4 = \$5,497$

58. **The correct answer is (B).** Choice (A) is the legal taking of a person's property as a result of a default on the mortgage. This is done to a person, whereas forfeiture is done by the person. Choice (C) does not necessarily involve real property, so it's not the most specific answer. Choice (D) is incorrect because it's what a realtor does in terminating a listing agreement before completion by performance or expiration of the agreement.

59. **The correct answer is (C).** Issuance of a deed, choice (A), is not part of the process of producing a marketable title, so it's incorrect. Choices (B) and (D) do not involve producing an abstract of title, which is a report. However, in some states, the title search ends with a binder, or a policy, for title insurance (if the premium is paid), and not an attorney's opinion.

60. **The correct answer is (C).** Choices (A), (B), and (D) are all lawful and, therefore, enforceable deed restrictions. Only choice (C) is illegal, and, therefore, unenforceable.

61. **The correct answer is (B).** Choices (A) and (C) are irrelevant. In order to work with the buyers about choice (D), the realtor needs to know the answer to choice (B).

62. **The correct answer is (D).** Choices (A) and (C) convey fee simple ownership of the property. Choice (A) is not a legal description, but a marketing description. Townhouse developments are typically PUDs. Choice (B) is a special type of ownership, but not a corporation.

63. **The correct answer is (C).**

3 months = 3/12 = 0.25

$2,300 \div (\$92,000 \times 0.25) = 0.1$, or 10

64. **The correct answer is (A).** Choices (B), (C), and (D) are all freehold estates. Choice (B) is a person's interest in an estate whose term of interest is dependent on the life of another person. If a condition relating to the use of the property is violated, the property reverts back to the grantor without a legal process, choice (C). Choice (D) is a category of freehold states that include all the estates in qualified fee.

65. **The correct answer is (A).** Littoral rights are the rights of beachfront property owners, choice (B). Choice (C) may seem reasonable, but the 12-mile limit refers to the limit of a nation's territorial boundary off its shoreline; this is a legal boundary accepted worldwide. Choice (D) is incorrect because shore communities have the right to zone any property within their jurisdiction—subject to state and federal regulations relating to the shoreline.

66. **The correct answer is (A).** Choices (B), (C), and (D) are common elements found in zoning ordinances. Choice (A) is not, so it's the right answer to the question.

67. **The correct answer is (B).** Choice (A) is an item that the buyer has asked to be left in the property, and the seller has agreed. Choice (B) is something so important that it will cause the buyer to cancel the contract if not done. Choice (D) is a distracter.

68. **The correct answer is (A).**

6 months = 6/12 = 1/2 = 0.5

$132,000 \times 0.8 = \$105,600$

$105,600 \times 0.0438 = \$4,625.28$

$4,625.28 \times 0.5 = \$2,312.64$

69. The correct answer is (D). Trendy clothing stores and gourmet restaurants will result in a higher value for housing stock than dollar stores and hot dog vendors. Choices (A) and (C) are economic factors that influence housing value. Choice (C) is an environmental factor.

70. The correct answer is (C). Choice (C) is not true. An ordinary life estate can be sold or mortgaged. Choices (A), (B), and (D) are true statements about an ordinary life estate.

71. The correct answer is (D). Choices (A), (B), and (C) are included in a Good Faith Estimate, but the commission paid to the seller's broker (and by agreement, the buyer's agent) is not included.

72. The correct answer is (B). Choice (A) is incorrect because the threshold is a 20 percent down payment and the mortgage can be ARM or fixed. Choices (C) and (D) are incorrect because neither is a test of whether a buyer is required to buy PMI.

73. The correct answer is (B). $1,342,900 × 0.73 = $980,317

74. The correct answer is (B). Choice (A) is a fixed-rate mortgage of any term. Choice (C) is an open mortgage. Choice (D) is an adjustable-rate mortgage.

75. The correct answer is (C). Choice (A) is a distracter from the correct answer. Choice (B) is incorrect because it's what a bond pays. Choice (D) is incorrect because it is the value of a property to an investor with specific goals for that property.

76. The correct answer is (C). Choices (A), (B), and (D) are members of protected classes under the Fair Housing Act. Choice (C), an active heroin addict, or anyone who is a current substance abuser, is not protected.

77. The correct answer is (A). Choices (B) and (D) are distracters. Choice (C) is incorrect because a Real Estate Commission does not have the power to regulate the form of a contract.

78. The correct answer is (D). Choices (A), (B), and (C) must be disclosed to a borrower, so they are incorrect answers to the questions. Choice (D) is incorrect, so it is the correct answer to the question. The purpose of the act is to help borrowers figure out the true cost of a loan. The credit score, choice (D), is of value to the lender, not the borrower, in terms of the transaction at hand.

79. The correct answer is (B). Choice (A) is incorrect because veterans are eligible. Choice (C) is incorrect because the mortgagor doesn't need to put any money down for a VA-guaranteed mortgage. Choice (D) is incorrect because there is no prepayment penalty with a VA-insured mortgage.

80. The correct answer is (A).

$751 ÷ 3 = $250.33

$250.33 ÷ 12 = $20.86

$20.86 ÷ 30 = $0.69

$250.33 × 1 = $250.33

$20.86 × 9 = $187.74

$0.69 × 20 = $13.80

$250.33 + $187.74 + $13.80 = $451.87

81. The correct answer is (C). You can eliminate choice (A) immediately because it omits the degrees, minutes, and seconds of a metes and bounds description. Choice (B) omits the south side of the property. Choice (D) mixes up the directions.

82. The correct answer is (D). Match the items in the key with the lines on the drawing to find which easement given in the answers is shown on the map.

83. The correct answer is (D). As soon as you see the phrase "point of beginning," you should recognize that the system used is metes and bounds.

84. The correct answer is (C). $82 - 25 = 67$

85. The correct answer is (D). Choice (A) is incorrect because size isn't a factor for a use variance. Choice (B) is incorrect because the correct name is "special use permit" and size doesn't involve use. Choice (C) is a distracter because it's close to nonconforming use, which isn't relevant here either.

86. The correct answer is (C).

$748,231 - $347,295 = $400,936

$400,936 ÷ $347,295 = 1.15

1.15 ÷ 15 = 0.08, or 8%

87. The correct answer is (A). With tenancy in common, a co-owner may dispose of his or her interest in the property in any way that he or she wishes. For this reason, choices (B), (C), and (D) are incorrect.

88. The correct answer is (B). Choice (A) is incorrect because this defines actual eviction. Choice (C) is incorrect because it defines retaliatory eviction. Choice (D) seems familiar because such an occurrence is typically covered in a lease, but it is not called constructive eviction. It is usually related to disaster clauses, if any, covering "acts of God," "the landlord's obligation to repair," and whether rent will be abated during reconstruction.

89. The correct answer is (A). The tax assessor's office for public tax records is the best source for choice (B). Choice (D) is what the appraiser is attempting to determine. Choice (D) is also best sourced through public records, usually the county recorder's office.

90. The correct answer is (D). Choice (A) is incorrect because it occurs when the landlord allows a tenant to occupy the premises

without a specified end date. Choice (B) refers to a legally valid will, but it is not the form of interest needed for the answer. Choice (C) is incorrect because it is the term used when a tenant stays past the end of the lease and the landlord has not agreed to the extension and starts eviction proceedings.

91. The correct answer is (B).

$465,380 ÷ 2,740 = $169.85

$169.85 × 2846 = $483,393

92. The correct answer is (D). Choices (A), (B), and (C) would still provide accurate market data in some instances. The exception would be a rapidly changing market similar to the recession market of 2007–09.

93. The correct answer is (C). Choice (C) is the value of replacing or reproducing an improvement. It does not include the cost of the land. Choice (A) refers to valuation for tax purposes. Choice (B) attempts to determine a market value, choice (D).

94. The correct answer is (B). Choices (A) and (C) seem as though they might be the correct answer, but they are distracters. Choice (D) is a new mortgage taken out by the buyer to include and pay off the unpaid balance of the seller's mortgage. The size of the wrap-around mortgage might be large enough to qualify as a jumbo mortgage, but the term is not the same as a jumbo mortgage.

95. The correct answer is (D).

90' × 363' = 32,670

32,670 ÷ 43,560 = 0.75

0.75 × $17,500 = $13,125

$13,125 × 0.63 = $8,268.75

$8,268.75 × 0.043 = $355.56

96. The correct answer is (B). A "for sale by owner" property is exempt from the requirements of the Fair Housing Act. Choice (A) is not exempt unless the landlord occupies one of the units in a four-unit building. Choice (C) would only be exempt if the townhouses were in an over-55 community. Choice (D) would only be exempt if they did not take public funding. Remember, however, that none of these scenarios are exempt from racial discrimination.

97. **The correct answer is (B).** Choice (A) is a distracter because "forfeiture" is a term used in real estate, but with contracts. Choice (C) is incorrect because there is not enough information to know if any of the creditors are government units. Choice (D) is incorrect because the property has not been taken from the Formans; they are selling it.

98. **The correct answer is (C).** Choice (A) is incorrect because the Truth-in-Lending Act has nothing to do with the GFE. Choices (B) and (D) may seem like good answers, but both are distracters. Choice (B) is not part of a mortgage.

99. **The correct answer is (B).** Choice (A) is a distracter. Choices (C) and (D) are types of judicial deeds and have a limited warranty. They warrant only that the entity selling the property has the right to sell it.

100. **The correct answer is (B).** Choice (A) is incorrect because a worn, dirty carpet is not an example of functional obsolescence. Choice (C) is incorrect because it is not incurable or an example of economic obsolescence. Choice (D) is correct because it is curable, but it's not functional obsolescence. Therefore, choice (D) is incorrect.

ANSWER SHEET PRACTICE TEST 3

1. Ⓐ Ⓑ Ⓒ Ⓓ	21. Ⓐ Ⓑ Ⓒ Ⓓ	41. Ⓐ Ⓑ Ⓒ Ⓓ	61. Ⓐ Ⓑ Ⓒ Ⓓ	81. Ⓐ Ⓑ Ⓒ Ⓓ
2. Ⓐ Ⓑ Ⓒ Ⓓ	22. Ⓐ Ⓑ Ⓒ Ⓓ	42. Ⓐ Ⓑ Ⓒ Ⓓ	62. Ⓐ Ⓑ Ⓒ Ⓓ	82. Ⓐ Ⓑ Ⓒ Ⓓ
3. Ⓐ Ⓑ Ⓒ Ⓓ	23. Ⓐ Ⓑ Ⓒ Ⓓ	43. Ⓐ Ⓑ Ⓒ Ⓓ	63. Ⓐ Ⓑ Ⓒ Ⓓ	83. Ⓐ Ⓑ Ⓒ Ⓓ
4. Ⓐ Ⓑ Ⓒ Ⓓ	24. Ⓐ Ⓑ Ⓒ Ⓓ	44. Ⓐ Ⓑ Ⓒ Ⓓ	64. Ⓐ Ⓑ Ⓒ Ⓓ	84. Ⓐ Ⓑ Ⓒ Ⓓ
5. Ⓐ Ⓑ Ⓒ Ⓓ	25. Ⓐ Ⓑ Ⓒ Ⓓ	45. Ⓐ Ⓑ Ⓒ Ⓓ	65. Ⓐ Ⓑ Ⓒ Ⓓ	85. Ⓐ Ⓑ Ⓒ Ⓓ
6. Ⓐ Ⓑ Ⓒ Ⓓ	26. Ⓐ Ⓑ Ⓒ Ⓓ	46. Ⓐ Ⓑ Ⓒ Ⓓ	66. Ⓐ Ⓑ Ⓒ Ⓓ	86. Ⓐ Ⓑ Ⓒ Ⓓ
7. Ⓐ Ⓑ Ⓒ Ⓓ	27. Ⓐ Ⓑ Ⓒ Ⓓ	47. Ⓐ Ⓑ Ⓒ Ⓓ	67. Ⓐ Ⓑ Ⓒ Ⓓ	87. Ⓐ Ⓑ Ⓒ Ⓓ
8. Ⓐ Ⓑ Ⓒ Ⓓ	28. Ⓐ Ⓑ Ⓒ Ⓓ	48. Ⓐ Ⓑ Ⓒ Ⓓ	68. Ⓐ Ⓑ Ⓒ Ⓓ	88. Ⓐ Ⓑ Ⓒ Ⓓ
9. Ⓐ Ⓑ Ⓒ Ⓓ	29. Ⓐ Ⓑ Ⓒ Ⓓ	49. Ⓐ Ⓑ Ⓒ Ⓓ	69. Ⓐ Ⓑ Ⓒ Ⓓ	89. Ⓐ Ⓑ Ⓒ Ⓓ
10. Ⓐ Ⓑ Ⓒ Ⓓ	30. Ⓐ Ⓑ Ⓒ Ⓓ	50. Ⓐ Ⓑ Ⓒ Ⓓ	70. Ⓐ Ⓑ Ⓒ Ⓓ	90. Ⓐ Ⓑ Ⓒ Ⓓ
11. Ⓐ Ⓑ Ⓒ Ⓓ	31. Ⓐ Ⓑ Ⓒ Ⓓ	51. Ⓐ Ⓑ Ⓒ Ⓓ	71. Ⓐ Ⓑ Ⓒ Ⓓ	91. Ⓐ Ⓑ Ⓒ Ⓓ
12. Ⓐ Ⓑ Ⓒ Ⓓ	32. Ⓐ Ⓑ Ⓒ Ⓓ	52. Ⓐ Ⓑ Ⓒ Ⓓ	72. Ⓐ Ⓑ Ⓒ Ⓓ	92. Ⓐ Ⓑ Ⓒ Ⓓ
13. Ⓐ Ⓑ Ⓒ Ⓓ	33. Ⓐ Ⓑ Ⓒ Ⓓ	53. Ⓐ Ⓑ Ⓒ Ⓓ	73. Ⓐ Ⓑ Ⓒ Ⓓ	93. Ⓐ Ⓑ Ⓒ Ⓓ
14. Ⓐ Ⓑ Ⓒ Ⓓ	34. Ⓐ Ⓑ Ⓒ Ⓓ	54. Ⓐ Ⓑ Ⓒ Ⓓ	74. Ⓐ Ⓑ Ⓒ Ⓓ	94. Ⓐ Ⓑ Ⓒ Ⓓ
15. Ⓐ Ⓑ Ⓒ Ⓓ	35. Ⓐ Ⓑ Ⓒ Ⓓ	55. Ⓐ Ⓑ Ⓒ Ⓓ	75. Ⓐ Ⓑ Ⓒ Ⓓ	95. Ⓐ Ⓑ Ⓒ Ⓓ
16. Ⓐ Ⓑ Ⓒ Ⓓ	36. Ⓐ Ⓑ Ⓒ Ⓓ	56. Ⓐ Ⓑ Ⓒ Ⓓ	76. Ⓐ Ⓑ Ⓒ Ⓓ	96. Ⓐ Ⓑ Ⓒ Ⓓ
17. Ⓐ Ⓑ Ⓒ Ⓓ	37. Ⓐ Ⓑ Ⓒ Ⓓ	57. Ⓐ Ⓑ Ⓒ Ⓓ	77. Ⓐ Ⓑ Ⓒ Ⓓ	97. Ⓐ Ⓑ Ⓒ Ⓓ
18. Ⓐ Ⓑ Ⓒ Ⓓ	38. Ⓐ Ⓑ Ⓒ Ⓓ	58. Ⓐ Ⓑ Ⓒ Ⓓ	78. Ⓐ Ⓑ Ⓒ Ⓓ	98. Ⓐ Ⓑ Ⓒ Ⓓ
19. Ⓐ Ⓑ Ⓒ Ⓓ	39. Ⓐ Ⓑ Ⓒ Ⓓ	59. Ⓐ Ⓑ Ⓒ Ⓓ	79. Ⓐ Ⓑ Ⓒ Ⓓ	99. Ⓐ Ⓑ Ⓒ Ⓓ
20. Ⓐ Ⓑ Ⓒ Ⓓ	40. Ⓐ Ⓑ Ⓒ Ⓓ	60. Ⓐ Ⓑ Ⓒ Ⓓ	80. Ⓐ Ⓑ Ⓒ Ⓓ	100. Ⓐ Ⓑ Ⓒ Ⓓ

answer sheet

Practice Test 3

100 Questions • 3 Hours

Directions: Read each question carefully and mark the letter of the best answer on the answer sheet.

1. Which of the following would NOT appear in a legal property description using the rectangular survey system?
   (A) Principal meridian
   (B) Location of physical features
   (C) Baseline
   (D) Direction

2. Condemnation of property in order to transfer it to a real estate developer is known as
   (A) adverse possession.
   (B) involuntary alienation.
   (C) escheat.
   (D) assignment.

3. Frank's Hardware Store has signed a gross lease. Frank will pay
   (A) rent based on the business's receipts.
   (B) rent, utilities, and real estate taxes only.
   (C) rent and possibly utilities.
   (D) rent, real estate taxes, and repair and maintenance to the premises.

4. Which of the following accurately describes plottage?
   (A) The process of acquiring land
   (B) Increase in the value of individual lots when combined
   (C) Another name for the lots in a planned unit development
   (D) The division of land in a rectangular survey system

5. Which of the following is NOT a cap for ARMs?
   (A) Annual cap on the interest rate
   (B) Life of loan interest rate cap
   (C) Payment cap
   (D) Index cap

6. The Jansen Outdoor Display Company wants to put up a billboard on the roof of the Mason Company's apartment building that fronts I-95. To gain access to the roof, the Jansen Company asks the Mason Company for a
   (A) lease allowing it to erect a billboard.
   (B) tenancy in common of the rooftop.
   (C) syndication.
   (D) sublease on the roof.

247

7. The Mason Company rejects the Jansen Company's request because of the clause in the deed that it received when it bought the land from Tracy Merrit. If it agreed to the Jansen Company's request, the Mason Company would lose the property. The clause must have conveyed what kind of ownership?

(A) Leasehold with conditions

(B) Qualified fee conditional ownership

(C) Estate at will

(D) Estate with qualifications

8. Agent Jeff Jackson receives a $7,488 commission on the sale of a house on Cherry Street. If he is contracted to get 45% of the commission on the sale of $256,000, what was the total rate of commission?

(A) 0.016

(B) 0.029

(C) 0.065

(D) 0.075

9. The homebuyers' tax credit of 2009–10 created a situation in which buyers were hurrying to close while the tax credit was in force. This resulted in a flurry of sales activities because of which economic factor?

(A) Change

(B) Highest and best use

(C) Competition

(D) Externalities

10. If a principal discharges a realtor, this is known as

(A) revocation.

(B) renunciation.

(C) reversion.

(D) release.

11. An aging elevator would be considered in an appraisal as a/an

(A) curable physical deterioration.

(B) curable economic obsolescence.

(C) incurable functional obsolescence.

(D) curable functional obsolescence.

12. Littoral rights give property owners all of the following rights EXCEPT

(A) to build a dock out into the water from their land.

(B) to launch a boat into the water from their land.

(C) to maintain an inland no-trespassing zone beginning at the high tide water mark.

(D) to refuse others the use of their shoreline to ground or launch boats.

13. A savings and loan gives the Fongs a 90% loan on the appraised value of $265,900. If the interest payment for the first month is $1,046.98, what is the interest rate on the loan?

(A) 3.22%

(B) 4.37%

(C) 5.25%

(D) 6.87%

14. Approval of a building permit requires a

(A) review by the zoning board.

(B) zoning variance.

(C) review by the planning board.

(D) review by the municipal building department or similar department.

15. Mortgage lenders must cancel PMI coverage on mortgages when the mortgagor has paid down the loan to

(A) 80 percent.

(B) 78 percent.

(C) 75 percent.

(D) 72 percent.

16. Anti-trust laws forbid which of the following actions?

   (A) A developer building four PUDs in a single city

   (B) Four real estate brokers deciding on the customary rate for sales commissions in their city

   (C) Four brokers sharing the costs of highway billboards advertising the benefits of living in their city

   (D) A mortgage broker offering the same interest rate on construction loans to two different developers

17. Which of the following is a provision of RESPA?

   (A) A certain amount of money equal to 6 months of taxes and insurance must be held in an escrow account.

   (B) Lenders must pay interest on the money held in mortgages escrow accounts.

   (C) A lender may be required to take out PMI on a borrower's mortgage, depending on the down payment.

   (D) The lender must tell borrowers why their loan has been turned down.

18. Selma McMullen owns the vacant lot next door to her home. It is valued at $45,000, and her home is valued at $135,000. If both are assessed at 85% of value and are taxed at a rate of 6.3 per thousand for schools, 4.2 per thousand for the county, and 2.2 per thousand for the borough, what is her yearly tax bill?

   (A) $9,693.90

   (B) $1,943.10

   (C) $642.60

   (D) $336.60

19. What are the taxes due on a $120,000 property assessed at 55% of value that has a tax rate of $3.20 per $100 of valuation?

   (A) $211.20

   (B) $2,112

   (C) $3,840

   (D) $384

20. A 52,000 square foot office building recently sold for $972,800. If the monthly income is expected to be $0.375 per square foot, what is the expected rate of return?

   (A) 2.4%

   (B) 24%

   (C) 2%

   (D) 20%

21. Which of the following established "innocent landowner immunity"?

   (A) SARA

   (B) CERCLA

   (C) Brownfields Program

   (D) LUST Trust Fund

22. An Mortgage Loan Disclosure Statement includes itemized costs for

   (A) loan amount, notary, disability insurance.

   (B) deed preparation, fire insurance, loan amount.

   (C) appraisal, disability insurance, deed preparation.

   (D) fire insurance, loan amount, title insurance.

23. The Zuckers are getting ready for the closing on their new home. They are paying four discount points. What is the purpose of paying discount points?

    (A) Paying points reduces the mortgage.

    (B) Paying points reduces the interest rate on the mortgage.

    (C) Paying points reduces the sales price of the property.

    (D) Paying points reduces the overall closing costs for the buyer.

24. Bill Clyde sells his house to Keisha Erwin for $376,875. He filled the 200-gallon oil tank on February 1. When he sold the house on May 15, there were 127 gallons left in the tank. If the oil cost $3.15 per gallon, how much does Keisha owe Bill for the unused oil?

    (A) $229.95

    (B) $342.87

    (C) $400.05

    (D) $0.00

25. Sal DeFalco has decided to buy a condo. Which of the following would be able to write him a mortgage?

    (A) Mortgage broker

    (B) Ginner Mae

    (C) FHA

    (D) Credit union

26. To appraisers, things like types of bathroom fixtures, countertops, and flooring come under the heading of

    (A) physical details.

    (B) environmental factors.

    (C) finishes.

    (D) interior design.

27. Private restrictions placed on a subdivision's deeds are enforceable by

    (A) federal law only.

    (B) federal and state law.

    (C) municipal governments only.

    (D) homeowner associations only.

28. The four characteristics of the highest and best use of property are legally possible, maximally productive, economically feasible, and

    (A) space-efficient.

    (B) time-efficient.

    (C) physically possible.

    (D) marketable.

29. Sonjay Singh is completing a URAR using the cost approach. He will fill in all of the following items EXCEPT

    (A) estimated site value.

    (B) gross adjustments.

    (C) total depreciation.

    (D) value of site improvements.

30. A townhouse sold on August 10 for $123,000. The taxes of $3,760.90 were due and paid in full on March 1, for the tax year March 1 to February 28. The monthly association fees of $189 were due and paid in full on August 1. What money, if any, is owed and to whom?

    (A) $2,215.40 to the buyer

    (B) $2,215.40 to the seller

    (C) $2,089.40 to the buyer

    (D) $2,089.40 to the seller

31. The Davidsons are buying a co-op. At the closing they will receive a

    (A) ground lease.

    (B) joint tenancy lease.

    (C) tenancy in common lease.

    (D) proprietary lease.

32. Which of the following describes an open listing?

    (A) Seller and agent sign an agreement that the agent will get whatever is the difference between the seller's desired price and the actual price.

    (B) The agent acts as an intermediary between seller and buyers.

    (C) The agent represents both the seller and the buyer.

    (D) The seller releases a listing to multiple realtors.

33. Under the federal Residential Lead-Based Paint Hazard Reduction Act,

    (A) the seller must have the property, if constructed before 1978, inspected for lead paint before putting the property on the market.

    (B) neither the seller's nor buyer's agent has a responsibility to tell the buyer about the possible presence of lead paint in a house that was constructed prior to 1978.

    (C) the seller must remediate any lead paint before selling a property built before 1978.

    (D) the seller must inform the buyer of the existence of lead paint on the property.

34. The Williams are buying a condo. All of the following are common areas of ownership EXCEPT

    (A) lobby.

    (B) fitness gym.

    (C) rooftop sun deck.

    (D) storage cage.

35. The buyer of a property will typically be debited which of the following?

    (A) Cost of the title insurance

    (B) Taxes paid to the time of the closing

    (C) Deed preparation

    (D) Escrow balance held by the seller's lender

36. If the sale of a foreclosed property fails to satisfy the mortgage, the lender

    (A) may file a deed in lieu of foreclosure.

    (B) may go to court and seek a deficiency judgment.

    (C) has no way to recover additional money from the person in default.

    (D) may allow the person in default of the mortgage to exercise the right of reversion.

37. Which of the following would NOT be covered under home warranty insurance given by the seller to the buyer?

    (A) Heating system

    (B) Dishwasher

    (C) Roof repairs

    (D) Foundation

38. Issac Jones sold his home for $587,000 in 2009. He had purchased the house in 1975 for $743,257. What is the rate of appreciation or depreciation per year?

    (A) 26.6% appreciates

    (B) 26.6% depreciates

    (C) 0.8% appreciates

    (D) 0.8% depreciates

39. In doing a competitive market analysis, a real estate agent should consider
    (A) only the prices of homes in your area that sold within the last 60 days.
    (B) only the prices of homes in your area that sold within the last 6 months.
    (C) the prices of homes that sold and did not sell in your area within the 6 months.
    (D) the prices of homes that sold and did not sell in your area within the shortest time practical based on the number of listings and sales.

40. The Stephens bought a house from the Jacksons who did not tell them that the woods behind the house were going to be torn down to build a 500-unit townhome community. The Stephens
    (A) can sue to void the contract because of nondisclosure on the part of the Jacksons.
    (B) can claim the contract is voidable because of fraud and sue to rescind it.
    (C) can claim that the contract is invalid because they have lost the right of quiet enjoyment of their property.
    (D) have only two options: to stay in the house or try to sell it.

41. When does a sales contract between buyer and seller become valid?
    (A) The buyer's agent gives the seller's agent the buyer's offer.
    (B) The seller accepts the buyer's offer.
    (C) The buyer's agent tells the buyer of the seller's acceptance.
    (D) The buyer's agent tells the seller's agent that the buyer has been notified.

42. Among the duties that a realtor handles are all of the following EXCEPT
    (A) providing information about local property taxes.
    (B) making sure that the inspections have been carried out.
    (C) having the title and mortgage recorded after the closing.
    (D) providing an estimate of closing costs.

43. Sam Schieffer is interested in renting an apartment for his elderly mother. He wants the landlord to allow him to install grab bars by the toilet and in the bathtub. The landlord must agree under the
    (A) Fair Housing Act.
    (B) Americans with Disabilities Act.
    (C) Rehabilitation Act of 1973.
    (D) Housing and Community Development Act of 1981.

44. Susan and Jay Morton have signed the sales contract to purchase the Ryans' house. The Mortons are told that they now have equitable title to the property, which conveys
    (A) complete ownership to the buyer.
    (B) property free and clear of encumbrances.
    (C) joint ownership to a married couple.
    (D) the right to complete ownership.

45. An appraiser's report includes all of the following EXCEPT
    (A) type of value estimated.
    (B) data gathered and analyzed in appraising the property.
    (C) insurance information.
    (D) the purpose for the appraisal.

46. Dina Stewart thought she wanted to move into the city from the suburbs, put her house up for sale, accepted an offer from the Phelps, and signed the sales contract. Then she had a change of mind. In the meantime, the Phelps learned they were having another baby and decided that Dina's house was too small. Both parties discussed their feelings and decided mutually to

    (A) remainder the contract.

    (B) liquidate the contract.

    (C) rescind the contract.

    (D) accept compensatory damages.

47. In Question 46, do the realtors get their commissions?

    (A) Yes, because the seller accepted the buyer's offer.

    (B) Yes, because the realtors brought together a buyer who at the time was ready, willing, and able to buy the house with a seller who was ready to sell at the time.

    (C) No, because the transaction never took place.

    (D) No, because there was no closing where commissions are paid.

48. Jack Patton has entered into an option to buy contract with the Allens to buy a 320-acre parcel of land to build condos on. Which of the following statements is true about this situation?

    (A) Patton has an obligation to buy the land.

    (B) The Allens are under no obligation to sell the land to Patton.

    (C) The Allens have an obligation to sell the land to Patton.

    (D) With an option to buy, the price is not set, so Patton and the Allens still have to negotiate a price acceptable to both parties.

49. Joe Spires wants to sell his farm for development. If the farm is 5,445,000 square feet, how many 1.5-acre lots can he propose to the developer?

    (A) 186

    (B) 189

    (C) 188

    (D) 187

50. In a state that bases its mortgage law on title theory,

    (A) the mortgagor turns over legal title to the mortgagee.

    (B) the mortgagor retains the legal title, and the mortgagee retains the deed.

    (C) a lien is placed on the property.

    (D) the mortgagee receives equitable title.

51. Which of the following is NOT covered by the federal rules regulating underground tanks?

    (A) Gas station oil tanks

    (B) Home heating oil tanks

    (C) Chemical plant tanks

    (D) Used motor oil tanks

52. Bill McCarthy is a real estate agent who is buying a home. He wants a general warranty deed on the property because it guarantees that

    (A) the current owner will convey any interest that she may get in the property in the future.

    (B) the grantor has legal title that can be conveyed and has not placed any encumbrances on the property while holding title.

    (C) the current owner has the right to sell it.

    (D) the current owner is able to convey title and that the title is free of all claims and encumbrances.

QUESTIONS 53 TO 55 ARE BASED ON THE FOLLOWING MAP.

FAIR HAVEN STREET

HARDY LAKE

BALL FIELDS | CLUB HOUSE | TENNIS COURTS

SUNSET ROAD

SHADE TREE LANE

PEAR STREET — APPLE LANE — PARKING — SHOPPING CENTER — ENTRANCE

53. The development, part of which is shown on the map, probably has which type of zoning?

(A) Cluster

(B) PUD

(C) Downsizing

(D) Density reduction

54. If the subdivision shown on the map was zoned inclusionary, it would

(A) have affordable housing units.

(B) be required to sell a certain number of units to minorities.

(C) be regulated under the Fair Housing Act.

(D) be required to sell a certain number of units to people over 55.

55. The map above is required to be filed by all developers of subdivisions and is called a

(A) lot and block map.

(B) plat map.

(C) plottage map.

(D) rectangular survey system map.

56. The local Mini Mart sold for $1,280,000, and the rate of commission was 7%. If the seller's broker received $51,072, what was the percentage of the commission?

(A) 0.57

(B) 0.67

(C) 0.77

(D) 0.87

57. What is the first month's interest on a one-year loan for $34,000 at 8.28%?

(A) $2,346.00

(B) $281.52

(C) $2,815.20

(D) $234.60

58. A loan that amortizes is one in which

    (A) the amount of principal that is paid down increases over time, while the amount of the interest paid stays the same.

    (B) the amount of principal that is paid down decreases over time, while the amount of the interest that is paid increases.

    (C) the amount of principal that is paid down increases over time, while the amount of interest that is paid decreases.

    (D) the amounts of both principal and interest remain the same for the term of the loan.

59. Regulation Z enforces

    (A) fair housing laws.

    (B) hazardous materials laws.

    (C) consumer credit laws.

    (D) the mortgage industry.

60. Among the bundle of rights of real property ownership are the rights to

    (A) sell interests in the property, lease the property, use the property.

    (B) bequeath the property, lease the property, depreciate the property.

    (C) sell interests in the property, appreciate the property, use the property.

    (D) donate the property, depreciate the property, do nothing with the property.

61. Earnest money is

    (A) another name for a down payment.

    (B) used for recording and transfer fees.

    (C) used to pay the seller's broker if the buyer defaults.

    (D) the amount requested by the seller to bind the buyer to the sales contract.

62. A mortgage that ranks below another mortgage for payment if the mortgagor defaults is called a

    (A) minor mortgage.

    (B) lower-grade mortgage.

    (C) subprime mortgage.

    (D) junior mortgage.

63. Prepaid items required by the lender at closing include all of the following EXCEPT

    (A) mortgage insurance premiums.

    (B) hazard insurance premiums.

    (C) appraisal fee.

    (D) property taxes.

64. Keishon DeVal's house was assessed at $2,204,000. The previous tax rate was $4.50 per $100. After a new school funding bill was passed, the new rate is $6.50 per $100. What is the difference in his monthly tax bill?

    (A) $3,673.33

    (B) $44,080

    (C) $9,918

    (D) $14,326

65. An advantage of a VA-guaranteed mortgage is

    (A) no private mortgage insurance is required regardless of the amount of the down payment.

    (B) the down payment can be as low as 3 percent.

    (C) that it can be used to buy a rental property as well as a primary residence.

    (D) that credit rating is not considered by the lender in determining eligibility for a mortgage.

practice test

66. The Kristols are buying a home in a community that has an assessment ratio of 52 percent. This means that they will pay
    (A) a tax rate of 52 percent.
    (B) a tax rate of $0.52.
    (C) taxes on 52 percent of the value of their home.
    (D) taxes on 48 percent of the value of their home.

67. For a real estate transaction to be an arm's length transaction, all of the following apply EXCEPT
    (A) all parties are ready, willing, and able to complete the transaction.
    (B) no pressure has been exerted on any parties.
    (C) everyone has the same set of facts about the transaction.
    (D) the transaction is an "as is" transaction.

68. Which of the following phases of an environmental assessment estimates the cost for cleaning up a site?
    (A) Phase I
    (B) Phase II
    (C) Phase III
    (D) Phase IV

69. In order to make sure that the terms of the mortgage at the time of the closing are what the borrower understood them to be, a buyer should ask for which of the following from the lender?
    (A) Certificate of Torrens
    (B) Certificate of estoppel
    (C) Certificate of title
    (D) Abstract of title

70. The rate of depreciation on Tamika Johnson's property over 18 years is 3% per year. If she bought the property for $132,000, what is its value now?
    (A) $60,720
    (B) $71,280
    (C) $83,265
    (D) $95,737

71. Jake and Marita Morales are buying their first home. They do not live in a community property state or a state that recognizes tenancy by the entireties, so they are most likely going to own their property by
    (A) joint tenancy.
    (B) tenancy in common.
    (C) tenancy in severalty.
    (D) tenancy at will.

72. The city buys a block of condemned houses, razes them, and establishes a park. In order to create the park, the city required
    (A) nonconforming use zoning.
    (B) density zoning.
    (C) spot zoning.
    (D) open space zoning.

73. If found guilty of two or more violations of the Fair Housing Act within 7 years, a realtor may be fined a maximum of
    (A) $11,000.
    (B) $22,000.
    (C) $55,000.
    (D) $100,000.

74. Sam Knowles, John Hudson, and Brian Morgan buy an apartment building as an investment. As a tenancy in common,

(A) each had to put in the same amount of money.

(B) each may sell his interest whenever he wishes.

(C) none of them can take out a mortgage on his interest without the consent of the others.

(D) should one of them die, the others will inherit his third.

75. In certain states, which of the following statutes protects property owners from having their homes taken to satisfy nonmortgage creditors?

(A) Homestead property exemption

(B) Nonprofit property exemption

(C) Nonprofit property tax exemption

(D) Fee simple ownership

76. All of the following apply to the exclusive right to sell listing EXCEPT

(A) ensuring that the seller's broker will be paid the commission regardless of who finds the buyer.

(B) giving the seller's broker the sole right to market the property.

(C) allowing the seller to sell his or her own property.

(D) not allowing the property to be listed on an MLS.

77. The rental on a local office building shows a monthly profit of $1,050. If this is a 7% return, what is the value of the property?

(A) $11,666

(B) $180,000

(C) $116,666

(D) $18,000

78. A judgment lien is a

(A) general lien.

(B) specific lien.

(C) voluntary lien.

(D) minor lien.

79. Which of the following statements is true about the secondary mortgage market?

(A) The secondary mortgage market provides mortgages to mortgagors.

(B) The secondary mortgage market requires that mortgages have PMI.

(C) Investors buy mortgage-backed securities on the secondary mortgage market.

(D) Fannie Mae insures mortgages that are sold on the secondary mortgage market.

80. The Barbers recently bought a property that has 110' of frontage on the river. If the property is 1/2 an acre, what is the depth of the property?

(A) 404'

(B) 198'

(C) 396'

(D) 202'

81. The Minhs bought their home 10 years ago for $175,000, paying 10 percent down and taking a mortgage for $157,500. Today, the outstanding principal is $98,900. What is the total equity that the Minhs have in their home?

(A) $17,500

(B) $58,600

(C) $76,100

(D) $116,400

82. Price fixing is
   (A) what an agent does in deciding at what price to list a property.
   (B) what the appraiser does in adjusting the value of comps to the subject property.
   (C) the collusion between two or more realtors in an area to set the sales commission rate.
   (D) the adjustment that a seller and agent do when they reduce the sale price of a property because it isn't moving.

83. The main components of a typical mortgage payment are
   (A) principal, interest, property taxes.
   (B) principal, interest, private mortgage insurance, property taxes.
   (C) principal, interest, homeowner's insurance, property tax.
   (D) principal, interest, points, property taxes.

84. The township has decided to put in a sidewalk on both sides of Cherry Valley Road. This will create what kind of easement?
   (A) Appurtenant easement
   (B) Easement in gross
   (C) Easement by prescription
   (D) Easement by necessity

85. Which of the following would be protected under the principle of familiar status when renting a property?
   (A) Elderly parent moving in with daughter and family
   (B) Roommates who are cousins
   (C) Pregnant single woman
   (D) Unmarried couple

86. Horace Jones wants to sell his seven-bedroom house on Elm Street. A similar house in the neighborhood with six bedrooms just sold for $75,000. What is the value of Horace's house?
   (A) $62,500
   (B) $75,000
   (C) $81,500
   (D) $87,500

87. The Mortons have accepted an offer on their property and are waiting for the contract to be signed. Which of the following statements accurately describes the situation?
   (A) The Mortons' agent may not continue to show the property.
   (B) The Mortons may not entertain any offers that other agents bring to them.
   (C) Other agents must stop showing the property.
   (D) The Mortons may accept back-up offers.

88. Peter James has hired Martinson Realty to find apartment buildings for him to buy, provide information about the properties to him, and negotiate on his behalf. Martinson Realty is acting as a/an
   (A) universal agent.
   (B) agent by estoppel.
   (C) special agent.
   (D) general agent.

89. Peter James is considering buying the Johnson Company's apartment building as an investment. Which of the following will help him decide how long the building will contribute to the value of the property?
   (A) Economic life
   (B) Physical life
   (C) Effective age
   (D) Actual age

90. All of the following come under federal municipal solid waste landfill regulations EXCEPT

(A) restrictions on locations of landfills.

(B) disposal of radioactive wasters.

(C) monitoring of groundwater.

(D) requirements related to the closure of landfills.

91. Sue Praker works for Resort Area Realty and has exclusive rights to sell its Woodlands development. She earns a 6% commission on the first $100,000 sold and 7% on every dollar over $100,000. What was her total commission check for March when she sold houses worth $89,000, $97,000, and $82,000?

(A) $6,000

(B) $17,420

(C) $17,760

(D) $22,780

92. To determine square footage,

(A) multiply length times width.

(B) add length and width and multiply by 2.

(C) add length and width.

(D) multiple length times width and divide by the cost per square foot.

93. Title XI of the federal Financial Institutions Reform, Recovery and Enforcement Act (FIRREA) regulates

(A) real estate licensing.

(B) real estate appraising.

(C) the secondary mortgage market.

(D) the primary mortgage market.

94. The civil penalty that HUD may impose for fraud in interstate land sales is a

(A) maximum of $1,000 in any one year.

(B) maximum of $10,000 in any one year.

(C) maximum of $1 million in any one year.

(D) $1 million lifetime maximum.

95. The Mays brothers are putting together parcels of land for a subdivision and have asked for a contract for deed on the Jasons' farm. This will allow the Mays to

(A) take title immediately while paying off the purchase price in installments.

(B) borrow the purchase price from a financial institution over a longer period of time.

(C) take title after a certain number of monthly payments have been made.

(D) negotiate for a wraparound mortgage with a bank.

96. A triangular lot measures 335' across the front and has a depth of 172'. What is the commission if the commission rate is 6% and the land sells for $2.55 per square foot?

(A) $4,407.93

(B) $440.79

(C) $44,079.3

(D) $440,793

97. The Floyds want to buy their first home. They have 20 percent to put down and need to borrow $200,000. They want a 30-year, fixed-rate mortgage and rates are 5.1 percent. Their monthly housing payments, including principal, interest, taxes, and homeowner's insurance, will be $2,340. If their total income is $80,090, what percentage of their monthly combined incomes will their housing payments be?

    (A) 2.85 percent

    (B) 28.5 percent

    (C) 3.5 percent

    (D) 35 percent

98. Would the Floyds qualify for a $200,000 loan under the generally accepted mortgage guidelines that the sum of the payments for the monthly mortgage, taxes, and nonhousing debt payments can be only "X" percentage of gross month income?

    (A) Yes, because the percentage of the sum of the payments less than the guidelines.

    (B) Yes, because the percentage of the sum of the payments is just equal to the guidelines.

    (C) No, because their housing payments are already at the limit without including the monthly nonhousing payments.

    (D) Can't answer the question because there is no information on the Floyds' other debt payments.

99. A deed to be valid must have all of the following EXCEPT

    (A) *habendum* clause.

    (B) defeasance clause.

    (C) granting clause.

    (D) consideration.

100. Which of the following should be shown as a disbursement to the seller on a broker's reconciliation worksheet?

    (A) Real estate commission

    (B) Mortgage recording fee

    (C) Amount of the balance on the purchase price

    (D) Pest inspection fee

ANSWER KEY AND EXPLANATIONS

1. B	21. A	41. C	61. D	81. C
2. B	22. D	42. C	62. D	82. C
3. C	23. B	43. A	63. C	83. C
4. B	24. C	44. D	64. A	84. B
5. D	25. D	45. C	65. A	85. C
6. A	26. C	46. C	66. C	86. D
7. B	27. D	47. C	67. D	87. D
8. C	28. C	48. C	68. C	88. C
9. A	29. B	49. D	69. B	89. A
10. A	30. B	50. A	70. A	90. B
11. A	31. D	51. B	71. A	91. C
12. D	32. D	52. D	72. C	92. A
13. C	33. D	53. A	73. C	93. B
14. D	34. D	54. A	74. B	94. C
15. B	35. A	55. B	75. A	95. C
16. B	36. B	56. A	76. D	96. A
17. D	37. D	57. D	77. B	97. D
18. B	38. D	58. C	78. A	98. C
19. B	39. D	59. C	79. C	99. B
20. B	40. B	60. A	80. B	100. C

1. **The correct answer is (B).** Choice (B) would be found in a metes and bounds system that used monuments for some of its boundaries or corners. Choices (A), (C), and (D) are elements that might be found in a legal property description that used the rectangular survey system.

2. **The correct answer is (B).** Choice (A) refers to a type of easement. Choice (C) is the taking of property by the state when the owner dies without a will and without relatives. Choice (D) is the giving of rights, duties, or obligations to another; for example, a tenant may assign his or her lease to another.

3. **The correct answer is (C).** With a gross lease, the tenant pays rent and may or may not pay his or her own utilities, depending on the lease. Choice (A) describes a percentage lease. Choice (B) describes a possible net lease, one in which the tenant pays more than rent and utilities. Choice (D) describes a possible double net lease.

4. **The correct answer is (B).** Choice (A) is simply buying property. Choice (C) seems

as though it might be correct if you didn't know the answer immediately, but it's a distracter. Choice (D) is incorrect because the rectangular survey system uses tier, range, township, and section.

5. **The correct answer is (D).** Choice (D) is a distracter; an index is used to compute the rate adjustment, but there is no such thing as an index cap on adjustable-rate mortgages. Choices (A), (B), and (C) are all caps on how much the interest rate or payments may change for an ARM.

6. **The correct answer is (A).** Choice (B) is a form of ownership, and the Mason Company would have no reason to ask to buy the roof (though it might ask to buy air rights), so this is not a reasonable answer. Choice (C) is also a form of ownership related to developing large parcels of land. Choice (D) is incorrect because the Mason Company owns the building; it's not subleasing it.

7. **The correct answer is (B).** There is also a qualified fee determinable, which also restricts the buyer, but no court proceeding is necessary to have the property reverted back to the original seller. Choice (C) is a form of lease in which the landlord allows the tenant to occupy a property without a specified end date. Choices (A) and (D) are distracters.

8. **The correct answer is (C).**

$7,488 \div 0.45 = $16,640

$16,640 \div $256,000 = 0.065

9. **The correct answer is (A).** You can figure that choice (C) is too easy to be correct. Competition in the economic sense relates to the competition between builders to take advantage of buyer demand. Choice (A) is the correct answer because it relates to how things, including government policies, change, such as the tax credit ending at a certain point. Choice (B) is incorrect because it relates to the use of property, not to the cost of the property. Choice (D) is incorrect because it relates to the fixed position of property, not to the cost.

10. **The correct answer is (A).** Choice (B) occurs when a realtor discharges a principal. Choice (C) is incorrect because it refers to the process by which a limited estate in a property is returned to the original owner. Choice (D) seems like a likely answer, but is not the correct term.

11. **The correct answer is (A).** Choice (B) is incorrect because while an aging elevator is curable, it's not economic obsolescence. This makes choice (D) incorrect also. The elevator is curable, but not an example of functional obsolescence. Choice (C) is incorrect on both counts. In an answer with two parts or details, check that both are correct.

12. **The correct answer is (D).** Choices (A), (B), and (C) correctly describe the littoral rights of people who own property that abuts a lake, ocean, or sea.

13. **The correct answer is (C).**

$265,900 \times 0.9 = $239,310

$1,046.98 \div ($239,310 \times 1/12) = 0.0525, or 5.25%

14. **The correct answer is (D).** Choice (D) is all that is necessary for a building permit—if the proposed building meets zoning ordinances. Choice (A) is incorrect because even if the proposed building was to be rejected by the building department, the request for a building permit wouldn't go before the zoning board—unless the application appealed the rejection because the building department said a variance was needed. Only a request for a zoning variance would be reviewed by the zoning board. A zoning variance, choice (B), is only required if the proposed building doesn't comply with the

zoning ordinances. Choice (C) is incorrect because a planning board doesn't approve building permits; it adopts the master plan and reviews and decides subdivision and site plan applications.

15. **The correct answer is (B).** Choice (A) is incorrect because it is the threshold for requiring PMI. If a mortgagor puts down 20 percent, then PMI is not required. Choices (C) and (D) are incorrect.

16. **The correct answer is (B).** Choice (A) is not an unusual business strategy for a developer in a large urban area. Choice (C) is incorrect because it doesn't involve any kind of illegal activity; each brokerage shares expenses and, they hope, the benefits of the advertising that their city is a great place to live. Choice (D) is incorrect because offering the same interest rate to different borrowers is a typical and legal business practice.

17. **The correct answer is (D).** Choice (A) is incorrect because RESPA doesn't require any money to be held in escrow; that's up to the mortgagee to decided, but RESPA does limit the maximum amount that can be required by the lender, approximately two months of escrow payments. Choice (B) is incorrect for mortgage escrow accounts. (Some state laws do require that interest be paid on these accounts.) Choice (C) is incorrect because having or not having PMI on a mortgage is up to the lender, not HUD.

18. **The correct answer is (B).**

$135,000 + $45,000 = $180,000

$180,000 × 0.85 = $153,00

0.0063 + 0.0042 + 0.0022 = 0.0127

$153,000 × 0.0127 = $1,943.10

19. **The correct answer is (B).**

$120,000 × 0.55 = $66,000

$66,000 × 0.032 = $2,112

20. **The correct answer is (B).**

52,000 × $0.375 = $19,500

$19,500 × 12 = $234,000

$234,000 ÷ $972,800 = 0.24, or 24%

21. **The correct answer is (A).** Choice (B), the Comprehensive Environmental Response, Compensation, and Liability Act of 1980, was the predecessor to SARA, the Superfund Amendments and Reauthorization Act of 1986, and held the current landowner responsible for any contamination, even if the landowner had nothing to do with the contamination. Choice (C) is the program that cleans up contaminated land and is administered under these two acts and the Small Business Liability Relief and Brownfields Revitalization Act of 2002.

22. **The correct answer is (D).** Choice (A) is incorrect because the purchase of disability insurance is not a requirement of getting a mortgage. Choice (B) is incorrect because deed preparation is a cost of the seller, not the buyer, so it would not appear on the MLDS. Choice (C) is incorrect because it includes disability insurance as well as deed preparation. To save some time in answering a question with a series in each answer choice, read each item in an answer first. If it is incorrect, check it off and go on to the next answer. Then read the second item in the remaining choices until you have eliminated all but one answer choice.

23. **The correct answer is (B).** Choice (A) is incorrect, but tricky. Paying less in interest reduces mortgage payments, but not the mortgage itself. Choice (C) is incorrect because discount points have nothing to do with the sales price. Choice (D) is incorrect because the discount points add to the closing costs of the buyer.

24. The correct answer is (C).

$127 \times \$3.15 = \$400.05$

25. The correct answer is (D). Choice (A) would put Sal in touch with a mortgagee, but couldn't write the mortgage. Choice (B) is part of the secondary mortgage market and sells packages of mortgages to investors, but doesn't write mortgages. Choice (C) insures mortgages, but doesn't write them.

26. The correct answer is (C). The level, or quality, of the finishes are taken into consideration when appraising a residential property. Choices (A) and (D) are distracters. Choice (C) may seem familiar, but environmental factors refer to economic factors that affect value.

27. The correct answer is (D). No government organization enforces private deed restrictions in subdivisions. However, any deed restriction that is illegal, such as refusing to allow a property to be sold to a particular group, cannot be enforced by an HOA, and the HOA could be sued for discrimination if it tried. An HOA can use the courts to enforce valid restrictions just as parties to a contract can use the courts to enforce it.

28. The correct answer is (C). None of choices (A), (B), and (D) is the fourth characteristic of the highest and best use of property.

29. The correct answer is (B). Choice (B) is found in the sales comparison section, so it's incorrect about the cost approach, but the correct answer to the question. The cost approach section on the Uniform Residential Appraisal Report also includes estimated reproduction costs of any improvements in addition to choices (A), (C), and (D).

30. The correct answer is (B).

$\$3,760.90 \div 12 = \$313.40$

$\$313.40 \div 30 = \$10.45$

$\$313.40 \times 6 = \$1,880.40$

$\$10.45 \times 20 = \$209.00$

$\$1,880.40 + \$209.00 = \$2,089.40$

$\$189 \div 30 = \$6.30$

$\$6.30 \times 20 = \$126$

$\$2,089.40 + \$126 = \$2,215.4$ to the seller

31. The correct answer is (D). People who buy into co-ops buy shares in the underlying corporation and they get a stock certificate; the shares give them the right to a certain unit. Choice (A) is incorrect because it is the rental of unimproved land to a tenant with the intention that the tenant will build on the land. Choices (B) and (C) are incorrect because they are forms of ownership, not leases.

32. The correct answer is (D). Choice (A) is incorrect because it is a net listing. Choice (B) describes a transactional agency. Choice (C) describes a dual agency.

33. The correct answer is (D). Choice (D) is correct to the best of the seller's knowledge. Choice (A) is incorrect because this is not a requirement of the federal law. Choice (B) is incorrect because an agent has a responsibility to disclose any material fact about a property. The presence of lead paint is such a fact. Choice (C) is incorrect because the seller must only disclose the information; it is up to the buyer to decide what to do about it. Removing it could become a condition of sale, especially if there are young children in the buyer's family, or a contingency.

34. The correct answer is (D). Choices (A), (B), and (C) are common elements of ownership in a condominium, so they are incorrect answers to the question. Choice (D) is a limited common element, that is, its ownership—and use—is limited to one owner.

35. **The correct answer is (A).** Choice (B) is typically a credit to the buyer. Choice (C) is typically a debit to the seller. Choice (D) is typically a credit to the seller.

36. **The correct answer is (B).** Choice (A) is incorrect because it would occur before any sale of a foreclosed property. The person in default of the mortgage transfers title to the property to the lender without any court proceedings. Choice (C) is incorrect because choice (B) is the way to recover additional money to satisfy the rest of the mortgage. Choice (D) is incorrect because it mixes up the right of equitable redemption (paying off the complete mortgage by the person in default before [or after] a foreclosure sale) and the process of returning an interest in a property back to the original owner after the interest that another has held in the property has ended.

37. **The correct answer is (D).** Structural elements such as a home's foundation, choice (D), are not covered under home warranty insurance, but might be covered by a regular homeowner's policy depending on the cause of the problem. Choices (A), (B), and (C) are covered, so they are not the correct answer to the question. Choice (B) is an example of built-in appliances, which are typically covered. Choice (C) may have limits on the type or cost of repairs covered.

38. **The correct answer is (D).**

$743,257 − $587,000 = $156,257

$156,257 ÷ $743,257 = 0.266

2009 − 1975 = 34

0.266 ÷ 34 = 0.008, or 0.8% rate of depreciation

39. **The correct answer is (D).** The more recent the dates of sale, the more accurate the CMA will be. Choices (A) and (B) are incorrect because a CMA includes both the homes that sold and those that did not. Choice (C) is not as good an answer as choice (D) because the idea is to use the most recent data available.

40. **The correct answer is (B).** The better answer between choices (A) and (B) is choice (B). Choice (A) is incorrect because nondisclosure of material information with the intent to deceive is fraud, not just misrepresentation. Choice (C) is incorrect because "quiet enjoyment" refers to an owner's or a tenant's right to occupy and have the undisturbed use of real property, but that's not the issue in this scenario. Choice (D) is incorrect because the Stephens do have another option, that is, choice (B).

41. **The correct answer is (C).** Choices (A) and (B) are actions that take place before the buyer's agent notifies the buyer of the seller's acceptance. Choice (D) takes place after there is a valid contract.

42. **The correct answer is (C).** Choice (C) is done by the buyer's attorney. Choice (A) may seem as though it's not a realtor's job, but property taxes can be a great concern to homebuyers and the realtor in relaying information about the property taxes is not offering any tax advice. Choices (B) and (D) are responsibilities of a realtor in overseeing the process to closing.

43. **The correct answer is (A).** Choice (B) deals with areas other than housing such as employment and access to public places. Choice (C) prohibits discrimination based on disability in any program or activity receiving federal funding. Choice (D) prohibits discrimination based on age or disability in new construction of more than four units.

44. **The correct answer is (D).** By signing the contract of sale, a buyer has an equitable title in a property, the right to complete ownership once the purchase price has been paid

to the seller. Choice (A) is not conveyed until the full purchase price has been paid. Choice (B) describes a marketable title. Choice (C) seems like a good answer, but it's a distracter.

45. The correct answer is (C). Choices (A), (B), and (D) are all typical entries in an appraiser's report, so they are the wrong answers to the question. Choice (A) may be market value, price, investment value, etc. Choice (B) is the type of data that the appraiser collected and analyzed, such as tax records, area rents, recent sales, etc. Choice (D), the purpose, may be to set a sales price or to determine value for a mortgage or for refinancing, etc.

46. The correct answer is (C). Choice (C) means that the situation is as though there never was a signed contract. Choice (A) is incorrect because it is an estate that is conveyed when a previous estate ends, usually through death. Choice (B) is incorrect; a contract can be liquidated, that is, paid off to settle a debt, but it doesn't apply to this situation. Choice (D) is a distracter.

47. The correct answer is (C). Choices (A), (B), and (D) are incorrect because there was no sale.

48. The correct answer is (C). Choice (A) is incorrect because it is the opposite of what is true. Patton is under no obligation to buy the land; that's why it's an option. Choice (B) is also incorrect because it is the opposite of choice (C) that is true as long as Patton exercises the option according to its terms, and the answer to the question. Choice (D) is incorrect because an option to buy already includes the purchase price.

49. The correct answer is (D).

$5,445,000 \div 43,560 = 125$ acres

$125 \div 1.5 = 187.5$

50. The correct answer is (A). With choice (A), the mortgagor retains equitable title for the term of the mortgage. Choice (B) is incorrect though the first half of the answer describes lien theory. Choice (C) describes the lien theory of mortgage law. Choice (D) is incorrect because it is the mortgagor (the borrower) who receives equitable title in place of legal title.

51. The correct answer is (B). Choices (A), (C), and (D) would be covered by the Resource Conservation and Recovery Act (RCRA) of 1984, so they are incorrect answers to the question.

52. The correct answer is (D). A general warranty deed, choice (D), provides the most protection to a property buyer. Choice (A) is incorrect because it describes a grant deed. Choice (B) is incorrect because it describes a special warranty deed. Choice (C) is incorrect because it describes a judicial deed of some type.

53. The correct answer is (A). The map shows that different types of uses, including open space, are clustered in the community. The map shows a PUD (planned unit development), but that is not the term used for its zoning. Choice (C) is a distracter; the correct zoning term is downzoning and might be applicable to this development, but the question doesn't give enough information. Choice (D) is incorrect because, like choice (C), the term is incorrect and if corrected to "density" alone, could be true, but the question doesn't give enough information.

54. The correct answer is (A). Choices (B) and (D) are incorrect because affordable housing is sold based on income, not protected classes. Choice (C) is incorrect because the Fair Housing Act applies to sales in subdivisions regardless of its zoning.

55. **The correct answer is (B).** Choices (A) and (D) are used for writing legal descriptions of property, but neither is the name of the map that developers must file. Choice (C) is incorrect because plottage is the process of combining smaller plots of land into a larger one and thus increasing the value of the assembled land.

56. **The correct answer is (A).**

$1,280,000 \times 0.07 = \$89,600$

$51,072 \div \$89,600 = 0.57$

57. **The correct answer is (D).** $\$34,000 \times 0.0828 \times 1/12 = \$234.60$

58. **The correct answer is (C).** Choice (A) is partially correct because the amount of principal that is paid down increases, but the amount of the interest payment decreases, so the answer is incorrect. Choice (B) is incorrect because the principal part of the payment increases whereas the interest part decreases. Choice (D) is incorrect because the payment proportions of the interest and principal payments alter over time.

59. **The correct answer is (C).** Regulation Z issued by the Federal Reserve Board of Governors enforces consumer credit laws related to the disclosure by lenders of the true cost of credit (borrowing), choice (C). Choice (A) is enforced by the Department of Housing and Urban Development. Choice (B) is enforced mainly by the Environmental Protection Agency, and the mortgage industry is regulated mainly by the Treasury Department and the Federal Deposit Insurance Corporation.

60. **The correct answer is (A).** Choices (B), (C), and (D) are incorrect because appreciation and depreciation of property have nothing to do with the bundle of rights. They are economic factors related to property ownership. The other answers in each answer choice are rights related to the bundle of rights. One way to save time in answering questions with multiple items in answer choices is to read the first item in each line; if it's incorrect, check that answer choice off and don't bother reading that choice again. Then read the second item in the remaining choices, checking off any answer choices in which the second item is incorrect. Continue until you eliminate all but one answer choice.

61. **The correct answer is (D).** The earnest money is usually a small amount to show that the buyer is "in earnest" about buying a property until a contract can be negotiated and signed. It will eventually be counted toward the down payment. Choice (A) is incorrect because the down payment is the amount the lender requires that the buyer pay the seller in order to get a mortgage, and the amount of the earnest money is what the seller requires. Choice (B) is incorrect although the seller may use the earnest money as he or she wishes. Choice (C) is incorrect because if the buyer defaults, the earnest money may or may not go to the seller as damages for breach of contract, depending on the contract, but it would not go to the seller's broker.

62. **The correct answer is (D).** A junior mortgage is also known as a subordinate or an inferior mortgage. Choices (A) and (B) are distracters; they seem reasonable, but are incorrect. Choice (C) is incorrect. A junior mortgage may be a subprime mortgage, but not because it's subordinate to another mortgage.

63. **The correct answer is (C).** Choices (A), (B), and (D) and also accrued interest on the mortgage and association dues if the property is a townhome (PUD), co-op, or condo are required to be paid at closing, so they are incorrect answers to the question. Choice (C) is not a prepaid item, so it is the correct answer to the question.

64. The correct answer is (A).

$2,204,000 \times 0.045 = \$99,180$

$2,204,000 \times 0.065 = \$143,260$

$143,260 - \$99,180 = \$44,080$

$44,080 \div 12 = \$3,673.33$

65. The correct answer is (A). Choice (B) is incorrect because in some cases no down payment is required. Choice (C) is incorrect because the property must be a primary residence. Choice (D) is incorrect because credit rating, steady income, and a maximum debt ratio of 41 percent are considered by a lender in determining loan eligibility.

66. The correct answer is (C). Assessment ratio is the ratio of assessed value to market value. The process of elimination would help in answering this question if you didn't know the answer. Choice (A) would result in a huge tax bill, so no one would buy property in that community. Choice (B) would also result in a huge number, and also doesn't indicate if the tax rate is per hundred dollars or thousands or what. Choice (D) is a distracter. After three answers with "52" in them, the item writer throws in "48."

67. The correct answer is (D). Choices (A), (B), and (C) are all characteristics of an arm's length transaction, which is what any real estate transaction should be, and so are incorrect answers to the question. Choice (D) is incorrect; this is a condition of sale, not a standard of the legitimacy of a transaction.

68. The correct answer is (C). Choice (A) identifies potential contamination. Choice (B) involves taking samples and analyzing them to confirm contamination. Choice (D) develops a site management plan if the contamination is too large or dangerous to remove.

69. The correct answer is (B). Choice (A) is used in certain states in lieu of a certificate of title, choice (B), or abstract of title, choice (D), which are used to guarantee title, and have nothing to do with the mortgage.

70. The correct answer is (A).

$132,000 \times 0.03 \times 18 = \$71,280$

$132,000 - \$71,280 = \$60,720$

71. The correct answer is (A). Choice (B) does not give the tenants right of survivorship, which is an important consideration for married couples. Choice (C) is ownership by one entity, which may be an individual or a group such as a corporation. Choice (D) is incorrect because it refers to a rental situation, not ownership.

72. The correct answer is (C). Spot zoning is property zoned for a different purpose than the surrounding area. It can be beneficial, but can also be "arbitrary, capricious, and unreasonable." A zoning variance is a better way to deal with a zoning issue. Choice (A) is incorrect because the park did not exist previously to the current zoning. Choice (B) refers to the number of houses that may be built on an acre of land. Choice (D) is a distracter.

73. The correct answer is (C). Choice (A) is the maximum penalty for a first violation. Choices (B) and (D) are incorrect.

74. The correct answer is (B). Choice (A) is incorrect because parties in a tenancy in common do not have to put in the same amount of money, which would give each the same share in the tenancy. Choice (C) is the opposite of what is true about a tenancy in common; each party has control over his or her share. Choice (D) is incorrect for two reasons. First, there is no right of survivorship with a tenancy in common, and second, the question doesn't state that each party has a third share in the investment.

75. **The correct answer is (A).** Some states exempt homeowners from having their homes taken to pay certain kinds of debts; this doesn't extend to default on mortgages though. Choices (B) and (C) are incorrect because both refer to entities that are not private homes. Choice (D) is a form of ownership.

76. **The correct answer is (D).** Choices (A), (B), and (C) are true about exclusive right to sell listings, so they are incorrect answers to the question. Choices (C) and (D) may be confusing, but the "right to market" is not the same as the right of the owner to sell the property himself or herself. Choice (D) is incorrect, so it is the right answer to the question.

77. **The correct answer is (B).**

$1,050 \times 12 = $12,600

$12,600 \div 0.07 = $180,000

78. **The correct answer is (A).** A judgment lien can be obtained by a creditor for any number of reasons, for example, unpaid credit card bills or unpaid home improvement bills, but not a mortgage default. It is placed against all property, whereas choice (B) is placed against one specific property. Choice (C) is incorrect because a judgment lien is involuntary; a mortgage is voluntary. Choice (D) is a distracter.

79. **The correct answer is (C).** Choice (A) is incorrect because the secondary mortgage market does not provide mortgages to homebuyers. Choice (B) is incorrect because the secondary mortgage market has no requirements about PMI in mortgages that it securitizes, buys, and sells. Choice (D) is incorrect because Fannie Mae buys mortgages on the secondary mortgage market; it's not an insurer of mortgages.

80. **The correct answer is (B).**

$43,500 \times 0.5 = 21,780$

$21,780 \div 110' = 198'$

81. **The correct answer is (C).** Choice (A) is incorrect because it is only the down payment. Choice (B) is incorrect because it represents only the amount that the mortgage has been reduced. Choice (D) is incorrect it represents the amount of the outstanding principal plus the down payment.

82. **The correct answer is (C).** Choice (A) is simply deciding the selling price. Choice (B) is simply adjusting the value of comps upward or downward in relation to the subject property in order to estimate the subject property's value. Choice (D) is simply adjusting the selling price to better reflect the market value of the property.

83. **The correct answer is (C).** Choice (C) lists the main components of the monthly mortgage payment and are abbreviated as the PITI. Choice (A) is missing homeowner's insurance, which some lenders make borrowers pay a year in advance. Choice (B) is incorrect because it's homeowner's insurance, not PMI. PMI may be true for some mortgages, but not all mortgages. Choice (D) might be a good guess, but points are a one-time only charge.

84. **The correct answer is (B).** Choice (A) is a permanent easement that runs with the property—both the dominant and servient properties. Choice (C) is continued use of someone else's property for a long period of time. Choice (D) is also called easement by implication. As a result of an owner's selling off land, a parcel becomes landlocked. In order to have access to that parcel, the new owner creates an easement by necessity across the parcel to which his or her land was once joined.

85. **The correct answer is (C).** Familial status refers to children under 18, so only choice (C) applies. Choices (A), (B), and (D) are not protected under the familial status class.

86. **The correct answer is (D).**

    $75,000 \div 6 = \$12,500$

    $12,500 \times 7 = \$87,500$

87. **The correct answer is (D).** While a property owner who has accepted an offer on his or her property may accept back-up offers, the offerors must be told that there is an accepted offer on the property and any other back-up offers as well. Choices (A), (B), and (C) are incorrect.

88. **The correct answer is (C).** Choice (A) has broad powers to act for a principal, whereas the authority given to the agency in this case is limited. Choice (B) occurs when an agent acts in such a way that a third party thinks the agent has more authority than the agent has; in this case, if the agent made an offer on a property without clearing it with Peter James, the seller would reasonably think the agent had that authority. Choice (D) has broader powers than a special agent, but less broad powers than a universal agent.

89. **The correct answer is (A).** Choice (A) is also called useful life. Choice (B) is the period of time during which an improvement is estimated to last. Choice (C) is the functional age of an improvement based on the condition of the improvement and market conditions. Choice (D) is the chronological age of an improvement.

90. **The correct answer is (B).** The Nuclear Regulatory Commission (NRC) regulates the disposal of radioactive wastes, so it is not part of the oversight of federal MSWLF regulations, and, therefore, the correct answer to the question. Choices (A), (C), and (D) are regulated by the federal government, so they are incorrect answers to the question.

91. **The correct answer is (C).**

    $\$89,000 + \$97,000 + \$82,000 = \$268,000$

    $\$268,000 = \$100,000 + 168,000$

    $\$100,000 \times 0.06 = \$6,000$

    $\$168,000 \times 0.07 = \$11,760$

    $\$6,000 + \$11,760 = 17,760$

92. **The correct answer is (A).** Choices (B) and (C) are common errors, but still wrong. Choice (D) is the process for finding cost per square foot, not square footage.

93. **The correct answer is (B).** In addition to FIRREA, which was passed in 1989, regulators have issued three sets of guidelines for real estate appraisers: the Interagency Appraisal and Evaluation Guidelines (1994), the Independent Appraisal and Evaluation Functions (2003), and Fannie Mae and Freddie Mac's Guidance for Lenders and Appraisers (2009). Choice (A) is incorrect because real estate licensing laws are state laws. Choices (C) and (D) are distracters.

94. **The correct answer is (C).** Choice (A) is incorrect because HUD may impose a fine of up to $1,000 for each violation. Choice (B) is the maximum amount of a fine in a criminal prosecution for fraud in interstate land sales. Choice (D) is a distracter because $1 million seems like a lot of money, but how would HUD know what someone's lifetime would be?

95. **The correct answer is (C).** Choice (A) is incorrect because the vendee doesn't get title to the property until a certain number of monthly payments have been made. Choice (B) is incorrect because the mortgagor is the vendor of the property, not a financial institution. Contract for deed is used when financing is difficult for the vendee to get. Choice (D) is incorrect for the same reason as choice (B). A wraparound mortgage is one in which the buyer takes out a mortgage

that includes the remaining amount on the seller's mortgage and makes payments to his or her lender that include payments on the original mortgage. This lender then pays the original seller's mortgage; it is usually a method of refinancing. The new loan is second to the original debt, but the whole is considered one obligation.

96. **The correct answer is (A).**

$$335' \times 172' \times \frac{1}{2} = 28,810$$

$$28,810 \times \$2.55 = \$73,465.50$$

$$\$73,465.50 \times 0.06 = \$4,407.93$$

97. **The correct answer is (D).**

$$\$80,090 \div 12 = \$6,674.17$$

$$\$2,340 \div \$6,6674.17 = 0.35$$

98. **The correct answer is (C).** Answering this question correctly requires knowing that the generally accepted guidelines are that the percentage of the sum of payments for monthly mortgage, taxes, and nonhousing debt payments cannot be more than 35 percent of gross monthly income. Even without knowing what the Floyds' other monthly expenses are, you can tell that they cannot afford this mortgage. They are already at 35 percent.

99. **The correct answer is (B).** Choice (B) is a mortgage clause, not a deed clause, used in some states. It promises that the borrower will gain title when the mortgage has been satisfied. Choice (A) states the interest that the deed is granting and reiterates choice (C). Choice (D) is necessary in order for the deed, which is a contract, to be valid.

100. **The correct answer is (C).** Choice (C) is the only item in the list paid to the seller. Choice (A) is a disbursement to the seller's broker. Choice (B) is paid to the appropriate government department. Choice (D) is paid to the pest inspection company.

answers practice test 3

ANSWER SHEET PRACTICE TEST 4

1. Ⓐ Ⓑ Ⓒ Ⓓ	21. Ⓐ Ⓑ Ⓒ Ⓓ	41. Ⓐ Ⓑ Ⓒ Ⓓ	61. Ⓐ Ⓑ Ⓒ Ⓓ	81. Ⓐ Ⓑ Ⓒ Ⓓ
2. Ⓐ Ⓑ Ⓒ Ⓓ	22. Ⓐ Ⓑ Ⓒ Ⓓ	42. Ⓐ Ⓑ Ⓒ Ⓓ	62. Ⓐ Ⓑ Ⓒ Ⓓ	82. Ⓐ Ⓑ Ⓒ Ⓓ
3. Ⓐ Ⓑ Ⓒ Ⓓ	23. Ⓐ Ⓑ Ⓒ Ⓓ	43. Ⓐ Ⓑ Ⓒ Ⓓ	63. Ⓐ Ⓑ Ⓒ Ⓓ	83. Ⓐ Ⓑ Ⓒ Ⓓ
4. Ⓐ Ⓑ Ⓒ Ⓓ	24. Ⓐ Ⓑ Ⓒ Ⓓ	44. Ⓐ Ⓑ Ⓒ Ⓓ	64. Ⓐ Ⓑ Ⓒ Ⓓ	84. Ⓐ Ⓑ Ⓒ Ⓓ
5. Ⓐ Ⓑ Ⓒ Ⓓ	25. Ⓐ Ⓑ Ⓒ Ⓓ	45. Ⓐ Ⓑ Ⓒ Ⓓ	65. Ⓐ Ⓑ Ⓒ Ⓓ	85. Ⓐ Ⓑ Ⓒ Ⓓ
6. Ⓐ Ⓑ Ⓒ Ⓓ	26. Ⓐ Ⓑ Ⓒ Ⓓ	46. Ⓐ Ⓑ Ⓒ Ⓓ	66. Ⓐ Ⓑ Ⓒ Ⓓ	86. Ⓐ Ⓑ Ⓒ Ⓓ
7. Ⓐ Ⓑ Ⓒ Ⓓ	27. Ⓐ Ⓑ Ⓒ Ⓓ	47. Ⓐ Ⓑ Ⓒ Ⓓ	67. Ⓐ Ⓑ Ⓒ Ⓓ	87. Ⓐ Ⓑ Ⓒ Ⓓ
8. Ⓐ Ⓑ Ⓒ Ⓓ	28. Ⓐ Ⓑ Ⓒ Ⓓ	48. Ⓐ Ⓑ Ⓒ Ⓓ	68. Ⓐ Ⓑ Ⓒ Ⓓ	88. Ⓐ Ⓑ Ⓒ Ⓓ
9. Ⓐ Ⓑ Ⓒ Ⓓ	29. Ⓐ Ⓑ Ⓒ Ⓓ	49. Ⓐ Ⓑ Ⓒ Ⓓ	69. Ⓐ Ⓑ Ⓒ Ⓓ	89. Ⓐ Ⓑ Ⓒ Ⓓ
10. Ⓐ Ⓑ Ⓒ Ⓓ	30. Ⓐ Ⓑ Ⓒ Ⓓ	50. Ⓐ Ⓑ Ⓒ Ⓓ	70. Ⓐ Ⓑ Ⓒ Ⓓ	90. Ⓐ Ⓑ Ⓒ Ⓓ
11. Ⓐ Ⓑ Ⓒ Ⓓ	31. Ⓐ Ⓑ Ⓒ Ⓓ	51. Ⓐ Ⓑ Ⓒ Ⓓ	71. Ⓐ Ⓑ Ⓒ Ⓓ	91. Ⓐ Ⓑ Ⓒ Ⓓ
12. Ⓐ Ⓑ Ⓒ Ⓓ	32. Ⓐ Ⓑ Ⓒ Ⓓ	52. Ⓐ Ⓑ Ⓒ Ⓓ	72. Ⓐ Ⓑ Ⓒ Ⓓ	92. Ⓐ Ⓑ Ⓒ Ⓓ
13. Ⓐ Ⓑ Ⓒ Ⓓ	33. Ⓐ Ⓑ Ⓒ Ⓓ	53. Ⓐ Ⓑ Ⓒ Ⓓ	73. Ⓐ Ⓑ Ⓒ Ⓓ	93. Ⓐ Ⓑ Ⓒ Ⓓ
14. Ⓐ Ⓑ Ⓒ Ⓓ	34. Ⓐ Ⓑ Ⓒ Ⓓ	54. Ⓐ Ⓑ Ⓒ Ⓓ	74. Ⓐ Ⓑ Ⓒ Ⓓ	94. Ⓐ Ⓑ Ⓒ Ⓓ
15. Ⓐ Ⓑ Ⓒ Ⓓ	35. Ⓐ Ⓑ Ⓒ Ⓓ	55. Ⓐ Ⓑ Ⓒ Ⓓ	75. Ⓐ Ⓑ Ⓒ Ⓓ	95. Ⓐ Ⓑ Ⓒ Ⓓ
16. Ⓐ Ⓑ Ⓒ Ⓓ	36. Ⓐ Ⓑ Ⓒ Ⓓ	56. Ⓐ Ⓑ Ⓒ Ⓓ	76. Ⓐ Ⓑ Ⓒ Ⓓ	96. Ⓐ Ⓑ Ⓒ Ⓓ
17. Ⓐ Ⓑ Ⓒ Ⓓ	37. Ⓐ Ⓑ Ⓒ Ⓓ	57. Ⓐ Ⓑ Ⓒ Ⓓ	77. Ⓐ Ⓑ Ⓒ Ⓓ	97. Ⓐ Ⓑ Ⓒ Ⓓ
18. Ⓐ Ⓑ Ⓒ Ⓓ	38. Ⓐ Ⓑ Ⓒ Ⓓ	58. Ⓐ Ⓑ Ⓒ Ⓓ	78. Ⓐ Ⓑ Ⓒ Ⓓ	98. Ⓐ Ⓑ Ⓒ Ⓓ
19. Ⓐ Ⓑ Ⓒ Ⓓ	39. Ⓐ Ⓑ Ⓒ Ⓓ	59. Ⓐ Ⓑ Ⓒ Ⓓ	79. Ⓐ Ⓑ Ⓒ Ⓓ	99. Ⓐ Ⓑ Ⓒ Ⓓ
20. Ⓐ Ⓑ Ⓒ Ⓓ	40. Ⓐ Ⓑ Ⓒ Ⓓ	60. Ⓐ Ⓑ Ⓒ Ⓓ	80. Ⓐ Ⓑ Ⓒ Ⓓ	100. Ⓐ Ⓑ Ⓒ Ⓓ

answer sheet

Practice Test 4

100 Questions • 3 Hours

> Directions: Read each question carefully and mark the letter of the best answer on the answer sheet.

1. Which of the following is NOT among the governmental factors that influence housing values?

   (A) Property taxes

   (B) Zoning

   (C) Interest rates

   (D) Building codes

2. John Hall left his estate, including his real property, for the care of his son with disabilities. When the son dies, the estate, including the real property, will pass to his daughter. The daughter is known as a

   (A) revertor.

   (B) sublessee.

   (C) remainderman.

   (D) subordinate inheritor.

3. A broker receives a 7% commission on the first $150,000 and 3% on any amount over $150,000 for each house sold. What would be the loss in commission if a house listed for $240,000 settled for 22% less?

   (A) $2,700

   (B) $10,500

   (C) $1,116

   (D) $1,584

4. Shirley Jordan was told that she retained equitable title to her newly purchased home, but the bank had legal title. She must live in a state that bases it mortgage law on

   (A) lien theory.

   (B) title abstract theory.

   (C) title theory.

   (D) transitional theory.

5. Anita Oshodi has decided to pay three points on her mortgage. If her mortgage is $354,000, how much is she paying for points?

   (A) $106.20

   (B) $1,062

   (C) $10,620

   (D) $106,200

6. In order to reduce the amount of interest that accrues before the first monthly mortgage payment, mortgagees try to close on

   (A) the first day of the month.

   (B) the fifteenth of the month.

   (C) the last day of the month.

   (D) When a closing occurs doesn't affect the amount of interest accrued.

7. In a housing discrimination case, an administrative law judge can impose all of the following EXCEPT

(A) payment of a fine to the federal government.

(B) payment of damages, which include humiliation, pain, and suffering, to the complainant.

(C) injunctive or other forms of relief such as making the property available to the complainant.

(D) closing the building.

8. The buyer in a contract for deed is called a

(A) vendor.

(B) vendee.

(C) lessor.

(D) lessee.

9. The service station on Mulberry Street has an assessed value of $52,000. The town has a business tax rate of 6.5 mills. Next year, the rate is going up to 8.2 mills. What is the difference in taxes that the station will pay?

(A) $426.40

(B) $88.40

(C) $126.40

(D) $27.40

10. An alienation clause in a mortgage does which of the following?

(A) States the type of foreclosure that can be used by the lender to take possession of the property if the mortgagee defaults

(B) Provides for how the ownership will be divided in a noncommunity property state should the owners divorce

(C) States the mortgagee will have full title to the property once the mortgage is paid in full

(D) Requires that a buyer assuming the mortgage on the property from the current buyer be approved by the lender

11. The Mayfields are the sellers in an escrow closing. They need to give the escrow agent which of the following before the closing?

(A) Certified check to pay off their mortgage

(B) Homeowner's insurance policy

(C) Executed deed to their property

(D) Proof of title insurance

12. Al Janssen works for a computer company and lives abroad for months at a time, so he sublets his apartment while he's gone. His last tenant has refused to leave at the end of the sublease, creating a/an

(A) periodic tenancy.

(B) estate at sufferance.

(C) estate at will.

(D) tenancy by possession.

13. The first month's interest on a 1-year loan for $34,000 at 8.2 percent is $234.60. If the monthly payments are $2,962.01, including interest, what is the amount of interest paid in the second month?

(A) $234.60

(B) $215.78

(C) $220.98

(D) $235.90

14. Which of the following would typically have to be paid off first at a closing?

    (A) Property tax lien dated September 15, 2009

    (B) Materialman's lien dated May 12, 2010

    (C) IRS income tax lien dated January 19, 2010

    (D) Lien for nonpayment of water and sewer utilities dated August 21, 2009

15. Ebony Baxter has signed a two-year lease on an apartment managed by Realty Inc. The lease has a 2 percent rent increase at the end of the first year. What kind of lease has she signed?

    (A) Percentage lease

    (B) Step lease

    (C) Graduated lease

    (D) Net lease

16. In the above example, Ebony has what kind of interest in her apartment?

    (A) Leased fee interest

    (B) Leasehold estate

    (C) Lessor interest

    (D) None

17. A farmhouse sold on May 30 for $687,432. If the real estate taxes of $6,038.60 are paid in arrears for one year on September 15, who owes whom how much?

    (A) $4,277.31 to the seller

    (B) $3,774.21 to the seller

    (C) $3,774.21 to the buyer

    (D) $4,277.31 to the buyer

18. Angelina Boccavich is trying to decide whether to buy a condo or use her savings to start an online jewelry business. In buying the condo, she gives up the chance to make money on a business, but the condo is good investment. Which economic principle is creating her dilemma?

    (A) Contribution

    (B) Increasing returns

    (C) Supply and demand

    (D) Opportunity cost

19. Which of the following is NOT considered in appraising unimproved land?

    (A) Location

    (B) Financing

    (C) Any restrictions on property rights

    (D) Siting

20. The local furniture store property sold and had an 8% rate of appreciation per year for 12 years. It was originally bought for $653,800. What was the latest sales price?

    (A) $627,648

    (B) $1,281,448

    (C) $607,104

    (D) $1,265,439

21. Win Farrell asks his neighbor Jack Straw, a realtor, to help him sell his house. Jack gives Win suggestions about staging the house and then brings some buyers through. One of the couples makes an offer that Jack presents to Win who accepts. Jack then shepherds Win through the closing. Jack has what kind of agency with Win?

    (A) Agency by ratification

    (B) Agency by estoppel

    (C) Express agency

    (D) Agency coupled with an interest

22. In the above example, Jerry March who lives next door to Jack takes him aside and says that he hopes that Jack doesn't show the house to any of "those people." Jack's response should be that he

    (A) will show the house to anyone who will fit into the neighborhood.

    (B) doesn't know what Jerry means.

    (C) will show the property to anyone who has adequate finances to buy the house.

    (D) has to show the house to anyone who wants to buy a house.

23. In the above example, if Jack showed the house only to young white married couples, he would be practicing

    (A) redlining.

    (B) discrimination based on familial status.

    (C) steering.

    (D) bundling.

24. A township contains how many acres?

    (A) 640

    (B) 4,840

    (C) 5,280

    (D) 43,560

25. Two neighboring farms are up for sale for development. One recently sold for $759,000 and contained 173 acres. If the other is 143 acres, what is its value?

    (A) $642,987

    (B) $918,230

    (C) $627,381

    (D) $759,000

26. All of the following are recorded after a closing EXCEPT

    (A) the mortgage.

    (B) liens.

    (C) inspection reports.

    (D) easements.

27. In terms of disclosure about material facts that affect the value or use of a property, a realtor

    (A) doesn't have to disclose anything more than is on the seller's disclosure form.

    (B) has to disclose anything that he or she knows is of a material nature regardless of what is on the form.

    (C) has a fiduciary duty to the seller to protect the seller's best interest and so must abide by what the seller discloses.

    (D) has no responsibility; it is the seller's responsibility only.

28. Termination by performance of a listing agreement occurs when

    (A) the term of the agreement has expired and the agent has worked conscientiously to bring buyers to the property.

    (B) an agent brings an offer from a ready, willing, and able buyer to a seller who accepts the offer.

    (C) the seller terminates the agency because of a perceived lack of interest in the listing by the realtor.

    (D) the seller and the broker agree to end the agreement because of a lack of concurrence on what the broker should be doing.

29. A joint tenancy requires unities of

    (A) time, title, interest, and control.

    (B) title, possession, interest, and consideration.

    (C) time, interest, title, and possession.

    (D) title, control, survivorship, and possession.

30. What is the cost of the concrete needed to pave the Lewis' driveway if it is 80' long by 14' wide and 6" deep? The concrete costs $105 per cubic yard.
    (A) $2,178.75
    (B) $2,205
    (C) $2,100
    (D) $26,133.33

31. Concurrent ownership is NOT a right of which of the following forms of ownership?
    (A) Tenancy in severalty
    (B) Tenancy by the entirety
    (C) Community property
    (D) Joint tenancy

32. In a dual agency, a real estate broker
    (A) acts solely as an intermediary between seller and buyer.
    (B) shares listings with other brokers.
    (C) represents both the seller and the buyer in a transaction.
    (D) sells real estate as well as acts as a property manager for some clients.

33. An aging elevator would be considered in an appraisal as a/an
    (A) curable physical deterioration.
    (B) curable economic obsolescence.
    (C) incurable functional obsolescence.
    (D) curable functional obsolescence.

34. A typical listing agreement will include all of the following EXCEPT
    (A) zoning.
    (B) property taxes.
    (C) type of agency created by the listing agreement.
    (D) closing date.

35. An assignment of a lease is a
    (A) partial transfer of rights between landlord and lessee.
    (B) partial transfer of rights from sub-lessor to sublessee.
    (C) total transfer of rights from lessee to a third party.
    (D) total transfer of rights from sublessee to sublessee.

36. Chris Phillips, a broker, has a contract to sell a lot on Oak Lane. He will receive 3% for the first $25,000 and 7.5% for every dollar over that. What was the selling price of the property if his commission is $1,800?
    (A) $14,000
    (B) $39,000
    (C) $25,000
    (D) $1,050

37. Which of the following statements accurately describes subprime mortgages?
    (A) Subprime mortgages originate in the subprime mortgage market.
    (B) Subprime mortgages are taken out by borrowers with good credit ratings.
    (C) Subprime mortgages are more likely to go to foreclosure than other types of mortgages.
    (D) Subprime mortgages are fixed-rate mortgages only.

38. The difference between earnest money and a down payment is that the buyer's
    (A) agent requires earnest money with the listing, and the seller requires a down payment with the sales contract.
    (B) lender requires a down payment, and the seller requires earnest money.
    (C) lender requires earnest money, and the seller requires a down payment.
    (D) lender requires earnest money, and the seller's lender requires a down payment.

39. Which of the following is considered fraud on the part of a realtor?

(A) Failure to display the Fair Housing poster

(B) Failure to submit all offers to the seller

(C) Acting as if one is employed by a seller or buyer when one is not

(D) Failure to maintain contact with one's principal between offer delivery and acceptance and the closing

40. Which of the following describes market allocation?

(A) Stan Bailey and Ed Jarowski of South Side Realty decide to carve up the South Side district between them looking for properties to list.

(B) Stan Bailey of South Side Realty and Bob Wood of First Rate Realty meet over lunch to discuss how they might combine their money to advertise listings on the South Side.

(C) Stan Bailey of South Side Realty and Bob Wood of First Rate Realty meet on January 2 to decide what commission rate their agencies will charge for the coming year.

(D) Stan Bailey of South Side Realty and Bob Wood of First Rate Realty meet on January 2 and decide which agency will sell duplexes and which will sell stand-alone homes in the district.

41. Al Simone will pay $5,000 in interest on a 2-year, $75,000 loan. What is the interest rate he is being charged?

(A) 0.278%

(B) $6\frac{2}{3}\%$

(C) $3\frac{1}{3}\%$

(D) $4\frac{1}{2}\%$

42. John Girardi's brother wants him to sell his vacation home in an adjoining state. Joe who is a licensed broker in his own state

(A) must decline unless he gets a license in the adjoining state.

(B) must ask a broker friend to sign him on as an independent contractor for that one sale.

(C) can sell the property on his own without any special arrangements.

(D) can get a temporary permit from the adjoining state's real estate commission for this one sale.

43. The owner of a real estate brokerage that is a franchisee of a national real estate corporation receives all of the following franchisee benefits EXCEPT

(A) national branding of his or her local office.

(B) a bonus if the office meets its sales goals.

(C) access to technology tools such as Internet marketing.

(D) attendance at sales training workshops.

44. The Penningtons have recently had their house reassessed and it was valued at $357,840. If the assessment rate is 63%, and the school district tax rate is 6.5 mills, and the county's tax rate is 3.25 mills, what is the actual value of the house?

(A) $348,894

(B) $553,008

(C) $568,000

(D) $687,439

45. Which of the following loans is exempt from Regulation Z?

(A) Commercial mortgages

(B) VA-guaranteed mortgages

(C) Mortgages on owner-occupied premises of 4 or fewer units

(D) FHA-insured mortgages

46. A Mortgage Loan Disclosure Statement must be delivered to the borrower

   (A) within 48 hours of applying for the mortgage.

   (B) within 3 days of applying for the mortgage.

   (C) within 10 business days of applying for the mortgage.

   (D) the day before the closing.

47. For a loan to meet the requirements of Fannie Mae and Freddie Mac, it must have a loan-to-value ratio of

   (A) 80/20.

   (B) less than 80 percent.

   (C) less than or equal to 80 percent.

   (D) more than 80 percent.

48. Your vacation home was valued new at $1,357,990. If you were to use straight-line depreciation to depreciate it over 25 years, what would be the depreciation each year?

   (A) $45,319.60

   (B) $54,319.60

   (C) $108.639.20

   (D) $81,639.20

49. Chet Murray is appraising a school property for a developer who wants to turn it into condos. Chet would probably use which approach as the main method of valuing the property?

   (A) Cost approach

   (B) Sales comparison approach

   (C) Use value approach

   (D) Income approach

50. An apartment building with 14 units renting for $1,250 each a month just sold. If the buyer was told to expect a 9.5% return, what was the cost of the building?

   (A) $2,210,526

   (B) $221,052

   (C) $210,000

   (D) $2,100,000

51. Jan Pearson works with Maxwell Real Estate, and Mary Fitz finds her a townhome. The property was listed by Roy Alexander in the same office. To avoid confusion over whom Maxwell Real Estate is representing, what kind of agency offers the best protection to both the seller and Jan Pearson?

   (A) Buyer agency

   (B) Designated agency

   (C) Dual agency

   (D) Alternate agency

52. The four characteristics of value are utility, scarcity, transferability, and

   (A) effective supply.

   (B) effective demand.

   (C) economic life.

   (D) effective age.

53. Louise Parkhurst owns three parcels of land that all share at least 1 common border. The first is a triangle with a front of 90' and a depth of 210', the second is a square with a depth of 210', and the third is a rectangle with a front of 170' and a depth of 210'. What is the total acreage of the three parcels?

   (A) 1.50 acres

   (B) 1.75 acres

   (C) 2.25 acre

   (D) 2.05 acres

54. Keeshawn James has an FHA-insured mortgage, so he must have a

   (A) conventional mortgage.

   (B) conforming mortgage.

   (C) nonconforming mortgage.

   (D) fixed-rate mortgage.

55. The City/County of Philadelphia has a transfer tax on real estate sales. If the transfer tax on $444,000 is $8,880, what is the rate per $1,000?

(A) 0.02 percent

(B) 0.2 percent

(C) 2 percent

(D) 20 percent

56. Which of the following is considered personalty in a real estate transaction?

(A) Breakfast nook

(B) Refrigerator

(C) Dishwasher

(D) Chandelier

57. Which of the following is a debit to the seller at closing?

(A) Earnest money

(B) Survey cost

(C) Property tax payment

(D) Prepayment penalty

58. What is the amount owed the seller at closing on prepaid taxes based on a sale of $765,832, with an assessment rate of 65% and a tax rate of 32 mills, if closing is on July 1?

(A) $632.22

(B) $1,327.44

(C) $7,964.65

(D) $15,929.30

59. Rochelle Nagucchi is buying the leather couch and chairs in the living room from the Dubinskis when she buys their house. She is including the price of the furniture in her mortgage. She is getting a/an

(A) open mortgage.

(B) blanket mortgage.

(C) package mortgage.

(D) wraparound mortgage.

60. The more land that is zoned for a particular use in an area

(A) results in a lower value for the land than if there were less land zoned for that use.

(B) has no effect on the value of the land.

(C) drives up the value of the land.

(D) affects the value negatively or positively depending on the zoned use.

61. A borrower receiving an MLDS would expect all the following costs itemized EXCEPT

(A) real estate commission.

(B) appraisal fee.

(C) life insurance.

(D) credit report.

62. A property with a rental cottage sells for $275,000 on July 5. If rent is due on the fifth, who owes what to whom?

(A) Not enough information

(B) Buyer owes

(C) Seller owes

(D) Neither owes

63. In looking at well-kept homes in Parkside, buyers typically refer to the kitchens and bathrooms as dated. This comment is an example of

(A) functional obsolescence.

(B) economic obsolescence.

(C) physical deterioration.

(D) economic life.

64. The Doyle family has owned oceanfront property for 93 years. During that time, the ocean has steadily encroached on the beach in front of their house until it is now 10 feet from the front door. This process is known as

(A) alienation.

(B) propulsion.

(C) erosion.

(D) accretion.

65. Charlie Samuels owned several parcels of land in addition to a house. He died without a will, but he left three daughters. In this case, which of the following applies?

(A) The government takes the property by escheat.

(B) The government takes the property by right of eminent domain.

(C) The daughters claim testamentary trust.

(D) The daughters claim title by descent.

66. In appraising a townhouse that is being bought to rent, the appraiser would most probably use the

(A) cost approach.

(B) sales comparison approach.

(C) reproduction and replacement approach.

(D) income approach.

67. Mortgagors who get an FHA-insured loan have to pay an initial insurance premium that is what percent of the value of the loan?

(A) 1.75 percent

(B) 2 percent

(C) 2.25 percent

(D) 3 percent

68. Jumbo mortgages are loans that

(A) are mortgages that permit the mortgagor to borrow additional money so that the mortgage can increase back to its original amount.

(B) are above the limit on mortgages for securitization on the secondary mortgage market.

(C) include senior and junior mortgages.

(D) are the same as a 30-year, fixed-rate interest-only mortgage.

69. If a house depreciates at a rate of 3.75% for 4 years and was worth $132,800 originally, what is it worth today?

(A) $106,420

(B) $110,870

(C) $112,880

(D) $157,720

70. The grantor in a real estate sale is the legal term for the

(A) buyer.

(B) seller.

(C) lending institution for the buyer.

(D) lending institution for the seller.

71. Which of the following is an example of nonconforming use?

(A) A convenience store in a commercial zone

(B) A bar and restaurant in a residential zone

(C) A gas station that predates garden apartments in the neighborhood

(D) An elementary school in a mixed-use zone

72. If land in a development goes for $45,675 an acre, how much would a 139,392 square foot lot sell for?

(A) $146,160

(B) $156,160

(C) $166,160

(D) $176,160

73. The Johnsons' attorney has told them that they need to order a complete history of the property that they are going to buy. They need to order a/an

(A) certificate of title.

(B) abstract of title.

(C) Torrens certificate.

(D) title company's opinion of title.

74. Joe Sanders is unable to pay his mortgage, so the First National Mortgage Company has gone to court for an order so First National can sell Sanders' home. What kind of foreclosure is this?

(A) Judicial foreclosure

(B) Strict foreclosure

(C) Default foreclosure

(D) Nonjudicial foreclosure

75. If the property in the above example sells for less than its mortgage, First National can ask the court for a/an

(A) deficiency judgment.

(B) default judgment.

(C) short sale judgment.

(D) underwater mortgage judgment.

76. All of the following are restrictive covenants that typically appear in subdevelopment deeds EXCEPT

(A) schedule for trash pickup.

(B) limitations on the number of pets.

(C) rules regarding the rental of a property.

(D) regulations regarding the setbacks of homes.

77. Taywana Johns sold a property for $452,850. After closing costs of $1,800 and Taywana's 5.63% commission, how much money did the seller net from the sale?

(A) $422,520.45

(B) $423,720.45

(C) $424,320.45

(D) $425,620.45

78. As part of their negotiations, the Millers included in the contract of sale that the seller would remedy before closing any pest problems that were found in the dwelling. The inspection found the presence of carpenter ants. At the walk-through, it was apparent that the seller had not remedied the problem. The Millers can do all of the following EXCEPT

(A) walk away from the deal if this is a contingency of sale.

(B) go through with the closing and take the house as-is.

(C) go through with the closing, but force the seller to pay for the remediation out of the proceeds of the sale.

(D) postpone the closing for 5 days while the seller remediates the problem.

79. Randy Jankovich has listed the Tubmans' 2,500 square foot, 3-bedroom, 3-and-a-half bath house. In order to determine a sales price, he will conduct a

(A) sales comparison analysis.

(B) comparative market analysis.

(C) highest and best use analysis.

(D) site valuation.

80. *Lis pendens* is a public notice that a lawsuit is pending

(A) between tenants.

(B) between a divorcing couple.

(C) involving a lien on property.

(D) by the owner of a property against the property manager.

81. Jack Wong and Kirby Loh own several apartment buildings together. Jack dies and Kirby takes over Jack's ownership of the business. The two must have had which of the following kind of ownership arrangement?

(A) Tenancy in common

(B) Joint tenancy

(C) Partnership

(D) Corporation

82. That listing agreements be in writing is required by
    (A) a state's real estate licensing laws.
    (B) a state's Statute of Frauds.
    (C) RESPA.
    (D) HUD.

83. The fiduciary responsibility of reasonable skill and diligence refers to an agent's duty to
    (A) alert prospective buyers to the presence of small animals so they aren't accidentally let out during a showing.
    (B) be careful not to damage anything when showing a house.
    (C) market a property accurately.
    (D) check with other agents about possible showings before arranging to take their buyers to a house.

84. What is the actual value of a house that has a tax bill of $4,485, if the tax rate is $0.45 per hundred and the rate of assessment is 67%?
    (A) $1,023,473.54
    (B) $1,085,555.56
    (C) $1,620,232.18
    (D) $1,852,893.53

85. Mary Jane Turo is a 60-year-old African American woman raising her grandson who is ten. She applies to rent an apartment in the Lakefront Apartment complex. She is protected under all the following classes EXCEPT
    (A) familial status.
    (B) race.
    (C) gender.
    (D) age.

86. The Ruizes are considering buying a riverfront property on the Mississippi River. Their realtor explains that they will have riparian rights. Which of the following definitions would the realtor choose?
    (A) They will own from the water's edge to 200 feet out into the river.
    (B) They will own to the water's edge or to the average or the mean high water mark.
    (C) They will own from the water's edge to the center of the waterway.
    (D) They will own from the water's edge to the ship channel wherever it begins.

87. Which of the following is an easement in gross?
    (A) Sewer line
    (B) Neighborhood child's cutting through your backyard to get to the bus stop though you have asked the parents to stop the child
    (C) Driveway through your side yard for a neighbor who has no other access to the street
    (D) Court-ordered right of way for a footpath through your beachfront property

88. A typical note for a mortgage contains
    (A) amount of the mortgage, interest rate, and schedule of payments.
    (B) schedule of payments, *habendum,* and acceleration clause.
    (C) acceleration clause, interest rate, and prepayment clause.
    (D) property tax rate, interest rate, and schedule of payments.

89. Which phrase in the following ad would be considered a violation of the Fair Housing Act: "Two-bedroom apartment for rent in elevator building with handicap-accessible bathroom. Husband and wife preferred. Children welcome."

(A) "Elevator building"

(B) "Handicap-accessible bathroom"

(C) "Husband and wife preferred"

(D) "Children welcome"

90. What is the principal on a loan that has an interest rate of 5.57% and a monthly interest payment of $763.98?

(A) $176,987.32

(B) $164,591.74

(C) $154,982.53

(D) $142,583.62

91. The Todds are buying their first home. Actual ownership of the home will be conveyed to them when the

(A) deed is recorded in the appropriate recording office.

(B) deed is delivered to the Todds at the closing.

(C) notary notarizes the deed.

(D) Todds hand over the check to the person conducting the closing.

92. The Todds have written a check for property taxes to be placed in an escrow account. This is shown at the closing as a

(A) credit to the seller.

(B) debit to the seller.

(C) credit to the buyer.

(D) debit to the buyer.

93. All of the following are trigger terms that require full disclosure in mortgage ads EXCEPT

(A) amount of a down payment.

(B) dollar amount of finance charges.

(C) term of the mortgage.

(D) APR.

94. Charlie Bartolli rents desk space and pays for all his expenses including advertising the properties that he lists. He receives 100 percent commission on his sales. Charlie is a/an

(A) franchiser.

(B) independent contractor.

(C) licensee.

(D) employee of a brokerage.

95. A fire insurance policy has an unused portion of 4 months and 16 days. If the policy cost $272 for 3 years, how much is the unused portion worth?

(A) $27.43

(B) $34.24

(C) $102.84

(D) $94.67

96. Recording the appropriate documents after a closing provides

(A) closure.

(B) constructive notice.

(C) actual notice.

(D) express notice.

97. Harold and Janelle Scott want to buy a house in an area that has easy access to the subway and bus systems. Which of the influences on housing values is this?

(A) Economic factor

(B) Environmental factor

(C) Political factor

(D) Social factor

98. When an appraiser is looking at the quality of interior finishes, the appraiser will evaluate all of the following EXCEPT

(A) countertops.

(B) walls.

(C) HVAC.

(D) presence or absence of molding.

99. Harvey McDonald has just moved into a townhome that is divided in the front from its neighbor by a narrow strip of land. The neighbor has been planting flowers in this strip for 20 years. The neighbor informs him that the land is hers and she intends to continue planting in it, regardless of what his deed says. She is claiming the land

(A) as a party wall.

(B) by adverse possession.

(C) by inverse condemnation.

(D) by voluntary alienation.

100. The Taylors are getting a general warranty on their home purchase. They expect that it will contain all of the following EXCEPT

(A) covenant of right to convey.

(B) covenant of right to grant.

(C) covenant of quiet enjoyment.

(D) covenant against encumbrances

ANSWER KEY AND EXPLANATIONS

1. C	21. A	41. C	61. C	81. B
2. C	22. C	42. A	62. D	82. A
3. D	23. C	43. B	63. A	83. C
4. C	24. A	44. C	64. C	84. C
5. C	25. C	45. A	65. D	85. D
6. C	26. C	46. B	66. D	86. B
7. D	27. B	47. C	67. C	87. A
8. B	28. B	48. B	68. B	88. A
9. B	29. C	49. D	69. C	89. C
10. D	30. A	50. A	70. B	90. B
11. C	31. A	51. B	71. C	91. B
12. B	32. C	52. B	72. A	92. D
13. B	33. A	53. D	73. B	93. D
14. C	34. D	54. B	74. B	94. B
15. C	35. C	55. A	75. A	95. B
16. B	36. B	56. B	76. A	96. B
17. D	37. C	57. D	77. C	97. B
18. D	38. B	58. C	78. C	98. C
19. D	39. C	59. C	79. B	99. B
20. B	40. D	60. A	80. C	100. B

1. **The correct answer is (C).** Choice (C) is an economic factor that influences housing values. Choices (A), (B), and (D) are political or governmental factors that influence housing values, so they are incorrect answers to the question.

2. **The correct answer is (C).** Choice (B) is a person who sublets an apartment. Choices (A) and (D) are distracters. They seem familiar so they might be the right answer, but they are meant to confuse.

3. **The correct answer is (D).**

    $100\% - 22\% = 78\%$ $\$240,000 = \$150,000 + \$90,000$

    $\$150,000 \times 0.07 = \$10,500$

    $\$90,000 \times 0.03 = \$2,700$

    $\$10,500 + \$2,700 = \$13,200$

    $\$240,000 \times 0.78 = \$187,200$

    $\$187,200 = \$150,000 + \$37,200$

    $\$37,200 \times 0.03 = \$1,116$

    $\$10,500 + \$1,116 = \$11,616$

    $\$13,200 - \$11,616 = \$1,584$

4. **The correct answer is (C).** In choice (A), the legal title passes to the buyer, and the mortgage is a lien on the property until it is paid off. Choices (B) and (D) are distracters. The third theory on which mortgage law is based is the intermediate theory, which is similar to title theory except in how foreclosure is done.

5. **The correct answer is (C).** $354,000 × 0.03 = $10,620

6. **The correct answer is (C).** Choices (A) and (B) open the mortgagee to a full month's or half month's worth of accrued interest. Choice (D) is incorrect because when a closing occurs does affect the amount of interest that accrues on the mortgage for the first monthly payment.

7. **The correct answer is (D).** Choices (A), (B), and (C), as well as ordering the respondent to pay reasonable attorney's fees for the complainant and court costs are penalties that can be levied in housing discrimination cases. There are also criminal penalties for violating the Fair Housing Act.

8. **The correct answer is (B).** Choice (A) is the seller. Choices (C) and (D) relate to rentals, not purchases. Choice (C) is the landlord, and choice (D) is the tenant.

9. **The correct answer is (B).**

    $52,000 × 0.0065 = $338

    $52,000 × 0.0082 = $426.4

    $426.4 – $338 = $88.4

    OR

    0.0082 – 0.0065 = 0.0017

    $52,000 × 0.0017 = $88.4

10. **The correct answer is (D).** Choice (A) is incorrect. Choice (B) is a distracter. Choice (C) is incorrect because it defines the defeasance clause in a mortgage.

11. **The correct answer is (C).** Choices (A), (B), and (D) are the responsibility of the buyer.

12. **The correct answer is (B).** Choice (A) is incorrect because it is for a specific period of time, and at the end of that time, the lease renews automatically. Choice (C) is incorrect because after the lease has ended with an estate at will, the landlord allows the tenant to remain. Choice (D) is a distracter.

13. **The correct answer is (B).**

    $2,962.01 – $234.60 = $2,727.41

    $34,000 – $2,727.41 = $31,272.59

    $31,272.59 × 0.0828 × 1/12 = $215.78

14. **The correct answer is (C).** Choice (D) is the earliest dated lien, but the IRS takes precedence and would be paid first. Choices (A), (D), and (B) would be paid in that order according to the order of priority. Materialman's lien is also called a mechanic's lien.

15. **The correct answer is (C).** Choice (A) refers to a commercial lease in which the renter pays a base rent plus a percentage of the gross sales of his or her business. Choice (B) is a distracter. Choice (D) is also a business lease in which the renter pays certain costs related to the premises such as the real estate taxes.

16. **The correct answer is (B).** Choices (A) and (C) refer to the landlord. Choice (D) is incorrect because once the lessee (Ebony) has signed the lease she receives an interest in the apartment, which is the right to occupy it.

17. **The correct answer is (D).**

    $6,038.60 ÷ 12 = $503.22

    $503.22 ÷ 30 = $16.77

    $503.22 × 8 = $4,025.76

    30 – 15 = 15

$16.77 \times 15 = \$251.55$

$4,025.76 + \$251.55 = \$4,277.31$

The seller owes the buyer because the taxes are paid in arrears.

18. **The correct answer is (D).** Choice (D) is the cost of doing something measured in terms of not doing something else. The cost is the loss of whatever the next best alternative use would bring. Choice (A) refers to the addition or subtraction of value that an item adds or subtracts, such as painting a room. Choice (B) refers to the increasing value that adding additional items will bring, with less value being added with each item. Choice (C) refers to the amount of property on the market at a certain price and the willingness of buyers to buy at that price.

19. **The correct answer is (D).** The land is unimproved, so choice (D), the location of the improvement on the land, doesn't apply. Choices (A), (B), and (C) are considered in appraising unimproved land. If the seller of comparison property provided financing or made other concessions about the sale, this can affect the value of the property.

20. **The correct answer is (B).**

$653,800 \times 0.08 = \$52,304$

$52,403 \times 12 = \$627,648$

$627,648 + \$653,800 = \$1,281,448$

21. **The correct answer is (A).** Choice (B) involves the agent doing more than the agreed-upon agency typically includes. There is no evidence of this in the scenario. Choice (C) is incorrect because there is no indication that Win and Jack signed an agreement. Choice (D) is incorrect because while Jack undoubtedly cares who moves in next door, he has no legal interest in the property.

22. **The correct answer is (C).** Discussing a prospective buyer's financing with the buyer is a legitimate activity for a broker. Choice (A) could be considered discriminatory because "fit" is subjective and could be used to keep people out of neighborhoods. Choice (C) is the professional response. Choice (D) is incorrect for the reason that choice (C) is the correct answer.

23. **The correct answer is (C).** Choice (A) refers to the practice of refusing mortgages to certain groups, especially African Americans. Choice (B) refers to the refusal to rent or sell to families with children, which is the opposite of the scenario. Choice (D) is a distracter.

24. **The correct answer is (A).** Choice (B) is the number of square yards in an acre. Choice (C) is the number of feet in a mile. Choice (D) is the number of square feet in an acre.

25. **The correct answer is (C).**

$759,000 \div 173 = \$4,387.28$

$4,387.28 \times 143 = \$627,381$

26. **The correct answer is (C).** Choices (A), (B), and (D) as well as the deed are recorded after a closing. Choice (C) is not recorded, so it is the correct answer to the question.

27. **The correct answer is (B).** Choice (B) is the only instance where the fiduciary responsibility is trumped by the law. Realtors must disclose anything of a material nature that affects the value or use of the property. Choices (A), (C), and (D) are incorrect.

28. **The correct answer is (B).** A termination by performance may also not occur until the closing, but that stipulation would be written into the contract. Choice (A) is incorrect; a listing agreement may simply end because of the expiration of the term of the agreement. Choice (C) is one reason that a seller may terminate a listing agreement, which

is called revocation, but it's not termination by performance. Choice (D) is a mutual termination of the agreement.

29. **The correct answer is (C).** Choice (A) is incorrect because control is not one of the four unities. Choice (B) is incorrect because consideration is not one of the four unities. Choice (D) is incorrect because control and survivorship are not unities required for a joint tenancy. To save time in checking answers, read the first item in each answer. If it's incorrect, check it off and don't read further on that line. Then read the second item in the remaining answers. Check any answers in which the second answer is incorrect. Continue until you have one answer choice left.

30. **The correct answer is (A).**

80' × 14' × 0.5' = 560 cubic feet

560 ÷ 27 = 20.75

20.75 × $105 = $2,178.75

31. **The correct answer is (A).** Choice (A) is not a form of concurrent or co-ownership; it is another name for sole ownership. Choices (B), (C), and (D) are different types of co-ownership.

32. **The correct answer is (C).** Choice (A) is incorrect because this is the definition of a transactional broker. Choice (B) is incorrect because it's the definition of a multiple listing service. Choice (D) is incorrect and is meant to be a distracter because it seems logical.

33. **The correct answer is (A).** Choice (B) is incorrect because while an aging elevator is curable, it's not economic obsolescence. This makes choice (D) incorrect also. The elevator is curable, but not an example of functional obsolescence. Choice (C) is incorrect on both counts. In an answer with two parts or details, check that both are correct.

34. **The correct answer is (D).** Choice (D) is incorrect; however, the termination date for the listing agreement is stated. Choice (A), (B), and (C) are typical elements of a listing agreement.

35. **The correct answer is (C).** The first part of choices (A) and (B) makes these answers incorrect regardless of the second part of the answer. An assignment of a lease is the total transfer of rights between a tenant and a third party, choice (C). Sublessor and sublessee, choice (D), are terms used in a subleasing arrangement, not an assignment of a lease.

36. **The correct answer is (B).**

$25,000 × 0.03 = $750

$1,800 − $750 = $1,050

$1,050 ÷ 0.075 = $14,000

$14,000 + $25,000 = $39,000

37. **The correct answer is (C).** Choice (A) may seem like a good answer, but it's a distracter. Choice (B) is the opposite of what is true; subprime mortgages are taken out by people with poor credit ratings. Choice (D) is incorrect because a subprime mortgage may be fixed or adjustable.

38. **The correct answer is (B).** Choices (A), (C), and (D) are incorrect. The buyer's lender wants the down payment in part to show the ability of the borrower to be able to make payments. The seller wants earnest money to show the commitment of the buyer because should the buyer default on the contract, the seller may be able to keep some or all of the earnest money.

39. **The correct answer is (C).** Choice (A) violates the Fair Housing Act, but it's not fraud. Choice (B) is a poor business practice, but in itself it is not fraud. Choice (D) is not a conscientious sales agent, but it's not fraudulent behavior.

40. The correct answer is (D). Choice (A) is not illegal; both agents work for the same agency. Choice (B) is not illegal because the brokers are not colluding to circumvent antitrust law. Choice (C) is illegal, but it's price fixing, not market allocation.

41. The correct answer is (C). $5,000 ÷ ($75,000 × 2) = 0.0333333, or $3\frac{1}{3}\%$

42. The correct answer is (A). Because real estate laws and regulations vary from state to state, a licensed broker or sales agent in one state may not sell real estate in another state without passing a licensing law. Choices (B), (C), and (D) are incorrect.

43. The correct answer is (B). Choices (A), (C), and (D) are among the benefits that a franchise owner receives. Choice (B) may be true if the owner pays himself or herself a bonus, but it's not a benefit that a franchise owner receives from the franchiser, so it's the correct answer to the question.

44. The correct answer is (C). $357,840 ÷ 0.63 = $568,000

Sometimes, the question will have more information than you need in order to answer it. Discard the unnecessary information like the millage for the county and the school district. This can't be important information because the municipal tax rate is omitted, and you would need that if millage was important in finding the answer.

45. The correct answer is (A). Credit extended for business, commercial, or agricultural purposes and nonmortgage loans in excess of $25,000, which are typically for business purposes, are exempt from Regulation Z. Choices (B), (C), and (D) are typically not exempt from Regulation Z, which are the regulations that implement the so-called Truth-in-Lending Act.

46. The correct answer is (B). As required by Regulation Z, the MLDS must be delivered in less than 3 business days if the borrower is expected to complete the loan sooner than 3 days. Choice (D) refers to timing for delivering the statement of closing costs to a buyer who is financing with an FHA-insured loan. Choices (A) and (C) are distracters.

47. The correct answer is (C). The best LTV ratio is less than or equal to 80 percent and does not require private mortgage insurance. Choice (A) is a distracter because it seems familiar; it is the financing of a mortgage by taking out two loans, one for 80 percent and one for 20 percent, which is used to cover the down payment. Choices (B) and (D) are incorrect.

48. The correct answer is (B). $1,357,990 ÷ 25 = $54,319.60

49. The correct answer is (D). Choice (A) is often used for appraising special-purpose or institutional buildings like a school, but in this case, the developer wants to turn the building into an income-producing business, so choice (D) is a better answer. Choice (B) is best used for estimating the value of residential property. Choice (C) is a distracter.

50. The correct answer is (A).

$1,250 × 14 = $17,500

$17,500 × 12 = $210,000

$210,000 ÷ 0.095 = $2,210,526.32

51. The correct answer is (B). Choice (C) offers less protection than choice (B) because the same agent handles the interest of both seller and buyer in a dual agency. Choice (A) is incorrect because it only protects the interests of the buyer. Choice (D) is a distracter.

52. The correct answer is (B). Choice (B) is demand combined with purchasing power. Choice (A) is a distracter. Choice (C) is the period during which an improvement is estimated to contribute value to the property. Choice (D) is the functional age of an improvement based on the condition of the improvement and the conditions in the market.

53. **The correct answer is (D).**

    $90' \times 210' \times 1/2 = 9,450$

    $210' \times 210' = 44,100$

    $210' \times 170' = 35,700$

    $9,450 + 44,100 + 35,700 = 89,250$

    $89,250 \div 43,560 = 2.05$

54. **The correct answer is (B).** Choice (A) is incorrect because it is a mortgage that is not government-insured. Choice (C) is a distracter; it seems familiar, but the correct real term is nonconforming use and refers to zoning. Choice (D) is incorrect because the question uses the word "must" and an FHA-mortgage may have a fixed rate or an adjustable rate.

55. **The correct answer is (A).** $8,880 \div$ $444,000 = 0.02$

56. **The correct answer is (B).** The custom may be to leave the refrigerator, but it is not considered real property. Choice (A) is a built-in. Choices (C) and (D) are fixtures.

57. **The correct answer is (D).** Choice (A) is a credit to the seller. Choice (B) is a debit to the buyer. Choice (C) is a credit to the seller.

58. **The correct answer is (C).**

    $765,832 \times 0.65 = 497,790.80$

    $497,790.80 \times 0.032 = 15,929.30$

    $15,929.30 \div 12 = 1,327.44$

    $1,327.44 \times 6 = 7,964.65$

59. **The correct answer is (C).** Choice (A) is incorrect because it is a mortgage that can

be paid off early without a prepayment penalty. Choice (B) is incorrect because it is a mortgage that covers more than one property. Choice (D) is incorrect because it includes the remaining amount on the seller's mortgage and makes payments to his or her lender that includes payments on the original mortgage.

60. **The correct answer is (A).** This is an example of the laws of supply and demand. The more supply, the less demand, and the lower the value. Choice (B) is incorrect because this is not an example of equilibrium. Choice (C) would be true if there were less supply and more demand. Choice (D) is incorrect because the economic principle is not dependent on use.

61. **The correct answer is (C).** An MLDS must contain a statement that a life insurance policy as a guarantee of repayment of the mortgage is not required, so choice (C) is the correct answer to the question. Choices (A), (B), and (D) must be itemized on an MLDS, so they are incorrect answers to the question. These are requirements of Regulation Z.

62. **The correct answer is (D).** Neither owes because the rent is due from the tenant on the day of the closing. If the question stated that the rent was due on the sixth, the answer would be the same. If the question stated that the rent was due on any day from the first of the month to the fourth, the answer would be choice (C), the seller.

63. **The correct answer is (A).** Choice (B), also called external obsolescence, refers to a loss in value because of factors outside a property. Choice (C) doesn't apply because the scenario states that the properties are well maintained. Choice (D) refers to the period of time during which a building is estimated to provide value.

64. **The correct answer is (C).** This is the slow wearing down of the surface of the earth by natural forces such as wind and water. Choice (A) is the transfer of the title to a piece of property. Choice (B) is a distracter. Choice (D) is the slow addition of water-borne sediment, which would add to the oceanfront and, thus, the opposite of the scenario.

65. **The correct answer is (D).** Choice (D) occurs when a person who owns property dies without a will, but is survived by heirs. Choice (A) occurs when a person who owns property dies without a will and with no heirs. Choice (B) refers to the right of the government to take property from an owner for a public use. Choice (C) is a trust that a person sets up through his or her will to manage property after the person's death for the benefit of heirs.

66. **The correct answer is (D).** While the sales comparison approach, choice (B), is typically used to appraise a residential property, the income approach could be used because the townhouse will be used as a rental property. Choice (A) is used typically for special-use properties such as a hospital or school. Choice (C) is actually called reproduction and replacement cost method and is a technique used to estimate cost for the cost approach, choice (A).

67. **The correct answer is (C).** In January 2010, the Federal Housing Administration raised the initial premium from 1.75 percent to 2.25 percent as a way to screen out risky borrowers as a result of the housing crisis that began in 2007. Choice (A) is the previous rate. Choice (B) is incorrect, and choice (C) refers to the maximum percentage of the buyer's loan that a seller could pay in points under the new regulations.

68. **The correct answer is (B).** Choice (A) is an open-end mortgage. Choice (C) is a distracter. Choice (D) is incorrect because a 30-year, fixed-rate, interest-only mortgage is one for which the mortgagor pays interest only for the first 10 years and then principal and accrued interest for the next 20 years.

69. **The correct answer is (C).**

$132,800 × 0.0375 × 4 = $19,920

$132,800 − $19,920 = $112,880

70. **The correct answer is (B).** Choice (A) is incorrect because the buyer is the grantee. Choices (C) and (D) are the same; the lending institution, whether for the buyer or seller in a real estate transaction, is the mortgagee. The buyer is the mortgagor.

71. **The correct answer is (C).** A nonconforming use is one that existed before some other type of use is zoned, in this case, a commercial use before a residential use. Choice (A) is incorrect because a convenience store is a commercial use of property. Choice (B) is incorrect because there is no information given about when the bar was built in relation to the residences, but it could have been given a variance by the zoning board. Choice (D) is incorrect because there is no information about when the school was built in relation to the other buildings, and a school in a mixed-use zone is not necessarily out of character for the zone.

72. **The correct answer is (A).**

139,392 ÷ 43,560 = 3.2

3.2 × $45,675 = $146,160

73. **The correct answer is (B).** Choice (A) is a written opinion by a title company or an attorney about the status of ownership and does not include the abstract, which is report. Choice (C) is a certificate that issued in states that use the Torrens land registration system. Choice (D) is the same as choice (A), a certificate of title.

74. **The correct answer is (B).** Choice (A) requires that the lender ask for a judgment against the mortgagee and then an order to sell property at public auction. Choice (C) is a distracter; a foreclosure occurs because the borrower is in default. Choice (D) is a clause in the original mortgage document that lists the steps to be taken in the event of a default on the mortgage.

75. **The correct answer is (A).** Choice (B) is one that is ordered by the court when a defendant fails to appear in court for a civil hearing. Choice (C) is a distracter; a short sale occurs when the purchase price is less than the outstanding mortgage and must be agreed to by the mortgagee. It is not a foreclosure procedure. Choice (D) refers to a mortgage on which the mortgagee owes more than the market value of the property. It is not a foreclosure procedure.

76. **The correct answer is (A).** Subdivisions can be very structured, but not so structured as to put into the deed the trash pickup schedule. Choices (B), (C), and (D) are just three of many typical restrictive covenants that can be included in a deed to a property in a subdivision.

77. **The correct answer is (C).**

$452,850 × 0.0563 = $28,529.55

$452,850 − $28,529.55 − $1800 = $424,320.45

78. **The correct answer is (C).** Choices (A), (B), and (D) are all options that the buyer has if a condition of sale is not met by the date of closing. Choice (C) won't work because once the buyer closes and pays the purchase price, there is no leverage to force the seller to make good on the unsatisfied condition of sale. This option could work only if the buyer withheld some of the purchase price until the seller fixed the problem, which can be done. The money is put in escrow.

Another alternative is to determine what it will cost to fix the problem and make that amount a credit to the buyer, thereby in effect reducing the selling price by that amount.

79. **The correct answer is (B).** Choice (B) looks at the prices of recently sold properties in the neighborhood that are similar. Choice (A) is an approach to estimating valuation used by appraisers. Choice (C) is a distracter; setting a sales price has nothing to do with estimating highest and best use. Choice (D) is a method used by appraisers to estimate the value of a site without including the value of existing or potential improvements.

80. **The correct answer is (C).** The lawsuit involving property may involve title to real property or an interest in real property such as a lawsuit involving a disputed estate of which the property is part, or involving a prior contract for sale in which the seller refused to perform. Choices (A), (B), and (D) are distracters.

81. **The correct answer is (B).** Only choice (B), a joint tenancy, has right of survivorship in which the surviving principal takes over the property. Choices (A), (C), and (D) do not confer this on the principals or shareholders.

82. **The correct answer is (A).** Choice (B) regulates whether contracts of sale must be in writing. Choice (C) is incorrect because the Real Estate Settlement Procedures Act deals with mortgage procedures and closings. Choice (D) stands for the federal Department of Housing and Urban Development, whose mission is to help communities "identify and overcome regulatory barriers that impede the availability of affordable housing."

83. **The correct answer is (C).** Choices (A), (B), and (D) are distracters. A realtor should do choices (A) and (B) and might choose to do choice (D), but they are not characteristics of the fiduciary responsibility of reasonable

skill and diligence, which refer to an agent's knowing about the features of a property and marketing that property competently and energetically.

84. **The correct answer is (C).**

$4,885 ÷ 0.0045 = $1,085,555.56

$1,085,555.56 ÷ 0.67 = $1,620,232.18

85. **The correct answer is (D).** The Fair Housing Act does not protect age. Age can be an exemption to the anti-discrimination provisions of the Fair Housing Act when the property is intended as an over-55 community, but that doesn't mean that age is a protected class in housing. Choices (A), (B), and (C) are protected classes.

86. **The correct answer is (B).** Choice (B) refers to the riparian rights in a navigable river, which the Mississippi is. Choice (C) refers to the riparian rights in a nonnavigable waterway. Choice (A) and (D) are distracters.

87. **The correct answer is (A).** Choice (B) is an easement by prescription. Choice (C) is an easement appurtenant. Choice (D) is an easement by necessity.

88. **The correct answer is (A).** For an answer to be wrong, only one piece of information needs to be wrong. Choice (B) is incorrect because the mortgage contains the *habendum* clause. Choice (C) is incorrect because the prepayment clause is in the mortgage. Choice (D) is incorrect because the property tax rate appears in neither document. The mortgage, however, obliges the mortgagee to pay the property taxes when due.

89. **The correct answer is (C).** Choice (C) states that married couples are preferred and implies that it's heterosexual couples that are preferred. Choice (A) and (B) are acceptable because they state facts and don't state or imply that people with disabilities are not welcome to apply. Choice (D) is not a negative either. Saying that a group is welcome

as long as it doesn't shut out other groups is not considered discriminatory advertising.

90. **The correct answer is (B).** $763.98 ÷ (0557

$\times \frac{1}{12}$) = $164,591.74

91. **The correct answer is (B).** Choice (A) is one of the last steps involved in a real estate transaction. Choice (C) takes place before the deed is delivered, that is, handed to the buyer. Choice (D) takes place before the deed is signed by the seller.

92. **The correct answer is (D).** An escrow account for property taxes relates to the buyer at a closing, not the seller, so choices (A) and (B) are incorrect. Choice (C) is incorrect because the buyer is paying this money out.

93. **The correct answer is (D).** Choice (D), annual percentage rate, is not a trigger in itself, but if any of the other terms, choices (A), (B), and (C), and the amount of each mortgage payment (the missing term) are used, then the APR must be included in the ad if applicable.

94. **The correct answer is (B).** This scenario describes an independent contractor in a brokerage that pays 100 percent commission. Choice (A) is incorrect because a franchiser is someone who sells franchises to franchisees. Choice (C) is incorrect because a licensee is someone who operates under a license and while a real estate agent must be licensed, the license is irrelevant to the scenario. Choice (D) is incorrect because an employee would receive a salary and would not pay expenses.

95. **The correct answer is (B).**

$272 ÷ 36 = $7.56

$7.56 ÷ 30 = $0.25

$7.56 × 4 = $30.24

$0.25 16 = $4.00

$30.24 + $4.00 = $34.24

96. The correct answer is (B). Choice (A) is a distracter. Choices (C) and (D) are legal terms denoting types of legal notices, but are not applicable in regard to recording documents related to the sale of real property.

97. The correct answer is (B). Choice (B) is physical factors and includes things such as transportation and location. Choice (A) would be factor such as the local economy. Choice (C) would be a factor such as limits on growth, which has economic consequences. Choice (D) includes access to recreational facilities and activities.

98. The correct answer is (C). HVAC, choice (C), is its own category for appraisals.

Choices (A), (B), and (D) are considered part of interior finishes.

99. The correct answer is (B). Choice (A) is a wall that separates two units that are owned individually; it's a type of easement. Choice (C) occurs when the government takes property for a public purpose and neighbors demand that their properties be taken as well because of the effects of the public purpose. Choice (D) is a distracter; taking one's property against the person's will (Harvey McDonald's in this scenario) is called involuntary alienation.

100. The correct answer is (B). The ownership of the title and the grantor's right to convey that title is found in the covenant of seisin; there is no covenant of right to grant. Choices (A), (C), and (D) are all found in a general warranty deed, and so are incorrect answers to the question.

answers practice test 4

ANSWER SHEET PRACTICE TEST 5

1. Ⓐ Ⓑ Ⓒ Ⓓ	21. Ⓐ Ⓑ Ⓒ Ⓓ	41. Ⓐ Ⓑ Ⓒ Ⓓ	61. Ⓐ Ⓑ Ⓒ Ⓓ	81. Ⓐ Ⓑ Ⓒ Ⓓ
2. Ⓐ Ⓑ Ⓒ Ⓓ	22. Ⓐ Ⓑ Ⓒ Ⓓ	42. Ⓐ Ⓑ Ⓒ Ⓓ	62. Ⓐ Ⓑ Ⓒ Ⓓ	82. Ⓐ Ⓑ Ⓒ Ⓓ
3. Ⓐ Ⓑ Ⓒ Ⓓ	23. Ⓐ Ⓑ Ⓒ Ⓓ	43. Ⓐ Ⓑ Ⓒ Ⓓ	63. Ⓐ Ⓑ Ⓒ Ⓓ	83. Ⓐ Ⓑ Ⓒ Ⓓ
4. Ⓐ Ⓑ Ⓒ Ⓓ	24. Ⓐ Ⓑ Ⓒ Ⓓ	44. Ⓐ Ⓑ Ⓒ Ⓓ	64. Ⓐ Ⓑ Ⓒ Ⓓ	84. Ⓐ Ⓑ Ⓒ Ⓓ
5. Ⓐ Ⓑ Ⓒ Ⓓ	25. Ⓐ Ⓑ Ⓒ Ⓓ	45. Ⓐ Ⓑ Ⓒ Ⓓ	65. Ⓐ Ⓑ Ⓒ Ⓓ	85. Ⓐ Ⓑ Ⓒ Ⓓ
6. Ⓐ Ⓑ Ⓒ Ⓓ	26. Ⓐ Ⓑ Ⓒ Ⓓ	46. Ⓐ Ⓑ Ⓒ Ⓓ	66. Ⓐ Ⓑ Ⓒ Ⓓ	86. Ⓐ Ⓑ Ⓒ Ⓓ
7. Ⓐ Ⓑ Ⓒ Ⓓ	27. Ⓐ Ⓑ Ⓒ Ⓓ	47. Ⓐ Ⓑ Ⓒ Ⓓ	67. Ⓐ Ⓑ Ⓒ Ⓓ	87. Ⓐ Ⓑ Ⓒ Ⓓ
8. Ⓐ Ⓑ Ⓒ Ⓓ	28. Ⓐ Ⓑ Ⓒ Ⓓ	48. Ⓐ Ⓑ Ⓒ Ⓓ	68. Ⓐ Ⓑ Ⓒ Ⓓ	88. Ⓐ Ⓑ Ⓒ Ⓓ
9. Ⓐ Ⓑ Ⓒ Ⓓ	29. Ⓐ Ⓑ Ⓒ Ⓓ	49. Ⓐ Ⓑ Ⓒ Ⓓ	69. Ⓐ Ⓑ Ⓒ Ⓓ	89. Ⓐ Ⓑ Ⓒ Ⓓ
10. Ⓐ Ⓑ Ⓒ Ⓓ	30. Ⓐ Ⓑ Ⓒ Ⓓ	50. Ⓐ Ⓑ Ⓒ Ⓓ	70. Ⓐ Ⓑ Ⓒ Ⓓ	90. Ⓐ Ⓑ Ⓒ Ⓓ
11. Ⓐ Ⓑ Ⓒ Ⓓ	31. Ⓐ Ⓑ Ⓒ Ⓓ	51. Ⓐ Ⓑ Ⓒ Ⓓ	71. Ⓐ Ⓑ Ⓒ Ⓓ	91. Ⓐ Ⓑ Ⓒ Ⓓ
12. Ⓐ Ⓑ Ⓒ Ⓓ	32. Ⓐ Ⓑ Ⓒ Ⓓ	52. Ⓐ Ⓑ Ⓒ Ⓓ	72. Ⓐ Ⓑ Ⓒ Ⓓ	92. Ⓐ Ⓑ Ⓒ Ⓓ
13. Ⓐ Ⓑ Ⓒ Ⓓ	33. Ⓐ Ⓑ Ⓒ Ⓓ	53. Ⓐ Ⓑ Ⓒ Ⓓ	73. Ⓐ Ⓑ Ⓒ Ⓓ	93. Ⓐ Ⓑ Ⓒ Ⓓ
14. Ⓐ Ⓑ Ⓒ Ⓓ	34. Ⓐ Ⓑ Ⓒ Ⓓ	54. Ⓐ Ⓑ Ⓒ Ⓓ	74. Ⓐ Ⓑ Ⓒ Ⓓ	94. Ⓐ Ⓑ Ⓒ Ⓓ
15. Ⓐ Ⓑ Ⓒ Ⓓ	35. Ⓐ Ⓑ Ⓒ Ⓓ	55. Ⓐ Ⓑ Ⓒ Ⓓ	75. Ⓐ Ⓑ Ⓒ Ⓓ	95. Ⓐ Ⓑ Ⓒ Ⓓ
16. Ⓐ Ⓑ Ⓒ Ⓓ	36. Ⓐ Ⓑ Ⓒ Ⓓ	56. Ⓐ Ⓑ Ⓒ Ⓓ	76. Ⓐ Ⓑ Ⓒ Ⓓ	96. Ⓐ Ⓑ Ⓒ Ⓓ
17. Ⓐ Ⓑ Ⓒ Ⓓ	37. Ⓐ Ⓑ Ⓒ Ⓓ	57. Ⓐ Ⓑ Ⓒ Ⓓ	77. Ⓐ Ⓑ Ⓒ Ⓓ	97. Ⓐ Ⓑ Ⓒ Ⓓ
18. Ⓐ Ⓑ Ⓒ Ⓓ	38. Ⓐ Ⓑ Ⓒ Ⓓ	58. Ⓐ Ⓑ Ⓒ Ⓓ	78. Ⓐ Ⓑ Ⓒ Ⓓ	98. Ⓐ Ⓑ Ⓒ Ⓓ
19. Ⓐ Ⓑ Ⓒ Ⓓ	39. Ⓐ Ⓑ Ⓒ Ⓓ	59. Ⓐ Ⓑ Ⓒ Ⓓ	79. Ⓐ Ⓑ Ⓒ Ⓓ	99. Ⓐ Ⓑ Ⓒ Ⓓ
20. Ⓐ Ⓑ Ⓒ Ⓓ	40. Ⓐ Ⓑ Ⓒ Ⓓ	60. Ⓐ Ⓑ Ⓒ Ⓓ	80. Ⓐ Ⓑ Ⓒ Ⓓ	100. Ⓐ Ⓑ Ⓒ Ⓓ

answer sheet

Practice Test 5

100 Questions • 3 Hours

Directions: Read each question carefully and mark the letter of the best answer on the answer sheet.

1. At the time of the sales contract signing, the buyer must hand over
   - (A) the down payment.
   - (B) earnest money.
   - (C) part of the down payment.
   - (D) a note for the down payment.

2. All of the following restrictive covenants in a townhome community probably add to the value of the properties EXCEPT
   - (A) the color of exterior front door and window trim.
   - (B) how long outdoor Christmas lights may be used.
   - (C) the type of planters that may be used outdoors.
   - (D) the distance that woodpiles may be kept from the dwellings.

3. The loan amount, granting clause, and covenant of seisin are typically found in the
   - (A) mortgage note.
   - (B) mortgage document itself.
   - (C) title to the property.
   - (D) deed to the property.

4. A typical listing agreement contains all of the following EXCEPT
   - (A) type of zoning.
   - (B) assessment and taxes.
   - (C) nondiscrimination clause.
   - (D) description of how the realtor arrived at the sales price.

5. An example of a material defect in a property is
   - (A) a 100-year-old electrical system.
   - (B) the addition of an attic fan that was not done to building code.
   - (C) cracked and peeling paint from water damage from an upstairs bathtub that overflowed.
   - (D) the presence of squirrel droppings in the attic.

6. The answer to Question 5 is an example of what kind of depreciation?
   - (A) Physical deterioration
   - (B) Functional obsolescence
   - (C) Economic obsolescence
   - (D) Effective age

7. Sara Jeffs has a contract with a local real estate firm that pays her 65 percent of its 45 percent of all commissions she generates. If Sara sold two houses in May for a combined total of $790,000 and both had 6 percent commissions to be split between broker and salesperson, how much was her commission check at the end of the month?

   (A) $1,386.45

   (B) $2,133.00

   (C) $13,864.50

   (D) $47,400.00

8. A designated agency is

   (A) one in which the buyer signs a buyer agency agreement and the seller signs a listing agreement with the same broker.

   (B) one in which a broker has exclusive rights to sell all the units for a developer

   (C) the same as a dual agency.

   (D) the same as an exclusive right to sell listing given by any principal to a broker.

9. The MPI is

   (A) a form of private mortgage insurance.

   (B) a one-time insurance premium on FHA-insured mortgages.

   (C) equal to one point on a mortgage.

   (D) an abbreviation for mortgage, principal, and interest.

10. At closing, the borrower turns over to the lender for deposit into an escrow account a certain number of months of all of the following payments EXCEPT

    (A) county property taxes.

    (B) municipal property taxes.

    (C) interest.

    (D) hazard insurance premiums.

11. An estate of indeterminate duration is a/an

    (A) estate from period to period.

    (B) freehold estate.

    (C) leasehold estate.

    (D) estate at will.

12. Joe Rosato just turned 75. In his township, this entitles him to a 20 percent rebate on his local taxes. If his house and property are worth $675,000, and the township assesses at a rate of 84 percent and taxes are assessed at a rate of $4.50 per thousand dollars, what will his new tax bill be?

    (A) $2,143.90

    (B) $2,987.20

    (C) $2,551.50

    (D) $2,041.20

13. Inclusion of which of the following words in an ad triggers full disclosure in loan advertising?

    (A) Terms of repayment

    (B) Annual percentage rate

    (C) Availability of FHA and VA loans

    (D) Dollar amount of finance charge

14. Cholly Berlind is an agent working for Schultz Realty. He is preparing a newspaper ad for one of the properties he is trying to sell. Which of the following items must by law be included in the ad?

    (A) Address of the property

    (B) Sales price

    (C) Property taxes

    (D) Name of the broker for whom he works

15. Which of the following must be given to mortgage applicants the day before the closing?

(A) Uniform Residential Appraisal Report

(B) Good Faith Estimate

(C) Uniform Residential Loan Application

(D) HUD-1, or Uniform Settlement Statement

16. If the sale of a foreclosed property fails to satisfy the mortgage, the lender

(A) may file a deed in lieu of foreclosure.

(B) may go to court and seek a deficiency judgment.

(C) has no way to recover additional money from the person in default.

(D) may allow the person in default of the mortgage to exercise the right of reversion.

17. The condo fees of $215.46 a month are due on the first of every month. If Erin Oskin sells her condo on October 16 to Jake Otis, how much does Jake owe Erin?

(A) $3,447.36

(B) $114.88

(C) $123.62

(D) $107.73

18. Mariel Rambias is using the cost approach to appraise a property. This approach includes cost to build, depreciation, and

(A) appreciation.

(B) value of the land.

(C) value of the improvement.

(D) income.

19. An agent stops to see if the Baileys might want to sell their farm. The Baileys agree and ask the agent to find a buyer. No listing agreement is singed. This oral agreement

(A) is not enforceable.

(B) may be enforceable if their state's Statute of Frauds recognizes oral contracts.

(C) is enforceable if the broker agrees to accept an oral contract.

(D) may be enforceable if their state's Real Estate Commission recognizes oral contracts.

20. A lender reserves the right to

(A) hire an appraiser during the term of a mortgage to ensure that the mortgagor is maintaining the property.

(B) approve any substantive changes to a property by the mortgagor during the term of the mortgage.

(C) approve the sale of the property.

(D) approve a lessee for the property during the term of the mortgage.

21. If a house sold for 165 percent of its original value of $431,970, what was its selling price?

(A) $261,800

(B) $316,782

(C) $587,920

(D) $712,750

22. At a closing, who writes the checks for prorated amounts credited to the seller?

(A) Buyer

(B) Buyer's broker

(C) Buyer's attorney

(D) Whoever is acting as escrow agent

23. In comparing multiple offers, sellers should consider all of the following in addition to price EXCEPT
   (A) closing dates.
   (B) amounts of the down payments.
   (C) contingencies.
   (D) whether the buyer is relocating.

24. Among the items that zoning ordinances regulate are lot size, building height, and
   (A) layout of municipal transportation systems.
   (B) distance between structures on adjoining properties.
   (C) weight limits on residential streets.
   (D) building codes.

25. A benefit of a VA-guaranteed loan is that
   (A) the VA guarantees that the home is free of defects.
   (B) the VA can order builders to fix problems with construction problems.
   (C) private mortgage insurance is waived.
   (D) down payments as low as 3 percent qualify for a mortgage.

26. An escrow account for a mortgage
   (A) is regulated under the Truth-in-Lending Act.
   (B) may not keep in the account more than one-sixth of the total amount necessary to be paid out, or approximately two months of escrow funds.
   (C) is mandated by RESPA.
   (D) must pay interest to the borrower on the money in the account.

27. Which of the following is NOT a duty of a real estate broker?
   (A) Hire home inspectors
   (B) Arrange for title searches
   (C) Help the buyer to obtain financing
   (D) Act as closing agent

28. A triplex sold for $329,000. If the property generates $37,500 a year in income, what is the rate of return?
   (A) 9.6%
   (B) 10.3%
   (C) 11.4%
   (D) 877%

29. The Ace Chemical Company has been told that the contamination in its old factory cannot be cleaned up. The company now needs to contract for what level of environmental study?
   (A) Phase I
   (B) Phase II
   (C) Phase III
   (D) Phase IV

30. A residential mortgage transaction for purposes of the Homeowner's Protection Act is one that
   (A) is a single-family dwelling.
   (B) has from 1 to 4 units.
   (C) has a VA-guaranteed or FHA-insured mortgage.
   (D) has a fixed rate mortgage.

31. The Hudsons have bought a parcel of unimproved land in a single-family residential area and wish to build a two-family building. They will live in one side of the building, and Mona Hudson's parents will live in the other side. The Hudsons need to seek a/an
   (A) nonconforming use variance.
   (B) area variance.
   (C) use variance.
   (D) accessory building variance.

32. Under RESPA, a homebuyer has all of the following rights EXCEPT the right to

    (A) compare the cost of mortgages from different lenders.

    (B) refuse to allow the mortgagee to sell the mortgage to a mortgage servicer.

    (C) know which charges are refundable if the buyer cancels the loan agreement.

    (D) know how much a mortgage broker is being paid by the lender.

33. A square plot of land originally sold for $2.55 per square foot. It now sells for $3.75 per square foot. How much has the plot appreciated if the plot has a frontage of 752 feet?

    (A) $664,706.90

    (B) $678,604.80

    (C) $682,763.90

    (D) $693,874.80

34. The FHA limits the amount of assistance that a seller may give a buyer to what percentage of the value of the property?

    (A) 2.25 percent

    (B) 3 percent

    (C) 6 percent

    (D) 10 percent

35. A mortgage note typically contains all of the following information EXCEPT

    (A) interest rate of the mortgage.

    (B) date on which the note was signed.

    (C) names of the seller and buyer.

    (D) day of the month on which mortgage payments are due.

36. An energy-efficient mortgage

    (A) can be used to fund a condo.

    (B) cannot fund improvements that increase the mortgage by more than $2,500.

    (C) cannot fund improvements that will add more than 10 percent to the value of the property.

    (D) enables a homebuyer to save money on future utility bills.

37. The correct order in paying off liens is

    (A) IRS, liens by contractors, property tax liens.

    (B) property tax liens, IRS, liens by contractors.

    (C) IRS, state tax liens, property tax liens.

    (D) property tax liens, IRS, state tax liens.

38. What would the total amount of interest be on a $265,000, 15-year loan with a monthly payment of $2,011.02?

    (A) $96,983.60

    (B) $9,698.36

    (C) $969,836.00

    (D) $9,698,360.00

39. The local gas station is sold for $953,252 on January 26. If the real estate taxes of $5,348.24 are paid quarterly on the first of January, April, July, and October, how much does the buyer owe the original owners?

    (A) $965.68

    (B) $1,139.74

    (C) $1,262.88

    (D) $4,976.89

40. Which of the following phrases in an advertisement for a rental unit would violate the Fair Housing Act?

    (A) "Master bedroom en suite"

    (B) "Older woman preferred"

    (C) "Walk to subway"

    (D) "Bachelor apartment"

41. Seepage from a leach field is a potential hazard from a/an
    (A) septic system.
    (B) fuel tank to supply oil to the furnace.
    (C) cesspool.
    (D) in-ground swimming pool.

42. Which of the following factors is NOT typically inspected during a home inspection?
    (A) Structural
    (B) Mechanical
    (C) Energy efficiency
    (D) Environmental

43. All of the following are typically found in a home inspection contingency clause in a sales contract EXCEPT
    (A) buyer satisfaction with the repairs.
    (B) statement of how any repairs will be made.
    (C) how many days the seller has to make the repairs after the home inspection report is received.
    (D) the buyer's choice to go ahead with the purchase even if the repairs are not made.

44. It cost $87,000 to build a house on a $17,000 lot 3 years ago. If the house depreciates at a rate of 1.7% a year and the land appreciates at a rate of 6.5% a year, what is the total property worth now?
    (A) $99,563
    (B) $102,878
    (C) $112,615
    (D) $107,315

45. A power line easement is an example of an
    (A) easement in gross.
    (B) easement by prescription.
    (C) appurtenant easement.
    (D) easement by necessity.

46. *Ad valorem* is a method used to
    (A) appraise property.
    (B) determine market value.
    (C) determine a listing price.
    (D) assess property.

47. An acknowledgement is a statement that a party to a contract
    (A) is authorized to enter into the contract.
    (B) is of sound mind.
    (C) entered into the contract freely.
    (D) is the party named in the contract.

48. James and Marie Pappas are looking to buy Mr. James's house, which has 3 bedrooms, 2.5 bathrooms, and 2,550 square foot. A comparable house around the corner recently sold for $375,600. It has 4 bedrooms, 2 baths and 2,500 square feet. What is the value of Mr. James's house if bedrooms are worth $15,000 and bathrooms are worth $7,500?
    (A) $356,838
    (B) $362,974
    (C) $387,963
    (D) $394,362

49. Under an exclusive agency listing, the realtor
    (A) receives a commission no matter who sells the property.
    (B) receives a commission only if he or she sells the property.
    (C) has to be paid a commission if the seller sells the property without any help.
    (D) receives a reduced commission if the seller sells the property himself or herself.

50. A conforming mortgage is all of the following EXCEPT it

(A) meets the criteria for sale to Fannie Mae and Freddie Mac.

(B) is a conventional mortgage.

(C) is a fixed rate mortgage.

(D) is a jumbo mortgage.

51. Lekha Chandra signed a contract of employment with Forest City Realtors. The contract includes a noncompete clause. Such a clause

(A) is unenforceable in some states.

(B) typically prohibits an agent from later working with clients they met through the agency, but does not proscribe an area in which they can work.

(C) is typically written for 90 days.

(D) has no force under the law because the agent signs under duress.

52. Which of the following is NOT an encumbrance on a property?

(A) A deed restriction on the use of a property as a child-care facility

(B) Mortgage

(C) Rent control regulations

(D) Party wall

53. Fitch Property Company is selling one of its office buildings. What will happen to the tenants in the building?

(A) The tenants will have to renegotiate their current leases with the new owner.

(B) The leases remain in force until the term of each lease ends.

(C) The new owners must act within 30 days to renew the leases, renegotiate them, or give the tenants notice to vacate.

(D) The new owners may renew or renegotiate the current leases, but cannot end leases before they expire.

54. Seller financing is also known as a

(A) shared equity mortgage.

(B) purchase-money mortgage.

(C) package mortgage.

(D) straight-term mortgage.

55. If it costs $22 a square foot to install thin-cut stone on a façade, what would it cost to cover the front of a house that measures 32' wide by 25' high?

(A) $16,900

(B) $17,600

(C) $18,600

(D) $19,900

56. In establishing the capital gains on a home sale, which of the following is subtracted from the sales price to determine the cost basis?

(A) Cost of a new HVAC system

(B) Accumulated depreciation

(C) Title fee for selling the house

(D) Real estate commissions for buying and selling the house

57. With a strict foreclosure,

(A) the lender takes possession in order to sell the property.

(B) the mortgagor may keep the property if the mortgage is paid in full.

(C) there is no court hearing involved in the foreclosure.

(D) the mortgagor has no right of appeal.

58. A buyer is looking at a townhouse and asks how old the HVAC is. The agent replies that it is 4 years old, but doesn't mention that it has the odor of stagnant water when it shifts from heat to air conditioning and vice versa. Is this fraud?

(A) Yes, because the agent intentionally withholds material information that might negatively affect the buyer's decision about the property.

(B) Yes, because the agent is misrepresenting how well the HVAC works.

(C) No, because the odor is not a material defect.

(D) No, because it would take an expert to detect the reason for the odor.

59. Which of the following violates Regulation Z's provisions related to appraisals?

(A) Asking the appraiser to correct factual errors in the appraisal report

(B) Requesting additional information to support the appraiser's valuation

(C) Withholding the appraiser's fee for breach of contract

(D) Telling the appraiser the minimum value of a seller's home that is needed to qualify for a mortgage

60. An agency agreement in writing between a broker and a principal would not be valid if which of the following was missing?

(A) Method of termination

(B) Expiration date

(C) The purpose of the agreement

(D) The sale price

61. All of the following are listed on a Good Faith Estimate EXCEPT

(A) points/loan discount.

(B) agent's commission.

(C) lender's inspection fee.

(D) credit report fee.

62. What is the interest paid over the course of a $562,980 mortgage at 6 percent with monthly payments of $10,883.98?

(A) $90,058.80

(B) $110,528.90

(C) $145,386.20

(D) $152,489.40

63. All of the following are breaches of an agent's fiduciary responsibilities to his or her seller EXCEPT

(A) failing to help the seller find a broker in the area where the seller is relocating.

(B) failing to submit offers to the seller in a timely manner.

(C) delaying the placement of a listing on the MLS.

(D) telling a potential buyer that the seller recently lost her job.

64. The original grant of title to real property and all transfers of the title and encumbrances on the property since then are contained in a property's

(A) deed.

(B) certificate of title.

(C) abstract of title.

(D) certificate of Torrens.

65. In which of the following could an owner have to pay taxes individually, but still have the liability protection of a corporation?

(A) Shah Brothers Property Management Company, Inc.

(B) Whiteside Property Developers, a general partnership

(C) Edward S. Peyton Real Estate Brokerage, a sole proprietorship

(D) Farzhad Realty LLC

66. What income is needed from a building valued at $475,692, if a return of 12.5 percent is desired?

    (A) $4,955.13

    (B) $59,461.50

    (C) $62,543.50

    (D) $64,253.50

67. An acceleration clause in a mortgage

    (A) enables a mortgagor to pay off the debt without a prepayment penalty.

    (B) requires that a mortgagor pay off the mortgage immediately.

    (C) reduces the term of the mortgage by rising the principal and interest paid each month.

    (D) increases the amount of principal that is paid each month.

68. A covenant of further assurances is found only in a

    (A) general warranty deed.

    (B) special warranty deed.

    (C) deed of trust.

    (D) quitclaim deed.

69. The settlement fee is

    (A) the entire cost of the closing.

    (B) the settlement agent/escrow holder's fee.

    (C) paid by the seller.

    (D) another name for the transfer tax.

70. Sonja Japsers buys her grandparents' home after her grandfather dies. She gives it to her mother to live in as a life estate. When Sonja's mother dies, Sonja will take the house back. Sonja must have what kind of interest in the property?

    (A) Beneficiary

    (B) Remainder

    (C) Reversionary

    (D) Grantor

71. A parcel of land can be broken into a rectangle and a triangle. The rectangle has frontage of 345' and a depth of 97'. The triangle shares the depth and has frontage of 83'. What is the total square footage of the lot?

    (A) 32,942.5

    (B) 34,987

    (C) 35,762.5

    (D) 37,670.5

72. The local university wants to move at its own expense the commuter train station that stands on its property, so it can expand its facilities on its property. The university must seek permission from the

    (A) zoning board.

    (B) city council.

    (C) planning board.

    (D) municipal building department.

73. The state government needs to expand its offices, so it moves to take over property by right of eminent domain. Some property owners refuse to accept the state's offer. The state then goes to court to ask for

    (A) an actual eviction.

    (B) a retaliatory eviction.

    (C) an injunction.

    (D) condemnation of the property.

74. Which of the following guarantees investors in the secondary mortgage market that the payment of principal and interest on their mortgage-backed securities will be paid in a timely manner?

    (A) Fannie Mae

    (B) Ginnie Mae

    (C) Freddie Mac

    (D) Federal Reserve

75. "Subject to a mortgage"

(A) is the same as assigning a mortgage.

(B) occurs when a purchaser takes over liability for the entire unpaid balance of the mortgage from the original mortgagor.

(C) occurs when a purchaser agrees to take over payments of a mortgage, but the original mortgagor remains responsible for the entire mortgage should the purchaser default.

(D) is a contingency clause in a sales contract that allows the purchaser to cancel the contract if his or her home is not sold before the closing on the new purchase.

76. It is estimated that the replacement cost for a 2,654 square foot house is $73.43 per square foot. If the land is worth $45,000 and the house is 2 years old with a 3.5 percent depreciation rate, what is the value of the whole property?

(A) $194,883

(B) $206,734

(C) $239,883

(D) $226,241

77. A salesperson who is working for a broker as an independent contractor

(A) does not receive paid disability insurance from the broker.

(B) does not need to work on the broker's premises.

(C) works the hours and days that the salesperson chooses.

(D) pays his or her own federal income tax.

78. Joe Hidalgo and Manny Sanchez are buying a small office building. In addition to the normal items that the seller brings to a closing, they expect the seller to also bring

(A) hazard insurance policy.

(B) rent control documents.

(C) letters from tenants authorizing the transfer of their leases to the new owner.

(D) leases and maintenance contracts.

79. The capitalization rate is the

(A) amount of money that an investor will have to put into a property to gain a certain rate of return.

(B) figure that represents the relationship between income and value.

(C) same as the rate of return on investment.

(D) cost of reproduction or replacement used in figuring the cost approach in appraisals.

80. The procuring cause of a transaction in real estate is the

(A) seller who brought the property to a broker.

(B) buyer who was ready, willing, and able to buy the property.

(C) realtor who listed the property.

(D) realtor who sold the property to the buyer.

81. What is the commission on the sale of a house that sold for $537,620, if the salesperson receives a 4.25% commission?

(A) $228,848.85

(B) $2,284.88

(C) $228.48

(D) $22,848.85

82. In zoning terms, a public park with tennis courts and ball fields between an area of single-family homes and a strip mall is a/an

(A) park zone.

(B) exception to zoning.

(C) buffer zone.

(D) recreation site.

83. Appraisers use three approaches to valuing a property. The final appraisal report

   (A) reconciles the different value indicators to present the appraiser's opinion of value.

   (B) offers all three approaches with support documentation so the entity that commissioned the appraisal can choose the appropriate value.

   (C) provides the appraiser's best estimate of the highest and best use.

   (D) gives the same weight to each approach.

84. The Masons are getting a divorce. Jim coerces his wife Judy into selling their house by telling her that without the proceeds of the sale, they can't afford to divorce. He is in a car accident and is in a prolonged coma. Although Judy was coerced, she decides to go ahead with the sale. This is an example of a contract that is

   (A) voidable, but enforceable.

   (B) valid and enforceable.

   (C) void.

   (D) void, but enforceable by agreement.

85. Both corporations that own property and tenancy in common are examples of

   (A) tenancy in severalty.

   (B) joint tenancy.

   (C) leaseholds.

   (D) estates in qualified fee.

86. Sam Gergiev is out of the country on business when the closing is set for his purchase of a condo. His brother-in-law appears at the closing to sign all necessary documents for him. The brother-in-law must have

   (A) power of attorney.

   (B) a legal directive.

   (C) a special agency.

   (D) a general agency.

87. In terms of antidiscrimination practices, a broker must do all of the following EXCEPT

   (A) display the Fair Housing poster.

   (B) enforce Fair Housing policies among the office's sales agents and other employees.

   (C) ensure that agents abide by RESPA.

   (D) hire licensed realtors regardless of race, color, religion, age, sex, familial status, disability, or national origin.

88. Taxes are due in full on June 1. There is a 1 percent late penalty for each month the taxes are late. How much in total will the Pattersons pay on their $876,300 house that is assessed at a rate of 58 percent, and a total tax rate of 29 mills, if they pay in full on the August 1?

   (A) $15,034.16

   (B) $12,354,87

   (C) $14,739.37

   (D) $22,546.91

89. Tom Yang decides not to rent a storefront for his clothing business when he finds out that the lease is an absolute net lease. What would he be paying in an absolute net lease?

   (A) Rent and a percentage of his sales

   (B) Rent and utilities

   (C) Rent, property taxes, utilities, and property insurance

   (D) Rent, property taxes, and utilities

90. Which of the following fees is typically included in a mortgage's APR?

   (A) Home inspection fee

   (B) Title fee

   (C) Prepaid interest

   (D) Credit report fee

91. All appraisal reports should contain all of the following EXCEPT

(A) the list of real property rights appraised.

(B) a range of sales prices for the property based on the appraisal.

(C) the assumptions on which the appraisal is based.

(D) the intended use for which the appraisal was commissioned.

92. National Bank is willing to make a 3.38 percent loan on 80% of the value of a property that has depreciated 3 percent a year for 5 years. If the original price of the property was $184,950, how much is the bank going to lend its customer?

(A) $126,843.50

(B) $147,960

(C) $137,766

(D) $172,207.50

93. In using the sales comparison approach to appraise a property, the appraiser considers the following exterior features:

(A) foundation, landscaping, patio, pool.

(B) foundation, driveway, patio, porch.

(C) foundation, landscaping, paint color, patio.

(D) foundation, windows, paint color, porch.

94. The Reynolds Homes Agency is buying up land to create a subdivision that will be built in phases. The best kind of mortgage for the developers to take out is a

(A) blanket mortgage.

(B) sale-and-leaseback.

(C) open-end mortgage.

(D) mortgage rate buydown.

95. Jim Schaeffer and Tony Janoff are setting up a real estate agency. To ensure that they are handling their escrow accounts properly, they should do all of the following EXCEPT

(A) set up separate escrow and operating accounts.

(B) keep all funds for a particular transaction until the transaction closes.

(C) be sure the person handling the escrow accounts is bonded.

(D) give one person responsibility for the escrow accounts.

96. According to statute, the presence of which of the following must be disclosed to a potential homebuyer if a property was built before 1978?

(A) Asbestos

(B) Lead paint

(C) Radon

(D) Air pollution that resulted in an outbreak of Legionnaire's disease

97. The Franklin Realty Company has three offers that came in almost simultaneously for the Putnams' house. One is $5,000 under the asking price, another is $6,000 under the price, and one is $17,000 less than the price. The broker should

(A) not tell the buyer about the offer that is $17,000 below asking price because it is too low.

(B) work with the agent of the second-highest offeror to get the buyer to make a higher offer and then present it to the seller.

(C) tell all three offerors that there are three of them and they should increase their offers before the broker presents them to the seller or they should drop out.

(D) submit all three offers to the buyer.

98. If the real estate taxes of $6,270 are paid in full on January 1 and the house closes on August 1, who is owed what?

(A) The buyer is owed $3,657.50.

(B) The buyer is owed $2,612.50.

(C) The seller is owed $2,612.50.

(D) The seller is owed $3,657.50.

99. All of the following should be included in a real sales contract EXCEPT

(A) name of the broker who will receive the commissions.

(B) what costs will be shared by buyer and seller and how the costs will be shared.

(C) the mortgage lender contact information.

(D) the right of the seller to cancel the contract if the seller cannot produce a marketable title.

100. Social factors that enhance residential property values include

(A) prestige, tennis courts, and low property taxes.

(B) tennis courts, proximity to museums, and high SAT scores.

(C) low property taxes, high SAT scores, and low interest rates.

(D) prestige, low interest rates, and zoning for large lots.

practice test

ANSWER KEY AND EXPLANATIONS

1. B	21. D	41. A	61. B	81. D
2. B	22. D	42. C	62. A	82. C
3. B	23. D	43. B	63. A	83. A
4. D	24. B	44. B	64. C	84. A
5. A	25. C	45. A	65. D	85. A
6. B	26. B	46. D	66. B	86. A
7. C	27. A	47. C	67. B	87. C
8. A	28. C	48. A	68. A	88. A
9. B	29. D	49. B	69. B	89. C
10. C	30. A	50. D	70. C	90. C
11. B	31. C	51. A	71. D	91. B
12. D	32. B	52. C	72. C	92. C
13. D	33. B	53. B	73. D	93. B
14. D	34. B	54. B	74. B	94. A
15. D	35. C	55. B	75. C	95. D
16. B	36. D	56. B	76. D	96. B
17. D	37. C	57. B	77. A	97. D
18. B	38. A	58. A	78. D	98. C
19. B	39. A	59. D	79. B	99. C
20. B	40. B	60. C	80. D	100. B

1. **The correct answer is (B).** Choice (A) is incorrect because the down payment is required by the lender, not the seller. Choice (C) is true; the earnest money is credited to the seller at the closing, but it is not part of the down payments. Choice (D) is incorrect because the note is signed at the closing along with the mortgage.

2. **The correct answer is (B).** Whether the lights come down on January 15 or February 15 does not affect the value of the property, especially because prospective homebuyers are less likely to be inspecting property after dark. Choices (A) and (C) speak to the economic factor of conformity; a house with pink trim in a suburban neighborhood in which the trim blends in with the wooded surroundings could affect property values in the neighborhood. Choice (D) is based on a practical concern; wood stored for fireplaces could harbor carpenter ants, termites, and other insects that could damage the buildings. Remember that one wrong answer in a list makes the entire answer incorrect.

3. **The correct answer is (B).** Choice (A) contains the loan amount, but not the other items. Choice (C) contains none of the items in the question. Choice (D) includes a granting clause and a covenant of seisin, but not the loan amount.

4. **The correct answer is (D).** Choice (D) is not part of a listing agreement, so it is incorrect about listing agreements, but the correct answer to the question. Choices (A), (B), and (C) are parts of a typical listing agreement, so they are incorrect answers to the question.

5. **The correct answer is (A).** A material defect is one that could affect the buyer's decision to purchase a property or affect a property's value. Choices (B), (C), and (D) can all be remedied: the wiring in the attic fan can be redone, the ceiling can be repainted, and a pest company can be hired to find where the squirrels are coming in and plug the hole. Choice (A) requires a great deal more money if rewiring the entire house is necessary.

6. **The correct answer is (B).** Choice (A) occurs with wear and tear and typically covers items such as paint, carpeting, and broken windows or doors. Choice (C) refers to items external to the property such as neighboring properties that are not being maintained. Choice (D) refers to the functional age of a property based on the condition of the property; in determining depreciation, an appraiser takes effective age into consideration, but effective age is not a form of depreciation.

7. **The correct answer is (C).**

   $790,000 \times 0.06 = \$47,400$

   $47,400 \times 0.45 = \$21,330$

   $21,330 \times 0.65 = \$13,864.50$

8. **The correct answer is (A).** Choices (B) and (D) are distracters. Choice (C) is incorrect because with a dual agency, which is illegal in some states, a single agent represents both the buyer and the seller. With a designated agency, it's the broker who is the same, but there will be two agents.

9. **The correct answer is (B).** Choice (A) is incorrect; private mortgage insurance is abbreviated as PMI. Choice (C) is incorrect because the mortgage insurance premium is not related to discount points, and the premium as of 2010 is 2.25 percent. Choice (D) is incorrect because MPI stands for mortgage insurance premium.

10. **The correct answer is (C).** Choice (C) is paid on an ongoing monthly basis with payment of the principal, and so is the correct answer to the question, which is asking for what is *not* included in escrow. Some number of months of choices (A), (B), and (D) are paid to the lender at closing and placed in an escrow account. (If the amount is larger than allowed under RESPA, an adjustment is made in the amount of the payments.)

11. **The correct answer is (B).** Choice (B) is the same as a freehold estate. Choice (A) is a form of leasehold that does not have a specified end date, but is for a specified period of time such as a week or a month. The leasehold automatically renews unless the landlord or the tenant wishes not to renew. Choice (C) is the large category of estates that grants the holder of the lease possession of the property for a set period of time. In choice (D), a tenant occupies a property without a specified end date and with or without a written lease.

12. **The correct answer is (D).**

   $675,000 \times 0.84 = \$567,000$

   $567,000 \times 0.0045 = \$2,551.5$

   $100\% - 20\% = 80\%$, or 0.80

   $2,551.5 \times 0.8 = \$2,041.20$

13. **The correct answer is (D).** Choices (A) and (B) represent information that must be included depending on the trigger words used in the ad. Choice (C) does not require full disclosure.

14. **The correct answer is (D).** Choices (A), (B), and (C) are important to prospective buyers, but the name of the broker for whom the ad is being placed—not the agent—must be identified in the ad. This is typically regulated under state law and regulation as well as the Federal Trade Commission (FTC).

15. **The correct answer is (D).** Choice (A) is used by professional appraisers hired by lenders to appraise the property in order to determine the value of the mortgage. The mortgagor is entitled to a copy of the report within 90 days of being informed of the lender's action on the mortgage request. Choice (B) is required to be given persons seeking a mortgage within 3 days of applying for a loan. Choice (C) is the form used to apply for a mortgage and is completed in order to apply for a mortgage, so it precedes choice (B). A new application form dated 6/09 must be used for all mortgage applications after July 1, 2010.

16. **The correct answer is (B).** Choice (A) is incorrect because it would occur before any sale of a foreclosed property. The person in default of the mortgage transfers title to the property to the lender without any court proceedings. Choice (C) is incorrect because choice (B) is the way to recover additional money to satisfy the rest of the mortgage. Choice (D) is incorrect because it mixes up the right of equitable redemption (paying off the complete mortgage by the person in default before—or after—a foreclosure sale) and the process of returning an interest in a property back to the original owner after the

interest that another has held in the property has ended.

17. **The correct answer is (D).**

$215.46 \div 30 = $7.18

$7.18 \times 15 = $107.73

18. **The correct answer is (B).** The cost approach is the cost to build minus depreciation plus the value of the land. Choices (A), (B), and (D) are incorrect.

19. **The correct answer is (B).** Choice (A) is not the best answer because there is not enough information in the question to determine if an oral contract is valid in the unnamed state. Choices (C) and (D) are incorrect because neither the broker nor the Real Estate Commission makes the applicable law, though both have a duty to see that it is carried out.

20. **The correct answer is (B).** Choice (A) is incorrect because a lender has a property appraised at the time of the mortgage origination, but not again unless there is a foreclosure. Choice (C) is incorrect, and choice (D) is a distracter to confuse the scenario with the assignment or assumption of a lease or mortgage.

21. **The correct answer is (D).** $431,970 \times 1.65 = $712,750

22. **The correct answer is (D).** The funds come from the buyer, but whoever is serving as the escrow agent writes and signs the check. Choices (A) and (B) are incorrect. Choice (C) may be true, but only if the buyer's attorney is acting as the escrow agent.

23. **The correct answer is (D).** Choices (A), (B), and (C) as well as discount points and other financing provisions such as whether the buyer is pre-approved or pre-qualified should be considered in analyzing competing offers. Choice (D) is incorrect because relocation is not a factor of importance in analyzing multiple offers.

24. **The correct answer is (B).** Choice (B) is called a setback and also includes the location of a structure in relation to a street. Choice (A) might be considered by the planning board. Setting weight limits on local streets, choice (C), is a function of the state department of transportation and/or local government. Choice (D) is a function of the building department.

25. **The correct answer is (C).** Choices (A) and (B) are incorrect because the VA does neither of these. Choice (D) is incorrect because under certain circumstances, no down payment is required. As little as 3 percent are required for an FHA-insured loan.

26. **The correct answer is (B).** Choice (B) is true, but if a state has a lower requirement, the lender cannot keep more than that lesser amount in escrow accounts. Choice (A) is incorrect because RESPA regulates escrow accounts. Choice (C) is incorrect because RESPA does not require that lenders establish and maintain escrow accounts. Choice (D) is incorrect.

27. **The correct answer is (A).** Choice (A) is incorrect. The broker may suggest home inspectors and other contractors, but the buyer hires them. Choices (B), (C), and (D) are duties that brokers carry out, so they are incorrect answers to the question.

28. **The correct answer is (C).** $37,500 ÷ $329,000 = 0.114 = 11.4\%$

29. **The correct answer is (D).** Choice (A) is the initial study of a site by reviewing the site's history. Choice (B) involves sampling of materials from the site. Choice (C) is the cleanup stage.

30. **The correct answer is (A).** HPA regulates private mortgage insurance. In addition to choice (A), a residential mortgage transaction according to HPA is one that generates a mortgage or deed of trust and whose purpose is to finance the acquisition, construction, or refinancing of the borrower's primary residence. Choice (B) is a dwelling that is covered under the Fair Housing Act, but not under HPA. Choice (C) is incorrect because VA-guaranteed and FHA-insured mortgages are not covered under HPA. Choice (D) is incorrect because HPA regulates residential mortgages that are ARMs also.

31. **The correct answer is (C).** Choices (A) and (D) are not variances, but uses. Choice (A) is a use that existed prior to the zoning that now prohibits it. Choice (D) is the addition of a structure to a property. Choice (B) is a variance that permits a larger building on a property than the property is zoned for.

32. **The correct answer is (B).** Choices (A), (C), and (D) are all homebuyers' rights under RESPA, so they are incorrect answers to the question. Choice (B) is not true in regard to RESPA or any government regulation, and so is the correct answer to the question. However, RESPA does require that a mortgagee notify a mortgagor if the company transfers the servicing rights for his or her loan to another servicer. This is the Servicing Transfer Statement.

33. **The correct answer is (B).**

$3.75 − $2.55 = $1.20

752' × 752' = 565,504

565,504 × $1.20 = $678,604.80

34. **The correct answer is (B).** The amount of seller-assist for FHA-insured loans dropped from 6 percent, choice (C), to 3 percent. Choice (A) is the new initial insurance premium that borrowers who get an FHA-insured loan must pay. Choice (D) is a distracter.

35. **The correct answer is (C).** The name of the buyer who is the person or persons taking out the mortgage and note must be included

on the note, but not the name of the seller of the property. Choices (A), (B), and (D) are all typical pieces of information that are found in a note, and they are, therefore, incorrect answers to the question.

36. **The correct answer is (D).** Choice (A) is incorrect; an EEM can be used to buy a 1- and 2-unit residence, but not a condo. Choices (B) and (C) are incorrect because the improvements may not be more than $4,000 or 5 percent of the value of the property, whichever is greater.

37. **The correct answer is (C).** IRS liens typically take precedence, and then come other tax liens, so choices (A), (B), and (D) are incorrect. One way to save time in answering series questions like this one is to read the first item in each series. If it's wrong, check off the answer choice and go on to the next answer. If the first item is wrong, check it off. Go through the first item in each answer in this way, and then do the same for the second item in the remaining answer choices until you have only one choice left.

38. **The correct answer is (A).**

$2,011.02 \times 12 \times 15 = $361,983.60

$361,983.60 - $265,000 = $96,983.60

39. **The correct answer is (A).**

$5,348.24 \div 4 = $1,337.06

$1,337.06 \div 3 = $445.69

$445.69 \div 30 = $14.86

$445.69 \times 2 = $891.38

$14.86 \times 5 = $74.30

$891.38 + $74.30 = $965.68

This is an instance where there is more information in the question than you need to answer it. The sales price is irrelevant.

40. **The correct answer is (B).** Choices (A), (C), and (D) according to HUD's own guidance do not constitute discriminatory advertising.

41. **The correct answer is (A).** Choice (B) could have an oil leak into the ground, but that's not related to a leach field. Choice (C) is an alternative way of disposing waste from a septic system; in other words, it serves the same purpose as a leach field, but a homeowner wouldn't have both. Choice (D) is a distracter.

42. **The correct answer is (C).** Choices (A), (B), and (D) are elements of a residential property that are typically included in a home inspection.

43. **The correct answer is (B).** Having this statement in the home inspection contingency clause gives away the buyer's leverage, though the buyer may choose to do this, but should negotiate to deduct some of the purchase price in order to have the repairs done after the closing. Choices (A), (C), and (D) are typically found in home inspection contingency clauses and are, therefore, the wrong answers to the question.

44. **The correct answer is (B).**

$87,000 \times 0.017 \times 3 = $4,437

$87,000 - $4,437 = $82,563

$17,000 \times 0.065 \times 3 = $3,315

$17,000 + $3,315 = $20,315

$82,563 + $20,315 = $102,878

45. **The correct answer is (A).** Choice (B) is incorrect because it relates to an easement that occurs without a property owner's permission, in plain sight, without interruption, and for a period of time that the state considers the prescribed statutory time for an easement by prescription. Choice (C) is incorrect because it relates to an easement given by one property to another. Choice

(D) refers to an easement over another's property in order to reach one's landlocked parcel.

46. **The correct answer is (D).** *Ad valorem* means "according to value." Choice (A) is incorrect; the three ways to appraise property are sales comparison, cost, and income. Choice (B) is determined through appraisal. Choice (C) is determined using competitive market analysis.

47. **The correct answer is (C).** The notary or person taking the acknowledgement must be satisfied with the identity of the person(s) signing. Choices (A), (B), and (D) are distracters.

48. **The correct answer is (A).**

    2,550 − 2,500 = 50

    $375,600 ÷ 2,500 = $150.24

    $150.24 × 50 = $7,512

    $375,600−$15,000+($7,500×0.5)−$7,512 = $356,838

49. **The correct answer is (B).** Choice (A) is an exclusive right to sell listing. Choice (C) is the same as choice (A) and the opposite of the correct answer, choice (B). Choice (D) is incorrect unless a seller and realtor negotiate this.

50. **The correct answer is (D).** A conforming mortgage is choices (A), (B), and (C) and can also be an ARM. Because a conforming mortgage can be sold to Fannie Mae and Freddie Mac, it cannot be a jumbo mortgage, choice (D), so it is incorrect, but the correct answer to the question.

51. **The correct answer is (A).** Because choice (A) is true, you need to find out your state's regulations on noncompete clauses in contracts of employment. Choice (B) is incorrect because a prohibition against the immediate area is typical in a noncompete

clause. Choice (C) is incorrect because the time period varies. Choice (D) is a distracter.

52. **The correct answer is (C).** Choice (C) is a state or municipal law, but not an encumbrance, which includes easements, liens, deed restrictions, and leases. Choice (A) is a deed restriction. Choice (B) is a lien. Choice (D) is an easement.

53. **The correct answer is (B).** A lease survives a property sale, so choices (A), (C), and (D) are incorrect.

54. **The correct answer is (B).** Choice (A) is a mortgage in which the buyer borrows money for the down payment and in return the lender gets a partial share in the property. Choice (C) includes both real property and personal property. In choice (D), only the interest is paid during the term of the mortgage, not the principal. Check your state law and banking regulations to see if shared equity and package mortgages are allowed.

55. **The correct answer is (B).**

    32' × 25' = 800

    800 × $22 = $17,600

56. **The correct answer is (B).** Choice (A) is an improvement and is added to the purchase price during the calculation. Choices (C) and (D) are added to the purchase price. No capital gains need to be sold on the main home if the profit is $250,000 for a single person and $500,000 for a married couple if it has been the primary residence for at least 2 years. Exceptions to the residency period can be made for job relocation and health reasons.

57. **The correct answer is (B).** Choice (A) describes a judicial foreclosure. Choice (C) describes a nonjudicial foreclosure. Choice (D) is incorrect. Remember that not all states recognize nonjudicial and strict foreclosures.

58. The correct answer is (A). Choice (B) would be negligent misrepresentation if the agent had not found out how old the HVAC was. Choice (C) is incorrect because to someone with bad allergies or asthma, the odor might be a material defect and cause the buyer to pass on the property. Choice (D) is incorrect because while it might take an expert to determine the cause, it is not a hidden defect so the agent has a duty to disclose it.

59. The correct answer is (D). Choices (A), (B), and (C) are all legitimate actions that a lender may take with an appraiser. Choice (D) is not.

60. The correct answer is (C). The agency agreement is a contract, and the purpose of a contract must be stated and it must be a legal purposed for the contract to be valid. Choices (A), (B), and (D) are not necessary in order for the agency agreement to be valid. If choice (D) were "commission," then it would be one of the five characteristics that make a contract valid.

61. The correct answer is (B). Choices (A), (C), and (D) are lines on the GFE; they are also all fees that the lender charges the buyer. Choice (B) does not appear on the GFE, so it is the correct answer to the question.

62. The correct answer is (A).

$10,883.98 × 60 = $653,038.80

$653,038.80 − $562,980 = $90,058.80

63. The correct answer is (A). Helping someone find a broker in a new area may be a courtesy, but it's not a fiduciary responsibility, so not doing it isn't a breach of a broker's fiduciary responsibilities. In other words, it's the correct answer to the question. Choices (B), (C), and (D) are breaches of obedience, reasonable care and diligence, and confidentiality respectively.

64. The correct answer is (C). Choice (A) is the document that conveys title, but it does not give a history of the title. Choice (B) is a document provided either after a title search resulting in an abstract of title or based on an attorney's opinion of title after a search that did not include an abstract. Choice (D) is incorrect because it is evidence that a change in title has been recorded, but it does not provide a history of the title.

65. The correct answer is (D). A limited liability company has the limited liability of a corporation, but its owner or owners have to pay taxes on profits individually, not at corporate tax rates. Choice (A) is a corporation and has liability limited generally to the amount of the shareholders' investment in the corporation. The corporation pays taxes on profits, and the shareholders pay taxes on the distribution of dividends. In a general partnership, choice (B), all partners share in the liability related to the actions of the partnership, and partners pay taxes in relation to the amount of their interest in it. Choice (C) is ownership by a single person who has unlimited liability under the law and pays taxes on profits as individual income.

66. The correct answer is (B). $475,692 × 0.125 = $59,461.50

67. The correct answer is (B). Choice (B) occurs when a mortgagor is in default of the mortgage. A mortgage can be paid off without a prepayment penalty, choice (A), but that's not the answer to the question. Choice (C) is a graduated payment mortgage. Choice (D) describes a graduated equity mortgage.

68. The correct answer is (A). Choice (B) guarantees only the actions of the person conveying the title, not the complete history of the property; nor does it warrant that the grantor will help the grantee should someone later lay claim to the property, which is what the covenant of further assurances, choice (A), warrants. Choice (C) is used by a trustor to convey title to a trustee who holds title while the property is being used as security for a loan. Choice (D) has no warranties attached to it and only conveys the interest that the grantor has in the property.

69. **The correct answer is (B).** Choices (A) and (D) are distracters. Choice (C) is incorrect because the seller or the buyer may pay the settlement fee. It is one of the items to be negotiated between buyer and seller.

70. **The correct answer is (C).** Choice (A) is incorrect because a beneficiary is someone who benefits from a trust. Choice (B) is incorrect because Sonja is taking the property back herself; she is not leaving it to someone else in her will. Choice (D) is a distracter.

71. **The correct answer is (D).**

$345' \times 97' = 33,465$

$97' \times 83' \times \dfrac{1}{2} = 4,205.5$

$33,465 + 4,205.5 = 37,670.5$

72. **The correct answer is (C).** Choice (A) is incorrect because there is nothing in the scenario that indicates a zoning variance is needed. Choice (B) is incorrect because it has no jurisdiction over this. Choice (D) would be correct only if the university already had permission and needed building permits to get started.

73. **The correct answer is (D).** Choice (A) is eviction of a tenant for cause such as nonpayment of rent. Choice (B) is eviction of a tenant as revenge for some action of the tenant such as complaining to the board of health because of poor building maintenance by the landlord. Choice (C) is incorrect because the property owners would go to court to ask for an injunction against the state;

an injunction is a court order to prohibit a person or an entity from doing some action.

74. **The correct answer is (B).** Choices (A) and (C) buy mortgages and package them as MBS to sell on the secondary mortgage market; they don't insure the MBS. Choice (D), in addition to regulating the nation's money supply through its monetary policies, regulates credit transactions, banks, and other depository organizations.

75. **The correct answer is (C).** Choice (A) occurs when a lender sells a mortgage to another financial institution. Choice (B) describes an assumption of a mortgage. Choice (D) accurately describes a typical contingency clause in a sales contract, but it's a distracter.

76. **The correct answer is (D).**

$0.654 \times \$73.43 = \$194,883.22$

$\$194,883.22 \times 0.35 = \$6,820.91$

$\$6,820.91 \times 2 = \$13,641.82$

$\$194,883.22 + \$45,000 - \$13,641.82 = \$226,241.40$

77. **The correct answer is (A).** An independent contractor receives no benefits like paid sick days, vacation, or holidays; pension plan; and medical or other insurance. Choices (B), (C), and (D) are criteria for any independent contractor. In addition to paying one's own quarterly federal income tax, an independent contractor also pays state income tax quarterly and FICA taxes. (FICA stands for Federal Insurance Contributions Act and funds Social Security and Medicare.)

78. **The correct answer is (D).** Choice (A) is incorrect in two ways: it is a typical item brought to a closing and it's the buyer that brings it. Choice (B) pertains to apartment rentals, not office rentals. Choice (C) is incorrect. A seller of a rental property would provide estoppel letters from tenants

indicating the rental amounts due on their leases—before the closing—so the closing agent can incorporate the amounts into the settlement statement.

79. **The correct answer is (B).** Net operating income is the method most often used to find the capitalization rate. Choice (A) seems right because people put money into a project when they capitalize it, but it's a distracter. Choice (C) is incorrect because the capitalization rate should reflect the expected rate of return for investors, but is not the same as the ROI. Choice (D) is similar to choice (A) and incorrect.

80. **The correct answer is (D).** Choice (D) is known as the procuring cause agent. However, in the real world, determining who is the procuring cause agent is not always clear cut, so it's important to explain the concept to buyers. Choices (A), (B), and (C) are incorrect.

81. **The correct answer is (D).** $537,620 × 0.0425 = $22,848.85

82. **The correct answer is (C).** Choice (C) is an area of land that is used to separate one type of land use from another. Its purpose is transitional. Neither choice (A) nor choice (D) is a zoning term. Choice (B) is incorrect because it defines a variance.

83. **The correct answer is (A).** Choice (B) is an example of the truism that the longest answer is often the wrong answer. The purpose of an appraisal is to provide the commissioning entity with a single valuation. Choice (C) is incorrect because highest and best use is one economic factor influencing value. Choice (D) is incorrect because the use of the property affects which appraisal approach (income, cost, sales comparison) receives more weight.

84. **The correct answer is (A).** A contract that is voidable is enforceable if the parties agree to act on it; in this case, the wronged party decides to act on it. Choice (B) is incorrect because coercion makes the contract voidable, so it can't be valid and enforceable. Choice (C) is incorrect because it's a voidable contract, which is not the same as void, and for this reason, choice (D) is also incorrect.

85. **The correct answer is (A).** A sole proprietorship is also tenancy in severalty. Choice (B) is an ownership arrangement for two or more individuals with right of survivorship. Choice (C) grants the holder of the lease possession, not ownership, of the property for a set period of time. Choice (D) is a qualified fee simple estates subject to certain conditions or contingencies that the grantor puts on the property.

86. **The correct answer is (A).** Having a power of attorney also gives the brother-in-law universal agency. Choice (B) is a distracter. Choice (C) bestows only limited authority on a person to act for another. While choice (D) enables an agent to take on many tasks for another person, those do not include power of attorney.

87. **The correct answer is (C).** Choice (C) is incorrect because RESPA stands for the Real Estate Settlement Procedures Act and doesn't deal with antidiscrimination policies, so it is the correct answer to the question. Choices (A) and (B) are true about antidiscriminatory housing policies, so they are incorrect answers to the question. Choice (D) is regulated by various federal employment laws such as the Equal Employment Opportunity Act.

88. **The correct answer is (A).**

$876,300 × 0.58 = $508,254

$508,254 × 0.029 = $14,739.37

$14,739.37 × 1.02 = $15,034.16

89. **The correct answer is (C).** Choice (A) is a percentage lease. Choice (B) is a gross lease. Choice (D) is a net lease.

90. **The correct answer is (C).** Choices (A), (B), and (D) are not typically included when calculating a mortgage's annual percentage rate, whereas choice (C) is.

91. **The correct answer is (B).** Choices (A), (C), and (D) are components of appraisal reports, so they are incorrect answers to the question. Choice (B) is not a part of an appraisal report. An appraiser estimates value, not sales price.

92. **The correct answer is (C).**

    $184,950 × 0.03 × 5 = $12,742.50

    $184,950 − $12,742.50 = $172,207.50

    $172,207.50 × 0.8 = $137,766

93. **The correct answer is (B).** Choice (A) is incorrect because the appraiser doesn't consider landscaping, which also makes choice (C) incorrect. It is also incorrect because the appraiser doesn't consider paint color, whereas he would note whether it was cracked and peeling and would need to be repaired or repainted. Choice (D) is incorrect because it includes paint color also.

94. **The correct answer is (A).** Choice (B) is commercial financing, not strictly a loan in which the owner of property sells it and agrees to remain as a tenant of the new owner. Choice (C) is a mortgage that permits the mortgagor to borrow additional money under the same mortgage up to the original amount. Choice (D) is also a type of financing, and it is offered by developers to help buyers purchase their new construction by paying a percentage of the monthly mortgage payment for the first year or two. Check to see if this is permissible in your state.

95. **The correct answer is (D).** It is safer to spread duties—depositing checks, writing checks, and reconciling accounts—to more than one person, so that each person acts as a check on the other. Choices (A), (B), and (C) are good policies to follow, according to the National Association of Realtors.

96. **The correct answer is (B).** While sellers must disclose the presence of lead paint in a home by law, they don't have to remediate it. It's up to the buyer to decide what to do. Choices (A) and (C) are other items that should be disclosed to potential buyers and in some states, a radon test is required when residential property is to be sold. Choice (D) may be a case where Legionnaire's disease might be considered a stigma on a property and should be disclosed for that reason, even if the problem has been eradicated.

97. **The correct answer is (D).** Choice (A) would only be correct if the seller told the broker not to submit an offer under a certain amount. Choice (B) is incorrect because a broker has a duty to treat all offers and buyers equally. Choice (C) is incorrect because it's up to the seller to decide what he or she wants to do; the realtor can't act without instructions from the seller.

98. **The correct answer is (C).**

    $6,270 ÷ 12 = $522.50

    $522.50 × 5 = $2,612.50

99. **The correct answer is (C).** Choices (A), (B), and (D) are typical inclusions in a real estate contract of sale, and so are not correct answers to the question. Choice (C) is not a typical inclusion, so it is the correct answer to the question.

100. **The correct answer is (B).** Choices (A) and (C) are incorrect because low property taxes are a political factor that enhances property values. Choice (C) is also incorrect because low interest rates are an economic factor that influences property values. Choice (D) is incorrect because zoning is a political factor that influences property values.

Practice Test 6: Do-It-Yourself Test

Each state's real estate licensing exams are different. In addition to a section that includes national content, which is similar content that a real estate salesperson or broker in any of the 50 states, the District of Columbia, and the U.S. Virgin Islands must know, there are licensing laws and real estate laws, rules, and regulations specific to each of these 52 jurisdictions. Throughout this book, you have read NOTEs, TIPs, and ALERTs reminding you to check your state's licensing and other real estate laws. This Do-It-Yourself Test will see how well you have learned this information.

Under each heading, write at least three facts for each topic. Don't look up the answers. If you don't know something, leave it blank. After you have completed the test, check your answers against the information that you have researched, correct any mistakes, and fill in the missing answers.

I. Your State Real Estate Commission

1. What is its purpose, powers, and composition? _____

2. What sanctions/penalties can the commission impose?
   _____

3. What duty does a salesperson/broker have to report violations of the law?
   _____

4. What is the process for investigations and hearings into violations?
   _____

5. What is the appeals process? _____

II. Licensing Requirements

1. What activities related to real estate require a license?
   _____

2. What licenses are available in your state? _____

3. What are the requirements for licensing as a salesperson?
   _____

4. What is the process for license renewal for salesperson/broker?
   _____

5. What type of continuing education is required of real estate salespeople/brokers?
   _____

6. Is bonding required, and if so, what kind? _____

7. What are the requirements for being considered an independent contractor vs. an employee of a broker? _____

III. Statutory Requirements Governing Activities of Licensees

1. What are the state requirements related to advertising?

   _____

2. What requirements govern the broker-salesperson relationship?

   _____

3. What disclosures are mandated by statute? _____

4. What is mandated in terms of commissions? _____

5. How must documents be handled? _____

6. How must monies be handled? _____

7. What requirements are there in terms of recordkeeping?

   _____

8. What constitutes the unauthorized practice of law? _____

9. What issues of confidentiality are involved in agency relationships?

   _____

10. What is a "permitted action" in terms of agency relationships?

    _____

11. What statutory duties are mandated in terms of agency relationships?

    _____

12. What are the state requirements in terms of marketing out-of-state properties for development? _____

13. What are the requirements in terms of property rentals?

    _____

14. What are the requirements for acting as a property manager?

    _____

IV. Statutory Requirements for Specific Topics

1. What are state regulations related to the sale/rental of condos, PUDs, and co-ops?

   _____

2. Is there a code of ethics for the landlord-tenant relationship? If so, what does it cover?

   _____

3. What types of ownership are recognized in your state?

   _____

4. What are the state laws regarding easements? _____

5. What are the state laws regarding adverse possession?

   _____

6. What are the state laws regarding riparian rights? _____

7. What are the state laws regarding property taxes including exemptions?

    _____

8. What types of titles are recognized in your state? _____

9. What types of deeds are recognized in your state? _____

10. What types of foreclosure are recognized in your state?

    _____

11. What type of closing is used in your state? _____

12. Does your state have its own fair housing act? If so, what does it cover?

    _____

13. Is seller financing allowed? If so, what type? _____

14. What are the requirements for signage? _____

15. How should transfer taxes/transfer stamps be handled?

    _____

16. What are state regulations about zoning and land use?

    _____

17. What system of legal property description is used? _____

18. What is the process for offers and counteroffers? _____

19. If your state has a consumer protection law that covers real estate, how does it handle

    • misrepresentation? _____

    • property disclosures? _____

20. What is your state's laws regarding hazardous materials such as

    • lead? _____

    • asbestos? _____

    • radon? _____

    • mold? _____

    • underground fuel storage tanks? _____

    • landfills? _____

    • private wells? _____

    • septic systems and cesspools? _____

    • smoke and carbon dioxide detectors? _____

    • wetlands protection? _____

V. Broker Only Issues

1. What are the eligibility requirements for licensing as a broker?

   _____

2. What are the issues related to supervision of salespeople?

   _____

3. What are the requirements related to changes on a license?

   _____

4. How are escrow accounts handled? _____

5. How are trust accounts handled? _____

6. Does your state recognize

   • dual agency? _____

   • designated agency? _____

7. What disclosures are specifically required of brokers?

   _____

8. Must contracts be in writing? _____

9. Must listing agreements be in writing? _____

10. How can a broker go about obtaining listings agreements?

    _____

11. Does your state recognize net listings? _____

12. What is the process for drafting and submitting offers?

    _____

13. What broker actions are prohibited by law, such as self-dealing?

    _____

14. Which legal forms may be used and how? _____

15. What are the restrictions on giving legal advice? _____

VI. Other

What are three other topics that differ in your state from what is explained in the content of this book?

_____

_____

_____

APPENDIXES

Glossary of Important Real Estate Terms

A

Absolute net lease: tenant pays the base rent and all expenses associated with operating and maintaining the building

Abstract of title: researched history of title to real property including owners, liens, easements, etc.

Acceleration clause: provides for full repayment of a mortgage if the mortgagor defaults on any aspect of the mortgage

Accessory building: secondary building on a property

Accessory use: secondary use for real property

Accretion: addition to land over time by the depositing of waterborne sediment

Acknowledgment: statement sworn to in front of a notary that the person freely and voluntarily entered into the contract

Actual age: the chronological age of an improvement

Actual eviction: expulsion of a tenant from the premises by filing a complaint with the court for an eviction notice, serving the notice, and holding a hearing to gather evidence from both sides; if complaint upheld, the tenant is served with a warrant to dispossess and must surrender the premises

Adjustable-rate mortgage (ARM): also known as a variable-rate mortgage; interest rate fluctuates based on certain conditions stated in the mortgage document

Ad valorem: in proportion to the value; a term in assessed value

Adverse possession: encroachment on real property; continuous, hostile, unopposed use of property by someone not the owner for a period of time that meets statutory requirements for adverse possession

Agency: relationship between buyer and seller and his/her real estate broker/agent

Agent: person acting for another

Alienation: see *involuntary alienation* and *voluntary alienation*

Alienation clause: clause in a mortgage or deed of trust that requires full payment of the balance of the mortgage if the mortgagor transfers title to the real property; type of acceleration clause

Amortization: a method of paying down a mortgage in which both principal and interest are paid in periodic payments on a regular basis

Appraisal: opinion of value

Appraiser: professional who develops an opinion of value of real property or personalty

Appreciation: increase in value or price over time

Appurtenant easement: right to pass through or use another's property that once negotiated is permanent; may be overhead, surface, underground; see also *easement appurtenant*

Area variance: exception from a zoning law that involves yard or lot size, floor area ratio, building height

"Arm's length agreement": agreement that is freely and independently entered into by two parties without any special relationship, side deal, or control by one party of the other

Asbestos: incombustible, chemical-resistant fibrous mineral used for insulation, fireproofing, etc., that has been found to be hazardous to health

Assessed value: value of property for tax purposes

Assignee: party to whom property, rights, or interest has been transferred

Assignment: transfer of ownership of a mortgage from one mortgage lender to another; transfer of a lease from one tenant to another in which the first tenant gives up all rights to the premises, but retains the obligations under the lease

Assignor: party transferring property, rights, or interest to another

appendix a

Assumption: transfer of a mortgage from one mortgagor to another in which the second mortgagor takes on responsibility for the entire unpaid portion of the mortgage; lender must agree

Avulsion: sudden shifting of soil from one property to another because of a shift in a stream or river or a flood

B

Bargain and sale deed: no warranties are included, but the grantor's interest is implied; may be used by executors, trustees, and officers of the court

Baseline: one of the imaginary lines used in the rectangular survey system, a method of determining the legal description of property; runs east and west

Bilateral contract: agreement between two parties that involves promises made by each party to the other

Bilateral rescission: decision of two parties to a contract to nullify the contract as though it never existed; unwinding of a contract by mutual agreement

Binder: temporary agreement secured by a payment to show good faith until a formal contract can take effect; temporary title insurance to be replaced by title insurance later

Blanket mortgage: covers more than one piece of property; often used by developers; see *partial release provision*

Blockbusting: attempting to persuade home-owners to sell, usually at a loss, by appealing to their fear that minority groups are moving into the neighborhood; the homes are resold usually at a high price

Breach of contract: failure to perform actions as promised in the contract

Broker: person with proper licensing who acts as an intermediary between buyer/lessee and seller/landlord in exchange for a commission

Brownfield: abandoned, idled, or underused industrial or commercial property where expansion or redevelopment is complicated by the presence or potential presence of contamination

Bundle of rights: rights that owners exercise over their property: the rights to occupy, use, enjoy, sell, bequeath, give, lease, or do nothing with their property

C

Capitalization rate: percentage used to convert income into value and represents the relationship between income and value

Certificate of estoppel: signed statements by tenants verifying the terms of their leases and any deposit agreements when a landlord is seeking a loan on the leased property

Certificate of title: statement by an abstract company, title company, or attorney stating the holder of title to real property based on a search of the public records.

Certificate of Torrens: certificate used by some states to show to whom title to real property is registered

Closing: see also *traditional closing, closing of escrow, escrow closing*

Closing of escrow: actual closing when the escrow closing method is used; see *escrow closing*

Cloud on the title: any claim or obstacle to a clear transfer of title from one party to another, such as a lien

Cluster zoning: grouping of different types of land use in certain areas

Commission: compensation charged by a broker for his/her service in facilitating a real estate transaction, which may be a sale or lease

Community property ownership: joint and equal ownership of property by husband and wife, but with no right of survivorship; limited to only a few states

Comparative market analysis: review of the prices of recently sold properties that are similar in the same neighborhood

Comparative unit method: estimate of cost based on square footage or cubic volume of a structure used as a method to valuing property under the cost approach

Compensatory damages: court-ordered payment of money in compensation for loss or injury; one recourse for the injured party in a dispute over a real estate contract that was breached

Competitive market analysis (CMA): method to determine listing price; comparison of property with similar properties in the area that have sold recently or are currently on the market

Comprehensive Environmental Response, Compensation, and Liability Act of 1980 (CERCLA): federal law that created a tax on the chemical and oil industries and provided broad federal authority to respond to releases or threatened releases of hazardous substances; established the Superfund to pay for cleanups of abandoned sites

Condemnation: seizure of property for public use

Conditional use application: see *special use permit*

Conditional use permit: see *special use permit*

Condition of sale: something that must be done or accomplished by one party or the other to a contract; something about the property that must be acceptable to the buyer

Condominium (condo) ownership: ownership of a specific unit in a property as well as ownership of common areas; condo owner pays a monthly maintenance fee and real estate taxes

Conforming mortgage: conventional mortgage (one that is not insured or guaranteed by a government agency) that is eligible for sale to Freddie Mac or Fannie Mae

Consideration: something that the parties to a contract agree is of value and what the parties exchange

Construction mortgage: provides funding for construction projects at different stages of completion

Constructive eviction: tenant's leaving a rental unit as a result of the landlord's neglect of the premises so it becomes inhabitable

Constructive notice: public notice of something having occurred; purpose for filing mortgage, deed, liens, and easements with the county office

Contingency: clause that describes some action that must be met in order for the contract to be valid; usually a material term of the contract that is so important to the buyer that the contract can/will be canceled if not met

Contract: agreement between two or more parties to do or not to do something that is enforceable by law

Contract for deed: form of financing the purchase of land; an initial payment of part of the sale price is made and the rest is paid over time with equitable title going to the buyer (vendee) with the down payment, full title may be transferred either with full payment of the sale price or a certain number of additional payments; also known as land contract, land

sales contract, installment sales contract, installment contract

Conventional mortgage: one that is not insured or guaranteed by a government agency

Conveyance tax: see *transfer tax*

Co-operative (co-op) ownership: ownership of shares in the underlying corporation that owns the property organized as a co-operative and that entitles the buyer to a proprietary lease to a specific unit; co-op owner pays a monthly fee that includes property taxes as well as maintenance

Cost approach: one method that appraisers use to estimate the value of property; analysis of replacement or reproduction cost of improvements minus depreciation plus the value of the land

Covenant against encumbrances: warrants that there are no encumbrances such as liens or easements against the property other than the easements stated in the deed

Covenant of further assurance: promise by the grantor to provide any documents or perform any actions needed to clear up any errors or problems with the deed

Covenant of quiet enjoyment: warrants that the title to the property will not be claimed by a third party and that the grantor will make good on any losses that the grantee suffers as a result of a third party's claim should one come forward in the future who has a better claim to the property

Covenant of seisin: guarantees the mortgagor the right to transfer title to the mortgagee

Covenants, conditions, and restrictions (CCRs): private restrictions on what a property owner is allowed to do with his/her property as opposed to public restrictions on private property owners; placed on property by developers and townhome, condo, and neighborhood associations; also known as deed restrictions, restrictive covenants

Credit: payment/money in a buyer's or seller's favor at closing

Curable depreciation: type of depreciation that can be fixed

Curtesy: life interest of a widower in his wife's estate acquired during their marriage if they had a child who could inherit; no longer widely used

D

Datum: point, line, or surface used as a reference in surveying

Debit: payment/money not in a buyer's or seller's favor at closing; money owed at closing by one or the other party that becomes a credit to the other

Declaration of restrictions: list of covenants, conditions, and restrictions in a deed

Deed: written legal document that conveys and is evidence of a person's legal right to possess property

Deed of release: used when a mortgage is paid in full to convey the title from the financial institution to the buyer

Deed of trust/deed in trust: see *trust deed*

Deed restriction: runs with the land; see *covenants, conditions,* and *restrictions (CCRs)*

Defeasance clause: in a mortgage clause that states the mortgagor will turn over to the mortgagee the title to the property when the loan is paid off

Deficiency judgment: a court order requiring the mortgagor who defaulted on his/her mortgage to pay the difference between what a foreclosed property sold for and the outstanding mortgage; other lienholders may also sue if the sale doesn't net enough to pay them off

Density zoning: zoning that identifies the number of houses that may be built on an acre of land; used in rural areas typically to control growth while supporting farmers

Depreciation: decrease or loss of value over time for a variety of reasons such as age, wear and tear, market conditions

Designated agency: a single brokerage represents both the buyer and seller in a real estate transaction, but the seller signs a listing agreement and the buyer signs one of the forms of buyer agency agreement and each is represented by separate agents; created to avoid potential conflicts of dual agency representation

Discount points: see *points*

Discriminatory advertising: advertising that violates the federal Fair Housing Act (and any state laws related to nondiscriminatory practices in advertising real estate sales or leasing); prohibits any advertising that indicates a limitation or preference based on race, color, national origin, religion, sex, familial status, or handicap and applies to single-family and owner-occupied housing that is otherwise exempt from the Fair Housing Act; indicates trigger words that are considered discriminatory

Doctrine of prior appropriation (water): system for allocating water rights in Western states

Dominant estate: real property that benefits from an easement given to it by another property (servient estate); usually an appurtenant easement

Double net lease: lessee pays rent, taxes, and insurance on the leased property

Dower: life estate to which a widow is entitled on the death of her husband; no longer widely used

Downzoning: zoning that typically reduces the amount of density or use that is allowed on a property

Dual agency: one brokerage represents both the buyer and seller in a real estate transaction

E

Earnest money: deposit that the buyer makes to seller to show that the buyer is "in earnest" about buying the property

Easement appurtenant: right to pass through or use another's property that once negotiated is permanent; maybe overhead, surface, underground; see also *appurtenant easement*

Easement by necessity: access to one's land-locked parcel of land through another's property

Easement by prescription: occurs without a property owner's permission, in plain sight, without interruption, and for a period of time that a state considers the prescribed statutory time for an easement by prescription

Easement in gross: right of way for a person, not a property, the person being a person in a legal sense such as a telephone, cable, water, power, or railroad corporation; there is no dominant estate, but the easement runs with the land

Economic life: the period during which an improvement is estimated to contribute value to the property

Effective age: functional age of an improvement based on the condition of the improvement and the conditions in the market

Effective demand: demand combined with purchasing power

Effective gross income (EGI): potential gross income minus a factor for vacancy and collection loss; used by appraisers with the income approach to valuation

Eminent domain: taking of private property by a unit of government—federal, state, local—for public uses, which are regulated by states and localities, and paying property owner's fair market value

Encapsulation: method for dealing with asbestos that is friable (disintegrating) without removing it

Encroachment: something that intrudes on another person's property, either accidentally or deliberately

Encumbrance: something that limits the title of a property; includes mortgages, liens, easements, leases, and restrictions

Environmental impact statement (EIS): study required by many states before a developer can get building permits to construct a subdivision, industrial part, or shopping mall; analyzes the project, the need for it, the area to be affected, a range of alternatives, the impact of each alternative; also required for federal agencies undertaking construction projects that would alter the environment; also called environmental impact report (EIR)

Environmental site assessment: study of a property to determine the presence, type, and extent of hazardous materials, clean up the area, or manage the hazardous materials if the area cannot be remediated

Equalization factor: factor used by the taxing authority to equalize the tax rate for different localities within a country of state

Equitable title: interest held by a buyer who has signed a contract of sale to purchase a property, but has not yet closed on the property; ownership interest held by the mortgagor in a state that uses the title theory until the mortgage is paid off and the mortgagor receives legal title

Equity: market value of a property minus the mortgage or other liability such as a home equity loan

Erosion: wearing away of the Earth's surface that can affect property lines

Escheat: reversion of real property by the state when a person dies without a will and heirs

Escrow: deposit of funds with a third party for a period of time while a real estate transaction is being finalized between two parties; trust account held in the borrower's name to pay obligations, such as property taxes and insurance premiums

Escrow agent: person who conducts an escrow closing; may be the buyer's attorney or an agent of the title company or an escrow company

Escrow closing: settlement in which buyer and seller turn over completed documents to an escrow agent before the closing date, all aspects of the contract of sale have been completed, and the agent handles the closing; see *closing of escrow, escrow agent*

Estate: one's interest in real property

Estate at sufferance: occurs when a tenant stays past the end of his or her lease, the landlord has not agreed to an extension or renewal, the lessee may or may not be trying to pay rent, but the landlord refuses it; also known as holdover tenancy

Estate at will: leasehold in which a tenant occupies a property without a specified end date and with or without a written lease

Estate for years: lessee and landlord agree to a lease for a term of years, the beginning and end dates of which are stated in the lease, and at the end of the term, the lessee vacates or a new lease must be negotiated

Estate from period to period (periodic tenancy): leasehold that does not have a specified end date, but is for a specified period of time such as a week or a month and automatically renews unless the landlord or the tenant wishes not to renew

Estoppel certificate: see *certificate of estoppel*

Eviction: removal of a tenant from the premises

Executed contract: a completely fulfilled contract

Executory contract: a contract that is still open, not yet fulfilled

Exclusive agency buyer agency agreement: gives the broker exclusivity over other agents to find a property for the buyer, but if the buyer on his or her own finds a property and buys it without the aid of the broker, the buyer does not have to pay the broker a fee

Exclusive agency listing: gives the broker the sole right to market the property during the term of the agreement, no commission is paid if the principal sells the property himself or herself

Exclusive buyer agency agreement: gives the broker the exclusive right to help a buyer find a property and must be paid his or her commission even if the buyer buys a property during the time period of the agreement without the broker's help

Exclusive right to represent agreement: see *exclusive buyer agency agreement*

Exclusive right to sell listing: gives the broker the sole right to market the property and assures the broker of the commission regardless of who sells the property during the term of the listing

Express contract/express written contract/express oral contract: parties to the contract clearly state and agree to the actions to be taken or not taken by each party

External obsolescence: factor outside the property that results in depreciation; incurable

F

Fair Housing Act of 1968 and Fair Housing Amendments Act of 1988: federal laws that prohibit discrimination on the basis of "race, color, religion, sex, handicap, familial status, or national origin in the sale, rental, or advertising of dwellings, in the provision of brokerage services, or in the availability of residential real estate-related transactions"

Fair market value: the price at which buyers and sellers are willing to do business with one another

Familial status: protected class under the Fair Housing Act; refers to families with children under 18, pregnant women, or adults in the process of adopting children under 18

Fannie Mae: government-sponsored entity that works with mortgage originators in the primary mortgage market to buy mortgages, bundle them, and sell them as securities to investors

Fee simple estate: ownership in which the owner has all rights to use, enjoy, and dispose of the property subject to public and private restrictions; most complete form of ownership

Fiduciary responsibilities (of agents): duties to an agent's principal include loyalty, obedience, disclosure, confidentiality, reasonable care and diligence, accountability

Final closing statement: records all the costs related to the purchase of property, prepared by one of the attorneys or the title company

Fixed-rate mortgage: mortgage that has an interest rate and a payment amount that remains the same for the life of the mortgage

Fixture: any article that is permanently attached to the property and, thus, becomes part of the real property; to determine the status of an article, four questions are asked: How is the item attached? What did the person who attached the item intend? Is there a contract stating what is considered real property and what is personal property? What is the relationship of the parties?

Foreclosure: see *judicial, nonjudicial, and strict foreclosures*

Four unities (requirements of joint tenancy): time, title, interest, possession

Fraud: intentional misrepresentation of information to a buyer

Freddie Mac: government-sponsored entity that works with mortgage originators in the primary mortgage market to buy mortgages, bundle them, and sell them as securities to investors

Freehold estate: grants ownership or property for an indeterminable period of time

Friability: ability of asbestos to crumble; factor that creates the problem with asbestos used in construction

Full covenant and warranty deed: see *general warranty deed*

Functional obsolescence: design defect; can be curable or incurable

G

General lien: lien that gives the lender the right to seize all the property of a borrower, not just the property on which the lien is placed

General listing: see *open listing*

General warranty deed: fullest protection to the buyer that the title is free and clear and the grantor (seller) has the right to convey the property; also called full covenant and warranty deed; see *covenants of seisin, of quiet enjoyment, against encumbrances, of further assurance*

Ginnie Mae (Government National Mortgage Association): government-backed corporation within Department of Housing and Urban Development; "guarantees mortgage-backed securities (MBS) backed by federally insured or guaranteed loans"

Good Faith Estimate (GFE): estimate of closing costs that must be given to a prospective borrower within 3 days of applying for a mortgage; required under RESPA

Government survey system: see *rectangular survey system*

Graduated lease: multiyear, long-term lease for which the rent varies; may be adjusted from time to time to reflect the changes in the appraised value of the premises, or it may be changed based on a benchmark rate such as the consumer price index

Grant deed: limits the warranties to the period the grantor owned the property and includes only that the grantor has not conveyed the property to anyone else, has encumbered the property only as noted in the deed, will convey to the grantee any interest in the property that the grantor may acquire later; used in only a few states

Granting clause: clause in a mortgage that gives the right to the mortgage to the mortgagee

Gross lease: lease in which the tenant pays the same amount of rent each month for a specified term of the lease, either the landlord or tenant pays the utilities, and the landlord pays the taxes, takes care of maintenance and repair, makes improvements, and buys liability insurance

Ground lease: typically multiyear, long-term leases for the rental of a parcel of unimproved land with the intention that the tenant will build on it within the term of the lease, when the lease is up the landlord takes possession of the land and improvements, in the meantime, the tenant pays all costs of the property and improvements

GSE (government-sponsored entity): chartered by Congress, such as Freddie Mac and Fannie Mae; not government-backed like Ginnie Mae

Guide meridian: adjusted line used in the rectangular survey system for legal property descriptions; runs north and south

H

Habendum **clause:** in a mortgage, the clause that reiterates the ownership specified in the granting clause

Handicap: as defined by the Department of Housing and Urban Development "a physical or mental disability which substantially limits one or more major life activities" including mental retardation; hearing and visual impairments; mobility impairments such as cerebral palsy and muscular sclerosis; cancer, diabetes, heart disease, epilepsy, and similar physical diseases; chronic mental illness; AIDS and AIDS-related illnesses; drug addiction from past illegal use of drugs; alcoholism; does not include current use of or addition to controlled substances

Hazardous material (hazmat): depends on the federal agency, but in terms of housing includes any health or physical hazard that is carcinogenic, toxic, corrosive, an irritant, or a sensitizer that acts on various parts of the body—human, animal, or plant—and that may get into the environment "through spilling, leaking, pumping, pouring, emitting, emptying, discharging, injecting, escaping, leaching, dumping, or disposing" according to According to the Institute of Hazardous Materials Management; EPA lists more than 350 such hazmats, may be in the form of "dusts, gases, fumes, vapors, mists, or smoke"

Highest and best use: the most profitable and legally permissible use for a property

Holdover tenant: a tenant who does not vacate the premises at the end of the lease

I

Implied contract: contract created by the actions of the parties; always an oral contract

Income approach: one method appraisers use to estimate the value of property; determination of value based on income generated by the property

Income capitalization approach: see *income approach*

Inclusionary zoning: zoning that seeks to provide low- and moderate-income housing new housing construction; affordable housing

Incurable depreciation: type of depreciation that cannot be remedied

Index: benchmark against which interest rates for adjustable- (variable-) rate mortgages are calculated; 1-year Treasury rates, LIBOR, COFI

Index method: least reliable method to estimate costs in the cost approach to valuing property; quick way to estimate costs in today's dollars if the original costs are known

Innocent landowner immunity: the current owner of a property if, at the time of the sale, had had a Phase I environmental study conducted and no hazardous materials were detected (though present), would not have to pay for site cleanup under the Superfund Amendments and Reauthorization Act

Installment contract: see *contract for deed*

Installment sales contract: see *contract for deed*

Interest: charge to the borrower for a loan, typically a percentage of the loan amount

Interstate Land Sales Full Disclosure Act: federal law regulating subdivision sales across state lines; developers must register with HUD and provide each potential buyer with a property report before the contract of sale is signed; the buyer has 7 days to cancel a contract and receive a refund; additional protections for consumers are built into the law and penalties for violation by developers are stiff

Inverse condemnation: occurs when the government takes property for a public purpose and neighbors demand that their properties be taken as well because of the effects of the public purpose

Investment value: value of property to a specific investor with a specific goal

Involuntary alienation: taking one's property against one's will

Involuntary lien: lien against a property because of an unpaid debt

J

Joint tenancy: ownership arrangement for two or more individuals who have right of survivorship typically; see *four unities*

Judicial foreclosure: judicial process that includes asking for a foreclosure order, setting a date for a mortgage payoff, court-ordered sale of the property if the mortgagor cannot meet the deadline

Judgment lien: lien that is placed on a property by a court order as the result of a lawsuit filed against the owner of the property

Jumbo mortgage: mortgage that is above the limit set by Fannie Mae and Freddie Mac

L

Laches: failure to enforce or exercise a right that then causes the right to be lost

Land contract: see *contract for deed*

Landfill: dumping grounds for variety of wastes: municipal sold wastes, wastes from factories, radioactive wastes; danger to the environment from waste products leaking into the environment; also known as MSWLF (Municipal Solid Waste Landfill)

Land sales contract: see *contract for deed*

Law of Agency: body of law that regulates the relationship between buyer or seller and his/her real estate broker/agent

Lead: common and highly dangerous ingredient in paint prior to 1978; can cause illness and disabilities, especially in children; regulated by the Residential Lead-Based Paint Reduction Act that requires sellers of homes built before 1978 to disclose to buyers or renters the presence of lead paint, provide a copy of *Protest Your Family From Lead in Your Home,* and buyers have 10 days to have an inspection done

Lead hazard screen: test to determine if lead is present in a home

Leaking Underground Storage Tank (LUST) Program: federal program under the Resource Conservation and Recovery Act that set up the LUST Trust Fund, oversees the cleanup of leaks, pays for cleanups when the party is "unknown, unwilling, or unable" to pay; Energy Policy Act of 2005 expands the use of the Trust Fund

Lease: contract usually in writing between a tenant/lessee and landlord/lessor that establishes a leasehold estate, usually for a specific period of time and for a specific consideration (rent)

Leasehold estate: grants the holder of the lease possession of the property for a set period of time (a renter's interest in a property)

Leasehold interest: see *leasehold estate*

Lease option/lease purchase option: see *option*

Legal property description: description that is made in accordance with accepted legal standards, is legally sufficient to identify the property, shows that this identity is unique and separate from all other real property; see *metes and bounds system, lot and block system, rectangular survey system*

Legal title: collection of rights of ownership of property; see *bundle of rights*

Lessee/tenant: renter, holder of an interest in a property for a period of time

Lessor: landlord, owner of a property being leased, that is, rented

Lien: financial claim against property

Life estate: interest in property that has an endpoint, which is the life of the person who is called the life tenant

Life estate *pur autre vie* with remainder: upon the death of the life tenant, the life estate is given to someone other than the person who set up the life estate

Life estate *pur autre vie* with reversion: upon the death of the life tenant, the life estate returns to the person who set up the life estate

Liquidation: selling of property in a relatively short time to satisfy debts

Lis pendens: public notice that a lawsuit has been filed that involves the title to real property or an interest in real property

Listing broker: broker that gains the right by contract to sell a property on behalf of the property owner

Listing contract/listing agreement: contract between a real estate broker, or agent acting in the broker's name, and a seller of real property to give the broker the right to market the seller's property

Living trust (*inter vivos*): trust established and operating during the grantor's life

Lot and block system: method for stating a legal property description in a subdivision; based on the lots and blocks shown on the map, or plat, of a subdivision

Lot block tract system: see *lot and block system*

M

Market allocation: illegal practice in which competitors (brokers or agents) divide up a market (area)

Market comparison approach: see *sales comparison approach*

Market value: "most reasonable price which a property should bring in a competitive and open market under all conditions requisite to a fair sale" (federal register); amount that a seller may expect to receive from a buyer in the open market

Marketable title: title that is free and clear of any significant liens and encumbrances

Master Plan: long-range plan developed by a government unit in consultation with the public to consider the most desirable development for the land that forms a particular governmental unit such as a city, town, or region; considers a variety of factors such as housing, transportation networks, public utilities, open spaces, and economic development

Material defect: defect that could affect either a buyer's decision to buy a property or the property's value; also called property defect

Materialman's lien: same as mechanic's lien

Mechanic's lien: lien a contractor attaches to a property for work done on the property for which the property owner has not paid the contractor; involuntary, specific lien

Meeting of the minds: see *mutual agreement*

Metes and bounds system: method for stating a legal property description; division of an area into the points of a compass, moving clockwise around the circle giving both compass points (direction) and measurement (distance), beginning with a "point of beginning" as the main reference point, which is also the point to which the boundary line must return; used mainly in the state that were originally settled by English colonists

Method of annexation: how a fixture is attached to real property

Millage: tax rate on property expressed as mills per dollar value of property

Monument system: method of determining legal description of property; use of natural or artificial objects (landmarks) to delineate a property's boundaries

Mortgage: promise to repay a loan on property; see also *trust deed*

Mortgage-backed security (MBS): bundle of mortgages that banks sell to Fannie Mae that then repackages them as securities and sells to investors

Mortgagee: lender

Mortgage insurance premium (MIP): the upfront fee and the percent of the mortgage that the Federal Housing Administration charges as an annual insurance premium until certain conditions on a loan are met

Mortgage-rate buydown: form of financing offered by developers to help buyers purchase their new construction by helping the purchaser pay a percentage of the monthly mortgage payment for the first year or two

Mortgagor: borrower

Multiple Listing Service/System (MLS): clearinghouse that posts listings for member brokers; marketing tool

Mutual agreement: all parties to a contract must agree to the terms and conditions of the contract; also meeting of the minds, offer and acceptance, reality of consent, mutual assent, mutual consent

Mutual assent: see *mutual agreement*

Mutual consent: see *mutual agreement*

N

Negligent misrepresentation: innocent misstatement or incomplete statement of a material fact

Net lease: tenant pays the base rent and some or all of the expenses of the property, not just utilities; typical commercial rental lease

Net listing: broker receives the difference between the selling price and the price that the owner wants for the property; may be exclusive or nonexclusive

Net operating income (NOI): part of the income approach to valuing property; gross income minus expenses, but not depreciation and principal and interest payments

Nonconforming mortgage: mortgage that can't be sold to Fannie Mae or Freddie Mac for reasons such as the mortgagor's poor credit rating, insufficient documentation, missing standard provisions required by Fannie Mae and Freddie Mac, or the loan is over their threshold

Nonconforming use: a use or structure that is out of character with the surrounding neighborhood, but the use or structure predates the zoning (variance is only required if the owner wants to expand the nonconforming use or structure)

Nonexclusive listing: see *open listing*

Nonjudicial foreclosure: a form of foreclosure that is described in a clause in the original mortgage document

Note: see *promissory note*

O

Offer and acceptance: see *mutual agreement*

Offeree: person to whom an offer is made

Offerer: person who is making an offer

Open buyer agency agreement: buyer enters into agreements with a number of brokers, but pays only the broker who actually finds the property that the buyer purchases, and no commission is paid if the buyer finds a property without the help of any broker

Open-end mortgage: mortgagor may borrow additional money under the mortgage so that the mortgage can increase back to its original amount

Open listing: right to market the property is given to several brokers with a commission going only to the broker who brings a buyer who closes on the property, unless the seller sells the property himself or herself and then no broker receives a commission; used more often in commercial real estate; unilateral contract

Open mortgage: can be paid off early without a prepayment penalty

Opportunity cost: cost of the next best alternative use of a resource when one choice is made rather than another

Option: gives a person the right to buy property within a stated period of time for a stated price, but the buyer doesn't have to buy, however, the seller must sell if the buyer decides to buy; unilateral contract

Optionee: person who receives a right to option property

Optionor: person who grants right to option property

Option to purchase/buy: see *option*

Ordinary life estate: estate that lasts for the life of someone and upon that person's death passes to another person

Ordinary life estate with remainder: life estate that upon the person's death passes to some person, not the grantor/owner

Ordinary life estate with reversion: life estate that upon the person's death passes back to the grantor/owner

P

Partial release provision (of a blanket mortgage): allows a builder to develop and sell lots separately, paying off part of the mortgage with each sale

Party wall easement: a wall that separates two units that are owned individually

Percentage lease: tenants pays rent plus a percentage of the gross sales of his/her business to the landlord; used primarily for retail rentals

Periodic tenancy: see *leasehold estate*

Personal property: see *personalty*

Personalty: personal property or chattel; not a fixture on real property

Phase I of Environmental Site Assessment: general assessment of a property that includes its history in terms of possible contaminants, the present use of the property, and identification of potential and existing problems

Phase II of Environmental Site Assessment: taking samples and analyzing them to confirm the presence of contamination on a property

Phase III of Environmental Site Assessment: additional testing to pinpoint the type, sources, and extent of contamination, a plan for cleanup is developed, and cleanup is undertaken

Phase IV of Environmental Site Assessment: a site management plan for containing the contamination and managing the site is developed if cleanup cannot be done

Physical deterioration: results from wear and tear on a property; may be curable or incurable

Physical life: period of time during which an improvement is estimated to last

Planned unit development (PUD): zoning classification that includes residential, commercial, industrial, and open space uses

Planning Board: adopts the master plan, reviews and decides subdivision and site plan applications (and may grant ancillary variances in connection with these), reviews and decides conditional use applications, recommends changes to the official map, recommends changes to the zoning code to the governing body (city council, for example) after reviewing the zoning report

Plat: map of the division of land—the lots—in a subdivision

Plottage: combining properties into one large property, thus raising the values of the whole, or the whole is greater than the sum of its parts

Point of beginning: first point of reference in a metes and bounds system, a type legal description of property

Points: prepaid interest on a mortgage that a borrower can purchase in order to lower the amount of interest that will be paid on the mortgage

Police power: right of government to regulate the use of private property

Potential gross income (PGI): income for a rental property based on 100 percent occupancy

Premises: rental property

Primary mortgage market: originates mortgages directly with mortgagors; includes commercial banks, savings and loan associations, credit unions, mutual savings banks, mortgage companies (mortgage bankers),

portfolio lenders (REITS [Real Estate Investment Trusts], insurance companies, and pension funds)

Priority of liens/priority of payments: order in which liens against property are paid off; order depends on the order in which liens were filed, but IRS liens take precedence

Procuring cause agent: broker/agent who brings the ready, willing, and able buyer to the transaction

Promissory note: promise to pay back a debt such as a mortgage; included with mortgage

Property defect: see *material defect*

Property manager: person who manages rental property for a landlord; duties include finding suitable tenants, advertising for tenants and checking references, negotiating leases, collecting rents, hiring and overseeing individuals and companies for maintenance and other services, appearing in court on behalf of the landlord in eviction proceedings, paying the bills; with the exception of resident property managers, must have a real estate license

Property report: under the Interstate Land Sales Full Disclosure Act: report that must be supplied to potential buyers before a contract of sale is signed in order to protect consumers from fraudulent practices in interstate land sales and leasing

Property stigma: anything in the history of a property that could hinder sale of a property

Property tax: local tax as opposed to state and federal taxes; used to fund local government services; based on value of real property

Property tax exemption: exception from having to pay property taxes in all or in part; major exemptions are government-owned property and may also be educational facilities and religious-owed properties, and certain classes of people such over 65, those with disabilities, and veterans

Proprietary lease: what a co-op buyer receives rather than a deed at the time of closing

Proration: process of determining the *pro rata* portions of something, that is, the amount that each party should pay

Protected class: category of people who are protected from discrimination under the law; race is protected in all circumstances; race, color, religion, sex, handicap, familial status, and national origin are protected against discrimination in housing; age is not a protected class in terms of housing, but in other circumstances

Public land survey system: see *rectangular survey system*

Puffing: describing something in an exaggerated or more flattering way; stretching the truth

Q

Qualified fee conditional: grantor/seller stipulates in the sale of a property that the buyer and his or her heirs may not use the property for a certain purpose and if this stipulation is violated, the grantor/seller has the right of reentry and reversion, the latter providing a court mechanism for reclaiming the property; form of fee simple estate

Qualified fee determinable: similar to qualified fee conditional, but the seller does not have to go to court to regain the property because reversion is automatic

Quantity survey method: most reliable method used in the cost approach to valuing property; cost of the materials of each component and the cost to install each is listed separately

Quitclaim deed: has no warranties, so it only conveys the interest that the grantor has in the property; used to clear up the cloud on the title when the buyer in a land contract defaults and the seller wants to resell the land

R

Radon: colorless, odorless, tasteless, radioactive gas that occurs naturally and is the second-leading cause of lung cancer in the United States; testing is recommended by the U.S. Environmental Protection Agency and the Surgeon General and mandated in many states before putting a house on the market

Range: land marked off into six-mile strips by range lines and meridians in the rectangular survey system

"Ready, willing, and able buyer": buyer who is ready to enter into a sales contract, wants to buy, and meets all requirements of the purchase including the ability to finance the purchase

Real estate: land and anything permanently affixed to it

Real Estate Settlement Procedures Act (RESPA): requires "that loan originators provide borrowers with a standard Good Faith Estimate that clearly discloses key loan terms and closing costs and that closing agents provide borrowers with a new HUD-1 settlement statement"; relates to all housing purchases for which the buyer takes out a mortgage loan and for refinancing

Real property: realty as opposed to personal property, or personalty

Reality of consent: see *mutual agreement*

Reconciliation: next-to-last-step in a real estate appraisal in which the estimates arrived at by the sales comparison, income, and cost approaches are compared and synthesized to come up with an estimate of value

Reconveyance deed: document that transfers title to real property secured by a deed of trust from the trustee to the trustor upon satisfaction of the debt

Recorded map system: see *lot and block system*

Recorded plat system: see *lot and block system*

Recording fee: charge to record documents in a real estate transaction including transfer of title and mortgage

Rectangular survey system: government survey system used for legal property descriptions in western states; uses meridians, base lines, tiers, ranges, and sections; divides land into 6-square mile townships

Redlining: illegal practice of denying mortgages and loans or limiting the amount of them to people in certain neighborhoods, particularly those with large numbers of certain groups

Regulation Z: implements Truth-in-Lending Act (Consumer Credit Protection Act) along with RESPA; regulates certain disclosures for mortgage loans including fees, charges, advertisements for mortgage financing, and information about variable rate mortgages

Remainderman: person who is entitled to an ordinary life estate with remainder upon the death of the life tenant

Rent control: law that regulates the amount of rent that landlords may charge

Rent stabilization: law that allows a landlord to raise the rent only a certain percentage a year and gives the tenant the right to renew the lease when it expires

Rescission: annulling of a contract so that the parties are where they were before the contract; it's as if the contract never existed

Restrictive covenant: see *covenants, conditions, and restrictions (CCRs)*

Retaliatory eviction: illegal expulsion of a tenant from a property as punishment for exercising a legal right

Rider: amendment to a contract

Right of quiet enjoyment: property is free of claims of others

Right of survivorship: right that allows the surviving party to automatically take ownership of the deceased party's share

"Run with the land": right or restriction that affects current and future owners of a property, for example, appurtenant easement

S

Sale-and-leaseback: financing for commercial enterprises in which the owner of a property sells it and agrees to remain as a tenant of the new owner; original owner gains the value of the property to use and the new owner is assured of rent for a period of time

Sales comparison approach: appraisal approach that compares the subject property (property being appraised) to similar properties, either recently sold or currently on the market; based on sales price

Section: division in the rectangular survey system consisting of 1 square mile/640 acres

Secondary mortgage market: buys mortgages from the primary mortgage market, bundles them, and sells them as investments

Selling broker: licensed real estate broker/agent who brings a buyer to a real estate transaction

Servient estate: real property that has an easement over it for the benefit of another property (dominant estate); usually an appurtenant easement

Settlement: see *traditional closing*

Short sale: sale of a property for less than the outstanding mortgage, must be agreed to by the lender, often occurs when the borrower cannot continue to make mortgage payments

Site valuation: method used by appraisers to estimate the value of a site without including the value of existing or potential improvements

Siting: location of an improvement on a parcel of land

Small Business Liability Relief and Brownfields Revitalization Act of 2002 (SBLRBRA): enlarges the classes under SARA that are protected from liability including those engaged in certain real estate transactions and further clarifies the innocent landowner immunity, enhances state brownfields programs, and provides financial assistance for brownfields revitalization

Sole owner: tenancy in severalty

Special assessment: flat-rate tax levied by a municipality or special district for an improvement

Special use permit: variance that would introduce a use into an area for which the area is not zoned

Special use variance: see *special use permit*

Specific lien: lien that applies to a single property

Specific performance: judgment handed down by a court that requires a party to a contract to execute the contract as agreed upon

Square foot method: see *comparative unit method*

Statute of limitations: state law that sets a maximum period of time after certain events in which legal proceedings based on those events may be initiated

Steering: illegal practice in which a realtor maneuvers a buyer or renter who is a member of a protected class away from a particular neighborhood

Strict foreclosure: process in which the mortgagee goes to court for an order demanding payment of the mortgage and setting a time period for payment, which if the mortgagor misses, the mortgagor loses all rights to the property, and the mortgagee gains title to the property; not allowed in all states

Subdivision: tract of land divided into lots to build houses on and sell

Subject to a mortgage: clause in a mortgage that affects assumption of the mortgage; original purchaser is responsible for the entire balance should the purchaser to whom the mortgage was transferred default on the mortgage

Sublease/sublet: tenant rents premises to another (sublessee) for a specific period of time with the intention of retaking possession of the premises at the end of that time; the tenant is ultimately responsible to the landlord

Sublessee: person who rents (sublets) premises from a tenant of a landlord, rather than the landlord; obligated to observe all terms of the original lease

Subprime mortgage: type of loan offered to people with low credit ratings who would not otherwise qualify for a mortgage; high rates of interest for these mortgages because of the high probability of loan defaults with this class of borrowers

Superfund Amendments and Reauthorization Act of 1986 (SARA): amended CERCLA; increased the amount of money in the Superfund, stresses the importance of permanent remedies and the use of new technologies to clean up hazardous waste sites, increases the involvement of the states in Superfund programs, establishes the public's right to know about the use and release of chemicals into the environment, encourages greater community participation in decisions about site cleanup, created the innocent landowner immunity provision

T

Tax assessor: person who calculates the value of property for the purpose of taxation

Tax lien: general lien placed against property for nonpayment of taxes

Tax rate: rate applied to the assessed value of property in order to calculate annual property taxes

Tenancy: having an ownership interest in a particular property; renting property

Tenancy in common: gives undivided interest in the property to each person, though the percentage of ownership may vary, and ownership in severalty, which means that each tenant may dispose of that interest as he or she chooses without the consent of the other tenant; no right of survivorship; most common form of co- or joint ownership

Tenancy in entirety: parties in a marriage own property as if they were one entity with undivided and equal interest and right of survivorship; four unities plus unity of the person are conditions of tenancy in entirely

Tenancy in severalty: each tenant may dispose of his or her interest as he or she chooses without the consent of the other tenant

Tenant's estate: see *leasehold estate*

Testamentary trust: trustor leaves instructions in his or her will about establishing a trust that will not be effective until after he or she dies

Tier: horizontal rows of townships in the rectangular survey system used for legal property descriptions

Timeshare: ownership of a fractional share in a property allowing a person the right to use the property for a period of time, usually one or two weeks every year; form of fee simple interest

Title: right of possession of property; ownership

Title by descent: transfer of title to heirs when a person dies without a will, but with heirs

Title insurance: protects the buyer in case someone claims an interest in the property in the future; lender may also buy title insurance, which the borrower pays for, to protect its investment in the property

Torrens system: land title registration system guaranteed by the state; title is indefeasible, that is, no one can void or annul the ownership of the title/property; used in some states only

Township: in terms of the rectangular survey system: unit of 36 sections, 36 square miles

Trade fixture: article attached to a rental property by a merchant for the purpose of the merchant's business

Traditional closing: signing of documents and handing over of checks to transfer the title of the property from the seller to the buyer; conducted by any of the nonprincipals

Transfer tax: Tax imposed on the transfer of the title from one entity to another

Triple net lease: tenant pays rent, utilities, taxes, and insurance

Trust: legal arrangement in which a person (trustor) gives fiduciary control of property to another (trustee) for the benefit of beneficiaries

Trust deed: used in some states instead of a mortgage when a GSE provides the mortgage

Trustee: lender in a mortgage transaction

Trustor: borrower in a mortgage transaction

Truth in Lending Act: see *Regulation Z*

U

Underground storage tank (UST): approximately 617,000 underground storage tanks in the United States store petroleum or hazardous wastes and are a danger to groundwater; regulated by the Resource Conservation and Recovery Act

Unilateral contract: one party promises to do something if the other party does something

Unilateral rescission: one party to a contract decides not to do what was promised in the contract

Unit-in-place method: method used in the cost approach to valuing property; appraiser measures the number and, in some cases, the area of various elements in a building and multiplies each by its unit cost

Use variance: exception to zoning based on a use that is not permitted in the zone in question and must be considered inherently beneficial or peculiarly fitted to the particular property

V

Vacancy decontrol: law that allows a landlord to charge the going market rate for a new tenant when a tenant who was living under rent control moves out

Value: relative worth of a thing expressed in monetary terms

Value in use: value of a property based on a particular use of, or purpose for, the property

Variable-rate mortgage: see *adjustable-rate mortgage*

Variance: see *zoning variance*

Vendee: buyer

Vendor: seller

Voidable contract: initially legal and enforceable, but misrepresentation of information, nondisclosure of material facts, undue influence on a party to the contract will cause a contract to be voidable

Void contract: contract based on a mistake of fact; unenforceable

Voluntary alienation: sale made voluntarily by the seller

Voluntary lien: lien that a property owner agrees to (mortgage)

W

Walk-through: property inspection just prior to closing

Z

Zoning: division of a geographic area into smaller areas based on use: primarily residential (single-family and multifamily), commercial, and industrial, but also mixed use

Zoning board/zoning board of adjustments/ zoning board of appeals: hears applications for relief from zoning ordinances and provides an annual report to the planning board of the variances granted

Zoning ordinance: law that regulates how private property owners may use their land

Zoning variance: exception from a zoning ordinance

State Real Estate Licensing Boards and Commissions

ALABAMA

Real Estate Commission
1201 Carmichael Way
Montgomery, AL 36106-3674
Phone: 334-242-5544
Fax: 334-270-9118
Web site: www.arec.alabama.gov

ALASKA

Real Estate Commission
Robert B. Atwood Building
550 W. 7th Avenue, Suite 1950
Anchorage, AK 99501
Phone: 907-269-8162
Fax: 907-269-1066
Web site: www.commerce.state.ak.us/occ/
    prec18.htm

ARIZONA

Department of Real Estate
2910 N. 44th Street
Phoenix, AZ 85018
Phone: 602-771-7799
Fax: 602-468-0562
Web site: www.re.state.az.us

ARKANSAS

Real Estate Commission
612 South Summit Street
Little Rock, AR 72201-4740
Phone: 501-683-8010
Fax: 501-683-8020
Web site: www.state.ar.us/arec/arecweb.html

CALIFORNIA

Department of Real Estate
2201 Broadway
Sacramento, CA 95818-2500

P.O. Box 187000
Sacramento, CA 95818-7000
Phone: 877-373-4542
Fax: 916-227-0925
Web site: www.dre.ca.gov

COLORADO

Department of Regulatory Agencies
Division of Real Estate
1560 Broadway, Suite 925
Denver, CO 80202
Phone: 303-894-2166
Fax: 303-894-2683
Web site: www.dora.state.co.us/real-estate

CONNECTICUT

Department of Consumer Protection
Connecticut Real Estate Commission
165 Capitol Avenue
Hartford, CT 06106-1630
Phone: 860-713-6050
Fax: 860-713-7239
Web site: www.ct.gov/dcp/site/default.asp

DELAWARE

Real Estate Commission
Cannon Building, Suite 203
861 Silver Lake Blvd
Dover, DE 19904
Phone: 302-744-4500
Fax: 302-739-2711
Web site: http://dpr.delaware.gov/boards/
    realestate

DISTRICT OF COLUMBIA

Board of Real Estate
941 North Capitol Street, NE
Washington, DC 20002
Phone: 202-442-4400
Fax: 202-698-4329
Web site: http://www.vue.com/dc/realestate

FLORIDA

Division of Real Estate
400 W. Robinson Street, N801
Orlando, FL 32801
Phone: 850-487-1395
Fax: 407-317-7245
Web site: www.myfloridalicense.com/dbpr/
    re/frec.html

GEORGIA

Real Estate Commission
229 Peachtree Street NE
International Tower, Suite 1000
Atlanta, GA 30303-1605
Phone: 404-656-3916
Fax: 404-656-6650
Web site: www.grec.state.ga.us

HAWAII

Real Estate Commission
King Kalakaua Building
335 Merchant Street, Room 333
Honolulu, HI 96813
Phone: 808-586-2643
Web site: www.hawaii.gov/hirec

IDAHO

Real Estate Commission
633 North 4th Street
P.O. Box 83720
Boise, ID 83720-0077
Phone: 208-334-3285
Fax: 208-334-2050
Web site: www.irec.idaho.gov

ILLINOIS

Bureau of Real Estate Professionals
320 West Washington Street
Springfield, IL 62786
Phone: 217-782-3414
Fax: 217-782-7645
Web site: www.idfpr.com/DPR/RE/realmain.asp

INDIANA

Professional Licensing Agency
Indiana Real Estate Commission
402 W. Washington Street, Room W072
Indianapolis, IN 46204
Phone: 317-234-3009
Web site: www.in.gov/pla/real.htm

IOWA

Real Estate Commission
1920 SE Hulsizer Road
Ankeny, IA 50021-3941
Phone: 515-281-7393
Fax: 515-281-7411
Web site: www.state.ia.us/government/com/prof/
    sales/home.html

KANSAS

Real Estate Commission
3 Townsite Plaza, Suite 200
120 SE 6th Avenue
Topeka, KS 66603-3511
Phone: 785-296-3411
Fax: 785-296-1771
Web site: www.kansas.gov/krec

KENTUCKY

Real Estate Commission
10200 Linn Station Rd., Suite 201
Louisville, KY 40223
Phone: 502-429-7050
Fax: 502-429-7246
Web site: www.krec.ky.gov/krec.gov

LOUISIANA

Real Estate Commission
9071 Interline Avenue
Baton Rouge, LA 70809

P.O. Box 14785
Baton Rouge, LA 70898-4785
Phone: 225-925-1923
Fax: 225-925-4501
Web site: www.lrec.state.la.us

MAINE

Real Estate Commission
35 State House Station
Augusta, ME 04333-0035
Phone: 207-624-8515
Fax: 207-624-8637
Web site: www.maine.gov/pfr/professionalli-
    censing/professions/real_estate/index.htm

MARYLAND

Real Estate Commission
500 N. Calvert Street, 3rd Floor
Baltimore, MD 21202-3651
Phone: 410-230-6230
Fax: 410-333-0023
Web site: www.dllr.state.md.us/license/occprof/
    recomm.html

MASSACHUSETTS

Real Estate Board
239 Causeway Street, Suite 500
Boston, MA 02114
Phone: 617-727-2373

Fax: 617-727-2669
Web site:
http://www.mass.gov/?pageID=ocasubtopic&
 L=4&L0=Home&L1=Licensee&L2=Divis
 ion+of+Professional+Licensure+Boards&
 L3=Board+of+Registration+of+Real+Esta
 te+Brokers+%26+Salespersons&sid=Eoca

MICHIGAN
Bureau of Commercial Services
Michigan State Board of Real Estate Brokers
 & Salespersons
2501 Woodlake Circle
Okemos, MI 48864-5955

P.O. Box 30018
Lansing, MI 48909
Phone: 517-373-7353
Fax: 517-373-1044
Web site: www.michigan.gov/realestate

MINNESOTA
Minnesota Department of Commerce
85 7th Place East, Suite 500
St. Paul, MN 55101
Phone: 651-296-6319
Fax: 651-284-4107
Web site: www.state.mn.us/portal/mn/jsp/
 content.do?subchannel=-536881740&id=-
 536881351&agency=Commerce

MISSISSIPPI
Real Estate Commission
2506 Lakeland Dr., Suite 300
Flowood, MS 39232

P.O. Box 12685
Jackson, MI 39236-2685
Phone: 601-932-6770
Fax: 601-932-2990
Web site: www.mrec.state.ms.us

MISSOURI
Real Estate Commission
3605 Missouri Blvd.
P.O. Box 1339
Jefferson City, MO 65102-1339
Phone: 573-751-2628
Fax: 573-751-2777
Web site: http://pr.mo.gov/realestate.asp

MONTANA
Board of Realty Regulation
P.O. Box 200513
301 South Park, Room 430
Helena, MT 59620-0513
Phone: 406-841-2320
Fax: 406-841-2323
Web site: www.realestate.mt.gov

NEBRASKA
Real Estate Commission
1200 N. Street, Suite 402
P.O. Box 94667
Lincoln, NE 68509-4667
Phone: 402-471-2004
Fax: 402-471-4492
Web site: www.nrec.state.ne.us

NEVADA
Department of Business & Industry
Real Estate Division

Las Vegas Office:
2501 E. Sahara Ave., Suite 102
Las Vegas, NV 89104-4137
Phone: 702-486-4033
Fax: 702-486-4275

Carson City Office
788 Fairview Drive, Suite 200
Carson City, NV 89701-5453
Phone: 775-687-4280
Fax: 775-687-4868
Web site: www.red.state.nv.us

NEW HAMPSHIRE
Real Estate Commission
State House Annex
25 Capitol Street, Room 434
Concord, NH 03301-6312
Phone: 603-271-2701
Fax: 603-271-1039
Web site: www.nh.gov/nhrec

NEW JERSEY
Real Estate Commission
20 West State Street
P.O. Box 328
Trenton, NJ 08625-0328
Phone: 609-292-7272

Fax: 609-292-0944
Web site: www.state.nj.us/dobi/division_rec/
index.htm

NEW MEXICO
5200 Oakland Avenue NE, Suite B
Albuquerque, NM 87113
Phone: 505-222-9820
Fax: 505-222-9886
Web site: www.rld.state.nm.us/realestatecom-
mission/index.html

NEW YORK
Division of Licensing Services
Alfred E. Smith Office Building
80 S. Swan Street, 10th Floor
Albany, NY 12210

P.O. Box 22001
Albany, NY 12201-2001
Phone: 518-474-4429
Web site: www.dos.state.ny.us/LCNS/
LICENSING.HTML

NORTH CAROLINA
Real Estate Commission
P.O. Box 17100
Raleigh, NC 27619-7100
Phone: 919-875-3700
Fax: 919-877-4216
Web site: www.ncrec.state.nc.us/

NORTH DAKOTA
Real Estate Commission
200 East Main Avenue, Suite 204
Bismarck, ND 58501

P.O. Box 727
Bismarck, ND 58502-0727
Phone: 701-328-9749
Fax: 701-328-9750
Web site: www.realestatend.org/

OHIO
Division of Real Estate and Professional
Licensing
77 South High Street, 20th Floor
Columbus, OH 43215-6133
Phone: 614-466-4100
Fax: 614-644-0584
Web site: www.com.ohio.gov/real

OKLAHOMA
Real Estate Commission
Shepherd Mall
2401 NW 23rd Street, Suite 18
Oklahoma City, OK 73107
Phone: 405-521-3387
Fax: 405-521-2189
Web site: www.ok.gov/OREC

OREGON
Real Estate Agency
1177 Center Street NE
Salem, OR 97301-2505
Phone: 503-378-4170
Fax: 503-378-3256
Web site: www.oregon.gov/REA

PENNSYLVANIA
Real Estate Commission
One Penn Center
2601 North 3rd Street
Harrisburg, PA 17110

P.O. Box 2649
Harrisburg, PA 17105-2649
Phone: 717-783-3658
Fax: 717-787-0250
Web site: www.dos.state.pa.us/bpoa/cwp/view.
asp?Q=433107

RHODE ISLAND
Department of Business Regulation
Real Estate Section
John O. Pastore Center
1511 Pontiac Avenue, Bldg. 69–1
Cranston, RI 02920
Phone: 401-462-9506
Fax: 401-462-9645
Web site: www.dbr.state.ri.us/divisions/com-
mlicensing/realestate.php

SOUTH CAROLINA
Real Estate Commission
Synergy Business Park
Kingstree Building
110 Centerview Drive, Suite 201
Columbia, SC 29210

P.O. Box 11847
Columbia, SC 29211-1847
Phone: 803-896-4400

Fax: 803-896-4404
Web site: www.llr.state.sc.us/POL/REC

SOUTH DAKOTA

Real Estate Commission
221 W. Capitol, Suite 101
Pierre, SD 57501
Phone: 605-773-3600
Fax: 605-773-4356
Web site: www.state.sd.us/sdrec

TENNESSEE

Real Estate Commission
500 James Robertson Parkway
Nashville, TN 37243-1151
Phone: 615-741-2273
Fax: 615-741-0313
Web site: http://tn.gov/commerce/boards/trec

TEXAS

Real Estate Commission
1101 Camino La Costa
Austin, TX 78752

P.O. Box 12188
Austin, TX 78711-2188
Phone: 512-459-6544
Fax: 512-465-3913
Web site: www.trec.state.tx.us

UTAH

Office of Professional Regulation
Division of Real Estate
Heber M. Wells Building
160 East 300 South, 2nd Floor
Salt Lake City, UT 84114

P.O. Box 146711
Salt Lake City, UT 84114-6711
Phone: 801-530-6747
Fax: 801-526-4387
Web site: http://realestate.utah.gov

VERMONT

Office of Professional Regulation
Real Estate Commission
National Life Building
North FL2
Montpelier, VT 05620-3402
Phone: 802-828-3228
Fax: 802-828-2465

Web site: http://vtprofessionals.org/opr1/
real_estate

VIRGINIA

Real Estate Board
9960 Mayland Drive, Suite 400
Richmond, VA 23233-1463
Phone: 804-367-8526
Web site: www.dpor.virginia.gov/dporweb/
reb_main.cfm

VIRGIN ISLANDS

Administrator, Boards and Commissions
Virgin Islands Board of Real Estate Commission
Department of Licensing and Consumer Affairs
Golden Rock Shopping Center, Suite 9
Christiansted, Virgin Islands 00820-4311
Web site: http://dlca.vi.gov/businesslicense/
steps/recrequirements/

WASHINGTON

Real Estate Commission
Department of Licensing
2000 Fourth Avenue West
Olympia, WA 98502

P.O. Box 9015
Olympia, WA 98507-9015
Phone: 360-664-6500
Fax: 360-586-0998
Web site: www.dol.wa.gov/business/realestate/
realestatecommission.html

WEST VIRGINIA

Real Estate Commission
300 Capitol Street, Suite 400
Charleston, WV 25301
Phone: 304-558-3555
Fax: 304-558-6442
Web site: www.wvrec.org

WISCONSIN

Department of Regulation and Licensing
1400 East Washington Avenue, Room 112
Madison, WI 53703

P.O. Box 8935
Madison, WI 53708-8935
Phone: 877-617-1565
Web site: http://drl.wi.gov

WYOMING

Real Estate Commission
2020 Carey Avenue, Suite 702
Cheyenne, WY 82002-0180
Phone: 307-777-7141
Fax: 307-777-3796
Web site: http://realestate.state.wy.us

State Real Estate Appraiser Boards

ALABAMA
Real Estate Appraisers Board
100 North Union Street, Suite 370
Montgomery, AL 36104

P.O. Box 304355
Montgomery, AL 36130-4355
Phone: 334-242-8747
Fax: 334-242-8749
Web site: www.reab.state.al.us

ALASKA
Board of Certified Real Estate Appraisers
P.O. Box 110806
Juneau, AK 99811-0806
Phone: 907-465-5470
Fax: 907-465-2974
Web site: www.commerce.state.ak.us/occ/
    papr.htm

ARIZONA
Arizona Board of Appraisal
1400 West Washington, Suite 360
Phoenix, AZ 85007
Phone: 602-542-1539
Fax: 602-542-1598
Web site: www.appraisal.state.az.us

ARKANSAS
Arkansas Appraiser Licensing &
    Certification Board
101 East Capitol, Suite 430
Little Rock, AR 72201
Phone: 501-296-1843
Fax: 501-296-1844
Web site: www.state.ar.us/aleb

CALIFORNIA
California Office of Real Estate Appraisers
1102 Q Street, Suite 4100
Sacramento, CA 95811
Phone: 916-552-9000
Web site: www.orea.ca.gov/

COLORADO
Board of Real Estate Appraisers
1560 Broadway, Suite 925
Denver, CO 80202
Phone: 303-894-2166
Fax: 303-894-2683
Web site: www.dora.state.co.us/Real-Estate/
    appraiserlicensing.htm

CONNECTICUT
Department of Consumer Protection
Real Estate & Real Estate Appraisal
165 Capitol Avenue
Hartford, CT 06106
Phone: 860-713-6150
Fax: 860-713-7243
Web site: http://www.ct.gov/dcp/cwp/view.
    asp?a=1624&Q=276078&PM=1

DELAWARE
Council on Real Estate Appraisers
Cannon Building, Suite 203
861 Silver Lake Boulevard
Dover, DE 19904-2467
Phone: 302-744-4500
Fax: 302-739-2711
Website: http://dpr.delaware.gov/boards/
    realestateappraisers

DISTRICT OF COLUMBIA
Department of Consumer and Regulatory
    Affairs
Business and Professional Licensing
    Administration
Board of Real Estate Appraisers
941 North Capitol Street, NE
Washington, DC 20002
Phone: 202-442-4400
Fax: 202-698-4329
Web site: http://www.vue.com/dc/appraisers

appendix c

FLORIDA

Department of Business and Professional
Regulation
Division of Real Estate
Real Estate Appraisal Board
400 West Robinson Street, N801
Orlando, FL 32801
Phone: 850-487-1395
Fax: 407-317-7245
Web site: www.myfloridalicense.com/dbpr/re/
freab.html

GEORGIA

Real Estate Appraisers Board
229 Peachtree Street, NE
International Tower, Suite 1000
Atlanta, GA 30303-1605
Phone: 404-656-3916
Fax: 404-656-6650
Web site: www.grec.state.ga.us

HAWAII

Department of Commerce and Consumer
Affairs
Professional and Vocational Licensing
Real Estate Appraiser
DCCA-PVL
Att: REA
P.O. Box 3469
Honolulu, HI 96801
Phone: 808-586-2701
Web site: http://hawaii.gov/dcca/pvl/programs/
realestateappraiser/

IDAHO

Real Estate Appraiser Board
1109 Main Street, Suite 220
Boise, ID 83702-5642
Phone: 208-334-3233
Fax: 208-334-3945
Web site: https://secure.ibol.idaho.gov/IBOL/
BoardPage.aspx?Bureau=REA

ILLINOIS

Division of Professional Regulation

Springfield Office:
320 West Washington Street
Springfield, IL 62786
Phone: 217-782-9300
Fax: 217-782-3390

Chicago Office:
James R. Thompson Center
100 W. Randolph Street, Suite 9–300
Chicago, IL 60601
Phone: 312-814-4500
Web site: www.idfpr.com/dpr/re/Appraisal.asp

INDIANA

Indiana Professional Licensing Agency
Real Estate Appraiser Licensure &
Certification Board
402 West Washington Street, Room W0702
Indianapolis, IN 46204
Phone: 317-234-3009
Web site: www.in.gov/pla/appriaser.htm

IOWA

Iowa Appraiser Examining Board
1920 SE Hulsizer Road
Ankeny, IA 50021-3941
Phone: 515-281-4126
Fax: 515-281-7411
Web site: www.state.ia.us/government/com/
prof/appraiser/home.html

KANSAS

Kansas Real Estate Appraisal Board
Jayhawk Tower, Roof Garden Level
700 SW Jackson, Suite 1102
Topeka, KS 66603
Phone: 785-296-6736
Fax: 785-368-6443
Web site: www.kansas.gov/kreab

KENTUCKY

Kentucky Real Estate Appraisers Board
135 W. Irvine Street, Suite 301
Richmond, KY 40475
Phone: 859-623-1658
Fax: 859-623-2598
Web site: www.kreab.ky.gov

LOUISIANA

Louisiana Real Estate Appraisers Board
9071 Interline Avenue
Baton Rouge, LA 70809

P.O. Box 14785
Baton Rouge, LA 70898-4785
Phone: 225-925-1923
Fax: 225-925-4501
Web site: www.lreasbc.state.la.us

MAINE

Department of Professional and Financial
    Regulation
Office of Licensing & Registration
Board of Real Estate Appraisers
35 State House Station
Augusta, ME 04333-0035
Phone: 207-624-8522
Fax: 207-624-8637
Web site: www.maine.gov/pfr/professionalli-
    censing/professions/appraisers/index.htm

MARYLAND

Commission of Real Estate Appraisers and
    Home Inspectors
500 North Calvert Street
Baltimore, MD 21202-3651
Phone: 410-230-6165
Fax: 410-333-6314
Web site: http://www.dllr.state.md.us/license/
    reahi/

MASSACHUSETTS

Division of Professional Licensure
The Board of Registration of Real Estate
    Appraisers
239 Causeway Street, Suite 500
Boston, MA 02114
Phone: 617-727-3055
Fax: 617-727-2669
Web site: www.mass.gov/?pageID=ocasubtopi
    c&L=4&L0=Home&L1=Licensee&L2=Di
    vision+of+Professional+Licensure+Boards
    &L3=Board+of+Registration+of+Real+Est
    ate+Appraisers&sid=Eoca

MICHIGAN

Department of Labor and Economic Growth
State Board of Real Estate Appraisers
P.O. Box 30018
Lansing, MI 48909
Phone: 517-241-8720
Fax: 517-373-1044
Web site: http://mich.gov/dleg/0,1607,7–154–
    35299_35414_35474—-,00.html

MINNESOTA

Department of Commerce
Real Estate Appraiser Advisory Board
85 7th Place East, Suite 500
St. Paul, MN 55101
Phone: 651-296-6319
Fax: 651-284-4107
Web site: www.state.mn.us/portal/mn/jsp/
    content.do?subchannel=-536893088&id=-
    536881352&agency=Commerce

MISSISSIPPI

Real Estate Appraisal Board
2506 Lakeland Drive, Suite 300
Flowood, MS 32932-7640

P.O. Box 12685
Jackson, MS 39236
Phone: 601-932-9191
Fax: 601-932-2990
Web site: www.mrec.state.ms.us/mab/index_
    mab.html

MISSOURI

Real Estate Appraisers Commission
3605 Missouri Boulevard
P.O. Box 1335
Jefferson City, MO 65102-1335
Phone: 573-751-0038
Fax: 573-526-3489
Web site: www.pr.mo.gov/appraisers.asp

MONTANA

Board of Real Estate Appraisers
301 South Park, 4th Floor
P.O. Box 200513
Helena, MT 59620-0513
Phone: 406-841-2354
Fax: 406-841-2323
Web site: http://bsd.dli.mt.gov/license/bsd_
    boards/rea_board/board_page.asp

NEBRASKA

Real Estate Appraiser Board
301 Centennial Mall South
P.O. Box 94963
Lincoln, NE 68509-2529
Phone: 402-471-9015
Fax: 402-471-9017
Web site: www.appraiser.ne.gov

NEVADA

Nevada Real Estate Division

Las Vegas Office:
2501 East Sahara Avenue, Suite 102
Las Vegas, NV 89104-4137
Phone: 702-486-4033
Fax: 702-486-4275

Carson City Office:
788 Fairview Drive, Suite 200
Carson City, NV 89701-5453
Phone: 775-687-4280
Fax: 775-687-4868
Web site: http://www.red.state.nv.us/
    Appraisal/appraisal.htm

NEW HAMPSHIRE

Real Estate Appraiser Board
State House Annex, Room 426
25 Capitol Street
Concord, NH 03301-6312
Phone: 603-271-6186
Fax: 603-271-6513
Web site: www.nh.gov/nhreab

NEW JERSEY

State Real Estate Appraiser Board
P.O. Box 45032
Newark, NJ 07101
Phone: 973-504-6480
Web site: www.njconsumeraffairs.gov/real/

NEW MEXICO

Real Estate Appraisers Board
Tony Anaya Building
2550 Cerrillos Road, 2nd Floor
Sante Fe, NM 87505
Phone: 505-476-4860
Fax: 505-476-4665
Web site: www.rld.state.nm.us/
    RealEstateAppraisers/

NEW YORK

Department of State
Division of Licensing Services
Alfred E. Smith Office Building
80 S. Swan Street, 10th Floor
Albany, NY 12210

P.O. Box 22001
Albany, NY 12201-2001
Phone: 518-474-4429
Web site: www.dos.state.ny.us/LCNS/
    REALESTATE/index.html

NORTH CAROLINA

North Carolina Appraisal Board
5830 Six Forks Road
Raleigh, NC 27609
Phone: 919-870-4854
Fax: 919-870-4859
Web site: www.ncappraisalboard.org

NORTH DAKOTA

Real Estate Appraiser Qualifications and
    Ethics Board
1725 Bonn Blvd.
Bismarck, ND 58504-7014

P.O. Box 1336
Bismarck, ND 58502-1336
Phone: 701-222-1051
Web site: www.governor.state.nd.us/boards/
    boards-query.asp?Board_ID=92

OHIO

Ohio Department of Commerce
Division of Real Estate and Professional
    Licensing
77 South High Street, 20th Floor
Columbus, OH 43215-6133
Phone: 614-466-4100
Fax: 614-644-0584
Web site: www.com.ohio.gov/real/AppMain.
    aspx

OKLAHOMA

Real Estate Appraiser Board
Shepherd Mall
2401 NW 23rd Street, Suite 28
Oklahoma City, OK 73107

P.O. Box 53408
Oklahoma City, OK 73152-3408
Phone: 405-521-6636
Fax: 405-522-6909
Web site: http://www.ok.gov/oid/Regulated_
    Entities/Real_Estate_Appraiser_Board_
    (REAB)/index.html

OREGON

Appraiser Certification & Licensure Board
3000 Market Street NE, Suite 541
Salem, OR 97301
Phone: 503-485-2555
Fax: 503-485-2559
Web site: http://oregonaclb.org/aclb_prod/
    index.php

PENNSYLVANIA

State Board of Certified Real Estate
    Appraisers
One Penn Center
2601 N. Third Street
Harrisburg, PA 17110

P.O. Box 2649
Harrisburg, PA 17105-2649
Phone: 717-783-4866
Fax: 717-705-5540
Web site: www.dos.state.pa.us/bpoa/cwp/view.
    asp?a=1104&q=432589

RHODE ISLAND

Department of Business Regulation
Division of Commercial Licensing and
    Regulation
Real Estate Appraisers Section
1511 Pontiac Avenue
Cranston, RI 02920
Phone: 401-462-9506
Fax: 401-462-9645
Web site: www.dbr.state.ri.us/divisions/com-
    mlicensing/realestate.php

SOUTH CAROLINA

Real Estate Appraisers Board
Synergy Business Park
Kingstree Building
110 Centerview Drive, Suite 201
Columbia, SC 29210

P.O. Box 11847
Columbia, SC 29211-1847
Phone: 803-896-4400
Fax: 803-896-4404
Web site: www.llr.state.sc.us/POL/REAB

SOUTH DAKOTA

Appraiser Certification Program
445 E. Capitol Avenue
Pierre, SD 57501-3185
Phone: 605-773-4608
Fax: 605-773-5369
Web site: www.state.sd.us/drr2/reg/appraisers/
    appraiser.html

TENNESSEE

Real Estate Appraiser Commission
500 James Robertson Parkway
Nashville, TN 37243-1166
Phone: 615-741-1831
Fax: 615-253-1692
Web site: www.state.tn.us/commerce/boards/
    treac/index.shtml

TEXAS

Appraiser Licensing and Certification Board
1101 Camino La Costa
Austin, TX 78752

P.O. Box 12188
Austin, TX 78711-2188
Phone: 512-459-2232
Fax: 512-465-3913
Web site: www.talcb.state.tx.us/agencyinfo/
    default.asp

UTAH

Division of Real Estate
Heber M. Wells Building, 2nd Floor
160 East 300 South
Salt Lake City, UT 84114

P.O. Box 146711
Salt Lake City, UT 84114-6711
Phone: 801-530-6747
Fax: 801-530-6749
Web site: http://realestate.utah.gov/#

VERMONT

Office of Professional Regulation
Board of Real Estate Appraisers
National Life Building
North FL2
Montpelier, VT 05620-3402
Phone: 802-828-3228
Web site: http://vtprofessionals.org/opr1/
    appraisers

VIRGINIA

Department of Professional and Occupational
    Regulation
Real Estate Appraiser Board
9960 Mayland Drive, Suite 400
Richmond, VA 23233-1463
Phone: 804-367-8552
Fax: 804-527-4298
Web site: www.dpor.virginia.gov/dporweb/
    apr_main.cfm

VIRGIN ISLANDS

Administrator, Boards and Commissions
Virgin Islands Board of Real Estate
    Commission
Department of Licensing and Consumer
    Affairs
Golden Rock Shopping Center, Suite 9
Christiansted, Virgin Islands 00820-4311
Web site: http://dlca.vi.gov/businesslicense/
    steps/recrequirements/

WASHINGTON

Department of Licensing
Real Estate Appraisers
2000 4th Avenue West
Olympia, WA 98502

P.O. Box 9048
Olympia, WA 98507-9048
Phone: 360-664-6504
Fax: 360-586-0998
Web site: www.dol.wa.gov/business/appraisers

WEST VIRGINIA

Real Estate Appraiser Licensing and
    Certification Board
2110 Kanawha Boulevard East, Suite 101
Charleston, WV 25311
Phone: 304-558-3919
Fax: 304-558-3983
Web site: www.wvappraiserboard.org

WISCONSIN

Real Estate Appraisers Board
Department of Regulation and Licensing
Real Estate Appraisers Board
Bureau of Business and Design Professions
1400 East Washington Avenue, Room 112

P.O. Box 8935
Madison, WI 53708
Phone: 608-266-2112
Web site: http://drl.wi.gov/board_detail.
    asp?boardid=51&locid=0

WYOMING

Certified Real Estate Appraiser Board
2020 Carey Avenue, Suite 702
Cheyenne, WY 82002-0180
Phone: 307-777-7141
Fax: 307-777-3796
Web site: http://realestate.state.wy.us

NOTES

NOTES

NOTES

NOTES

NOTES

NOTES

NOTES

NOTES

NOTES

NOTES

NOTES

NOTES

NOTES